D0908988

URBAN AND SOCIAL GEOGRAPHY SERIES

General Editor
J. H. Johnson, M.A., Ph.D., Professor of Geography, University of Lancaster

OFFICE

LOCATION

CE

OFFICE LOCATION

An Urban and Regional Study

P. W. DANIELS

Lecturer in Geography
University of Liverpool

LONDON
G. BELL AND SONS LTD
1975

009560

COPYRIGHT © 1975 BY
G. BELL AND SONS LTD
York House, Portugal Street
London, WC2A 2HL

All Rights Reserved

No part of this publication may be reproduced, stored in
a retrieval system, or transmitted, in any form or by any
means, electronic, mechanical, photocopying, recording or
otherwise, without the prior permission of
G. Bell and Sons Ltd.

HF
5547
.D254
1975

ISBN 0 7135 1901 0

Printed in Great Britain by
Butler & Tanner, Ltd,
Frome and London

To
Carole

Foreword

This new series of studies in urban and social geography is designed to be complementary to the well-known Bell's Advanced Economic Geographies, edited with distinction for many years by Professor R. O. Buchanan. The two series are not intended to be mutually exclusive, but this new development is designed to reflect the considerable growth in research and teaching of urban and social geography over the past decade.

The basic strategy in the series will be to occupy the difficult middle ground between first-year university textbooks and more esoteric research monographs. The aim will be to encourage those books that will assist more advanced undergraduate teaching and will also provide helpful introductions to topics in urban and social geography for the growing body of graduate students in human geography and in associated disciplines.

Dr Daniels' book attempts to place the growth of office employment in cities in a broader context than a purely economic study of this phenomenon might involve. He thus fills an important gap in the urban studies that have so far been published by geographers. He also succeeds in making comprehensible a massive body of research literature and, at the same time, presents his own personal enquiries in an easily readable form. In short, he provides an excellent indication of many of the aims of the series.

University of Lancaster   James H. Johnson

Preface

In many ways office studies are still at the pioneer fringe of economic and urban geography. There has been a longstanding interest amongst geographers in the location of manufacturing industry but little or no interest in office location. Twenty, or even fifteen, years ago few observers of the urban scene seemed to be aware of the impending impact of the rapidly expanding office function on the employment structure, land use patterns, transport, land values or redistribution of economic activities within cities and their surrounding regions. Offices remain a comparatively minor user of space in cities, where they are mainly concentrated, but their contribution to the urban economy as well as to some contemporary urban problems is out of all proportion to their propensity to consume space. Visually, office buildings have increasingly dominated the urban landscape. Activities which utilize office space now provide employment for more than 25 per cent of the labour force in the most economically advanced countries. Office occupations continue to grow faster than almost all other types of employment and this differential is likely to remain for some time into the future. Yet, surprisingly little is understood about the factors which have influenced the growth and location of office activities and their consequences for contemporary and future urban development.

The first objective of this volume is to integrate and systematize those aspects of office activities and their location which have interested geographers and others, particularly during recent years. In some respects it is an introduction to 'office geography' with reference to the spatial distribution of office activities, the factors which contribute to the observed patterns, and the part played by offices in the creation, as well as the solution, of some of the problems which confront urban and regional planning at the present time. Some selection and compression of the themes which are discussed has been inevitable and not everyone will agree with the final choice of material for inclusion. But if this book stimulates more interest in the study of office activities and helps to give it a clearer status within urban and economic geography, then its second objective will have been achieved.

The people who have contributed in many different ways to the preparation of the book are too numerous to mention individually but I owe them all my sincere gratitude. The material included has rested partly upon the published work of others but has also depended upon the interest, co-operation and information provided by the staff of the Location of Offices Bureau, Department of the Environment, Department of Employment, Civil Service Department, Office of Population Censuses and Surveys, the Greater London Council, and other local authority planning departments in Britain. The Regional Plan Association (New York) and various City Planning Commissions in the United States have also been most helpful in providing data and clarifying queries. Much of my initial interest in office activities was nurtured at University College, London, and parts of a Ph.D. thesis awarded by the University of London are included in the text.

I am also grateful for the encouragement received from my colleagues at the University of Liverpool and for the opportunities and facilities placed at my disposal to allow the study to be completed. I am also indebted to those who read parts of the manuscript and provided valuable suggestions and comments, in particular Professor J. H. Johnson in his capacity as Editor. Cartographic advice was provided by Miss Joan Treasure who also drew most of the maps and

ix

diagrams with help from Miss Sandra Pierce and Mr A. G. Hodgkiss. The final version of the manuscript was typed most efficiently and at very short notice by Mrs E. Sullivan and Mrs Burke.

Last, but by no means least, I would like to acknowledge the infinite patience, kindness, and understanding of my wife who has had to endure many lonely hours while I sat in my study wondering what to write next. The task would have been impossible without her help and constant encouragement.

December, 1974   P.W.D.

Contents

List of Tables

List of Figures

CHAPTER 1

Introduction

The office building has come to replace the factory as the symbol of contemporary urban economic development. It accommodates the disproportionate growth in 'those occupations that do not produce or process goods but service either production and processing industries or the consumer and all his diversified needs'.[1] The nineteenth-century city was heavily dependent upon factory employment as the cornerstone of its economy but during the twentieth century this role has been taken over by service, and particularly office, employment. This is the employment provided in construction, transport and communications, distributive trades, banking and finance, professional services, and public administration in local and central government.[2] Office employment is by no means confined to service industries, but is found in association with almost every kind of economic activity although its absolute importance is considerably lower in most manufacturing industries than in services. The 1971 Census shows that approximately 25 per cent of Great Britain's workers are in office occupations.[3]

The transformation from manufacturing to service-dominated economies is well developed in the larger cities of advanced industrial societies. These cities seem able to attract an unequal share of the rapid expansion of service activities and employment which has taken place since the last war. Automation (and the improved methods of production, increased efficiency, and higher productivity that result from it) is just one of the major changes which has reduced the demand for industrial labour. At the same time it has placed new claims upon man's managerial, organizational, and transactional abilities which form the basis for office-based activities. Urban economies have therefore become more complex as the workforce has become more specialized in parallel with an increasing division of labour through time. Probably the best single expression of this process of structural change in urban, as well as in regional and national, economic structure is the office.

The growing importance of non-industrial or 'white-collar' employment has been described as 'the quiet revolution'[4] which has been under way since the turn of the century. The significance of this growth extends far beyond its implications for occupation structure, female activity rates or gross national product, in that most of it has been concentrated within small areas inside major cities, particularly the central business district (C.B.D.). The office component of white-collar employment has a far higher level of centrality than was ever attained by manufacturing industry when it too was concentrated at the heart of urban areas. Many office activities depend for their successful operation upon much personal inter-communication and rapid exchange of information, and this is best achieved by clustering. The high density, strongly vertical component of a growing number of C.B.D.s is largely a response to the centrality demands of office activities. Offices have come to dominate city centres, in both a physical and economic sense, while they are also appearing in ever increasing numbers in suburban locations and beyond.

An index of the rapid growth of office activity is the massive increase in office floorspace in many major cities. Over 191 m. ft^2 was added to the national inventory of office floorspace in the United States in 1969, with 30 m. ft^2 in Manhattan alone.[5] This is more than 75 per cent of the 40 m. ft^2 per annum added to the floorspace stock of 100 other cities outside the United States and the Soviet Union. Paris and Tokyo–Yokohama have averaged 4 m. ft^2 per annum since 1965 while central London, despite stringent planning restrictions, added 2·5 m. ft^2 in one year between 1967 and 1968.[6] While cities such as London and Paris have recorded losses in their stock of industrial floorspace, there is no sign of a retardation in their accumulation of office

floorspace, although redistribution within the urban fabric is becoming more important.

THE NEGLECT OF OFFICE STUDIES

Despite their undoubted importance to city structure and planning and to the operation of the modern economy, office activities remain the most neglected facet of urban studies. Although offices have become a distinctive part of the urban scene only during the last 100 years, they are probably the single most important centripetal force in urban development at a time when centrifugal movement of retailing and industry, as well as of population, is characteristic of most metropolitan areas.

Reference to the literature in urban and economic geography, or in urban and regional planning, soon reveals a surprisingly limited discussion of office activities. Even when they are discussed, they are referred to implicitly rather than explicitly and there is a general failure to grasp their function and importance for city growth and development.[7] This compares very unfavourably with the large number of studies by geographers and others of the manufacturing, retail or residential structure of cities. Most of this work can be divided into two main groups comprising, first, descriptive/empirical studies, and secondly, the development and testing of techniques and models which attempt to explain and predict the location of these activities in urban space.[8] Examples of the latter include central place models, the identification of hierarchies in the retail structure of cities, and the development of retail potential models.[9] Although, by comparison, models of industrial location in urban areas are not well developed, they have still reached a level of sophistication which far exceeds anything which exists for office location.[10] Studies of the office sector have been largely descriptive and have concentrated on identifying location patterns and the factors influencing their distribution. A trend towards more comprehensive theoretical and explanatory study has only just begun[11] so that our understanding of the office system is in its infancy compared with progress in our knowledge of the

role of retail or industrial land uses, for example, in the function and structure of cities.

It is a poignant fact that 'more research has been done on the planting of peanuts and the marketing of toothbrushes than on the location of and the market for office buildings'.[12] Prior to the publication of Cowan's work on office growth and location in London,[13] and a more recent monograph on the office industry in the New York region[14] there have been few studies solely devoted to the office sector.[15] Each of these volumes are pioneers of their kind in Britain and the United States, respectively, despite the fact that the importance of offices and their employment to the urban economy had already been appreciated by Haig, working in New York, as far back as 1927.[16]

Haig attempted a general explanation for the location of financial offices in Manhattan with particular reference to the influence of accessibility. His ideas, however, were not examined further until publication of the findings of the New York Metropolitan Region Study from 1956 onwards. Particularly notable were the contributions of Hoover and Vernon in the *Anatomy of a Metropolis*[17] and of Robbins and Terleckyj.[18] The particular value of their work is not only its elaboration of the factors influencing the growth of office work and the location and distribution of offices, but also its role in making society at large aware of the magnitude of the growth of office employment generally during the post-war years. This theme was continued by Gottman[19] who took a more detailed look at the emergence of the 'white-collar revolution'. Gottman suggested, and has subsequently reiterated the view, that within non-production employment a differentiation should be made between tertiary services, such as retailing or transport, and a group of service activities described as 'quaternary'.[20] These are the activities which involve a large proportion of transactions, decision-making, analysis, and generally demand more intellectual training and responsibility. It is the quaternary sector which is most closely aligned to office employment in its narrowest sense.

In all these examples, the analysis of office activities is part of a much larger body of material, with the result that it tends to be submerged by the wealth of other information included. These analyses are also largely presented in subjective terms, which is a useful first step. The second step, systematic analysis of specific facets of office activities, has only recently been made, particularly by research workers in Britain and Sweden. Studies of office communications and their influence on location by Goddard in London and by Törnquist in Sweden[21] are representative of this trend. It can only be hoped that these, and work currently in progress, represent the tip of the iceberg.

SOME REASONS FOR THE NEGLECT OF OFFICE STUDIES

There appear to be three main reasons for the neglect of office studies. One of these has already been mentioned: the office and its associated employment have emerged comparatively lately as an identifiable component of urban economic and physical structure. This has led to an excessive preoccupation with trying to understand the location of manufacturing industry, at the expense of the service sector. This characteristic has retained its momentum into the second half of this century, even though manufacturing employment is now growing more slowly than service employment in all of the advanced economies.

The second reason is rather more fundamental. This revolves around the failure to appreciate the growing role of office-based activities in the internal structure, integration and co-ordination of organizations of all sizes and levels of complexity. At the same time there has been a rapid growth of specialist services in areas such as banking, insurance, finance, advertising, marketing, and market research, which meet the requirements of the large number of firms and individuals in need of expertise but which cannot, on economic grounds, retain the appropriate personnel on a permanent basis. Many of these specialist services are occupiers of office space and because of their particular locational requirements they have tended to accumulate at the centre of cities. This has had important effects upon the structure of the inner city while, more recently, offices as a whole have played a new role in the development of suburban areas in our major cities and in the formulation and implementation of regional development policies in some countries such as Britain and France.

But few geographers have grasped the opportunities which these processes of change provide for making a contribution to our understanding of the emerging office system. The causes and consequences of contemporary office location patterns or the relationship between city size and the role of office employment in the occupation structure have all been neglected. Indeed, the way in which offices imprint their particular locational attributes upon individual cities and on inter-regional employment structures are also worthy of more detailed scrutiny.[22]

A third reason for the neglect of office studies arises from the acute shortage of accessible and suitable data. At the national level, the census reports and some individual Government Departments dealing with legislation which affects office activities, are the main sources of information on employment and floorspace.[23] It was not until 1968, however, that the General Register Office issued a recommended standard definition of office occupations, which was first used in the 1966 Census.[24] The United States Census does not provide specific data on those office jobs which are contained within the employment figures for individual manufacturing or service industries.[25] Perhaps the main problem is that 'whereas manufacturing, transportation, retail trade, and wholesale trade are economic activities whose existence is easily recognized and catalogued, many aspects of office activity are more difficult to classify'.[26] Data can also be obtained from independent surveys by individual local authorities or cities but there are wide variations in the amount, detail, and reliability of the information relating to office

employment, floorspace, rents, occupants, and vacancy rates. These important problems will be discussed further in subsequent chapters.

DEFINING AN OFFICE

At this point it is useful to attempt a definition of offices and the work performed in them. Offices may be defined with reference to the functions which they perform or in terms of the space or types of buildings which they occupy.

The minimum function of an office is to direct and co-ordinate the activities of an enterprise.[27] Every enterprise either has an office as part of its physical infrastructure or is linked to some office elsewhere. This, in turn, is linked with other offices and activities outside the organization. Private companies, local government, central government, and the wide range of public undertakings all generate office work of some kind or other. Consequently, 'scattered throughout the political economy, the office is the peak of a pyramid of work and money and decision'.[28]

Although there will be detailed variations between different types of office, the office function can be categorized into five activities:[29]

1. *Receiving information.* This arrives along various channels of communication such as letters, telephone messages, memoranda, orders, invoices, telex, computer print-out, and records/minutes of meetings and transactions.

2. *Recording information.* Every item of information received must be documented, filed or destroyed, as appropriate. The information which is retained must then be stored in such a way as to be easily retrievable and intelligible to future users who are unlikely to have been involved in the recording process.

3. *Arranging information.* Before it becomes useful every piece of information normally needs to be combined with other information, or needs to be duplicated, summarized and edited, and certainly checked.

4. *Giving information.* This activity reflects the role of communications in the office function. Information needs to be passed both within an organization and between it and other organizations. At one end of the spectrum, this might be done at face-to-face meetings, or at the other, it might be passed around by electronic office machinery. The range of office services is wide and many of them are concerned with communications. The more efficient these communications are, the better will management be able to make the right decisions. Much of the information which is exchanged or distributed within an office is designed to help in decision-making at each level of responsibility within the firm.

5. *Safeguarding assets.* This is an important function of the office. Its staff must ensure that the cash and stock which represent the assets of any business are fully accounted for and that any debits have been collected.

The statutory definition of the office function transforms the above classification into an occupational framework and it includes administration, clerical work, handling money, the operation of telephone and telegraph facilities, and the use of computers.[30]

Office work therefore assists an organization to achieve its aims as efficiently as possible, as well as allowing it to fulfil its legal obligations. The office is responsible for initiating the various business elements necessary to the successful functioning of the organization. In the fiercely competitive framework within which most businesses operate, the office must capture the gains for any individual organization by maintaining good intelligence and communications links with the outside world. These comments are particularly relevant to the office activities of industries and services in the private sector. But they also apply, in a different working context, to the bureaucratic machine represented by central and local government.

The functional definition of an office is fairly straightforward but its physical characteristics are more difficult to isolate. Rausch warns us that it is a mistake to regard an office as a specific place.[31] He argues that an office exists anywhere that certain kinds of work, such as duplicating, typing, filing or book-keeping, are performed. The office should be regarded as an activity or group of activities with a functional rather than physical expression, so that an office can be said to exist wherever record-keeping is co-ordinated or performed. This view of the office is probably most applicable to the period when physical separation of production and administrative units of an organization was uncommon. The effect of this was to blur the 'physical' identity of the office section.

Today, the large number of free-standing skyscrapers and other office buildings in most large cities testify to the marked physical separation of offices from other urban land uses. It is in these buildings, specially designed to meet the needs of office users, that much of the rapid growth of office employment during this century has been concentrated. Despite the emergence of a distinctive physical form, not all offices are located in free-standing, unifunctional, buildings. It will be shown later that offices share buildings with other uses, such as retailing or manufacturing plants. Consequently, the *Offices Act 1960* refers to an office as 'including any room of which the substantial use is for clerical work ... except any room in premises of which the substantial use is as a private residence or for private domestic purposes'.[32] This is the broadest possible definition but more recently offices have been considered as 'premises whose sole use is to be used as an office for office purposes'.[33] This definition is narrower than the first and can result in the exclusion of buildings in which offices are not the principal users of space. Hence, an office is a place where 'people sit at desks or tables, equipped or supported in their work by paper and pens, typewriters, dictating machines, telephones, telex, calculating machines and more advanced data-processing machines'.[34]

When attempting a physical definition of an office it is also necessary to take into account the hierarchy of office functions and activities. In the office hierarchy the headquarters and regional offices of large organizations form a distinct group in terms of their locational and space attributes. Examples include central Government offices, large insurance companies, the banks or commodity exchanges, all of which occupy free-standing prestigious office space in the centre of major cities. The next level in the hierarchy is represented by the local offices of banks, solicitors, estate agents or accountants. These are normally considerably smaller and serve a more limited purpose than their larger counterparts. Hence, they are less commonly found in specialist office blocks but are scattered throughout the building fabric in space shared with other uses. A third level in the hierarchy, although not necessarily the lowest, are offices attached to manufacturing plants or warehouses. These are locationally tied although they often occupy distinctive, if not separate, office structures attached to the production plant. Each of these levels in the hierarchy occupies different types of office space which has distinctive physical and locational attributes.

OUTLINE OF THE BOOK

The last decade has produced a growing volume of literature on office activities.[35] This book attempts to identify and systematize some of the important themes to emerge from this, and earlier, work in a way which might stimulate further interest and research in the office sector. An analysis of the emergence of the office function since the turn of the century is followed by an examination of the growth of office employment and office floorspace at both the urban and regional level. The factors influencing supply and demand for office space and employment are then discussed along with some methods which have been used to estimate values for each variable under a given set of circumstances. The regional and urban attributes of the location of office activities, with particular reference to Britain and the United States, are considered in more detail in Chapters 6 and 7. Communications and office location have received a great deal of attention in recent years and these are discussed in Chapter 8. Decentralization of office activities from the centre of metropolitan areas has also become an important feature of urban growth since 1945. The final chapters therefore consider the causes and consequences of this process for offices, their employees, and for the surburban and other areas which receive them.

This approach stresses the dynamic character of office growth and location throughout this century. The traditional location of offices in the C.B.D. is being partially replaced by a more dispersed distribution, which reflects the impact of modern technology and the changing goals of urban society. At the same time, office employment is absorbing a larger share of total employment in urban areas and regions alike. It is therefore crucial that planned growth at the metropolitan or regional scale should make adequate allowance for office activities and their continuing expansion in the future.

REFERENCES

1 J. Gottman, *Megalopolis: The Urbanised North-eastern Seaboard of the United States* (Cambridge, Mass.: The M.I.T. Press, 1961), p. 568. The division of economic activities into primary, secondary and tertiary, or service, sectors was first introduced by A. G. B. Fisher, 'Economic implications of material progress', *International Labour Review*, vol. 32 (1935), pp. 5–18. See also C. Clark, *The Conditions of Economic Progress* (London: Macmillan, 1940), pp. 6–7.

2 G. J. Stigler, *Trends in Employment in the Service Industries* (Baltimore: The Johns Hopkins Press, 1956). P. Deane and W. A. Cole, *British Economic Growth, 1688–1959* (London: Cambridge University Press, 1962). R. E. Galtman and T. J. Weiss, 'The service industries in the nineteenth century', in V. R. Fuchs (ed.), *Production and Productivity in the Service Industries* (New York: Studies in Income and Wealth, 1969). M. Lengelle, *The Growing Importance of the Service Sector in Member Countries* (Geneva: Organization for Economic Co-operation and Development, 1966). M. Abramovitz and V. F. Eliasberg, *The Growth of Public Employment in Great Britain* (London: National Bureau of Economic Research, 1957). H. I. Greenfield, *Manpower and the Growth of Producer Services* (New York: Columbia University Press, 1966). R. Lewis, *The New Service Society* (London: Longman, 1973).

3 Office of Population Censuses and Surveys, *Census 1971, Great Britain, Summary Tables (1% Sample)* (London: Her Majesty's Stationery Office, 1973).

4 R. B. Armstrong, *The Office Industry: Patterns of Growth and Location* (Cambridge, Mass.: The M.I.T. Press, 1972), p. 2.

5 *100 'International Cities': Office Space Study of 60 Countries* (New York: E. Rene Frank Associates Ltd, 1970).

6 Department of the Environment, *Statistics for Town and Country Planning, Series II, Floorspace* (London: Her Majesty's Stationery Office, 1972), Table 31.

7 E. Schultz and W. Simmons, *Offices in the Sky* (New York: Bobbs-Merrill, 1959), p. 290.

8. See B. Garner and M. H. Yeates, *The North American City* (New York: Harper & Row, 1972).

9 For a review see R. L. Davies, 'The location of service activity', in M. Chisholm and B. Rodgers (eds.), *Studies in Human Geography* (London: Heinemann, 1972), pp. 125–72.

10 See F. E. I. Hamilton, 'Industrial location models', in R. J. Chorley and P. Haggett (eds.), *Models in Geography* (London: Methuen, 1967), pp. 361–424. B. H. Stevens and C. A. Bracket, *Industrial Location* (Philadelphia: Regional Science Research Institute, Bibliographic Series, no. 3, 1967).

11 P. Cowan *et al.*, *The Office: A Facet of Urban Growth* (London: Heinemann, 1969), pp. 209–56. J. B. Goddard, 'Multivariate analysis of office location patterns in the city centre: A London example', *Regional Studies*, vol. 2 (1968), pp. 64–85.

12 R. B. Armstrong, *op. cit.*, p. 2.

13 P. Cowan *et al.*, *op. cit.*

14 R. B. Armstrong, *op. cit.*

15 R. M. Fisher, *The Boom in Office Buildings: An Economic Study of the Past Two Decades* (Washington: The Urban Land Institute, Technical Bulletin, no. 58, 1967). J. H. Dunning and E. V. Morgan (eds.), *An Economic Study of the City of London* (London: Allen & Unwin, 1971). E. Schultz and W. Simmons, *op. cit.*

16 R. M. Haig, *Major Economic Factors in Metropolitan Growth and Arrangement* (New York: Committee on Regional Plan for New York and Its Environs, Regional Survey, vol. 1, 1927).

17 E. Hoover and A. Vernon, *Anatomy of a Metropolis* (Cambridge, Mass.: Harvard University Press, 1959).

18 S. M. Robbins and N. E. Terleckyj, *Money Metro-*

polis (Cambridge, Mass.: Harvard University Press, 1960).

19 J. Gottman, *op. cit.*, pp. 565–630.

20 J. Gottman, 'Urban centrality and the interweaving of quaternary activities', *Ekistics*, vol. 29 (1970), pp. 322–31.

21 J. B. Goddard, 'Office communications and office location: A review of current research', *Regional Studies*, vol. 5 (1971), pp. 268–80. G. Törnqvist, 'Flows of information and the location of economic activities', *Geografiska Annaler*, vol. 50 (1968), pp. 99–107.

22 See E. M. Burrows, 'Office employment and the regional problem', *Regional Studies*, vol. 7 (1973), pp. 17–31.

23 See, for example, General Register Office, *Sample Census 1966, Great Britain, Economic Activity Tables* (London: Her Majesty's Stationery Office, 1968). Ministry of Labour, *Growth of Office Employment* (London: Her Majesty's Stationery Office, Manpower Studies, no. 7, 1968).

24 Ministry of Labour, *op. cit.*, p. 7.

25 R. B. Armstrong, *op. cit.*, p. 3.

26 R. Vernon, *The Changing Economic Function of the Central City* (New York: Committee for Economic Development, Supplementary Paper, no. 1, 1959), p. 55. See also Economic Consultants Limited, *Office Classification Systems* (London: Location of Offices Bureau, 1974).

27 C. W. Mills, *White Collar* (New York: Oxford University Press, 1953), p. 190.

28 *Ibid.*, p. 190.

29 G. Mills and O. Standingford (eds.), *Office Administration* (London: Pitman, 1966), p. 5.

30 *Town and Country Planning Act 1971* (London: Her Majesty's Stationery Office, 1971), s. 73 (5).

31 E. R. Rausch, *Principles of Office Administration* (Columbus: Merrill, 1964), pp. 7–8.

32 *Office Act 1960* (London: Her Majesty's Stationery Office, 1960).

33 *Offices, Shops and Railway Premises Act 1963* (London: Her Majesty's Stationery Office, 1963).

34 Economic Consultants Limited, *op. cit.*, p. 21.

35 Location of Offices Bureau, *Offices: A Bibliography* (London: Location of Offices Bureau, 1973). Greater London Council, *Offices in London* (London: Greater London Council, Department of Planning and Transportation, Research Bibliography, no. 48, 1973).

CHAPTER 2

Genesis of the Office

BEFORE THE INDUSTRIAL REVOLUTION

Throughout the early history of cities the office played an extremely minor role in the economy. The main function of cities right up to the beginning of the industrial revolution was one of defence, of trade, or of political and religious administration. Although these activities demanded a certain amount of transactional work or documentation they were relatively unimportant in the exchange of goods or in the organization of the church or local governing body. Scale is probably an important controlling variable here, in that most of the transactions between individuals or small groups were small scale and lacked the complexity typical of the business activities of the modern industrial corporation or central government department.

The information field within which entrepreneurs made decisions about the price at which to sell a good, or what new kinds of goods or products competitors were planning to make available on the market, was much more limited than at the present time. Communications beyond the immediate sphere of personal contact were poorly developed and sporadic. Most of the information relevant to decision-making was obtained on a purely verbal basis. The simplicity of the production process and the predominance of one- or two-man organizations precluded the need for space reserved for the use of office activities. As late as 1793, the administration of affairs of state in England involved a very low proportion of civil servants to total population; the Treasury, for example, employed just 37 people.[1] The average number of clerks in Liverpool commercial offices in 1871 was four.[2] Most office work took place in the homes of merchants or in the coffee houses and markets so that it did not need to occupy purpose-built space.[3] It was a rather submerged and

scattered, although still necessary, activity at a time when functional specialization was increasing in the cities of Europe and was later to occur more rapidly in North American cities.

The typical office employee of the medieval period, and indeed of more recent periods, was the clerk. His task was to copy the manuscripts, to write the correspondence, and to keep the records, many of which were concerned with accounts. Much of an office's work revolved around the ledgers in which the clerks painstakingly and meticulously recorded the company's monetary and other transactions. The clerk often enjoyed a privileged position in the community and had a measure of job security that was not typical of the workforce as a whole. But the lot of the clerk was not as pleasant as the job security suggested because 'some firms ... hard and coarse, suspicious and parsimonious, treating their clerks as slaves, forbidding them to approach the fireplace in frosty weather, and keeping them in busy seasons until nine or ten o'clock at night without allowing them refreshment, can obtain as many clerks as they wish, and secure instant submission by a hint of dismissal'.[4] Cobbett described the office in which he worked for a short period as a place which 'was so dark that on cloudy days we were obliged to burn candles. I worked like a galley slave from five in the morning until eight or ten at night, and sometimes all night long. I never quitted this gloomy recess except on Sundays.'[5] Clerks were therefore expected to work very hard for employers who did not particularly care for their contribution to the business. Although there were 'better clerical appointments, the holders of which emerged as a superior and more prosperous clerical class not only envied by their fellow clerks but by an aspiring section of the manual workers, who struggled to place their sons and later their daughters in white-collar employment',[6] most clerks seem to have attracted pity and scorn rather than admiration.

THE EFFECT OF THE INDUSTRIAL REVOLUTION

Fortunately for clerical workers, the conditions of work in offices were to improve dramatically with the coming of the industrial revolution. As we know, the industrial revolution changed the role of the city, and one of the side effects was to give offices a more prominent role in the economic structure. From the late eighteenth century onwards economic activity, particularly manufacturing industry, became concentrated close to the centre of towns and cities in Western Europe; a process which was later repeated in other continents, particularly North America. The growth of industry in the cities acted as a magnet for population migrating from rural areas where the enclosure movement was creating high levels of unemployment amongst the agricultural labour force.

At the same time, there were major changes in the organization and scale of industry which stemmed from the various technological developments of the period. Small manufacturing establishments employing a handful of men began to be replaced by units employing tens, sometimes hundreds, of people. This trend was encouraged by improvements in the organization of production and in the design and productivity of machines. Such concentrations of labour and production inevitably led to an increasing demand for the management of, and communication between, growing and complex organizations which might comprise several production units within the same city or in a number of cities throughout the country. These same units were also in competition with other firms which produced similar products and there arose a need for more detailed information about competitors, the efficiency and productivity of plants within the organization, developments in overseas markets, and the possibilities for future expansion. This was the environment which stimulated the demand for clerical workers, as well as for professional and managerial personnel, and which allowed the office to create a niche for itself as a vital cog in the smooth operation of urban and regional economies.

The plethora of industrial activities in the rapidly growing cities of the nineteenth century and the accelerating expansion of ports, with their import and export trades, required considerable finance, insurance, and other services. The growth of London's commodity markets is typical of these trends. It 'was natural that merchants and brokers should have their premises somewhere between the London quays and the Royal Exchange ... and the growth of trade led in time to the need for central premises'.[7] These were the demands which created office-based employment providing a wide range of specialist facilities. Such offices were usually separate from units of production and characteristically occupied the most central locations within the city and these were amongst the earliest examples of premises used solely for office purposes.

Nevertheless, the majority of offices were still attached to their parent manufacturing plants. The owners of new production plants usually set aside a room or rooms within their factory buildings for office use.[8] These rooms were often used for counting money and became known as 'counting rooms' and since the officials of the factories used them they also became known as 'officers' rooms. Hence, the terms 'accounting' and 'office' could well have been derived from these expressions. Rausch goes on to explain that 'as trade expanded in proportion to the growth of manufacturing, various commercial "counting houses" were set up to keep records of the volume of trade and the amounts owed for goods and these establishments contained a number of "counting rooms" manned by the predecessors of modern office staff'.[9]

OFFICE MECHANIZATION

Improvements in techniques of communication and data processing also influenced the rate at which office activities established their own identity and become separated from other urban functions. This phase in the evolution of offices has often been called 'office mechanization' based on an analogy with the mechanization of manufacturing.[10] Such an analogy should not be taken too far, however, because the 'important difference between office "machines" and machines used in "production" is that the former were not to the same degree associated with the phenomenon of separation of management and workers. Conveyor belt methods of production were not used in the office nor do we find there the extreme case of the creation of a proletariat who felt they were "cogs in the machine" with very little discretion of liberty and movement.'[11]

Office machines have been mainly used to minimize the amount of effort required to perform routine tasks as well as to increase the speed with which these tasks can be performed. In most cases the operators of office machines have considerable discretion over their use and they determine the efficiency of their contribution to the smooth operation of an office. The data and information used by offices is often complex and this has led to a wide variety of machines which have an interesting chronological sequence of development which forms an integral part of office genesis.

Most of the major developments in office equipment technology took place at the end of the nineteenth century when Dickensian quill pens were replaced by the typewriter, telephone, telegraph, and stencil duplicators. The typewriter made a very early appearance; some 150 years before it was patented in America, a patent was received in 1714 from Henry Mill, a British inventor, for an artificial machine or method for the impressing or transcribing of letters singly or progressively in such an exact fashion as not to be distinguishable from print.[12] But European inventors of office equipment rarely utilized the commercial potential of their inventions and it was left to North America to provide the real advances of commercial significance.

Sholes, Glidden, and Soule patented the first typewriter in 1868, although it took some years for it to be accepted as an essential adjunct to the successful conduct of business. The main reason was that it represented a rather impersonal method of communication compared with the hand-written letters typical of the day.[13] Any initial hostility to the typewriter was shortlived, however, as demonstrated by the sales figures for the Remington 2 which stood at 146 in 1879 and rose to an annual figure of 65,000 in 1890.[14] In general the diffusion of the typewriter was a slow process which is hardly surprising when it is remembered that on the early models the typist could not see the finished typescript. This made errors difficult to spot and correct, and the manufacturers resorted to providing their own specially trained operators in the same way as many computer firms do today. Working at the typewriter was also a noisy, laborious task, until the electric machine was finally introduced commercially in the 1920s, even though Edison had developed an electric typewriter as early as 1872.

The main value of the typewriter was that it permitted an increase in the speed at which business could be transacted on paper. The real benefits of this did not accrue until other media of communication had been developed. One of the most important of these was the telegraph, which preceded the typewriter in its commercial application by several years. The original telegraph consisted of a string of semaphores on hill tops which could only be used to transmit messages efficiently if the weather conditions were favourable. Such a system was clearly unreliable, inefficient, and restricted to communication between towns, rather than individual office premises, in areas where physical conditions happened to be suitable.[15]

Difficulties of this kind were overcome in 1837 when Cooke and Wheatstone invented an electrical instrument, the needle telegraph, which was subsequently exploited commercially by Watson in 1846.[16] The operation of the telegraph was first demonstrated by Morse in 1838 when a line between Washington D.C. and Baltimore was opened, to be followed by the first demonstration in Britain by Gray and Wheeler in 1853. In 1866 the Atlantic cable finally linked Europe and in 1862 there were already 15,000 miles of telegraph wires in Britain and 48,000 miles in America. Almost all the major towns were linked by 1868.[17] Commercial companies providing telegraphic facilities date back to 1846, but prior to 1845 it had only been possible to transcribe the messages by hand. The need for transcription reduced the efficiency of the telegraph as a medium for conveying information until the arrival of 'House's printing telegraph' which allowed messages to be printed directly they were received. This device was developed in the United States and it is interesting to note that it probably inspired the commercial exploitation of typewriters. Many of the typewriter entrepreneurs were also associated with the telegraph industry.[18]

With the typewriter facilitating greater speed in the recording and reproduction of information and the telegraph permitting exchange of information over greater distances at lower cost, the last two decades of the nineteenth century saw a rapid increase in the number of typewriters in offices and of telegraph lines linking headquarters offices with scattered branches. The dispersal of office facilities to several locations, in order to improve services to clients now became feasible because branch offices could communicate quickly and more comprehensively with headquarters.

Communications had emerged as one of the key factors in the emerging office function and their role was made complete by the telephone. Although based on much earlier European inventions, the telephone was patented by Bell in the United States in 1876.[19] There were over a million telephones in the United States before the end of the century. The first telephone company in Britain was formed in 1878 and although originally visualized as a means of oral communication between two points, represented by telephone exchanges, conversations between any pair of local subscribers eventually became possible. This opened the way for telephone lines between towns and the development of a national network.[20]

The impact of the telephone on the office was immense. It undoubtedly promoted the rapid expansion of the typist's function because it permitted oral contact to be made without face-to-face meetings. This was especially useful for dealing with more routine matters when the relevant arrangements, information or data could be confirmed or exchanged by letter. The speed with which these processes could be undertaken led to an increase in the volume of office work in parallel with the industrial and economic expansion of the late nineteenth century. The place of the office in the organization of economic activity was now assured. Indeed, the consequences of the telephone, as well as the telegraph, for the office function had 'geographical significance in providing more or less instantaneous contact with branch offices and warehouses or the docks, and with stock or commodity exchanges, all of which therefore were no longer as strongly restricted to adjacent situation as they were previously'.[21]

Another development with implications for office work was stencil duplicating. Its main asset was that it would allow the wide distribution of letters, memoranda and other papers within and between organizations. Duplicating also encouraged the reproduction of publicity and advertising leaflets for promotional and sales purposes and this extended the range of the office function. The man at the heart of this particular revolution in office work was Gestetner who started his own duplicating business, based in a small room in Sun Street, City of London, in 1861.[22] Gestetner invented a toothed wheelpin for writing on waxed stencils which used superior quality Japanese paper. This was a valuable step forward from the hectograph, for example, which was a purple jelly process of copying which created more problems than duplicates for its users. Duplicating problems had attracted enquiry before Gestetner's time but most of the methods used were slow and had limited output. Brunel patented a multiple writing machine in 1799 which used two quills carried by vertical swinging arms on a horizontal wooden frame with a separate ink-well. Probably the most practical of these early inventions was that made by Watt in the late eighteenth century. He devised a screw press which held together for a few minutes the original and the damp tissue paper on to which the duplicate copy would be impressed. This was useful for the exchange of technical documents attached to letters, for example, but only allowed a limited run of duplicates. Most of the early methods also involved clumsy equipment which was impractical for office use. Gestetner resolved all these problems and added a further essential item in most offices' equipment.

An increase in the flow of information on paper was therefore the main product of these technical innovations in office machines. Consequently, it has been suggested that all the activities in the metropolis have ultimately become connected with paper, not the least being offices which Merciar, writing in the eighteenth century, likened to the metropolitan form of the White Plague.[23] With the passage of time the dependence of offices upon paper has dramatically increased in a way which is 'economically out of all proportion to the intrinsic importance of the matter recorded' and this results in a 'ravaging flood of paper'[24] which has all been generated along Parkinsonian principles by expanding office activities. This process has been encouraged by the increasing size of firms and the transition from private business to the larger, and more complex, limited liability and joint stock companies and corporations as well as by the emergence of business and government bureaucracy. It has been suggested that this took place without the business world really being aware of what was happening but 'plainly, no great corporate enterprise with a worldwide network of agents, correspondence, market outlets, factories and investors, could exist without relying upon the services of an army of patient clerkly routineers in the metropolis'.[25]

Improvements in communications and methods of exchanging information also encouraged the development of machines for processing data more rapidly and accurately. These machines relieved mental rather than physical effort and, initially, the majority were essentially counting machines. In 1883, Burroughs, who had abandoned his profession as a book-keeper to invent a device which would avoid, and detect, errors in book-keeping, was able to launch a machine on the market. The machine printed the results as well as carrying out the additions and subtractions, and in the

1890s it became widely used in American banks.[26] Burroughs's calculating machine was subsequently improved and could be used for purposes other than cost calculations such as sales, production figures or purchases. These machines had one important side effect. They were essentially labour saving and simplifying devices and they caused a lowering of the level of skill required to carry out calculations. This reduced the status of clerical work and, because the qualifications required for such work also became lower, an increase of women in office employment began to occur. This trend was already under way at the turn of the century and was firmly established by the 1930s, especially amongst the lower tier jobs in the office occupation structure. Whilst the earlier inventions had created new office occupations such as telephonists or typists, the calculating machines had no such effect, despite the attempts by manufacturers to create specialist occupations for their operation.[27] Even so, by 1930, at least 30 per cent of female office workers in the United States used machines other than typewriters.[28]

The introduction of punched card systems during the early years of the present century did give rise to new office occupations. Most of the jobs involved were routine, such as key punch operators or sorters, but the result was increased demand for office workers. The use of these machines relied on data which were in precise and standardized form before sorting. This required careful pre-planning of the way in which data could be used and what was relevant for particular purposes. There was, therefore, substantial scope for 'support' as well as the more routine jobs.

The prototype electro-mechanical device for sorting punched cards was patented by Hollerith in 1889. It was based on Babbage's 'analytical machine' which was never completely built but probably represented the first general purpose computer. Hollerith's inspiration was also derived from the experiences of the United States Bureau of the Census which took nine years to compute the returns of the 1880 Census. It was anticipated that with increasing population the 1900 Census would have been taken before the 1890 figures had been processed.[29] The Hollerith machine transmitted numerical values derived from the punched card codes fed into it, at approximately 400 cards per minute, and then transferred them to a counting device which formed part of the machine. The device was subsequently incorporated in a wide range of other office machines and in 1913 it was said that a bank statement machine allowed 'one clerk to do the work of two book-keepers' and the improved calculators could 'literally devour figures'.[30] But these machines were only as accurate as the data fed into them and there remained a considerable demand for labour to process and prepare the appropriate material.

Between 1920 and 1950 new office machines appeared on the market in literally hundreds each year. During the decade 1940–50, in the United States alone, the influx was so great that the number of operators increased 138 per cent and 3000 office machines were exhibited annually as mid-century approached.[31] Such figures point to the vitality of office growth both as a physical and occupational entity during this period but the process seems to have passed comparatively unnoticed.

Such large-scale office mechanization, particularly by the more sophisticated electronic machines, precipitated extensive internal restructuring of offices.[32] In order for the machines to be used efficiently it was necessary for offices to be more systematically organized. This invariably involved the requisition of more office space for filing and recording systems. As the number of clerks as well as specialized office labour increased to manage these systems it became necessary to organize them into departments, each with their own clearly defined functions 'as if part of a well oiled machine'.[33] Hence, in the 1920s and 1930s anything up to 100 typists, stenographers and others might be found in one large room within the office, a phenomenon which some observers reported as resembling a factory.[34] Such layouts were the predecessors of the modern open plan or 'burolandschaft' design of office interiors.[35]

ADVENT OF OFFICE COMPUTERS

The most recent automatic or electronic data processing systems (E.D.P.) are computers which have been increasingly used in commercial and government offices during the last 15 years. Electronic digital computers were originally developed during the Second World War to aid scientific and engineering calculations connected with weapons' technology and it was not until the early 1960s that the potential of computers for handling office data processing problems was realized.[36] The significance of the computer is that it has encouraged further systematization of office work flows and data processing. Much of the straightforward processing work in dealing with large numbers of company customers, for example, could be completed in a fraction of the time taken by earlier electronic devices and the back-up clerical workers. As the systems have been developed, computer software has also become a very efficient, space saving, method of storing data and information for records or for future use. All this can be achieved with a high level of accuracy and a reduction in clerical inputs.

Computers were first used for office work in Britain towards the end of 1953. Subsequent growth rates were slow and as late as 1966 there were still fewer than 1000 computers in British offices (Table 1).[37] There has been a substantial absolute increase in the rate of installation since 1966 with projected net additions in 1974 and 1975 of 600 and 700 computers respectively. These figures only represent new projects and do not include computers delivered as replacements. But it is clear that the rate of increase per annum is in fact declining and is expected to drop from 40 per cent in 1967 to 5 per cent in 1978. This does not mean that the use of computers in offices will decline but it represents more efficient use of existing installations by time-sharing between companies or the use of computer bureaux providing services to offices unable to support their own systems. The size of individual computer installations has also increased over the years and these can handle larger volumes of work more rapidly than smaller systems. Therefore, the volume of office work effected by computers is likely to increase even though

TABLE 1
COMPUTERS IN OFFICE WORK,
1959–69—GREAT BRITAIN

Year (1 January)	No. of computers[2]	Net additions during year	Increase per annum (%)
1959[1]	26	10	—
1960	36	34	94
1961	70	55	79
1962	125	103	82
1963	228	162	71
1964	390	215	55
1965	605	284	47
1966	889	290	33
1967	1179	468	40
1968	1647	461	28
1969	2108	502	24

Notes: 1. The number of computers in 1959 is the total for years prior to that date.
2. Very small systems costing less than £20,000 and computers in service bureaux have been excluded. At 1 January 1969 these totalled 1600 and 180 respectively.

Sources: Ministry of Labour, *Manpower Studies No. 4—Computers in Offices* (London: Her Majesty's Stationery Office, 1965), Appendix 16, p. 53. Department of Employment, *Manpower Studies No. 12—Computers in Offices, 1972* (London: Her Majesty's Stationery Office, 1972), Table 2, p. 10.

TABLE 2
ELECTRONIC COMPUTERS IN USE,
1955–69—UNITED STATES

Year (1 January)	No. of computers	Net additions during year	Increase per annum (%)
1955	214[1]	532	148
1956	746	544	73
1957	1290	860	67
1958	2150	950	44
1959	3100	1000	32
1960	4100	2600	63
1961	6700	3700	55
1962	10400	3500	34
1963	13900	5700	41
1964	19600	5400	28
1965	25000	7900	32
1966	32900	11200	34
1967	44100	12400	28
1968	56500	14100	25
1969	70600	12600	18

Note: 1. Includes non-office computers.
Source: International Data Corporation, in R. B. Armstrong, *The Office Industry: Patterns of Growth and Location* (Cambridge, Mass.: The M.I.T. Press, 1972), Table 1.2, p. 11.

growth in the number of installations is slowing down. The decline in the growth of installations can also be attributed to underestimation by office management of the limitations of E.D.P.[38] Many have not appreciated the lack of flexibility and time-delays which can occur in processing data by computer while some firms have been over-optimistic about the range of work which can be undertaken on computers as a substitute for human action. The slow diffusion of computer 'education' amongst office management is largely responsible for these difficulties.

Computer installations have been adopted at similar rates by offices in the United States (Table 2). Following a period of rapid annual growth up to 1963, the proportional increase per annum has declined to 18 per cent in 1969 which is lower than the equivalent figure for Great Britain (Table 1). In absolute terms, however, the number of computer installations added each year is considerably larger than for British offices, although it should be noted that the figures in Table 2 include computers in educational and research establishments. The number of non-office computers in Great Britain totalled 1000, or approximately 50 per cent of the number of office computers, in 1969.[39] Using this proportion as a guideline, there were at least 35,000 office computers in the United States in 1969 and even allowing for difference in total population of offices this suggests wider use of computers than in British offices. Such comparison must remain subjective, however, because most of the published figures for different countries do not specify the types of computers included. There were over 1000 small calculators in British offices at the end of 1964, for example, but these are excluded in the Ministry of Labour survey.[40] The remainder of this discussion will therefore be devoted to computers in British offices.

The installation of E.D.P. systems by offices is a selective process reflecting the various data

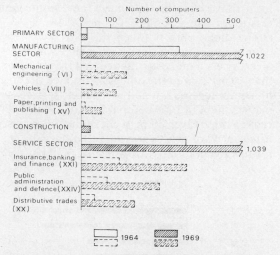

Fig. 1   Number of Office Computers, Great Britain—
By Major Industry Orders and Selected Sub-Orders,
1964 and 1969 (Data: Department of Employment,
Computers in Offices, 1972, 1972)

processing requirements of different economic
activities (Fig. 1).[41] Although the number of
computers in both 1964 and 1969 in the manufacturing and service sectors are almost identical,
individual industries within the service sector are
characterized by a larger number of computers
and faster growth rates. Hence, in 1964 over 18
per cent of the installed computers were in insurance, banking, and finance offices and there
was only a small decrease in this proportion in
1969 to just under 17 per cent. The number of
computers in these offices increased by 173 per
cent between 1964 and 1969. In the industrial
sector, offices in the electrical and engineering
goods industries had approximately 12 per cent
of all computers in 1964 and 1969. The concentration of computers in the service industries is
a product both of the proportion of total
national employment which they represent and
the greater relative importance of office work
within individual industries such as public administration or insurance, banking, and finance.
Similar patterns of distribution amongst industrial groups in Canada have been noted by
McDonald.[42] One-third of the computers in
Canada in 1962 had been installed by manufacturing industry with community/business services and banking/finance accounting for a
further one-third.

If the installed computers are analysed by size,
service sector offices again dominate the distribution (Fig. 2). Large installations represent 16

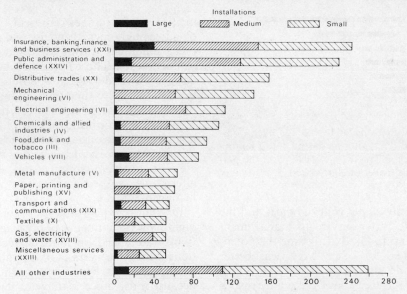

Fig. 2   Size of Computer Installations, Great Britain—By Industry Order,
1969 (After Department of Employment, *Computers in Offices, 1972*, 1972,
with the permission of the Controller of Her Majesty's Stationery Office)

and 18 per cent of the E.D.P. systems used by offices in insurance, banking and finance, and in gas, electricity, and water.[43] Only the offices of the vehicle industry had a similar proportion of large installations in 1969. Medium and small installations dominate in every industry, however, and only large organizations can either afford, or require, large installations. Large organizations with over 3000 employees had 49 per cent of all E.D.P. installations in 1969. If these organizations are further categorized according to the number of office staff, those with over 1000 personnel had 35 per cent of all installations in 1969, including 94 per cent of the large and over half of the medium-sized systems.[44]

The reasons given by office organizations for installing E.D.P. systems have changed through time.[45] During the early 1960s the reasons given largely mirrored the rationale for using the already existing electro-mechanical devices such as the punched card sorter. The need to reduce the cost of data processing and to speed the work amounted to 30 per cent of the prime reasons given in a 1964 survey of British offices (Fig. 3).[46] By 1969, these two reasons were listed as most

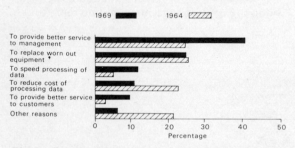

Fig. 3 Principal Reasons for Installing Office Computers—1964 and 1969 (After Department of Employment, *Computers in Offices, 1972*, 1972, with the permission of the Controller of Her Majesty's Stationery Office)

important by only 20 per cent of offices and the need to provide better service to management had become paramount. By this time the potential of computers for office work was better appreciated while Fig. 3 also shows that offices were also much clearer about the main reasons for installing computers. 'Other reasons' had declined from over 20 per cent in 1964 to 5 per cent in 1969. The need to provide better service

to customers has also become a more important reason for using computers since 1964.

The dichotomy between the 1964 and 1969 data becomes much clearer when all the reasons given by each office are aggregated (Fig. 4). Less than 40 per cent of the offices mentioned the role of computers as an aid to better service to management in 1964 compared with over 90 per cent in 1969. Over 80 per cent of the offices also listed speed of processing data as a relevant factor in 1969 compared with just over 40 per cent

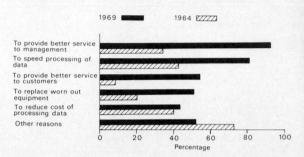

Fig. 4 Reasons for Installing Office Computers — By Frequency of Mention, 1964 and 1969 (After Department of Employment, *Computers in Offices, 1972*, 1972, with the permission of the Controller of Her Majesty's Stationery Office)

in 1964. Such changes represent the continuum of increasingly specialized use and application of office machines during the course of the last seventy years. The early office machines were designed to undertake low order, routine office tasks which were time consuming and wasteful of educated manpower. As the machines have become more sophisticated they have been used not only as substitutes for clerical office work and in data processing but also as an aid to more efficient problem solving and evaluation of alternative courses of action by company management.

One factor which surveys of this kind cannot quantify is the influence of prestige on the adoption of advanced office machines by organizations. Most observers of office automation refer to the prestige factor but cannot go further because most office managements are reluctant to admit the importance of this motive.[47] It seems that some firms use computers in their offices because they are 'impelled by the course of events' or 'because some other firm had preceded them'.[48] Some firms are reluctant to examine objectively the cost implications of using a computer in their operations and this also lends some weight to the view that prestige and related factors do play some part in decision-making about the installation of office computers.

Up to the middle and late 1960s, at least, the computers installed in British offices seem to be an extension of office mechanization rather than true automation.[49] Both on the basis of application to different types of work and time spent,

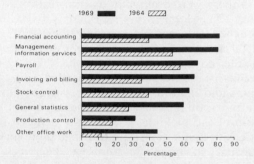

Fig. 5 Applications of Office Computers, Great Britain — 1964 and 1969 (After Department of Employment, *Computers in Offices, 1972,* 1972, with the permission of the Controller of Her Majesty's Stationery Office)

payroll work, management information services, and financial accounting amounted to at least 60 per cent of E.D.P. use in 1965 (Fig. 5). It was also found that the ratio of routine to other tasks performed had not changed very much in offices which had used computers for several years. This was probably encouraged by the need to overcome shortages of suitable office staff or because the computers replaced older and out-dated office machinery. Computer use had therefore been concentrated on the jobs which were most repetitive and largest in volume so that the more advanced applications, the benefits of which are less tangible, tended to be postponed. By 1969 the type of work processed by E.D.P. had become more evenly distributed but with a notable increase in management information services and financial accounting. These two computer applications could be regarded as the more sophisticated types of office work which were less widely manipulated by computer during the pre-1965 period. It would appear, however, that these changes still represent advanced mechanization rather than automation which has remained most applicable to manufacturing processes where the need to consider alternative courses of action or the implications of different decisions is less frequent.

OFFICE BUILDINGS

Physical changes in the buildings used to accommodate office work paralleled the process of functional evolution. Before offices emerged with a separate functional identity the need for specialist space and buildings did not arise, but once organizations became more complex and the volume of transactional activity began to increase during the nineteenth century the demand for purpose-built offices increased dramatically. Some of the earliest examples are found in central London where they date from the eighteenth century. These include the headquarters building of the East India Company opened in the City in 1726, the offices of the Admiralty, 1726, and the Bank of England completed in 1732. Somerset House was completed in 1789 and formed part of a complex of Government offices in the Strand.[50]

The pace of office building activity increased during the nineteenth century. Amongst the earliest to realize the significance of this expansion were the insurance companies who built a number of offices in the Strand and along Fleet Street between 1813 and 1815. These were followed by a series of Exchanges such as the Coal Exchange (1849), the Stock Exchange (1854), and the Wool Exchange (1874).[51] This marked the beginning of the long standing involvement of the institutions in providing and financing office buildings in our major cities. As the number of separate office buildings increased and the telephone, the typewriter, and the telegraph permitted further functional separation of offices from factories, clustering began to occur and this resulted in distinctive 'office quarters' such as parts of the City in London or Lower Manhattan in New York. Such agglomeration tendencies were already firmly established in the 1850s in central London and in the years following 1880 in New York.

Clustering of office building implies close spatial association within a limited area. But most of the early office buildings did not exceed 4 storeys in height because of the tedium of moving between, and getting up to, the floors. The relative simplicity of the building methods used also effectively limited the maximum height of buildings. In consequence, the number of office workers that could be accommodated in the expanding office clusters was limited by the volume of accommodation available in essentially low-rise structures. As the demand for space increased it had to be met by expansion around the fringes of the clusters or along arterial routes leading to them; Victoria Street (1852–71), Shaftesbury Avenue (1877–86), Queen Victoria Street (1867–71) and the Kingsway-Aldwych scheme (1905) were almost completely devoted to office frontages.[52] The outward spread of office quarters negated the advantages of proximity which many of the offices were seeking. Some locations benefited from superior accessibility both internally and externally to the office quarter compared with other areas. Some locations therefore became more attractive than others and there was clearly scope for taller buildings to cope with the pressures of demand at the most favoured points within cities.

Improvements in building techniques subsequently helped to resolve the space and location problems of office activities. Initially, however, construction of taller buildings required provision of thick walls at the base, tapering upwards so that the weight was supported by the base walls. The earliest examples of these proto-skyscrapers were built in Chicago where the architects allowed for a wall 12 in. thick for the support of a 2-storey building.[53] A further 4 in. of thickness was allowed for each additional storey. Ten storeys was considered the limit as this would result in a wall 4 ft thick at the base. Masonry-bearing walls of this type still permitted a major advancement in building height but the walls had so much to do in terms of load bearing that the windows had to be narrow, therefore cutting out valuable daylight for office

work. The sheer weight of building materials also placed enormous demands on the foundations and the taller the building the more costly it became to provide foundations. These buildings were also wasteful of space in that the letting space/building volume ratio was low.

In the 1870s and 1880s buildings with cast iron skeletons were being planned and this idea was to be used in the Home Insurance Building in Chicago, completed in 1885.[54] But this was not to be; during the design stage of the building the technique of rolling steel columns was perfected and these were eventually used instead of cast iron.[55] The Home Insurance Building was therefore the first true steel frame office building. The metal skeleton represented a major step forward in the construction of tall office buildings because the walls could be suspended from the frame and be of uniform thickness throughout (curtain walling). This reduced the height/weight ratio of the building, reduced the demand for extensive foundations, and provided more internal space for office uses and related services. A steel frame only weighed about one-third as much as wall-bearing masonry. These buildings also allowed an increase of up to 100 per cent in window space and therefore considerably improved the daylighting conditions of the offices.[56]

The tall buildings made feasible by improved construction technology were comparatively inefficient without rapid, energy saving, modes of transport between the ground and upper floors. This difficulty was resolved by the development of the passenger lift which was first installed in a relatively small building in New York in 1857 by the Otis Elevator Company.[57] This event 'inspired the entire vertical development of the American city'.[58] This, and other lifts mostly incorporated in hotels during the 1860s, was hydraulically operated and not very efficient in terms of speed, about 50 ft/min, and it could only service buildings with a maximum of 20 storeys. In 1873 the 10-storey Western Union Building in New York was the first office to be installed with hydraulically operated Otis elevators. Electric powered lifts were introduced in 1887 and these finally eliminated the remaining restrictions on building height. In 1904 the Otis Elevator Company installed three electric gearless traction lifts in the Beaver Building, New York, followed by two more in the Majestic Building, Chicago. By 1907 this type of lift had proved its supremacy and a new era in office building was under way.[59] The lift can be viewed as the verti-

cal component of the larger transport system serving the city centre. In New York alone there are over 30,000 passenger lifts covering more than 125,000 mile/day within buildings, many of them in the giant office blocks of Manhattan.[60]

SKYSCRAPERS

Buildings which 'express the need to accumulate floorspace for offices and related activities'[61] at high densities are known more commonly as skyscrapers. The Metropolitan Life Insurance Company of New York was an early convert to the skyscraper building (Table 3).[62] In about 1892 it built an 11-storey building at the north-east corner of Madison Avenue and 23rd Street which proved a success and followed this with a second building constructed in the late 1890s. The two buildings represented 850,000 ft^2 of office floorspace; large by the standards of Manhattan at the time. Skyscrapers of more than 18 storeys were common in Manhattan by the turn

of the century and with the caisson-type founda-tions developed in the 1880s, higher buildings of 25–30 storeys were possible. The 47-storey Singer Building completed in 1908 is an early example to be followed in 1913 by the Wool-worth Building which, for a time, had the distinc-tion of being the tallest skyscraper in New York. By 1915 there were six other towers of over 400 ft in Manhattan. Even so, it should be remembered that these office buildings repre-sented a small proportion of all the office build-ings in New York or Chicago; the remainder were low-rise unspectacular office premises. But the skyscraper represented an attempt to make the most efficient use of a scarce resource—land—in the most accessible areas of cities, the C.B.D.

Skyscraper office buildings have given the centres of major world cities a new and distinc-tive cityscape, particularly in North America. In the absence of really effective planning restric-tions in the United States, office blocks have been constructed in strongly clustered groups within the central areas of cities. This is best represented by Manhattan but is repeated on a smaller scale in Chicago, Detroit, Pittsburgh, Philadelphia, San Francisco or Seattle, to name a few. The scarcity of sites having high levels of accessibility within the central area has pushed up the value of such sites to extreme levels. The desire to maximize the use of such sites has forced office developers to construct as much space as possible in order to produce satisfactory returns on investment. Consequently, the World Trade Centre owned by the Port of New York Authority and completed in 1972 provides 9 m. ft^2 of floorspace in two tower blocks 1350 ft high. The office space provided covers 230 acres and can accommodate 50,000 office workers and generate more than 80,000 visitors to the build-ing every day.[63] This building dwarfs earlier

TABLE 3
PROGRESS OF TALL OFFICE BUILDINGS IN NEW YORK AND CHICAGO, 1872–1974

City	Year	Building	No. of storeys
Chicago	1872	Portland block	6
Chicago	1883	Montauk block	10
Chicago	1888	The Rookery	11
New York	1888	Tower building	11
Chicago	1891	Monadnock building	16
New York	1892	Metropolitan building	11
New York	1908	Singer building	47
New York	1909	Metropolitan Life Insurance Co. building	50
New York	1913	Woolworth building	60
New York	1931	Empire State building	102
New York	1932	Chrysler building	77
New York	1971	World Trade Centre	110
Chicago	1974	Sears building	109

Sources: Compiled from information in E. Schultz and W. Simmons, *Offices in the Sky* (New York: Bobbs-Merrill, 1959). W. McQuade, 'A daring new generation of skyscrapers', *Fortune*, vol. 87 (1973), p. 78.

skyscrapers such as the Empire State Building or the Pan-Am Building which in their own periods dwarfed earlier blocks. Brought together, such office buildings give the modern C.B.D. its strong vertical character.

Bailey has suggested a classification of office skyscrapers in the United States into First Era (1885–1919), Second Era (1920–44) and Third Era (post-1945).[64] The groups are largely based on design criteria such as types of elevator, heating system, capacity of electric system, and efficiency of ventilation. But the First Era was largely represented by 'experimental' office buildings in which new materials, techniques and facilities were developed without a backlog of previous experience. The Second Era was marked by a wide range of structural improvements, superior building designs and the economic skyscraper began to crystallize. Well equipped, safely designed skyscrapers are the hallmark of the Third Era with the main improvements facilitated by the perfection and acceptance of air-conditioning and fluorescent lighting.

Only since 1945 have skyscraper office buildings appeared in the centre of European cities. Prior to the *Town and Country Planning Act 1947* the maximum height of an office building in London was limited to 80 ft although if two additional floors were set back, this rose to 100 ft. Controls on building height were introduced in the *London Building Act 1894* largely because of objections to the 151 ft high Queen Anne's Mansions next to St James's Park underground station overlooking Buckingham Palace.[65] Only two pre-war buildings in central London exceeded this limit; Cooper's ornamental Port of London Authority Tower and the Senate House of the University of London (210 ft) completed in 1932. The general height of office buildings in the City of London before the war was under 70 ft with many less than 35 ft.[66] The 'taller' buildings in the City were also widely dispersed so that the central area retained its low-rise character in marked contrast to its North American equivalents.

Since the relaxation of building height controls in 1954 and the abolition of height limits in 1963 office skyscrapers have been added to the London skyline in increasing numbers. They remain small by North American standards, however, and only the 52-storey National Westminster Bank Building in the City at 600 ft, at present under construction, exceeds 500 ft. In central London, the Commercial Union Building, Centre Point, Euston Centre, Millbank Tower, and Britannia House in the Barbican area are examples of office buildings higher than 300 ft, but they are still far from achieving the density of jobs and the congested skyline of New York or Chicago.[67] Paris has held out even longer than London against the skyscraper but has eventually given way to a 685 ft office building at Maine–Montparnasse. There are several other blocks over 500 ft along the banks of the Seine and in the La Défense scheme on the fringes of the central area.

While skyscrapers have been getting higher, their physical form has been controlled by daylight codes and associated measures. Apart from controlling height of buildings, the London Building Acts also stipulated that street width should be related to height of building elevation. For example, in most of the City of London the sheer height permitted was one and a half times street width.[68] Various Town Planning Acts since 1947 have given local authorities power to determine building height, daylighting codes, density, siting, car parking, and the appearance of office building as part of the implementation of development control for planning purposes. Skyscrapers built too close together create canyon-like conditions between them. This is again well demonstrated in unplanned Manhattan where the amount of light and sky space visible from the lower floors is severely curtailed because of the shadows cast by adjacent buildings. This problem was especially acute in the areas of early skyscraper development and was made worse by the collection of exhaust and other pollutants in the stagnant air between the buildings. Such difficulties can be resolved by careful spacing of the buildings or by setting back the upper floors of skyscrapers above a certain height. But developers, and others interested in optimizing their returns, are unlikely to utilize these alternatives unless there is mandatory planning legislation in operation.

New York was the first city to respond to problems of this kind. The Commission on Congestion of Population brought out a voluminous report in 1911 citing towering office buildings as breeders of congestion and traffic problems. The Committee was reporting at a time when office development in New York was proceeding without the guidance of a general plan for the city and it recommended that height restrictions be imposed during the interim.[69] During subsequent years the opposition to skyscrapers gained momentum and an advisory body, the Heights of Buildings Commission, was set up to examine the problem.[70] On the basis of recommendation made by this, and other Commissions, the New York Zoning Ordinance 1916 was adopted by the Board of Resolution. This introduced conceptually very new zoning regulations pertaining to the height, area, and bulk of buildings on individual sites. These regulations forced architects 'to fit the building mass into an envelope resembling a Babylonian ziggurat, with the upper storeys progressively set back above a certain height to allow sunlight to penetrate the street'.[71] The economies of construction and the developers' individual whims for different sites and buildings now had to be tailored to the zoning requirements. This improved matters considerably and produced the characteristic stepped form of most New York skyscrapers built during the inter-war years. Provided that individual skyscrapers only occupied 25 per cent or less of their site areas, they could be constructed to any height. Where buildings exceeded this limit, the set-backs demanded restricted the height which could be achieved. In this way the bulk of office buildings was controlled.

The resistance to skyscrapers was not removed. There remained several complaints against them, some of which still apply today. The most longstanding argument is that they give rise to congestion of office workers, of movement between buildings, and in the journey to work.[72] This problem was considered in some detail in the Regional Survey of New York (1928).[73] A simple measure of the congestion of office workers and people was provided by the estimated number of workers converging on three recently completed buildings in Manhattan; the Chanin, Chrysler, and Lincoln buildings. These comprised 2,403,000 ft^2 of rentable floorspace with an estimated workforce of 18,400. It was further assumed that each office worker would generate four visitors per day. Hence, the total number of trips to these buildings was swollen by 74,000 to 92,400 per day. All these journeys would not converge on the three office buildings at the same time but they provide a measure of the employment and, more important, the traffic congestion generated by such buildings. The same survey stressed that time in movement has to be weighed against the factor of distance when attempting to evaluate the impact of skyscrapers on the central business district and the degree of proximity of buildings which is most efficient. These factors relate to three types of movement: those within the office building, those between different office buildings, and those between residences and office buildings. If the undoubted benefits of skyscrapers for office activity were to be retained it was essential not to overload one locality with the bulk of office buildings and their related movement patterns. The report did concede, however, that 'skyscrapers are not responsible for all types of congestion but when they bulk too closely together they contribute in a large degree to the kinds from which New York suffers'. In 1961 a new zoning resolution was introduced which, for the first time, introduced controls on building intensity by the use of a floor area ratio.[74]

Restriction on the height and bulk of skyscrapers does not necessarily resolve the congestion problem. If a 40-storey office building is restricted to 4 storeys, ten times as much space is required. Not only would this mean that there would be insufficient space to create sufficiently compact office clusters to generate economies of scale but impossible volumes of traffic, pedestrian and motorized, would be generated. Much of this traffic is at present confined to vertical movement within office buildings. The main difficulty occurs when all the office workers converge upon, or depart from, the offices at approximately the same time during the day.

Anti-skyscraper groups have also suggested that the buildings are uneconomic. This was also an early idea which was difficult to test until data became available, after the 1930s, from the National Association of Building Owners and Managers. Although based on an analysis of data from 624 office buildings in 1955, the basic conclusions could still be applied to modern sky-scrapers. The figures available included total income, the net income, and the average rent, per square foot. It was found that there is a 'definite increase in real income from the lowest to the tallest and from the smallest to the largest buildings'.[75] There are several reasons but the main ones are: it is only economic to construct tall or large buildings at the best locations because the cost of acquiring such sites is high, these large buildings can provide the best range of office services (lifts, etc.) and can therefore attract clients prepared to pay high rents, there is prestige to be derived from occupying skyscraper buildings and organizations are again prepared to pay for it, and because of the high rents which such buildings command developers can accumulate sufficient funds to provide the best facilities. Unless rents are actually controlled, therefore, or there is excess of supply over demand, there is no reason why skyscrapers should be uneconomic. The main disadvantage of height is construction financing cost which can sometimes effectively keep down building height.

The third major criticism is the effect of closely clustered skyscrapers on light and air. The early opposition on these grounds was that the conditions were a hazard to health but there has never been any medical evidence to support this contention. Artificial light has always been available to substitute for inadequately lit office areas. Before the development of neon and similar lighting, artificial lights were not a good substitute for natural light and the set-back provisions were certainly necessary. Many office organizations were anxious to provide natural lighting because of the effect on the morale of staff not only in terms of internal working conditions but because of the views provided. More recently lighting in all types of office building has been controlled in Britain by legislation which permits either natural or artificial lighting.[76] But the light problem is by no means confined to skyscrapers. It is found in any of the older office areas of our cities where narrow streets are closely flanked by buildings no more than 4 or 5 storeys in height. Modern air-conditioning systems are now standard equipment in most new office buildings and this has reduced the need for air or ventilation in the traditional sense.

Skyscrapers were also considered to be fire hazards. This may have been true of the early buildings in the United States but improvements in construction and the provision of adequate fire prevention devices has mitigated this problem. Indeed, Schultz and Simmons refer to experiences which show that office buildings have actually served as barriers in severe fires such as that in the Burlington Building, Chicago.[77] There have been very few fires in modern skyscrapers but there is still widespread concern amongst engineers, officials, and the public.[78] Some new building codes in the United States require installation of fire sensing and sprinkler devices which add 4 per cent to the total cost of a building.

Tall office buildings have also been seen as the main cause of the disequilibrium in the distribution of retail and other activities both within and outside the central area of cities. This kind of objection is likely to come from tenants or land-owners unable to obtain the best locations where they can benefit from proximity to higher value buildings.

Most recently of all, the impact of skyscraper offices on the urban landscape has been closely scrutinized, particularly in cities with historic cores such as London or Paris.[79] Much of Paris's old skyline has been replaced by the proliferation of skyscrapers along the Seine. There has been growing criticism and anger amongst Parisians about the impact of skyscrapers on the city and this has resulted in a plan to limit buildings in the centre to between 15 and 24 m (50–80 ft) which would lead to office buildings of 8 or 9 storeys at most. Centre Point, Euston Tower, the Millbank Tower, and New Zealand House have all, at various times, been the subject of controversy in central London. Their impact on traditional vistas such as along the Thames or Oxford Street (Millbank Tower and Centre Point) has been substantial and not made any easier to accept by the unimaginative architecture and design, a characteristic of many of the buildings involved. In the City of London there is clearly a conflict between the traditional architecture and historic buildings of the eighteenth and nineteenth century and the tall, glass and concrete slabs embodied by the modern office. The situation is aggravated in London by the scattered distribution of tall office buildings within the central area to produce an uncontrolled, confused skyline. In many ways the result is less satisfactory, visually, than in North American cities.

Skyscraper technology continues to improve. In really tall office buildings much of the space on the lower floors is occupied by lift shafts. This considerably reduces the rentable floor area and can make the difference between an economic and uneconomic building. Hence, many skyscrapers are being divided into separate units of 20–30 storeys, each unit being served by its own lift shaft facilities, with interchange facilities for movement between units. The 109 storey (1450 ft) Sears Building in Chicago uses this system of 'sky lobbies' combined with double deck lift cabs which can lift twice as many people on each trip.[80] If this building had used conventional lift

shafts they would have sterilized 45 per cent of its interior space. The weight of skyscrapers has also been reduced by using less masonry, wider interior spans and stiff exterior walls or 'tube structures' in order to reduce swaying to a minimum. These and other developments in skyscraper technology suggest that the 170–180-storey office building (2000 ft +) may yet appear in some of our major cities.

The functional evolution of offices and the development of a distinctive physical form to accommodate their activities has left a well established mark on the internal structure and character of the modern city. The skyscraper has become the edifice of office activity in cities. It now remains to examine, in greater detail, the growth and location of office activity at the regional and urban level.

REFERENCES

1 W. T. Morgan, *The Growth and Function of the General Office District in the West End of London* (Northwestern University, Illinois, unpublished Ph.D. Thesis, 1960).

2 B. G. Orchard, *The Clerks of Liverpool* (London: Collinson, 1871), p. 7.

3 The role of the coffee houses in the early development of the insurance industry in London is described in G. Clayton, *British Insurance* (London: Elek, 1971), pp. 15–16.

4 B. G. Orchard, *op. cit.*, p. 15.

5 W. B. Pemberton, *William Cobbett* (London: Penguin Books, 1949).

6 J. R. Dale, *The Clerk in Industry* (Liverpool: Liverpool University Press, 1962), p. 3.

7 G. Rees and J. Wiseman, 'London's commodity markets', *Lloyds Bank Review*, January (1969), p. 23.

8 E. R. Rausch, *Principles of Office Administration* (Columbus: Merrill, 1964), pp. 4–5.

9 *Ibid.*, p. 5. See also D. Lockwood, *The Black-coated Worker* (London: Allen & Unwin, 1958), pp. 19–35.

10 H. A. Rhee, *Office Automation in Social Perspective* (Oxford: Blackwell, 1968), p. 33.

11 *Ibid.*, pp. 35–6.

12 The history and social impact of typewriters is given in S. Bliven, *The Wonderful Writing Machine* (New York: Random House, 1954).

13 M. McCluhan, *Understanding Media* (New York: McGraw-Hill, 1964).

14 H. A. Rhee, *op. cit.*, p. 38.

15 E. T. Elbourne, *Fundamentals of Industrial Administration* (London: MacDonald & Evans, 1934), p. 47.

16 *Idem.*

17 T. K. Derry and T. I. Williams, *A Short History of Technology* (Oxford: Clarendon Press, 1960), pp. 626–7.

18 H. A. Rhee, *op. cit.*, p. 41.

19 *Ibid.*, p. 42.

20 T. K. Derry and T. I. Williams, *op. cit.*, p. 628.

21 W. T. W. Morgan, *op. cit.*

22 W. B. Proudfoot, *The Origin of Stencil Duplicating* (London: Hutchinson, 1972), p. 94.

23 L. Mumford, *The Culture of Cities* (London: Secker & Warburg, 1939), p. 256.

24 Town and Country Planning Association, *The Paper Metropolis* (London: Town and Country Planning Association, 1962), p. 3.

25 L. Mumford, *op. cit.*, p. 227.

26 H. A. Rhee, *op. cit.*, p. 44.

27 *Ibid.*, p. 45.

28 C. W. Mills, *White Collar* (New York: Oxford University Press, 1953), p. 193.

29 E. F. Baker, *Technology and Women's Work* (New York: Columbia University Press, 1964), p. 213.

30 G. M. Smith, *Office Automation and White-Collar*

Employment (Rutgers University: Institute of Management and Labour Relations, Bulletin, no. 6, 1959), p. 5.

31 E. F. Baker, *op. cit.*, p. 216.

32 C. W. Mills, *op. cit.*, pp. 195–8.

33 G. L. Coyle, *Present Trends in Clerical Occupations* (New York: The Woman's Press, 1928), p. 8.

34 *Ibid.*, pp. 9–10.

35 P. Manning (ed.), *Office Design: A Study in Environment* (Liverpool: Pilkington Research Unit, 1965), pp. 42–3. F. Duffy and D. Wankum, *Office Landscaping: A New Approach to Office Planning* (London: Anbar Publications, 1966). D. Canter, 'Reactions to open plan offices', *Built Environment*, vol. 1 (1973), pp. 465–7.

36 H. A. Rhee, *op. cit.*, p. 54.

37 Ministry of Labour, *Manpower Studies No. 4—Computers in Offices* (London: Her Majesty's Stationery Office, 1965), pp. 9–10. Department of Employment, *Manpower Studies No. 12—Computers in Offices, 1972* (London: Her Majesty's Stationery Office, 1972), pp. 9–10.

38 Department of Employment, *op. cit.*, p. 10.

39 Non-office computers used in scientific, design, and technical work, in educational establishments, for process control and in medical, defence, data communications, message switching and non-office computer service bureaux. See Department of Employment, *op. cit.*, Table 3, p. 11.

40 Ministry of Labour, *op. cit.*, pp. 10–11.

41 Department of Employment, *op. cit.*, Appendix 6, p. 68.

42 J. C. McDonald, *Impact and Implications of Office Automation* (Ottawa: Department of Labour, Occasional Paper, no. 1, 1964), p. 10.

43 Installations were classified according to the capital cost of their E.D.P. equipment. Large: over £500,000; Medium: over £100,000 to £500,000; Small: £20,000 to £100,000. Department of Employment, *op. cit.*, Appendix 1, p. 42.

44 *Ibid.*, p. 12.

45 Ministry of Labour, *op. cit.*, pp. 11–13. Department of Employment, *op. cit.*, pp. 12–14.

46 Ministry of Labour, *op. cit.*, p. 12.

47 *Idem.*

48 *Ibid.*, p. 13.

49 Department of Employment, *op. cit.*, pp. 13–14.

50 D. F. Stevens, 'The central area', in J. T. Coppock and H. C. Prince (eds), *Greater London* (London: Faber, 1964), p. 182. P. G. M. Dickson, *The Sun Insurance Office, 1710–1960* (London: Oxford University Press, 1960).

51 D. F. Stevens, *op. cit.*, pp. 181–3.

52 *Ibid.*, pp. 182–3.

53 E. Schultz and W. Simmons, *Offices in the Sky* (New York: Bobbs-Merrill, 1959), p. 26.

54 J. Gottman, 'Why the skyscraper?', *Geographical Review*, vol. 51 (1966), p. 191.

55 E. Schultz and W. Simmons, *op. cit.*, p. 37.

56 *Ibid.*, p. 38.

57 J. Gottman, *op. cit.*, p. 191.

58 E. Schultz and W. Simmons, *op. cit.*, p. 43.

59 *Ibid.*, p. 46.

60 J. H. Johnson, *Urban Geography* (Oxford: Pergamon Press, 1967), p. 111. See also J. H. Johnson, 'The geography of the skyscraper', *Journal of Geography*, vol. 55 (1956), pp. 349–56.

61 J. Gottman, *op. cit.*, p. 199.

62 E. Schultz and W. Simmons, *op. cit.*, p. 57. A. E. J. Morris, 'Skyscrapers', *Official Architecture and Planning*, vol. 32 (1970), pp. 55–7. A. Dickens, *Structural and Service Systems in Office Buildings: A Background Review* (Cambridge: Department of Land Use and Built Form Studies, Working Paper, no. 35, 1970), pp. 1–4. L. R. Ford, *The Skyscraper: Urban Symbolism and City Structure* (University of Oregon, unpublished Ph.D. Thesis, 1970). L. R. Ford, 'Individual decisions in the creation of the American downtown', *Geography*, vol. 58 (1973), pp. 324–7.

63 D. Rock, 'The architecture of compromise', *Built Environment*, vol. 1 (1973), p. 453.

64 G. R. Bailey, 'Functional design of office buildings', *Appraisal Journal*, vol. 24 (1956), pp. 175–9.

65 O. Marriott, *The Property Boom* (London: Hamish Hamilton, 1967), p. 30. See also D. Hawkes, *Building Bulk Legislation: A Description and Analysis* (Cambridge: Department of Land Use and Built Form Studies, Working Paper, no. 4, 1969), pp. 25–38.

66 Corporation of London, *Preliminary Draft Proposals for Post-War Reconstruction of the City of London* (London: Improvements and Town Planning Committee, 1944), p. 12.

67 For the distribution of buildings taller than 150 ft in the City of London see 'Towers in context', *Official Architecture and Planning*, vol. 32 (1970), pp. 333–5.

68 Corporation of London, *op. cit.*, p. 12.

69 M. Scott, *American Town Planning Since 1890* (Berkeley: University of California Press, 1969), pp. 153–4.

70 *Report of Heights of Buildings Commission* (New York: 1913).

71 M. Scott, *op. cit.*, p. 156. For a more detailed discussion of the effects of the Ordinance on office development see D. Hawkes, *op. cit.*, pp. 17–22.

72 E. Schultz and W. Simmons, *op. cit.*, pp. 274–5. F. A. Delano, 'Skyscrapers', *American City*, vol. 34 (1926). pp. 1–9.

73 *Buildings: Their Uses and Spaces About Them* (New York: Regional Survey of New York and Its Environs, 1931), pp. 69–92.

74 D. Hawkes, *op. cit.*, pp. 22–5.

75 E. Schultz and W. Simmons, *op. cit.*, p. 277. See also C. Thomsen, 'How high to rise', *Appraisal Journal*, vol. 32 (1966), pp. 585–91.

76 *Offices, Shops and Railway Premises Act 1963* (London: Her Majesty's Stationery Office, 1963).

77 E. Schultz and W. Simmons, *op. cit.*, p. 276.

78 For a more detailed discussion see W. McQuade, 'A daring new generation of skyscrapers', *Fortune*, vol. 87 (1973), pp. 150–2.

79 A. Ling, 'Skyscrapers and their siting in cities', *Town Planning Review*, vol. 34 (1963), pp. 7–18.

80 W. McQuade, *op. cit.*, p. 82.

CHAPTER 3

The Growth of Office Employment

The evolution of the office has already been considered because of the important contribution made by the various improvements in communications, office machine technology, and building techniques to the growth of office work. Brought together, these changes have resulted in rapid growth of office employment in most advanced economies and in extensive restructuring of the office labour force, both in terms of its sex structure and the range of occupations represented. Before analysing the growth of office employment it is necessary to consider the definition of the term and the sources of data which can be used for work in this field.

BLUE-COLLAR/WHITE-COLLAR

The limitations of published statistics relating to office employment have, until fairly recently, made it necessary to make *ad hoc* delimitations of office work. The most frequently used is the blue-collar/white-collar dichotomy which has formed the basis of so many studies of changing employment structure at national level.[1] Manual work is generally associated with blue-collar jobs and this category has been in existence far longer than the white-collar group. White-collar workers are non-manual and undertake the 'intellectual' jobs. This idea of the work function of white-collar workers probably has its origins in the emergence of a group of workers towards the end of the nineteenth century with neither managerial or manual occupations. Before this period most companies were small and the manual/non-manual function was indistinct. Many managers also undertook production work but as businesses grew occupational distinctions became clearer. The owner of the factory would be the manager while he might use members of his family to organize and control the production work. These represented the beginnings of clerical occupations and the emergence of a distinctive white-collar group. The sales staff, the administrative personnel or the accountants all occupied an intermediate position between the entrepreneur and the production workers. White-collar workers are therefore employees who perform supervisory, analytical, administrative, mercantile and other functions delegated to them by their employers.[2] White-collar workers can therefore be viewed as a separate social or socio-economic group.[3]

This does not resolve any difficulties of identification. The boundary between blue- and white-collar work may be drawn with reference to the type of work performed, but the distinction between manual and intellectual work is not always clear. It is also possible to distinguish between the groups on the basis of distinctions in conditions of work; white-collar workers receive monthly salaries, sick pay, pension and superannuation schemes, and other fringe benefits not enjoyed by most blue-collar workers. But there are many exceptions to this general rule, relating to both groups. There are also many blue-collar workers with more demanding and responsible jobs than their white-collar colleagues.

Using census information, white-collar jobs are normally identified as comprising the following major groups: professional, technical, and related workers; administrative, executive, and managerial workers; clerical workers; and sales workers.[4] This classification is used by the International Labour Office in an attempt to standar-

26

dize data on employment but individual national censuses vary considerably. Two of the censuses nearest to adopting this classification are those of the United States and Britain.[5] The blue-collar category includes craftsmen, operatives and labourers, while the U.S. Census also has a third group defined as service workers who work in household and other jobs which cannot be classified as white-collar or blue-collar. These are broad categories which conceal considerable internal variation which often leads to under-representation of office employment.[6]

The increase in the number of white-collar workers during this century has often been equated with the rapid expansion of service industries. These include commerce, transport and communications, insurance, banking and finance, and the public utilities—gas, electricity, and water.[7] These are sometimes referred to as the tertiary industries, as distinct from the secondary industries involved in manufacturing or the primary industries of agriculture, mining, and quarrying. But it would be inaccurate to directly relate the growth of white-collar employment to the expansion of service industries.[8] The utilities, for example, employ more blue-collar than white-collar workers while some of the secondary industries include a large proportion of white-collar workers.[9]

The terms 'white-collar' or 'service industry' are therefore not specific enough to be equated with office employment. It is necessary to find a narrower definition which still permits use of census statistics. Hence, Gottman has proposed the term 'quaternary' sector which in occupational terms includes managerial, professional, and higher level technical personnel.[10] This would correspond with administrators and managers (XXIV) and professional, technical workers, artists (XXV) in the British Census. But there are still occupations included in these two categories which are not necessarily office or white-collar workers. Clerical workers are also excluded although Gottman recognizes that they should be included in the quaternary rather than the tertiary sector. The latter would only be concerned with the transportation and manipulation of goods and with sales and distributive activities. It is conceded, however, that the quaternary sector is not only derived from service industry but also occurs in the secondary sector. A good example is publishing which is included in the manufacturing sector but includes a large number of managerial and editorial staff who should be included in the quaternary sector.[11]

OFFICE EMPLOYMENT BY OCCUPATION

The term 'office employment' refers to an individual's occupation rather than to the industry in which he works. Office work comprises a particular kind of job, the content of which does not vary substantially between different types of organization or business. It is unfortunate, therefore, that sources of information on office occupations are of limited scope and detail. The U.S. Census does not report office jobs as such while the British Census only produced a standard definition of office occupations in 1968.[12] This definition was first used in the 1966 Census on a selective basis. Prior to this time it was necessary to classify office occupations according to the individual researcher's requirements. Certain occupation groups, particularly clerical workers, are ubiquitous to all the census reports since 1921, while other occupations such as stenographers or office machine operators have only been added more recently.[13] This makes the task of analysing temporal changes in office employment very difficult and open to some subjective assessment. In addition, all the data prior to 1966 is by place of residence rather than place of work. In view of the locational characteristics of office employment, the latter is much more useful.

Although occupation questions were included in the first census in 1801, the detail and depth of analysis has changed with each successive census.[14] Up until 1911 the classification of occupations was a compromise between an occupation and industrial grouping and a clear distinction between the two was not made. Office occupations were not a major component of the employment structure, particularly before 1900,

TABLE 4
SELECTED DEFINITIONS OF OFFICE WORKERS—GREAT BRITAIN

Occupation	Census code 1960	1966	1970	1963 Inter-Dept	1966 Inter-Dept	G.L.C.	M.R.U. 1968
TRANSPORT AND COMMUNICATIONS (XIX)							
Telephone operators	201	128	127	*	*	*	N
Telegraph and radio operators	202	129	128	*	*	N	N
Messengers	204	131	130	N	*	*	N
CLERICAL WORKERS (XXI)							
Office managers n.e.c.	—	—	138	N	N	N	N
Typists, shorthand writers, secretaries	220	139	141	*	*	*	*
Clerks, cashiers	221	140a	139	*	*	*	*
Office machine operators	221	141b	140	*	*	*	*
Civil service executive officers	222	142	142	*	*	*	N
Civil service, L.A. officers	223	143	—	*	*	*	N
SALES WORKERS (XXII)							
Finance, insurance brokers	238	152	149	*	*	*	N
Salesmen, services; valuers, auctioneers	239	153	150	N	*	*	N
ADMINISTRATORS AND MANAGERS (XXIV)							
Ministers, M.P.s n.e.c., senior Government officials	270	172	173	*	*	*	N
L.A. senior officers	271	173	174	*	*	*	N
Managers in engineering and allied trades	272	174	175	N	*	*	N
Managers in building and contracting	273	175	176	N	*	*	N
Managers in mining and production	274	176	177	N	*	*	N
Personnel managers	275	177	178	*	*	*	N
Sales managers	276	178	179	*	*	*	N
Company directors	277	179	—	*	*	*	N
Managers n.e.c.	278	180	180	*	*	*	N
PROFESSIONAL, TECHNICAL AND ARTISTS (XXV)							
Civil, structural and municipal engineers	288	189	195	*	*	*	N
Mechanical engineers	289	190	196	*	*	*	N
Electrical engineers	290	191a	197	*	*	*	N
Electronic engineers	290	192b	198	*	*	*	N
Work study, progress engineers	—	—	199	N	N	N	N
Planning, production engineers	—	—	200	N	N	N	N
Engineers n.e.c.	—	—	201	N	N	N	N
Metallurgists	—	—	202	N	N	N	N
Technologists n.e.c.	291	193	203	*	*	*	*
Chemists			204	N	N	N	N
Physical and biological scientists	—	—	205	N	N	N	N
Authors, journalists	293	196	206	*	*	*	N
Accountants, professional	296	199	209	*	*	*	N
Company secretaries and registrars	—	—	210	N	N	N	N
Surveyors	—	—	211	N	N	N	N
Architects, town planners	—	—	212	N	N	N	N
Judges, barristers, solicitors	299	202	214	*	*	*	N
Social welfare and related	310	203	215	*	*	*	N
Officials of trade or professional unions	—	—	216	N	N	N	N
Professional workers n.e.c.	311	204	217	*	*	N	N
Draughtsmen	312	205	218	*	*	*	N
Technical and related workers n.e.c.	314	208b	220	N	*	*	N

Notes: 1. G.L.C.—Greater London Council (no date available); M.R.U.—Manpower Research Unit (Department of Employment, formerly Ministry of Labour); N—not included in definition.

2. *a*: revised occupation unit; *b*: new occupation unit.

Sources: General Register Office, *Sample Census 1966 England and Wales, Economic Activity Leaflets, General Explanatory Notes* (London: Her Majesty's Stationery Office, 1968). South East Joint Planning Team, *Strategic Plan for the South East* (London: Her Majesty's Stationery Office, 1971). Appendix 3.B, p. 119. Office of Population Censuses and Surveys, personal communication, September 1973.

so that this was not a major disadvantage. Since 1911 there have been gradual additions to the list of occupations which could be considered office employment and which were published separately from industrial groupings. Since the 1961 Census office occupations have been grouped to give aggregate figures for office work in administrative areas with 50,000 population and above and for larger areas such as counties and Economic Planning Regions. There were a number of additions in the 1966 Census (Table 4) while the most recent census classification also includes new groups such as work study and progress engineers or planning and production engineers.[15] A number of other definitions of office employment, based on census occupation groups, have also been in use during the last decade (see Table 4).[16] Widening the definition of office occupations is useful but the point is fast approaching where non-office occupations are being included.[17]

As an alternative to the census classification a system which 'has been made simple to operate and broadly compatible with other national and international classifications' has been introduced by the Department of Employment.[18] An occupation is defined as a collection of jobs sufficiently similar in their main tasks to be grouped under a common title for classification purposes and 3500 occupations are identified in this way.[19] Office-type occupations are listed but are not grouped accordingly; they are therefore scattered throughout the classification and have yet to be officially identified, which partly reflects the Department's concern with producing data appropriate to its own requirements.

This detailed classification also provides a frame for an abbreviated set of occupational statistics derived from selected key occupations in the list of 3500 individual occupations. But unfortunately the List of Key Occupations for Statistical Purposes does not handle office occupations comprehensively.[20] The classifications of office occupations used by various official sources also utilize a uni-dimensional grouping of occupations according to job content. But an individual's office job may comprise several facets and multi-axial classifications are now receiving more attention.[21] These take into account job skill, job activity or job knowledge, for example,

and result in a composite classification based on four or five axes.

The Regional Plan Association devised several major categories of office employment, representing a successively smaller component of a family of white-collar activities linked to offices, for its study of the New York Region.[22] Office-type occupations were defined as all white-collar occupations except sales workers. In common with the British experience, occupations not directly related to the performance of office work, such as pharmacists or musicians, were therefore included. Therefore these were excluded, mainly on the basis of subjective judgement, leaving office jobs as all office occupations minus certain deleted categories (Table 5). The study was especially concerned with office jobs in detached office buildings, particularly those in headquarters offices and for the New York Region these were obtained by matching geographical occupation data against available inventories of floorspace. For other metropolitan regions it was necessary to use a proxy in the form of central administrative office and auxiliary employment (C.A.O.&A.) which is reported by the U.S. Census for several selected industry groups. It is the only available source for tracing changes in employment in headquarters office activity over a relatively recent time period.

There are other sources of data on office employment but most of them relate to specific geographical areas. Some city planning departments undertake their own employment surveys which incorporate reference to offices but differences of definition and the collection of data for different time periods often makes such surveys difficult to compare with the census or with each other in an objective way. The Department of Employment publishes employment figures on a monthly basis and in its annual statistical reviews but the principal concern is with blue-collar employment.[23] Information about the numbers of administrative, technical, and clerical employees in manufacturing industries is given twice a year using returns provided by certain employers under the *Statistics of Trade Act 1947*.[24] These returns are used to estimate the total number of white-collar employees in each manufacturing industry group. The exclusion of service industries is clearly a major limitation of

TABLE 5
DEFINITION OF OFFICE WORKERS—UNITED STATES

Occupation	Occupation
PROFESSIONAL AND TECHNICAL WORKERS	CLERICAL AND KINDRED WORKERS
Accountants and auditors	Agents
Architects	Attendants
College faculty	Bank tellers
Designers	Book-keepers
Draftsmen	Cashiers
Editors and reporters	Collectors
Engineers	File clerks
Lawyers and judges	Insurance adjusters
Personnel and labour relations	Messengers and office boys
Public relations and publicity	Office machine operators
Social workers ($\frac{1}{3}$ of total)	Payroll clerks
	Postal clerks
	Receptionists
MANAGERS, OFFICIALS AND PROPRIETORS	
Buyers in stores	Secretaries
Credit men	Shipping clerks
Public administration officials	Stenographers
Purchasing agents and buyers	Stock clerks
Society, lodge and union officials	Telegraph operators
Selected salaried managers and officials ($\frac{1}{2}$ of total)	Telephone operators
	Typists
	Other clerical workers

Source: U.S. Bureau of the Census, *U.S. Census of Population: 1960, Detailed Characteristics* (Washington: U.S. Government Printing Office, 1962).

these statistics. It is also possible to extract figures for office employment for individual organizations from the annual returns provided under the auspices of the *Offices, Shops and Railway Premises Act 1963*. The task is arduous, however, and is only really feasible for detailed studies such as that undertaken for the City of London.[25]

These examples have been given in order to illustrate both the difficulties of defining office employment and the variety of definitions in use. It is therefore important to establish the precise definition used before commenting upon, comparing, or deriving relationships from statistics for different time periods or for different countries.

The censuses are clearly the main sources of information on office employment but separate totals for 'office occupations' are extremely recent. In order to extract similar statistics from previous years it is necessary either to adopt a very narrow definition of office employment or estimate figures from the available information. Contingency solutions of this type are very unsatisfactory and there is considerable scope for an improvement in office employment statistics.

GROWTH OF WHITE-COLLAR OCCUPATIONS

It has already been suggested that the growth of office employment is intimately associated with the growth of the broader group of white-collar occupations. Comparison of the trends over a similar 50 year period in the United States and Great Britain shows that white-collar occupations have doubled their share of all occupations (Table 6). Even allowing for differences in definition of occupation groups the statistics for each country are remarkably similar. In 1911 white-

nations are bound to evolve in the same direction'.[26] Blue-collar occupations still outnumbered the white-collar groups by approximately 2:1 in Great Britain in 1961 but the balance is changing in favour of the latter and could eventually arrive at a similar position to the United States.

White-collar occupations are proportionally most important in the advanced economies (Fig. 6).[27] Statistics for a selection of ten countries

TABLE 6
DISTRIBUTION OF WHITE- AND BLUE-COLLAR OCCUPATIONS IN
GREAT BRITAIN AND THE UNITED STATES—1911–61 AND 1910–60 (millions)

Great Britain					United States				
Year	White-collar[a]	Blue-collar	Total[1]	White-collar (%)	Year	White-collar[b]	Blue-collar	Total[2]	White-collar (%)
1911	3·4	13·7	18·3	18·7	1910	8·0	14·2	37·3	21·4
1921	4·1	13·9	19·3	21·2	1920	10·5	17·0	42·2	24·9
1931	4·8	14·8	21·0	23·0	1930	14·3	19·3	48·7	29·4
1941	*	*	*	*	1940	16·1	20·6	51·7	30·9
1951	6·9	14·4	22·5	30·9	1950	21·6	24·3	59·0	36·6
1961	8·5	14·0	23·6	35·5	1960	28·7	25·6	68·0	42·2

Notes: 1. Total includes employers and proprietors.
　　　2. Total includes service and farm occupations excluded from blue- or white-collar groups.
　　　a. Comprises: Managers and Administrators, Higher Professional, Lower Professional, Foremen and Inspectors, Clerks, Salesmen, and Shop Assistants.
　　　b. Comprises: Professional, Managerial, Clerical, Sales occupations.
Sources: Great Britain: G. S. Bain, *The Growth of White Collar Unionism* (Oxford: Clarendon Press, 1970), Table 2.1, p. 12, United States: R. B. Armstrong, *The Office Industry: Patterns of Growth and Location* (Cambridge, Mass.: The M.I.T. Press, 1972), Table 1.5, p. 16.

collar occupations comprised 18·7 per cent of the labour force in Great Britain; the equivalent for the United States was 21·4 per cent. These proportions had increased to 35·5 and 42·2 per cent by 1961 and 1960 respectively. In the United States the number of white-collar jobs increased by more than 200 per cent between 1910 and 1960 while blue-collar jobs grew by less than 50 per cent. Indeed, by the 1960 Census, the absolute number of white-collar jobs exceeded blue-collar jobs for the first time and 'once one of the larger countries in the world has achieved such new structural characteristics many other

representing a range of economic development show that in 1970 the United States had four times as many workers in white-collar occupations as Pakistan in 1968. In Pakistan, white-collar occupations only increased from 7·9 per cent in 1961 to 10·8 per cent in 1968 and in Hungary from 17·4 to 25·9 per cent. Although Venezuela compares more favourably with Great Britain or Japan, for example, this is because it has a large proportion of sales workers, many of whom would not be included in a narrower definition of white-collar occupations. It is more difficult to generalize about the annual growth rates of white-collar occupations in different countries. The number of white-collar workers in Pakistan increased by 89 per cent between 1961 and 1968; an annual rate of 12·7 per cent. Some equivalent figures for other countries shown in Fig. 6 are: Hungary, 1·2 per cent per annum (1960–70), Japan, 4·0 per cent per annum (1965–70), Canada, 5·0 per cent per annum (1961–71), and the United States, 4·3 per cent per annum (1960–70). Detailed analysis of the causes of the variations in growth rate would probably reflect differences in economic systems, capitalist

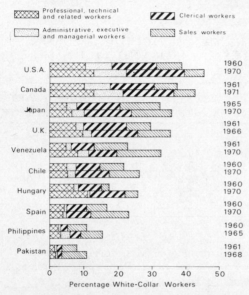

Fig. 6   White-Collar Occupations as a Proportion of All Occupations—Selected Countries (Data: International Labour Office, *Yearbook of Labour Statistics,* 1971)

or socialist; and the wider range of economic activities in the more advanced countries which generate a growing demand for professional and administrative occupations. White-collar occupations are growing fastest in the countries with high *per capita* incomes while the countries at the other end of the scale are still at the stage where blue-collar occupations are the fastest growing group.[28]

The expansion of white-collar occupations has also been selective (see Fig. 6). The two higher order occupation groups, professional, technical and related workers, and administrative, executive and managerial workers, have increased their share of all white-collar occupations. They accounted for 47·7 per cent of white-collar occupations in the United States in 1960 compared with 50·5 per cent in 1970. In Canada they increased from 48·1 to 52·1 per cent and in Great Britain from 32·1 to 35·1 per cent between 1961 and 1966. These two groups of occupations coincide with the quaternary sector suggested by Gottman and it is clear that the trends he observed in Megalopolis in the early 1960s have spread elsewhere.[29] The proportion of clerical workers has either remained constant or declined slightly in the occupation structure of these advanced economies but in countries such as Spain and Chile they are the fastest growing group.

The growth of white-collar occupations is therefore a cyclical process which can be linked to stages of economic development. In the early stages, exemplified by the industrial revolution, blue-collar occupations predominated as industrial production expanded and diversified. The second phase in the cycle was represented by a reduction in the growth rate of blue-collar occupations as the organization, transactional, and marketing activities required for efficient absorption of industrial and other goods into national and international trade began to increase in importance. This stage has been illustrated for the United States and Great Britain in Table 6. A third stage, involving proportional dominance of white- over blue-collar occupations has only been reached in the United States but this will eventually occur in other countries such as Great Britain or Japan in the near future. The final stage involves further differentiation of the white-collar work into quaternary and non-quaternary occupations. The quaternary occupations are now growing more rapidly than any other group as education, government, transactional activities, decision-making, research and analysis become even more important to the smooth operation of advanced economies.

CLERICAL WORKERS AND OFFICE EMPLOYMENT GROWTH

Much of the growth in white-collar occupations can be attributed to an increase in office-based activities. Probably the best single index of the growth of these activities during the last century is the number and proportion of clerical workers. These can almost exclusively be considered office workers although not all of them will be employed in office buildings.

The number of clerical workers increased faster than the number of people employed in professional occupations during the second half of the nineteenth century (Table 7).[30] Between 1871 and 1881 the number of commercial clerks in England and Wales increased by 99 per cent compared with 36 per cent for civil engineers and 9 per cent for solicitors. In 1881, however, there were over 317,000 employees in 17 different professional occupations and only half as many com-

mercial clerks.[31] But by 1911, there were more commercial clerks than professional workers; 477,000 and 473,000 respectively, and while the former increased by 163 per cent between 1881 and 1911, the latter increased by just 50 per cent. The pattern of growth for clerical workers was similar in the United States at this time with an increase of 69 per cent between 1870 and 1880. The decade of most rapid growth also occurred at the same time in Great Britain and thereafter the decennial growth rates decreased.

It was at this time that the telegraph, the typewriter, and the telephone were beginning to make their impact on office-based activities. With such small base totals, the rates of growth of clerical occupations during these early decades were inevitably high. Although in subsequent decades, especially during this century,

TABLE 7

PERCENTAGE INCREASE OF CLERICAL WORKERS IN
ENGLAND AND WALES AND THE UNITED STATES—
1841–1901 AND 1870–1900

Census Year	No. of Clerks (000s)	Increase (decade) (%)	Share of total labour force (%)
ENGLAND AND WALES			
1841	46689[1]	—	0·6
1851	60353	29	1·0
1861	56132	−7	1·5
1871	91475	63	1·9
1881	182457	99	2·6
1891	246761	35	3·4
1901	362710	47	3·9
UNITED STATES			
1870	305502[2]	—	2·4
1880	518439	69	3·0
1890	801505	54	3·5
1900	1068993	33	3·7

Notes: 1. Figures for England and Wales refer to commercial clerks only and exclude clerks attached to industrial establishments.
2. Based on estimates for all clerks, including those in industrial establishments.

Sources: England and Wales: W. J. Reader, *Professional Men: The Rise of the Professional Classes in Nineteenth Century England* (London: Weidenfeld & Nicolson, 1966), Tables I and II, Appendix I, p. 208 and p. 211.
United States: G. R. Terry, *Office Management and Control* (Homewood: Irwin, 1962), Table 2.6, p. 30.

the growth rate has slowed down the absolute number of clerical workers has increased steadily to represent a growing proportion of the total labour force. Even by the turn of the century, however, clerical workers only formed 4 per cent of the employed population in both Britain and the United States (Table 7). Although this represented considerable advancement from the estimated proportion of 1 per cent in England and Wales in 1841, national employment was very much the domain of blue-collar workers and other occupations such as the professions.

The trends triggered off when the first mechanical aids to office work were invented have continued up to the present time. The continued growth of the clerical function in offices may be explained in terms of the need for communication. Therefore, 'if a message takes a channel of x frequencies to travel y time, one can usually use $2x$ frequencies and, by simultaneous trans-

mission achieve $\frac{1}{2}y$ time. This is essentially what happens in the staff-clerical function. Unable to speed up transmission, we duplicate messages and transmit simultaneously achieving a measure of the desired speed.'[32] The development of the postal system or internal telephone systems would illustrate this process. As methods of communication have improved, this explanation for the clerical function becomes less satisfactory, but it certainly helps to explain the rapid increase in clerical occupations up to the recent past.

The continued expansion of clerical employment is clearly illustrated in Table 8. The main periods of expansion in both Britain and the United States occurred at approximately the same time, between 1930 and 1960, and annual growth rates of between 4 and 5 per cent were normal in the United States. In Britain, the equivalent figure was 3–4 per cent per annum.

TABLE 8

GROWTH OF CLERICAL EMPLOYMENT IN GREAT BRITAIN AND THE UNITED STATES, 1911–71 AND 1910–64

Census year	Nos. in Employment (000s)	Change per annum (%)	Clerical workers (000s)	Share of total labour force (%)	Change per annum (%)
GREAT BRITAIN					
1911	18350·2	—	832·4	4·5	—
1921	19158·5	0·4	1185·6	6·2	0·7
1931	20837·8	0·8	1381·7	6·6	1·5
1951	22116·1	0·3	2304·5	10·4	2·6
1961	23309·4	0·5	2992·6	12·8	2·6
1966	24102·4	0·7	3244·9	13·5	1·6
1971	23518·2	−0·5	3486·7	14·8	1·5
UNITED STATES					
1910	38167·3	—	1718·5	4·5	—
1920	41614·3	0·9	3111·8	7·5	8·1
1930	48829·9	1·7	4025·3	8·2	2·9
1940	45166·1	−0·7	4612·5	10·2	1·5
1950	55835·3	2·4	6866·7	12·3	4·9
1960	66681·5	1·9	9783·6	14·6	4·2
1964	70357·0	1·4	10667·0	15·2	2·3

Sources: Great Britain: Ministry of Labour, *Manpower Studies No. 7—Growth of Office Employment* (London: Her Majesty's Stationery Office, 1968), Appendix 1, p. 48. General Register Office, *Sample Census 1966, Economic Activity Tables* (London: Her Majesty's Stationery Office, 1968). Office of Population Censuses and Surveys, *Census 1971, Great Britain, Summary Tables (1% Sample)* (London: Her Majesty's Stationery Office, 1973).
United States: U.S. Bureau of the Census Reports, after G. R. Terry, *Office Management and Control* (Homewood: Irwin, 1962), Table 2.6, p. 30.

More important, the growth of the total work-force was at least 50 per cent less than for clerical occupations. Even during the period largely dominated by the war, 1931–51, clerical employment in Britain increased by 2·6 per cent per annum compared with 0·3 per cent for all workers in employment. The demand for clerical workers seems to be more independent of national economic fluctuations than many other types of work, particularly in manufacturing industry.[33] Hence, during the Depression in the United States employment decreased by 0·7 per cent per annum between 1930 and 1940 but clerical work continued to increase its share of all employment by 1·5 per cent annually.

In terms of their share of the total labour force, clerical workers in the United States are now more important than in Britain. Job control and evaluation has, however, led to more careful use of clerical labour and the advent of the computer has reduced the demand for the traditional skills of the clerical employee. Since 1960, therefore, there is some evidence of a slowing down in the growth of clerical employment following the peaks of 1950 and 1960, although its proportional share of all employment has continued to increase.[34] This does not mean that office employment as a whole is following a similar pattern. The declining growth of clerical employment is more than compensated by an increase in higher order office occupations. The expansion and acceptance in Britain of consumer credit, pension plans, life insurance schemes, the wide range of social security and other benefits, the growing range of consumer services of every description, and a rising standard of living, will ensure that office work will at least retain, if not increase, its share of total employment during the coming decades. Indeed, office work seems to grow along Parkinsonian principles as the range and number of job opportunities continues to expand.

GROWTH RATE VARIATIONS BETWEEN INDUSTRIES

While aggregate figures for the growth of clerical employment are interesting in themselves, they conceal important variations in growth rates between industrial sectors. The proportion of clerical workers in Great Britain increased from 6·2 per cent in 1921 to 13·5 per cent in 1966 and approximately 14·8 per cent in 1971 (Fig. 7).[35] Only the service industries have consistently had a larger proportion of their employees in clerical jobs than the national average. The three other sectors have always been below the national average and in the primary sector only 3·6 per cent of the workers were classed as clerical in 1971 compared with 18·8 per cent in services. Such differences reflect the structural variations between these sectors, particularly the predominance in the service sector of industries requiring large numbers of office workers.

The service industries are a major source of clerical employment (Fig. 7). More than 54 per cent of the working population was employed in the service sector in 1971 while in manufacturing the proportion employed has steadily decreased since 1961 and in the primary industries since 1921. The dominance of service industries in the overall employment structure is reflected in the concentration of clerical workers in this group. Approximately 65 per cent of all clerical workers are in service activities and the proportion has fluctuated by only 2–3 per cent since the peak of 69·9 per cent in 1921. The slight downward trend since that time to 65·9 per cent in 1966 is a crude measure of the impact of office mechanization on office work. Its effect has been absorbed by the increased demand for clerical workers in rapidly growing service industries where the number increased by 158 per cent from 828,300 in 1921 to 2,140,000 in 1966. Although the manufacturing industries employed a smaller proportion of clerical workers in 1971 than in 1951, the absolute increase of 200 per cent since 1921 has been even faster than for services. Therefore, although the distribution of clerical workers between industrial sectors has changed, there has been a substantial increase in absolute numbers in both services and manufacturing.

There are only two manufacturing industry orders which have consistently had a higher proportion of clerical workers than the national average (Fig. 8). In 1971 almost 17 per cent of

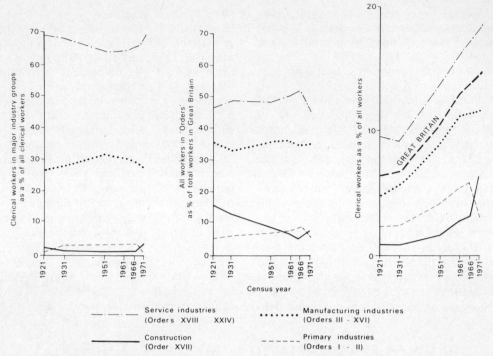

Fig. 7   The Industrial Distribution and Growth of Clerical Employment in Great Britain—
1921–71 (Data: Ministry of Labour, *Growth of Office Employment*, 1968; General Register Office,
Sample Census 1966, Great Britain, 1968; Office of Population Censuses and Surveys, *Census
1971, Summary Tables* (1% *sample*), 1973)

the workers in paper, printing, and publishing (XV) were clerical, reflecting the extensive support teams required by editors and journalists and by the advertising and related activities which form part of this industry. Clerical workers comprised 16·2 per cent of the workers in chemicals and allied industries (IV) in 1971, a decrease since 1961 but still above the national average. The large multi-national oil and chemical companies represented in this group require a large component of administrative and clerical personnel for their organization as well as operating research and development establishments which also generate some clerical employment. Elsewhere in the industrial sector, the proportion of clerical workers has been consistently below the national average, particularly in the older, traditional industries such as shipbuilding and marine engineering (VII), textiles (X), and clothing and footwear (XII). The proportion of clerical workers tends to be highest in the growth industries such as vehicles (VII) or engineering and electrical goods (VI).

In the service sector, only miscellaneous services (XXIII) has had a lower proportion of clerical workers than the national average (Fig. 8). But the discrepancy in 1971 is small compared with those which exist in the manufacturing sector. Foremost amongst the service industries in the growth of clerical employment is insurance, banking, and finance (XXI) in which approximately 55 per cent of the labour force was clerical in 1971, followed by public administration (XXIV) with 29·3 per cent. If all the other office jobs not classified as clerical were added to these figures, then 85·9 per cent of the workers in insurance, banking, and finance in 1966 were in office occupations and 37 per cent in public administration and defence.[36] The significance of these statistics will become clearer when the location of these industries will be considered in a later chapter.

TABLE 9
ANNUAL RATES OF CHANGE IN THE NUMBERS OF CLERICAL WORKERS IN
GREAT BRITAIN—BY INDUSTRY ORDER, 1951–61 AND 1961–6

	1951–61			1961–6		
Industry Order	Change (%)	Absolute change	Total clerical workers (000s)	Change (%)	Absolute change	Total clerical workers (000s)
MANUFACTURING						
III. Food, drink and tobacco	2·3	17·9	86·3	0·3	1·4	87·7
IV. Chemicals and allied industries	1·6	11·4	79·2	−0·5	−2·1	77·1
V. Metal manufacture	1·8	9·7	60·2	−0·6	−1·7	58·7
VI. Engineering and electrical goods	3·2	73·7	268·6	1·7	23·1	291·7
VII. Shipbuilding and marine engineering	0·6	0·8	14·6	−3·7	−2·5	12·1
VIII. Vehicles	3·1	26·3	99·0	−0·8	−3·9	95·1
IX. Metal goods n.e.s	1·7	8·1	51·4	1·8	4·8	56·2
X. Textiles	0·5	3·0	54·3	−0·7	−1·9	52·3
XI. Leather, leather goods and fur	−0·2	−0·1	4·6	−2·0	−0·4	4·2
XII. Clothing and footwear	—	0·2	33·6	—	−0·1	33·5
XIII. Bricks, pottery, glass, cement, etc.	3·1	7·5	28·3	2·3	3·6	31·9
XIV. Timber, furniture, etc.	2·6	5·2	23·3	1·9	2·3	25·6
XV. Paper, printing and publishing	3·2	23·6	87·1	1·1	4·8	91·9
XVI. Other manufacturing industries	1·9	5·9	34·2	0·9	1·6	35·8
SERVICES						
XVIII. Gas, electricity and water	2·3	14·2	68·8	0·7	2·5	71·3
XIX. Transport and communication	1·2	28·8	249·6	—	−0·6	248·8
XX. Distributive trades	2·7	104·1	444·2	1·1	24·6	468·8
XXI. Insurance, banking and finance	3·7	100·8	330·9	2·0	49·8	381·6
XXII. Professional and scientific services	2·8	67·3	277·3	3·4	50·6	327·9
XXIII. Miscellaneous services	5·3	152·2	269·1	4·0	57·9	327·0
XXIV. Public administration and defence	−0·4	−11·4	299·3	1·0	15·2	314·5
CONSTRUCTION (XVII)	4·2	29·0	84·3	5·4	25·3	109·6
Total[1]	2·6	678·2	2948·0	1·6	254·3	3203·2

Note: 1. Total excludes primary industries.
Sources: 1951–61—Ministry of Labour, *Manpower Studies No. 7—Growth of Office Employment* (London: Her Majesty's Stationery Office, 1968), Appendix 4–27, pp. 50–73.
    1961–6—Department of Employment, unpublished statistics based on *Census of Population, 1966*.

The characteristic growth curve for clerical employment in individual industries is made up of three components. The first stage is a period of relatively slow rates of growth in all industries between 1921 and 1931. The full impact of office mechanization was not evident until the second phase from 1931 to 1961 when the growth curve becomes much steeper, especially for service industries (Fig. 8). Since 1961 there has been a third phase consisting of slower growth in response to changes in demand for clerical workers reflecting the impact of computers and an organization and methods approach to the use of clerical labour. In insurance, banking, and finance, for example, the annual growth of clerical workers was 3·7 per cent between 1951 and 1961, but this decreased to 2·0 per cent in the years up to 1966 (Table 9). Similarly, in chemicals and allied industries and in engineering and electrical goods the annual growth rates were 1·6 and 3·2 per cent respectively in 1951–61, reducing to −0·5 and 1·7 per cent between 1961 and 1966. Even so, the

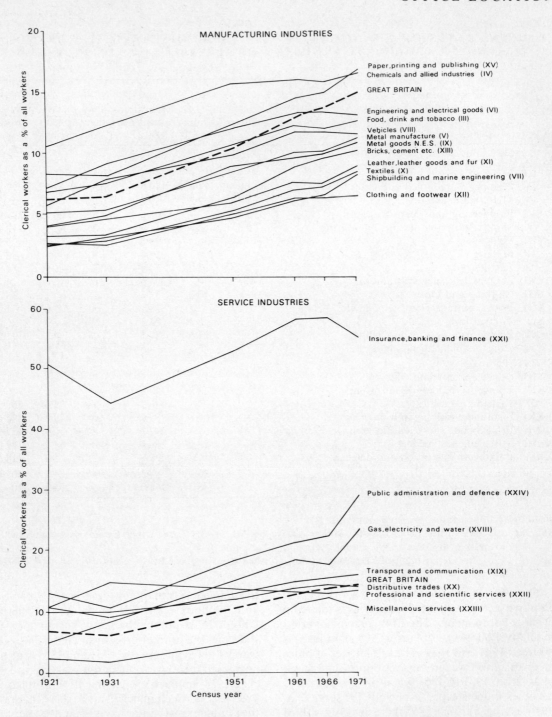

Fig. 8   Changes in the Proportion of Clerical Workers in Manufacturing and Service Industries, Great Britain—1921–71 (Data: as for Fig. 7)

growth rates amongst service industries have continued to remain positive with the exception of transport and communications (XIX). Exactly half of the manufacturing industry orders recorded negative changes between 1961 and 1966.

Hence, by 1971, the inter-industry distribution of all office and other non-manual occupations in Great Britain is heavily weighted in favour of, although by no means completely synonymous with, service industries (Fig. 8). It is likely that this pattern of inter-industry distribution will persist for some time into the future, although the rate of growth of both male and female office employment may be reduced as service indus-

tries improve output per head. Fuchs has shown that, in comparison with other sectors of the economy, output per man during the period 1929–65 grew much more slowly in the service industries of the United States. This was the cause of the high level of demand for office and other non-manual jobs in that sector compared to manufacturing. The reduction of recent growth rates of service and office employment in Britain and the United States in parallel with improvements in productivity per service worker suggests that industry output differentials are no longer an important stimulus to high office employment growth rates.

ROLE OF FEMALE OFFICE WORKERS

Throughout most of the nineteenth century office work had been the domain of male employees. Yet there were women employed as clerks and copy-typists in Washington, D.C. before the invention of the typewriter. They trimmed and clipped notes in the Treasury Department or copied speeches and other documents for members of Congress.[37] The numbers involved were small, however, and the 1841 Census recorded only 159 female commercial clerks in England.[38] In 1880 an advertisement for a typist or a telegrapher would have invariably elicited a response from men, but by 1910 such work had become dominated by female employees.[39] Prior to this time the scope for female employment was restricted to professional occupations. The majority were found in teaching jobs but by the end of the century women stood a better chance of earning a living than fifty years earlier. This was especially true of the new, but non-professional, office occupations such as telephonists, typists or office machine operators.[40] The typewriter lured many females into paid work for the first time, a form of emancipation explained by the high respectability of the typewriter as a 'woman's machine' which did not create factory-like conditions of work.[41]

The working environment was certainly more congenial in offices than in the factories. Tasks such as telephone operation presented more variety than watching machinery all day and the

hours were shorter.[42] But there remained a wide gap between the conditions of employment of a female clerk in a reputable shipping company and a clerk employed in a back-street warehouse where conditions of work and tenure were far from satisfactory.[43] Despite such problems it became apparent by the turn of the century that female labour would come to dominate the male/female employment balance of many offices. They could adequately perform the range of routine tasks involved in office work and there were machines to help them as well as to generate more work. The first telephone lines between Chicago and New York were opened in 1892 and by 1900 the telephone service had expanded so rapidly that the number of operators had increased to more than 22,000 and 29 per cent of them were females. By 1903 female telephone operators numbered 37,000 with just 2500 males.[44] The Twelfth U.S. Census of 1900 showed that there were 85,000 stenographers and typists, 75 per cent of them female, while 13 per cent of the nation's clerks and copy-typists were also women.[45] Women were therefore making rapid inroads into traditional male employment enclaves, a process encouraged by the lower rates of pay accepted by females and the possibility of taking part-time work which was not normally considered by men. The division between male and female salaries of office workers has, however, persisted through to the present and although the rates of pay for women generally increased by 5 per cent between 1969 and 1971, for example, they were still less than 80 per cent of male wage rates.[46] There are therefore some fiscal advantages derived from employing female labour wherever possible.

The lower wage rates of female office workers also reflects their dominance of the more routine clerical tasks. Because the qualifications required are not high there are large pools of labour potentially available. The higher level office jobs demand better qualifications which

female workers in all industries in Great Britain and is a measure of the major role played by office activities in affecting female employment rates. Women office workers in the United States first outnumbered men in the 1930 Census when they totalled over 2 m. By 1960 two out of every three clerical workers were female, a close parallel with the situation in Great Britain.[48]

In common with clerical work as a whole, there has been differential growth of female clerical employment within individual industrial

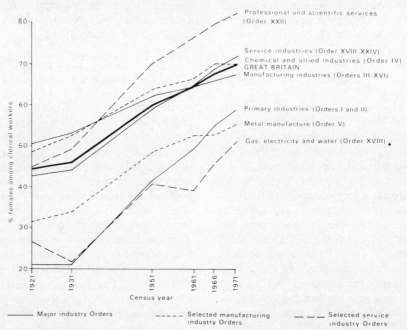

Fig. 9   Proportion of Females Amongst Clerical Workers, Great Britain— 1921–71 (Data: as for Fig. 7)

can be offered by fewer individuals so that organizations must be prepared to pay higher salaries in order to attract or retain such office personnel. The administrative and professional office occupations are almost exclusively male-orientated, so that in 1966 under 6 per cent of 2·5 million female office workers were in this category compared with almost 59 per cent of the males.[47] Female clerical workers first outnumbered their male counterparts sometime between the 1931 and 1951 Census and by 1971 there were more than two females for every one male clerk. This is the complete opposite of the ratio of male to

orders (Fig. 9). During the 50 years between 1921 and 1971 the number of female clerical workers has increased by 7·0 per cent per annum, while the number of male clerks has only increased by 1·2 per cent. Hence, in 1971 over 70 per cent of all clerical workers were female but in some industries, such as professional and scientific services, over 81 per cent of the workers are women. This represents an annual growth rate of 3·6 per cent since 1921. One of the most interesting features shown in Fig. 9 is the late emergence of service industries as employers of female clerks compared with the manufacturing industries which were above the national average until 1961. But the service industries have since increased their female clerical labour force at 7·1 per cent annually and manufacturing at 6·5 per cent. It again emerges that services have played a more important role in promoting the growth of female office employment than any other sector. The delayed impact of this growth may be derived from the large legacy of traditional male occupations in some of the service industries, particularly in insurance, banking, and finance or in some areas of public administration.

GROWTH OF OFFICE WORK IN INDIVIDUAL ORGANIZATIONS

An alternative measure of the changing relationship between white-collar work and other types of employment is the structure of individual organizations. This would appear to be an easy task involving time series data from as far back in the history of an organization as possible, but there are a number of problems which make this mode of analysis difficult. The first of these is the failure of many organizations to keep records of employees and their jobs over a large number of years; even firms less than ten years old may not keep employee records from the date of founding. Secondly, as organizations expand their activities they acquire other organizations or are themselves taken over by larger units. This often involves assimilation or merging of disparate employment structures which produces distortion or failure to keep pre-takeover records of

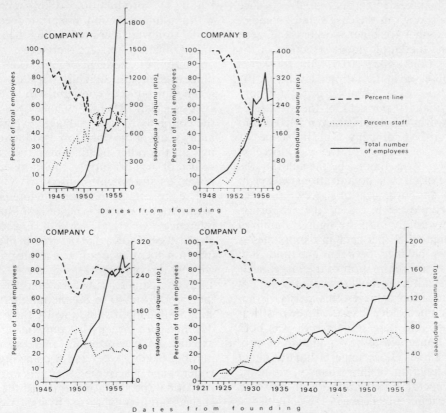

Fig. 10   Changing Employment Structures of Organizations Through Time (After M. Haire, *Modern Organization Theory*, 1959, with the permission of John Wiley and Sons, Inc.)

employees. Thirdly, new techniques in management and new job specifications make it difficult to evaluate structural changes in employment through time and make data retention even less necessary for the organizations concerned. Consequently, there is minimal published information on the changes in employment structure of individual organizations, even at the most generalized level of production/non-production workers.

An insight into this method of analysing the growth of office work has been provided by Haire.[49] He has made four case studies of American organizations and the employment changes within them from the date of founding until 1958, the year of study. He distinguished between 'line' and 'staff' personnel; the former including those who directly make and sell a product and the latter providing the specialist support which can reasonably be taken to consist largely of office personnel, although in the case studies some of the line personnel are office workers.[50] Traced through time the employment structure of the four organizations appears to be a microcosm of the trends observed at the national level (Fig. 10). In the early years of each firm's growth, staff constitute less than 10 per cent of the workforce whether the firm was established in 1950 (Company B) or 1922 (Company D). The scope for functional specialization of the workforce in these early years was limited by the fact that the average size of all four organizations was eight people. As the organizations grew and the number of employees increased, the proportion of staff grew rapidly until the figures stabilized at approximately 50 per cent in Companies A and B. This balance between line and staff workers is an approximation of the larger scale distribution within the modern economy but not every organization achieves this parity. Company D was much older than the three post-war organizations and here staff growth was both slower and continued to be dominated by production personnel. Haire suggests that this might be more a function of time than of economic growth in general. Equally important, however, must be the difference between the activities of these organizations which will result in a larger demand for office, or staff, personnel in some companies than others. The differences between

the proportion of clerical workers in different industrial orders has already been noted.

It appears that the growth of production, or line, personnel in an organization takes place on a linear scale, while staff grow according to an exponential function. The precise form of the exponential function varies according to the type of organization.[51] In general, the curve is steepest during the intermediate years between founding and balance in the employment structure (Fig. 10). In the later stages of growth the two groups expand in parallel although, as with white-collar employment in general, staff 'resist' negative changes when companies are reducing the number of personnel for economic or other reasons. This is clearly important when attempting to explain the continuing expansion of office work as other types of employment grow more slowly. In the case histories analysed by Haire, 311 production workers were laid off without any reduction in staff; indeed, 14 additional staff were recruited during the lay-off periods. Office workers are therefore crucial to the operation of modern organizations, even in times of economic difficulty. An additional factor is the reluctance of companies to lose specialist staff, especially where they have been trained by the company or have valuable experience after many years in the same job. Production personnel, on the other hand, unless they are highly skilled or in short supply, can more easily be replaced as and when required.

The growing proportion of white-collar work within organizations is again best illustrated by reference to clerical workers (Fig. 11). It has already been shown that the growth of the clerical function does not continue at a rate concomitant with white-collar work as a whole. In the case study companies, as the total number of workers increased from 40 to 80, the number of clerical staff doubled, but subsequently the growth rate declined even though the companies continue to expand. As organizations increase their total number of employees and become involved in a wider range of activities, they generate increased functional specialization amongst the staff. This specialization is expressed by increased demand for professional and managerial staff rather than clerical workers. Provided the latter form 15–20 per cent of the total labour force they provide

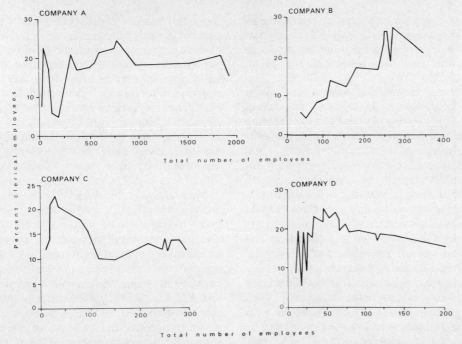

Fig. 11   Relationship Between Total Employment of an Organization and Proportion of Clerical Workers (After M. Haire, *Modern Organization Theory*, 1959, with the permission of John Wiley and Sons, Inc.)

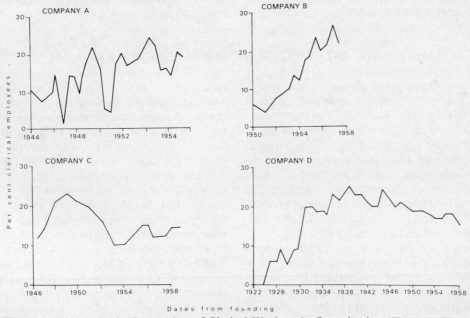

Fig. 12   Changes in the Proportion of Clerical Workers in Organizations Through Time (After M. Haire, *Modern Organization Theory*, 1959, with the permission of John Wiley and Sons, Inc.)

support for the smooth operation of
This accords well with the proportion
workers in the national labour force
growth rates have also slowed down in
recent years.

The increase in clerical personnel through time may be viewed as an 'agglutinative accretion' (Fig. 12).[52] Every new line worker creating an increase in production also produces work for an extra clerk or secretary. As with total employees, the proportion of clerical staff increases rapidly during the early years of each company but once it reaches 20–25 per cent it stabilizes or decreases (Companies C and D). As the effects of automation and mechanization are absorbed by office activities the proportion of clerical workers will probably continue to decrease, a trend already present in 1958.

An alternative approach has been used by Baker and Davis.[53] They have traced the growth and emergence of staff in 211 companies of various sizes at a single point in time rather than by examining the life history of individual firms. They suggest that every time a firm adds 100 direct, or line, workers, the number of indirect, or staff, workers increases by 75, regardless of the size of firm before the addition. This conclu-sion corroborates in general terms the pattern of parallel growth which emerged in the later years of the companies examined by Haire. Accounting tends to grow at the fastest rate, 4·6 people for every 100 additional line workers; the equivalent for clerical personnel is 1·46. The emergence of various staff functions as differentiated groups in an organization proceeds at varying rates so that, for example, accounting and purchasing functions only become separate when firms reach 75–99 workers in total.

Micro-level analysis of office employment growth embodied in studies of the type undertaken by Haire or by Baker and Davis provide a valuable insight to some of the processes and trends taking place at the macro-level. They cannot provide the complete answer because of the substantial variations between companies; in terms of whether they are primarily producer or service-orientated, in terms of their economic performance, and in terms of utilization of personnel. There is certainly scope for more detailed case study work of some British companies with a view to better understanding of the growth of office employment and its future role in the economy.

IMPACT OF COMPUTERS ON OFFICE EMPLOYMENT

One of the most discussed reasons for the downturn in the growth of clerical employment, and office work in general, is the effect of computers on labour demand. Most of the office aids developed prior to the computer may have changed the tasks performed by clerks to some degree, as well as increasing efficiency in handling information, but the consequence was higher demand for clerical workers to handle the massive growth of paper, data, and information which the improved machines generated.

Computers created anxiety about clerical work partly because the powers and speed of the early models were greatly overstated. One of the directors of a large insurance company in the United States estimated that the calculation of 80,000 Ordinary Department bonuses, which took about 4000 man hours using the punched card system, would only take nine hours by com-puter.[54] Such a calculation was far from accurate because it totally ignored the fact that, even if the computer could undertake such an operation in that time, it still required a substantial number of personnel, admittedly with slightly different skills to clerical workers, to feed it with the necessary information in the correct form and to operate the system efficiently. A further reason for anxiety was that the computer, which was used earlier for office work in America than in Britain, was introduced at a period which coincided with high unemployment rates. Although clerical workers were least affected by fluctuations in employment, it was widely believed that the advent of computers would change this situation. The memory of the Great Depression of the 1930s was also important, as well as the speed with which technical changes were taking place. These changes were too rapid for offices to absorb without causing a few employment problems.

The actual impact of computers on clerical and office work generally does not lend support to the prejudices evident during the early years. Indeed, virtually 'all the research studies on office automation conducted to date have been at the level of the individual firm. None of these have revealed substantial clerical lay-offs attributable to the introduction of electronic data processing.'[55] The kinds of job superseded by E.D.P. installations are the clerical, punching, and keyboard accounting activities. McDonald quotes an estimate that the introduction of a large-scale computer into a head office employing 2000 staff might be expected to eliminate 200–500 clerical jobs over a five-year period if it is assumed that the volume of work handled remains constant.[56]

The main effect of computers has been to slow down the growth of clerical work but rarely has it involved substantial laying-off of personnel. Many firms have been able to guarantee the jobs of their employees even though the work of as many as two-thirds may be affected by the installation of an E.D.P. system. The main reason for this is that E.D.P. systems have created a new group of office occupations, many of which can be filled by re-trained clerical workers, e.g. the operation of console and peripheral equipment, some categories of maintenance work, card punching, organization and administration of tape libraries and, in some cases, programming. A further factor helping to cushion the effects of E.D.P. on clerical staff is, given the youthful age structure (particularly of female staff) and the time lag of at least five years between the ordering of a computer and the complete changeover, that it is likely that the rate of annual turnover of such staff will reduce the need to actually declare employees redundant.[57]

The transition period during the installation of an E.D.P. system may actually increase, rather than decrease, the demand for clerical support.[58] At an early stage it is necessary to track down errors, omissions and inconsistencies which are unacceptable to a computer but which the old system happily absorbed. In the Department of Employment survey only 105 organizations (6 per cent of the total sample) had discharged staff as a result of installing computers and, on average, less than ten employees were involved.[59] In some offices E.D.P. has generated extra demand for office workers in other parts of the organization so that the net effect of the average computer project is an increase of 8 per cent in the total number employed.

The interrelationship of the several changes

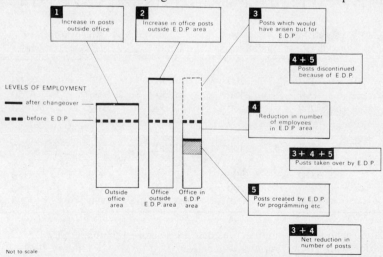

Not to scale

Fig. 13   Effect of the Installation of E.D.P. on Levels of Employment in a Hypothetical Organization (After Ministry of Labour, *Computers in Offices*, 1965, with the permission of the Controller of Her Majesty's Stationery Office)

occurring in the numbers of personnel and posts during the installation of an E.D.P. system is shown in Fig. 13. This simple model provides a picture of what happens to employment in an average organization adopting an E.D.P. system. The office posts in an organization can be sub-divided into those inside and outside the E.D.P. area. If E.D.P. had not been adopted the levels of employment in both parts of the office would have risen to that shown for the office outside the E.D.P. area. E.D.P. not only replaces posts which might have arisen but also causes a decrease in the number of employees in that part of the office directly affected by its introduction. The net result is partly improved, however, by new posts created by E.D.P. so that the reduction in the number of office workers in the E.D.P. area is more than adequately counterbalanced by the increases in other parts of the office. Hence, the Ministry of Labour survey showed that the average net reduction in the number of posts in the E.D.P. area was 90. Some of these would have occurred anyway, leaving just 40 jobs lost through E.D.P. But 188 new jobs were created outside the E.D.P. section of the office so that the net effect was an increase of 148 jobs in the average organization.[60]

The more recent Department of Employment survey prefers to deal in aggregate figures and attempts to isolate the types of office job most affected (Table 10). Up to January 1969 an estimated 143,500 office jobs have been taken over by E.D.P., excluding small computers and service bureaux. At least 100,000 of these would have been filled by female staff, mostly in the clerical occupations. Over 60 per cent of the jobs replaced were clerical, followed by calculating and accounting machine operators (14·8 per cent). The pattern for well established and new installations is very similar and the number of males whose jobs have been replaced only exceeds females in the enclaves of male-dominated office occupations, forming the managerial, executive, and supervisory categories.

By 1972 it is estimated that E.D.P. will have taken over 275,000 office posts but will have created 150,000 new jobs (Table 11). This results in a net reduction of 2·4 per cent, or 125,000 jobs, compared with 0·75 per cent in 1964. The trend is undoubtedly towards more jobs being lost through E.D.P., amounting to some 6·5 per cent in 1979, excluding professional and technical jobs. But this is unlikely to create major problems for individuals, particularly in the clerical

TABLE 10
OFFICE POSTS TAKEN OVER BY E.D.P. IN GREAT BRITAIN—1954–69

Occupation	Well established installations[1]	New installations[2]	Total	All installations %	Males	Females
Management and executive	1250	500	1750	1·2	1600	150
Supervisory	5800	2450	8250	5·7	6750	1500
Clerical	62000	26500	88500	61·7	41000	47500
Typing	9000	3750	12750	8·9	50	12700
Calculating/accounting machine operation	14800	6400	21200	14·8	900	20300
Other office machine operation	6850	2900	9750	6·8	850	8900
Other office work	900	400	1300	0·9	850	450
Total	100500	43000	143500[3]	100·0	52000	91500

Notes: 1. An installation whose first computer was delivered before 1 January 1967.
2. An installation whose first computer was delivered on or after 1 January 1967.
3. The total excludes 2000 posts taken over by very small computer systems and 12,500 posts by service bureaux.
Source: Department of Employment, Manpower Studies No. 12 — Computers in Offices, 1972 (London: Her Majesty's Stationery Office, 1972), Table 7, p. 47.

TABLE 11
CUMULATIVE EFFECTS OF E.D.P. ON OFFICE WORK IN
GREAT BRITAIN — 1953–79 (000s)

	Jan. 1969	Jan. 1972	Jan. 1974	Jan. 1979
Total volume of office work assuming no E.D.P. (in terms of equivalent no. of office posts)[1]	4919	5250	5500	6200
Office posts taken over by E.D.P.[2]	158	275	390	670
Office posts created by E.D.P.	99	150	190	270
Net reduction	59	125	200	400
No. of office posts remaining	4860	5125	5300	5800
Proportion of office work taken over by E.D.P.	1·2	2·4	3·6	6·5

Notes: 1. Includes all office computers (small and service bureaux systems).
  2. Office work refers to all office activity except professional and technical jobs.
Source: Department of Employment, *Manpower Studies No. 12 — Computers in Offices, 1972* (London: Her Majesty's Stationery Office, 1972), Table 8, p. 49.

grades, because the rate of loss is increasing relatively slowly and will incorporate natural wastage as well as some channelling of labour into E.D.P.-orientated jobs. Over the period up to January 1979 the number of office jobs in Britain is expected to increase by 2·4 per cent per annum, an additional 1·3 m. jobs between 1969 and 1979. Office posts are therefore being created faster than E.D.P. can take them over or divert growth.

The impact of the computer is not restricted to its effect on clerical employment. The relationship between clerical personnel and their superiors is changed, in that the primarily supervisory tasks at some levels of middle management are no longer necessary because there are no clerical staff to supervise.[61] At the same time there are opportunities to create new types of professional and technical jobs, although many of these must be recruited from elsewhere because of the difficulty of training existing middle management in the new techniques demanded by the operation of an E.D.P. system. Even so, 83 per cent of the offices in the Department of Employment survey had experienced no relative changes in the numbers of junior and middle management posts as a result of E.D.P. There were probably a few more posts created and an increase in levels of responsibility rather than a decrease in the number of employees.[62] At the higher points in the management hierarchy the changes caused are generally less dramatic. Senior management is usually more remote from

the E.D.P. system in an office, although intimately involved with interpreting, creating, and making policy decisions from the information it provides. The computer has substantially changed the quality of information available to upper management. The sophistication of computer operations and the ability to undertake more than just routine accounting and similar tasks means that the new generation of top managers need to understand the operation and limitations of E.D.P. installations to a much greater extent than their predecessors.

Other studies of small and large organizations in America, Japan, Australia, and West Germany come to broadly similar conclusions about the effect of E.D.P. on office work.[63] Estimates of the future impact are problematical because of advances in machine technology which might alter the manpower requirements of installations. In broad terms, E.D.P. might take over about 15 per cent of all office work in the next 30 years.[64] This is a conservative estimate compared with that made by Hoos who suggests that for every five jobs replaced only one will be created.[65] This estimate is based on extensive research in small and large offices and if it is correct a very high rate of growth of office employment would be required to continue past trends of expansion. Any estimates are also difficult because E.D.P. installations are too new to provide accurate 'before and after' figures of the type used by the Department of Employment. The problem is compounded by the fact that many companies have not yet attained anywhere near the level of automation which they foresee.[66] Many of the jobs which do not disappear also undergo drastic changes while the new ones are quite unlike the white-collar occupations traditionally associated with the office.

Whatever the future growth of office employment perhaps we should not overstate the role of computers. It is unlikely, for example, that clerical workers will be completely replaced because 'computers and common language machines have definite limitations. They will serve as receptionists only in a very limited way and run errands not at all. Although automatic telephone answering devices exist and it is possible for machines to analyse speech and select the information content, we are some distance from the application of such principles to business systems. Meeting the public, tracing exceptions, and preparing input for an office work system are jobs which people will continue to do. While the preparation of input is capable of considerable mechanization, there are practical limits to replacement of human endeavour.'[67] It should also

be borne in mind that the volume of work that is worth programming for computers is limited and that there is a reluctance to standardize office activity to enable package programmes to be produced for tasks common to different offices. A large proportion of the obvious applications of E.D.P. have already been implemented by the larger office organizations. Finally, there may be limits to the expression of human activity in all its facets in mathematical terms in logical flow charts.[68] The scope for expanding E.D.P. in office work is still large, however, particularly at the frontiers of development. Long distance data transmission or the use of terminals for remote operation of large computers are still in their infancy but their development should be accommodated without great hardship to office staff. More important, in the context of later chapters, such innovations in computer technology have major consequences for communications between office activities and their location both within urban areas and between regions.

REFERENCES

1 A. Sturmthal (ed.), *White-Collar Trade Unions* (Chicago: University of Illinois Press, 1966). G. S. Bain, *The Growth of White-Collar Unionism* (Oxford: Clarendon Press, 1970). J. Gottman, *Megalopolis: The Urbanized Northeastern Seaboard of the United States* (Cambridge, Mass.: The M.I.T. Press, 1961), pp. 565–630. E. M. Hoover and R. Vernon, *Anatomy of a Metropolis* (Cambridge, Mass.: Harvard University Press, 1959), pp. 78–112.

2 F. Croner, 'Salaried employees in modern industry', *International Labour Review*, vol. 44 (1954), pp. 97–110.

3 C. W. Mills, *White Collar* (New York: Oxford University Press, 1953). M. Crozier, *The World of the Office Worker* (Chicago: University of Chicago Press, 1965).

4 International Labour Office, *Yearbook of Labour Statistics* (Geneva: Bureau of Labour Statistics, 1971). International Labour Office, *International Standard Classification of Occupations* (Geneva: International Labour Office, 1958).

5 White-collar workers in the British Census would comprise: clerical workers (XXI), sales workers

(XXII), administrators and managers (XXIV), professional, technical workers, artists (XXV), see General Register Office, *Sample Census 1966, Great Britain, Economic Activity Tables* (London: Her Majesty's Stationery Office, 1968). In the U.S. Census: professional, technical and kindred workers, clerical and kindred workers, sales workers, managers, officials and proprietors (except farm), see Bureau of the Census, *U.S. Census of Population: 1960, U.S. Summary* (Washington, D.C.: Government Printing Office, 1962).

6 Hence, sales workers in the British Census include street vendors, hawkers or roundsmen (bread, milk, laundry, and soft drinks), as well as finance, insurance brokers, financial agents or valuers and auctioneers. The latter are clearly white-collar, and therefore broadly office, workers, while the former are not. Similar examples could be extracted from other censuses and they would illustrate the difficulty of using aggregate figures for white-collar jobs as a proxy for office employment. In the case of sales workers, the problem could be resolved by reject-

ing them from the aggregate figures but, with the exception of administrators and managers, and clerical workers, this would also be necessary for the much larger group of professional, technical workers, artists.

7 The service industries are: gas, electricity and water (XVIII), transport and communication (XIX), distributive trades (XX), insurance, banking and finance (XXI), professional and scientific services (XXII), miscellaneous services (XXIII), public administration and defence (XXIV), see Central Statistical Office, *Standard Industrial Classification* (London: Her Majesty's Stationery Office, 1968).

8 J. Gottman, *op. cit.*, p. 566.

9 Most offices are classified with the industry which they serve because they do not have 'any measureable output of their own but contribute to that of the establishments which they serve'. Only businesses producing office products for sale to other organizations or individuals are classified as office establishments *per se*. It is possible to identify 'office M.L.H.s' (minimum list headings) and these are 860–6, 871, 873, 901, and 906 but, at best, these only provide very incomplete white-collar statistics. See Central Statistical Office, *op. cit.*, p. iv and pp. 37–42.

10 J. Gottman, 'Urban centrality and the interweaving of quaternary activities', *Ekistics*, vol. 29 (1970), p. 325.

11 *Idem*.

12 R. B. Armstrong, *The Office Industry: Patterns of Growth and Location* (Cambridge, Mass.: The M.I.T. Press, 1972), p. 20. General Register Office, *Sample Census 1966, England and Wales, Economic Activity County Leaflets, Explanatory Notes* (London: Her Majesty's Stationery Office, 1968). Office of Population Censuses and Surveys, *Classification of Occupations 1970* (London: Her Majesty's Stationery Office, 1971).

13 Ministry of Labour, *Manpower Studies No. 7— Growth of Office Employment* (London: Her Majesty's Stationery Office, 1968), Appendix 37, pp. 83–5.

14 *Guides to Official Sources No. 2, Census Reports of Great Britain 1801–1931* (London: Her Majesty's Stationery Office, 1951), pp. 27–65. E. Devons, *British Economic Statistics* (London: Cambridge University Press, 1961), p. 51.

15 Office of Population Censuses and Surveys, *op. cit.*

16 The inter-departmental definition used by Government departments and first agreed in 1963 excludes those occupations which might be considered marginal such as messengers, or managers in mining and production (n.e.c.). But in 1966 the inter-departmental definition was revised to include all the occupation groups in Table 4 listed in the 1966 Census. Meanwhile, the Greater London Council produced its own definition which excluded telegraph and radio operators and professional workers (n.e.c.). Yet another definition of office employment was used for a study by the Ministry of Labour of occupational changes 1951–61. It included non-office professional and managerial staff while a later study from the same Ministry utilized an extremely narrow definition based on just three occupation orders: typists, shorthand writers, secretaries; clerks, cashiers; and office machine operators. See Ministry of Labour, *Manpower Studies No. 6—Occupational Changes 1951–61* (London: Her Majesty's Stationery Office, 1967). Ministry of Labour, *op. cit.* (1968).

17 For example, chemists and physical, biological scientists are included in the 1970 classification.

18 Department of Employment, *Classification of Occupations and Directory of Occupational Titles* (*CODOT*) (London: Her Majesty's Stationery Office, 1972).

19 There are 378 unit groups, or a basic group of occupations in which the main tasks are similar; 73 minor groups comprising a collection of unit groups which are related in terms of work performed; and 18 major groups which are a convenient collection of minor groups to assist in comprehension of the classification as a whole, *ibid*.

20 'List of Key Occupations for Statistical Purposes (KOSP)', *Department of Employment Gazette*, vol. 80 (1972), pp. 799–803. Under CODOT, clerical occupations form eight separate unit groups, thus acknowledging the wide range of jobs performed by clerks, but under KOSP they are telescoped into three categories with the majority, representing six CODOT unit groups, in one category: 'Clerks'. This category contains more workers than any other in the KOSP system and a substantial amount of detailed information about clerical office occupations is therefore lost in the published statistics.

21 Institute of Manpower Studies, *Introduction to Institute of Manpower Studies System of Occupational Classification* (Brighton: Institute of Manpower Studies, 1972).

22 R. B. Armstrong, *op. cit.*, pp. 20–1.

23 *Department of Employment Gazette*, published monthly by Her Majesty's Stationery Office. Formerly (pre-1971) the *Ministry of Labour Gazette*.

24 *Department of Employment Gazette*, vol. 79 (1971), p. 261.

25 J. H. Dunning and E. V. Morgan, *An Economic Study of the City of London* (London: Allen & Unwin, 1971), pp. 56–7.

26 J. Gottman, *op. cit.* (1961), p. 567.

27 The International Labour Office Statistics used in Fig. 6 are derived from census returns and official estimates.

28 This has also been noted in the context of tertiary and secondary employment growth in countries with large differences in *per capita* incomes by W. Galenson, 'Economic development and the sectoral expansion of employment', *International Labour Review*, vol. 87 (1963), pp. 505–19.

29 J. Gottman, *op. cit.* (1961), pp. 576–7.

30 W. J. Reader, *Professional Men: The Rise of the Professional Classes in Nineteenth Century England* (London: Weidenfeld & Nicolson, 1966), p. 208.

31 *Ibid.*, p. 211.

32 M. Haire, 'Biological models and empirical histories of the growth of organizations', in M. Haire (ed.), *Modern Organization Theory* (New York: John Wiley Ltd, 1959), p. 302.

33 This is an important characteristic of service industries, see C. W. McMahon and G. D. N. Worswick, 'The growth of services in the economy', in D. H. Aldercroft and P. Fearon (eds), *Economic Growth in Twentieth Century Britain* (London: Macmillan, 1969), pp. 125–50. R. M. Hartwell, *The Industrial Revolution and Economic Growth* (London: Methuen, 1971), pp. 201–25. V. R. Fuchs, *The Service Economy* (New York: Bureau of Economic Research, 1968).

34 Department of Employment, unpublished tabulations based on Census of Population 1966.

35 Ministry of Labour, *op. cit.*

36 These figures only apply to England and Wales.

37 E. F. Baker, *Technology and Women's Work* (New York: Columbia University Press, 1964), p. 71.

38 *Occupational Abstract of Census Returns—1844*, pp. 31–44. B. Lockwood, *The Black Coated Worker* (London: Allen & Unwin, 1958), p. 36.

39 P. F. Drucker, *Technology, Management and Society* (London: Heinemann, 1970), pp. 67–8.

40 W. J. Reader, *op. cit.*, p. 181.

41 C. W. Mills, *op. cit.*, p. 207.

42 E. F. Baker, *op. cit.*, p. 69.

43 J. R. Dale, *The Clerk in Industry* (Liverpool: Liverpool University Press, 1962), p. 5.

44 E. F. Baker, *op. cit.*, p. 216.

45 U.S. Bureau of the Census, *Statistics of Women at Work* (Washington: Government Printing Office, 1907), pp. 102–8.

46 The Institute of Administrative Management, *Clerical Salaries Analysis 1972* (Beckenham: Institute of Administrative Management, 1972).

47 General Register Office, *Sample Census 1966, Great Britain, Sub-Regional Tables* (London: Her Majesty's Stationery Office, 1970).

48 E. F. Baker, *op. cit.*, p. 217.

49 M. Haire, *op. cit.*, pp. 277–93.

50 'Production' workers and 'staff' in Britain.

51 M. Haire, *op. cit.*, p. 292.

52 *Ibid.*, p. 291.

53 A. W. Baker and R. L. Davis, *Ratios of Staff to Line Employees and Stages of Differentiation of Staff Functions* (Columbus: Ohio State University Bureau of Business Research, 1954). Some general case studies of firms along the lines used by Haire are also discussed in J. Woodward, *Industrial Organization: Theory and Practice* (London: Oxford University Press, 1965), pp. 28–9, 55–7. E. T. Penrose, *Theory of the Growth of the Firm* (Oxford: Blackwell, 1959). An aggregate analysis for U.S. manufacturing industries is given in D. Gujarati and L. Dors, 'Production and non-production workers in U.S. manufacturing industries', *Industrial and Labor Relations Review*, vol. 26 (1972), pp. 660–9.

54 H. A. Rhee, *Office Automation in Social Perspective* (Oxford: Blackwell, 1968), pp. 159–62.

55 J. C. McDonald, *Impact and Implications of Office Automation* (Ottawa: Department of Labour, Occasional Paper, no. 1, 1964), p. 9. See also I. R. Hoos, 'When the computer takes over the office', *Harvard Business Review*, vol. 38 (1960), pp. 102–12. H. F. Craig, *Administering a Conversion to Electronic Accounting: A Case Study* (Cambridge, Mass.: Harvard University Press, 1955). B. H. Bagdikian, *The Information Machines: Their Impact on Man and Media* (London: Harper & Row, 1971).

56 J. C. McDonald, *op. cit.*, p. 11.

57 Ministry of Labour, *Manpower Studies No. 4— Computers in Offices* (London: Her Majesty's Stationery Office, 1965), Appendix 9, p. 48.

58 J. C. McDonald, *op. cit.*, pp. 13–14.

59 Department of Employment, *Manpower Studies No. 12—Computers in Offices, 1972* (London: Her Majesty's Stationery Office, 1972), p. 16.

60 Ministry of Labour, *op. cit.* (1965), pp. 18–19.

61 R. Stewart, *How Computers Affect Management* (London: Macmillan, 1971).

62 For a fuller discussion of the impact of computers on office jobs see H. A. Rhee, *op. cit.*, pp. 62–157.

63 Bureau of Labour Statistics, *Impact of Office Automation on the Insurance Industry*, Bulletin,

no. 1468 (Washington D.C.: Government Printing Office, 1966). IFO Institut für Wirtschaftsforschung, *Soziale Auswirkungen des Dechrischen Fortschritts* (Berlin: Dunker & Humboldt, 1962). Japan Computer Usage Development Institute (ed.), *White Paper on Electronic Computers* (Tokyo: Development Institute, 1967). J. T. Dunlop, *Automation and Technological Change* (Englewood Cliffs: Prentice Hall, 1962). Parliament of New South Wales, *Inquiry into Recent Mechanization and Other Technological Changes in Industry* (Sydney: Government Printer, 1967). I. R. Hoos and B. L. Jones, 'Office automation in Japan', *International Labour Review*, vol. 87 (1963), pp. 551–72.

64 Department of Employment, *op. cit.*, pp. 40–1.

65 I. R. Hoos, *op. cit.* (1960), p. 103.

66 *Idem.*

67 H. S. Levin, *Office Work and Automation* (New York: John Wiley, 1956), p. 192.

68 Department of Employment, *op. cit.*, p. 41.

CHAPTER 4

The Supply of Office Floorspace

The growth of office employment discussed in the last chapter is inextricably linked with changes in the supply of floorspace to accommodate it. The supply of office floorspace is the product of demand and the structure of this will be discussed in the next chapter. For the present, attention is focused on the factors which influence the supply of floorspace at any point in time, and the factors which contribute to change through time. In common with office employment, one of the initial problems to be overcome is the availability of suitable data for analysing the supply of office floorspace.

AVAILABILITY OF FLOORSPACE DATA

The supply of office floorspace comprises two components: available and total supply. The former represents the actual and immediately available supply of floorspace, including new buildings completed but not let as well as vacant space in older buildings. The latter incorporates space in buildings under construction and space permitted under existing plot ratios or zoning regulations, as well as available supply. The total supply is therefore the maximum space permitted by planning control. Its value will tend to fluctuate through time if changes are made to zoning in district plans, for example, or to floorspace allocations in structure plans. The available supply will also fluctuate, but at a higher rate than total supply, in response to changes in market conditions which determine the use of floorspace. Ideally, office floorspace statistics should allow these two facets of supply to be examined for a time series and up to the most recent dates possible. In practice, the statistics available are far from satisfactory, containing gaps in coverage and problems of comparison between different sources. Published statistics have only very recently been available and analysis of the changes in supply in Britain before 1964 is virtually impossible.

The first office floorspace statistics for local authorities in England and Wales were published in 1969 but these only traced the changes in supply between 1964 and 1967 (April).[1] Total stock figures for the same local authorities only became available in 1972 and then only as at 1 April 1967.[2] The statistics are provided for selected use classes which include commercial, local government, and central government offices but these categories do not cover all offices.[3] These divisions are not, unfortunately, mutually exclusive. Allocation depends to some extent on the purposes for which offices were built rather than the actual use. A speculative office subsequently occupied by a local authority or central government is included as a commercial office. The commercial office category covers all hereditaments where the major use is for normal commercial office purposes.[4] The key word is 'major use' in that the floorspace figures are obtained from valuation lists prepared by the Inland Revenue which classifies hereditaments according to the dominant use. Hence, office space in factories will be classified as industrial floorspace and some major commercial office activities will not be included in the 'commercial' category and vice versa. A further major exclusion from this category occurs under the rating classification 'other undertakings'. This includes the various utilities such as gas and water undertakings, the National Coal Board and various transport undertakings, all of which occupy substantial areas of office floorspace. The situation is further confused in the case of the larger cities such as London and Manchester by the inclusion, as normal practice by Inland Revenue valuers, of very large 'head office' buildings of all types of activity under the commercial offices category. This leads to further discrepancies between smaller and larger cities.[5] The statistics for 1964–7 have also been found to be so much lower than the 1967–8 figures that a reliable annual series can only be considered to begin from 1 April 1967.

The data for local government offices are also incomplete in that they only include those hereditaments where the main use is for normal office purposes. It is therefore possible for major portions of town halls to be excluded whilst office accommodation rented by local government from the private sector will be included. The office floorspace of some local authorities is recorded for adjacent, and often larger authorities, because their offices are physically outside the areas they administer. Central government office floorspace is extracted from the rating category 'Crown occupations' which covers a wide variety of uses. 'Crown' relates to any ministry, department or institution listed in the Imperial Calendar. The separation of offices from other main uses in Crown occupation is also based on the dominant use so that none of the subsidiary office uses of any type of Crown hereditament is included.[6]

The total stock count for 1 April 1967 is based on a special count of all hereditaments. This will be repeated at quinquennial intervals rather than on the basis of annual counts. This largely reflects the difficulties of handling the large volume of returns each year and the accumulation of errors if the stock counts are based on an accumulation of figures for each year. Even the quinquennial figures may be difficult to produce because of the changes in local authority boundaries following reorganization of local government in 1974. It should also be noted that the total floorspace only relates to hereditaments which have been or are at present in occupation; new buildings which have not been occupied for the first time are excluded unless they occur in local authorities which charge 50 per cent of the annual rateable value to the owners of unoccupied properties.

The floorspace statistics published by the Department of the Environment (D.O.E.) therefore have many limitations, yet they are the only source of comparable statistics for England and Wales as a whole. Many, although by no means all, of the major local authorities have been making their own land use surveys during the last decade.[7] Few of them produce directly comparable statistics because of variations in standards and methods of data collection. Furthermore, it is difficult to compare the D.O.E. statistics with those produced by individual local authorities. The best example of this is the Greater London Council (G.L.C.) Land Use Survey 1966 which uses a definition of office floorspace and methods of measurement which are so different from those of the Inland Revenue as to lead to very large discrepancies in the floorspace statistics for the same administrative areas.[8] The G.L.C. identified all the different uses within surveyed areas instead of identifying the major use. Hence, office space which the Inland Revenue classifies as industrial because it is not the dominant use of a hereditament would be classified separately under the G.L.C. scheme. The G.L.C. also uses a separate category for the offices of nationalized bodies and institutions.

The measurement of floorspace by the G.L.C. is also different to the method used by the Inland Revenue. The latter use the Effective Floor Area (E.F.A.) of each hereditament which is the net internal area of buildings excluding piers, staircases, lifts, etc.[9] The former use the Reduced Cover Area (R.C.A.) which is based on the external measurement of buildings multiplied by the number of storeys and basements with an allowance for courtyards, etc. These two systems can produce large differences in measurement for the same property. Comparison of the two methods on some commercial office property in central London has shown that E.F.A. is approximately 66 per cent of R.C.A.[10] It is therefore important to know which method of measurement is being used for any floorspace statistics. The G.L.C. also measured 'parcels' rather than individual hereditaments which are sometimes aggregates of properties which appear to be in one main use. New buildings which had not been occupied for the first time were more likely to be included in the statistics because they were surveyed at an earlier stage than normal for the Inland Revenue. The stock count by the G.L.C. Land Use Survey also predates the D.O.E. count by 12 months.

The D.O.E. data represent substantial underenumeration of office stock and floorspace changes. There were 140 m. ft^2 of occupied office floorspace in Greater London in 1967 according to the Inland Revenue figures published by the D.O.E., while according to the G.L.C. Land Use Survey the figure was 296 m. ft^2 in 1966. The D.O.E. total for the G.L.C. is less than the total floorspace in the central area alone according to the G.L.C. statistics. Major discrepancies of this kind make the interpretation and comparison of office floorspace statistics a hazardous affair. This will only be improved either by centralized collection and publication of statistics of sufficient depth, and to fit its own requirements, by the D.O.E., or by standardization of definitions and measurement techniques for use in all land use surveys. In this context, it seems that the D.O.E. has much to gain from local authorities like the G.L.C., rather than depending on 'second-hand' statistics from other Government departments. But even the G.L.C.'s Land Use Survey and Decision Analysis programme does not provide a complete record of changes in supply of office floorspace.[11] The Decisions Analysis system has only operated since 1965 so that planning permissions granted before that date are excluded. This method of analysing changes in supply by monitoring permissions and completions for office buildings is a long-term, time-consuming task but it allows the G.L.C. to follow quite accurately the floorspace trends within its boundaries. At present, only the larger local authorities can afford to finance such advanced schemes which are a vital adjunct to planning strategies for floorspace provision for office and other activities.

Data problems are also evident in the United States. There are no national statistics for office floorspace and it is left to organizations like the Building Owners and Managers Association or local Chambers of Commerce to collate and publish rather incomplete data for the larger cities.[12] As in Britain, information about office building and floorspace leaves much to be desired. The scarcity of good statistics is a product of the variety in types of office buildings, the fragmented structure of the office industry, and the absence of public programmes directed towards offices.[13] There is no official agency in the United States responsible for comprehensive reporting of additions and removals from the office stock and the statistics published by various miscellaneous sources usually fall short of giving complete coverage of all relevant information.[14] For their recent study of the office industry in the New York Region, the Regional Plan Association had to purchase floorspace data on commercial office contracts from an information systems company. The figures they produced were much more comprehensive than data available in the U.S. Census, for example, because the floorspace of individual projects down to county level are listed.[15] But it should not be necessary to purchase data in this way. In view of the important role of office floorspace in terms of employment provision, as a source of rateable value income, or in its contribution to national wealth and in capital formation, more vigorous efforts are required to produce central and standardized data banks as part of the normal routine of national data collection. While individual studies by City Planning Commissions are undoubtedly useful it is almost impossible to compare the results for different cities and to compare city trends with national characteristics of floorspace supply.[16]

TRENDS IN SUPPLY

With these important data limitations in mind, some of the characteristic features of the supply of office floorspace can be identified. The supply of floorspace reflects the demands expressed by

the office market which, in turn, has expanded steadily as the growth of office employment has continued. But the supply of office floorspace is a cyclical process which responds to the economic climate at any point in time (Fig. 14). Although complicated by building height restrictions, the graph for Chicago between 1870 and 1970 illustrates clearly the cyclical trends in the supply of office floorspace. Particularly important is the large trough in construction between the early 1930s and 1950. This feature is characteristic of office construction in the major cities of Britain and America during the same period and represents the effects of, initially, the Depression and subsequently the Second World War, when building materials were diverted to other uses. In the case of Britain, demand was also stifled by the threat of bombing in the major cities. But since approximately 1950 there has

was inevitable that the supply of floorspace would proceed apace. In 1949 there were only 31·5 m. ft² of offices in the City of London compared with 37·8 m. ft² in 1939.[17] By 1957 the stock of office floorspace had reached its pre-war level and during the next ten years the annual increment of floorspace was approximately 1 m. ft² (Table 12). These figures only apply to the 1 mile² of the City of London; the West End, where the post-war increases in floorspace have been equally rapid, is excluded. Table 12 also shows how the supply of office floorspace has not only increased consistently each year but also at a faster rate than other uses, some of which have not returned to pre-war levels, e.g. warehousing

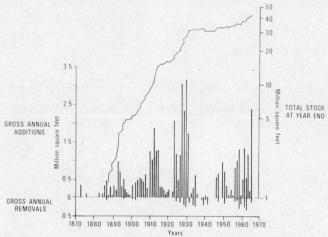

Fig. 14   The Supply of Office Floorspace in Chicago—1870–1970 (After R. M. Fisher, *The Boom in Office Buildings*, 1967. Reprinted with permission from ULI—the Urban Land Institute, 1200 18th Street, N.W., Washington, D.C. 20036. Copyright 1967)

been a boom in office construction as a result of the subdued demand during the previous 15–20 years, as well as from the general expansion of office activities.

Towards the end of the war the shortage of space was demonstrated by the high level of occupancy rates for office buildings; there were few vacant offices and 100 per cent occupancy was common in the more important cities. The opportunities for expansion and mobility of office activities was almost nil and as soon as building licence restrictions and other Government controls on construction were removed it

and industry. During the period 1949–68 office floorspace increased by 52·1 per cent compared with only 6·1 per cent for industrial floorspace. In this respect, the City is a microcosm of land use and floorspace trends in the central business districts of all our major cities.

Recent floorspace statistics for Greater London show similar growth trends, although tempered by office development controls since 1964 (Table 13).[18] In 1961 there were 271 m. ft² of occupied office floorspace in Greater London, of which more than 62 per cent was concentrated in the 11 mile² of central London. By 1971 the

TABLE 12
DISTRIBUTION OF FLOORSPACE IN
SELECTED USES — CITY OF LONDON, 1939–68

Floorspace standing	(m. ft^2)				
	Offices	Warehouses	Industry	Shops	Residential
1939	37·6	22·3	9·9	4·1	1·0
1949	31·5	10·3	4·9	2·7	0·7
1957	37·8	10·4	5·0	2·8	0·7
1958	39·7	10·4	5·0	2·9	0·7
1959	40·7	10·4	5·2	2·9	0·7
1960	42·0	10·5	5·3	2·9	0·7
1961	42·9	10·6	5·3	3·0	0·7
1962	43·7	10·4	5·3	3·0	0·7
1963	44·7	10·2	5·3	3·0	0·7
1964	46·0	10·2	5·2	3·1	0·7
1965	46·5	10·1	5·3	3·2	0·8
1966	46·9	10·3	5·3	3·2	0·8
1967	47·8	10·3	5·3	3·2	0·8
1968	47·9	10·3	5·2	3·2	0·8
Percentage change 1949–68	+ 52·1	no change	+ 6·1	+ 18·5	+ 14·3

Source: J. H. Dunning and E. V. Morgan (eds), *An Economic Study of the City of London* (London: Allen & Unwin, 1971), Table 1.1, p. 32.

TABLE 13
ESTIMATED GROWTH OF OFFICE FLOORSPACE
IN GREATER, INNER, OUTER AND
CENTRAL LONDON — 1961–76

Floorspace (m. ft^2, gross)

Occupied floorspace	Central London	%[1]	Inner London	%	Outer London	%	Greater London	%
1961	168	—	44	—	59	—	271	—
1966	179	6·5	48	9·1	69	16·9	296	9·2
1971	187	4·5	50	4·2	80	15·9	317	7·0
1976[2]	199	6·4	55	10·0	92	15·0	346	9·1

Notes: 1. Percentage change. Unless indicated all values are positive.
2. 1976 figures are based on target net completions 1972–6. Figures for earlier years are based on probable net completions.
Source: Greater London Development Plan Inquiry, *Industrial and Office Floorspace Targets, 1972–76* (London: Greater London Council, Background Paper, B.452, 1971), p. 94.

Greater London figure had increased to 317 m. ft² with 59 per cent of the total in the central area. Some 57 per cent of the office floorspace in Greater London will be concentrated in the centre by 1976 but the overall trend will be continued growth with a growing disparity between the inner and outer areas of the city (see Table 13). The latter is part of the national pattern in the growth of office floorspace since 1945. Approximately 120 m. ft² of office building received planning approval in England and Wales between 1946 and 1962 for example.[19] Over 41 per cent of the approvals related to buildings already constructed, or under construction, in London while most of the remaining office approvals in the provinces were concentrated in the major centres such as Liverpool, Manchester, Birmingham, and Leeds. Further scrutiny of this data would probably reveal further concentration of the approvals into small areas of the individual cities. These spatial components in the supply of office floorspace at the regional and intra-urban level have important consequences for the distribution of office employment and regional planning. This theme will be discussed more fully in later chapters.

An office boom has also occurred in the United States since the early 1950s. As might be expected, one of the first places to be affected was Manhattan where 20 new office buildings had already been started after 1945 and completed by the end of 1950.[20] Different cities were affected by the office floorspace explosion at different times, depending on the rate at which buildings under construction were completed. Major new buildings were not added to the stock of San Francisco and Los Angeles until 1955, Chicago and Minneapolis in 1957, and Baltimore in 1962.[21] Although the impact of the office boom has been most obvious in the centre of larger cities, they have only accounted for a relatively small proportion of the total increase in floorspace since 1945. Suburban areas and smaller communities outside the major cities have attracted a growing proportion of office construction although, as in Britain's S.E. Region, the New York Region will continue to have the largest amount of total office floorspace in the United States (Table 14). Estimates of the national growth of office floorspace between 1963 and 2000 reveal a possible increase of more than 200 per cent, compared with 137 per cent in the New York Region and 97 per cent in Manhattan. It took 63 years for the office floorspace in Manhattan to increase from 40 to 203 m. ft² but only a further 12 years to add a further 53 per cent (106·6 m. ft²) to its office stock. Similarly, between 1957 and 1970 approximately 1300 m. ft² of new private office space was constructed in the United States; this represents more than half of the floorspace which existed at the beginning of the period.[22]

FACTORS INFLUENCING SUPPLY

The supply of office floorspace is the product of an amalgam of factors which include the influence of public controls, vacancy/occupancy rates of existing office premises, the rate of demolition and conversion of buildings, and the influence of property developers. The diversity of office building design, size, and height is indicative of the most distinctive feature of this part of the construction industry; almost all office buildings are one-off jobs. They represent investment of substantial capital sums, designed on one hand to provide the best possible returns for the owner, and on the other hand to be as attractive as possible to potential tenants as prestigious, desirable places to conduct their office activities.

Each office building, particularly in the high land value locations of the central area, is designed to make available as much functional floorspace as possible so that the best possible returns can be obtained. This is especially important in speculative office development, as distinct from custom constructed buildings, where the specific requirements of the owner may outweigh the need to provide maximum space.

Finance

Probably some 40–45 per cent by value of all construction in Britain comprises offices build-

TABLE 14

PAST AND PROJECTED GROWTH OF OFFICE FLOORSPACE
IN THE UNITED STATES, NEW YORK REGION AND
MANHATTAN—1900–2000

Floorspace (m. ft² gross)

Year	United States	New York Region	% of U.S.	Manhattan C.B.D.	% of Region
1900	—	—	—	40	—
1920	—	—	—	70	—
1940	—	—	—	130	—
1963	2200	411	18·7	203	49·4
1967	2600	455	17·5	221	48·6
1975	3400	594	17·5	310	52·2
1985	5000	735	14·7	340	46·3
2000	7000	975	13·9	400	41·0

Note: Based on data collected by the Regional Plan Association and trends in public
and private office construction reported by F. W. Dodge Inc. Government administration buildings as well as private offices and banks are included. The projected
figures are derived from office employment and office construction trends for the
various levels of data presented.

Source: R. B. Armstrong, *The Office Industry: Patterns of Growth and Location* (Cambridge, Mass.: The M.I.T. Press, 1972), Table 5.8, p. 120 and Fig. 5.3, p. 121.

ings. Most of the building is undertaken by construction and property companies specializing in
offices. Only the largest manufacturing and other
companies can afford, or can obtain, the necessary funding for construction of their own buildings. In contrast with the house construction
industry, for example, the office industry involves
much higher risks in that the demand for office
space can fluctuate widely in response to various
economic parameters. Most office buildings are
rented rather than purchased because developers
need time to recoup the large capital sums vested
in buildings for which few purchasers could
afford to pay directly. Office space is therefore a
commodity subject to the vagaries of supply and
demand and because of this the supply will be
a matter of public interest and control to an
extent not typical of some other types of land use
in the city.[23] Public involvement is necessary in
order to control the amount of land available for
office development, its location relative to other
uses, and, given the tendency towards a high level
of centrality, the opportunity to influence the
spatial disposition of the commodity in a way
which will reduce congestion and other community-borne costs to an acceptable level.

The construction of an office building depends
upon the availability of a site, capital, labour,
and raw materials.[24] The most important of
these four factors are site and capital although
even if these are available they are of little use
without architectural and construction expertise, and building materials.

Unless large, existing office buildings are being
replaced, most city-centre sites are not large
enough for economic office development. This
problem occurs in all but the very youngest cities
such as Brasília or Canberra where sites of
appropriate size can be allocated to offices at
the planning stage. Sites which are sufficiently
large for development must therefore be
acquired by amalgamation of several contiguous
units which might be owned by local authorities, institutions, property companies or individual occupants or former occupants not belong-
ing to any of these categories. Site acquisition by
a development company may take many years
and involve extensive negotiations mainly with
a view to obtaining the freehold rather than the
leasehold of the sites. This permits the development company to proceed comparatively unhindered with its office project. If leasehold

arrangements remain there is likely to be less flexibility and in cases where the existing owner/s of a site allow development but retain the freehold, the development company will have to share profits, etc. with its partners. Development companies will go to great lengths to assemble sites as cheaply as possible so that they do not form a major part of construction costs. Even so, in 1969 there were some sites in the Broad Street area of Manhattan fetching $500/ft^2 with construction costs of the building at only $40/ft^2. In the areas of intense competition for sites, land alone may cost two-thirds as much as the cost of putting up the office building.[25] The complexities of site acquisition in London have been illustrated by Marriott with respect to the Euston Tower site on the northern side of Euston Road.[26]

The capital requirements of office projects are of two main types, purchasing funds and bridging finance.[27] The purchasing funds are required for site acquisition and are normally the larger of the two in terms of the sums involved. They represent long-term finance where the objective is investment. Because property represents one of the most secure investments, many of the institutions operating insurance and pension funds will provide the necessary funds either for site purchase directly and granting a long lease to the development company, or by providing a mortgage against the property already owned by the company.[28] An increasing number of institutions have also been demanding an equity as well as fixed income arrangements in office development. The insurance companies have been particularly important in the provision of purchasing funds since the war.[29] Immediately after the war they financed many property companies directly and then during the credit squeeze of 1955–8 they participated in the sale and leaseback system. Under this arrangement owners or developers were able to obtain capital by selling their property to the insurance company and then leasing it back again. This could result in the developer paying more than he took in rent if the market for office space declined but this system was undoubtedly important in retaining the momentum of office development in most British cities at a time when demand was expanding rapidly. Since 1958 insurance companies have continued

to play an important, but indirect, role in office development, only investing in office buildings if they are to be used for their own purposes, e.g. the Royal Insurance Building in Liverpool. Local authorities are also a source of purchasing funds but less so for office development then for other types of land use.[30]

Joint stock and merchant banks are the main source of bridging finance for office development.[31] These, essentially short-term, loans cover the cost of construction, loss of rent during redevelopment, or company expenses and many other items which occur following site acquisition. During the last 15 years the merchant banks have taken on an increasing proportion of short-term funding. They usually require a return on their loan of 5–6 per cent above base rate in addition to a share of the profits from the development. They maintain strict control over the process of development in order to protect their interest. The banks are prepared to lend on the assumption that inflation and demand will guarantee satisfactory returns for the development company and, therefore, for the repayment of loans. By and large, property has been the most secure area for investment since the war and most of the banks have profited from their involvement in office development in this way. The importance of finance in the supply of office floorspace is much more complicated than a brief review may suggest but it has been shown that however difficult the access to capital may be, office developers are still prepared to provide new floorspace in areas of well established demand such as Manhattan.[32] To some extent, the opportunities for obtaining bridging finance depend on whether it represents construction, refinancing, or rehabilitation of office buildings. Sources will also depend on the type of ownership, private or public, and type of tenure, owner or tenant.[33]

The role of developers

During the preceeding discussion frequent reference has been made to development companies.[34] Most of them are involved with speculative rather than custom-built offices and are usually referred to as the 'developers'. As the initiators of most new office building and replacement, the developers clearly have a vital role in the supply equation, as well as affecting demand. Individual office buildings can cost several million pounds in site acquisition, and to construct, and the task of co-ordinating land purchase, the raising of capital, and finding a construction company has increasingly come under the control of development companies. It is estimated, for example, that Centre Point in London cost at least £3·5 m. in construction and mortgage interest exclusive of the £500,000 required to purchase the site. Therefore Marriott has likened the developer to an impressario who catalyses others into transforming his raw material, land, into something more useful for somebody else while at the same time increasing the value of the land to himself.[35] The entrepreneurial developers of the boom period for office development in the 1950s actually produced nothing which was tangible; they acted as the middle-men. Many developers began as estate agents who, once they became familiar with the operation of the land market, could easily specialize in the office, or any other, sector. Contemporary development companies are usually more involved in the total process of office space provision and are much more sophisticated in their operations.

Most of the office development companies in Britain are found in London where much of the demand for office floorspace is generated. They are also close to the money market in the City and over 50 per cent of the respondents (50 companies out of 204 in the sample) to a survey of development companies in London were located within the City or West End and only five had their head offices outside London, in Manchester and Birmingham.[36] Of the 21 companies which had participated in office development during the last ten years, only seven had produced more than 500,000 ft^2. This may be because many development companies are of recent formation but it also reflects a real concentration of large scale projects in the hands of a small number of companies.[37] This is also true of office development in New York where the Rockefeller group, Uris Buildings or H. B. Helmsley have dominated new construction in 1971 and 1972.[38] Moreover, the office development controlled by

these developers involves the largest buildings and consequently, provided the market is satisfactory, the largest potential profits. Although some development companies were in existence before the war, the majority are a by-product of the post-war office boom during which the limited number of pre-war companies could not cope with the demand.

When undertaking the task of supplying a new office building, or of rehabilitating an existing one, the developer is making a number of assumptions about long-term trends in the property market. He is managing an end-product which might take ten or more years to complete from site assemblage to letting the building. The decision to build a speculative office involves calculations of anticipated total income and total costs.[39] The former will depend upon rents per square foot and the vacancy rates of existing office floorspace in the city. The lower the vacancy rate, the tighter the market is likely to be and the better the opportunities for letting a building quickly at the top prevailing rent.[40] If the vacancy rate is high it will not be possible to obtain the highest rent prevailing at the time, but the developer must project current rents to the levels expected to occur when an office building is completed. It should also be noted that the highest prevailing rent will be much higher than the average rent due to the lags in renewing long leases. The vacancy rate also suggests the prospects for rent rises in existing offices as well as in the prediction of future income by the developer. Normally, the developer can achieve the highest rent more easily than owners of older buildings because a new product is being offered which is not bound by the terms of existing leases.

Total costs to the developer comprise variable and fixed components. Variable costs operate in similar ways for different developers and include heating, lighting, decorating, etc. and this will not influence the supply of office space. The fixed costs are much more influential because they involve the financial bases of office projects, along the lines already discussed. In terms of whether or not to proceed with an office project, it is construction costs, rather than fixed charges, which act as the deterrant or stimulus to office construction in any one year.[41] Construction costs per ft^2 in Manhattan have increased by 100 per cent from \$20 in the early 1960s to \$40 in 1969.[42] Add to this the increases in labour charges, 40 per cent between 1969 and 1972, the rising cost of borrowing money, and the fact that construction is taking longer per unit of space than before, then the risks to the developer in speculative office development are indeed heavy. Developers in Britain now work for a 20–30 per cent profit margin, particularly the smaller companies who cannot support a large loss or are unable to undercut larger competitors. Some of the larger companies will go down to 15 per cent or even less. This increases the risks as profit margins are eroded by the increasing cost of land purchase, rising construction costs or changes in mortgage rates. The problem of land purchase is also becoming more acute as more landowners become aware of the value of their property to developers. The developer is often held responsible for high land values but it is increasingly due to excessive demands by landlords for the best possible prices. The developer must live with short-term fluctuations or lulls in the economy, while planning to meet long-term growth which he has every reason to expect over a longer period.

However sophisticated the decision making by development companies may appear to be, in the end the selection of a site for an office is largely dependent on whether it 'feels right'. Only subsequently, if the decision is questioned by way of a planning refusal, for example, will an attempt be made to justify the choice of site.

All office development is not speculative. Custom-built offices for financial institutions or major manufacturing companies have also played an important part in the post-war office boom. The Commercial Union and Shell Buildings in London or the Seagram and Chase Manhattan Buildings in New York are examples of custom-built structures. Such offices provide an opportunity for prestigious buildings which can easily be associated with the companies concerned and they are often monumental in conception. Such buildings add variety and quality to office buildings in our cities by comparison with the standardized structures generally associated with speculative development. Custom-built offices often contain more space than initially required by the owners. This surplus is usually sub-let until such time as the company requires it for its own use. This can represent valuable short-term additions to the supply of office floorspace. The risks involved in these buildings are lower than those faced by developers. Many of the companies are large enough to provide their own funds or can negotiate loans or sales-leaseback arrangements at favourable terms. Construction costs are also likely to be less of a deterrent because the types of company engaging in these exercises are likely to view such investment as small relative to their total funds. A custom-built office also allows companies to centralize their activities and this consideration may outweigh costs, as well as allowing the use of funds which might otherwise be lying idle.

However, only 15–25 per cent of office floorspace is custom-built. The proportion fluctuates between major cities. In Washington D.C., where public sector activities are very important, more than 50 per cent of the new office space completed since the war has been largely owner occupied and constructed. By comparison, the non-competitive supply of floorspace is far less important in Manhattan where over 75 per cent of all new offices since the war have been speculative.[43] The balance between private and public sector demand for office space in individual cities will clearly influence the level of custom-built construction. In Britain, however, the Government leases a surprisingly large proportion of speculative office space.[44] At the end of December 1972, Government Departments occupied 14·4 m. ft^2 of office floorspace in central London and 69·2 per cent was leased from non-Government sources. For areas outside central London but within the G.L.C. the equivalent figure was 63·2 per cent.[45] The construction of custom-built offices also fluctuates more than speculative development. When vacancy rates are low and there is general business expansion in an economy, a large proportion of new office development during the early years of increasing supply of floorspace will be in the form of owner occupied buildings and vice versa.[46]

Vacancy rates

The role of vacancy rates in the supply of office floorspace has already been mentioned. The existence of vacant space in the total stock of offices allows the market to operate with more flexibility than when supply and demand are exactly matched. The desirable vacancy rate is at least 5 per cent of total floorspace. Vacant space permits mobility of firms within and between cities, allows expansion of organizations and the establishment of new office activities. But the supply of vacant space is often biased towards older office buildings which are less attractive and more difficult to let, despite the lower rents which they command. Therefore, although the overall vacancy rate in a city may be 5 per cent, the true vacancy rate may be as low as 1 or 2 per cent because new space is more attractive than old. A special study carried out after the Land Use Survey 1966 of offices in central London showed 11·6 m. ft^2 of vacant space but the amount previously occupied was approximately 10 m. ft^2 and a large proportion of this could be described as 'old' vacant space.[47] The overall vacancy rate also assumes that all empty space will be available to all potential clients. It is assumed that rents are at a level which can be paid by at least some of the organizations in the market for space. But in London, and elsewhere, this is not always the case because some of the completed offices are not accessible on short-term leases, will not be let in sub-divided units, or require rents which are well above the highest prevailing rents for the city. The classic example of this is Centre Point in London which was completed in 1964 but is only now being occupied. Other examples include Space House, London Bridge House and, until mid-1973, half of Telstar House in Paddington. Between them, these buildings represent over 600,000 ft^2 of new office floorspace, the kind of space most in demand. In 1972 the Greater London Council estimated that over 2 m. ft^2 of new office space in London had never been occupied and over 50 per cent of it was in the central area.[48] Vacancy rates therefore require careful examination before assessing their important role in the supply of office floorspace. Yet there is no systematic monitoring by planning departments and other interested groups.[49]

Vacancy rates depend to some extent on the turnover of occupancy.[50] Compared to other types of land use, turnover rates for office space are low; normally less than 5 per cent per annum in most cities. Typical office leases run for 21 years for rented space while owner occupiers will clearly be tied to the offices they possess. The opportunities for high levels of turnover are therefore restricted, and to some extent discouraged by the flexibility of space in individual buildings. If an office needs to expand but cannot move to other premises the additional staff can usually be accommodated in the existing space provided that the regulations relating to working conditions are satisfied. As the amount of occupied floorspace increases the absolute volume of turnover will rise even if the rate itself remains constant and this will encourage additional new construction.

Conversion and demolition

Apart from new buildings, the supply of office space will also depend on how much is removed through demolition and how much is added through conversion.

The potential opportunities for demolition are substantial in that many offices occupy premises over 50 years old which are not suited to modern office requirements. Approximately 42 per cent of the occupied office floorspace in central Manchester is in property built before 1914 and only 16 per cent of the present occupied space was built during the inter-war period.[51] As a result many of the smaller office establishments do not occupy purpose-built premises. In Leeds, 23·1 per cent of the offices in a sample survey occupied converted houses, 5 per cent occupied commercial warehouses, and 14 per cent were in other types of converted property.[52] Only some 50 per cent of the establishments were located in purpose-built premises. Long-term loss of floorspace as a result of demolition is exceptional, especially in high cost, high rent central areas where demolition of an office building is likely to involve replacement by the same use. Most planning authorities cannot afford to pay compensation to developers seeking planning permission on the basis of existing use. Planning controls allowing, the replacement building will usually be larger and will add more floorspace than prior to demolition. Any shortfall in supply through demolition is therefore essentially short term although it may involve five years or more before the demolished space is replaced by a new structure. Demolition is a costly method of supplying new office space, particularly in cases where the developers need to obtain planning permission for a higher density replacement.

Conversion within the existing shell of an old building has recently become more attractive than to demolish and rebuild. This approach to supply has gained ground during the last five years in the face of planning control problems such as the difficulties of getting office development permits for central area sites. These controls have forced up rents for office space and thus made conversion financially more attractive.[53] Corporate prestige is another reason for the growing importance of conversion and some companies go to the extent of heading their notepaper with motifs of their Georgian or Victorian office buildings. Much of the demand for older converted offices comes from professional organizations, societies, and institutions. Because of their size these buildings are not really attractive to the large corporate organizations. Historically, conversion of buildings from non-office to office uses has also been an important source of supply while there has been a much lower propensity to convert office space to other uses. Victorian and Edwardian residential areas within and on the fringes of the C.B.D. are frequently subject to this kind of land use change.

Scale

A final component in the supply equation is the changing scale of office buildings. Although there are many small office projects of less than 1000 ft^2 associated with shop and other developments in suburban areas and parts of city centres, most new floorspace is supplied in a small number of large buildings. This is well illustrated in Manhattan where 227 new buildings were erected between 1950 and 1971. They contained approximately 110 m. ft^2 of which 1·8 m. ft^2 was produced in the first five years with an average building size of 250,000 ft^2.[54] During the last five years of the period 47·5 m. ft^2 were built and the average size of building was 765,000 ft^2. In downtown Chicago more new space was added in four buildings completed in 1965 than stood vacant in 160 older buildings in 1964.[55] Between 1951 and 1966 the average size of buildings completed in central London has fluctuated between a low of 30,100 ft^2 in 1961 to a high of 55,300 ft^2 in 1966 (Table 15).[56] This has occurred even though the number of buildings completed in any one year has declined from 142 in 1959 to 79 in 1966. The more recent Euston Tower at the north end of Tottenham Court Road contains 1 m. ft^2 of office floorspace which is more than the 900,000 ft^2 provided in 21 buildings completed in 1954. This building is large by contemporary London standards but the World Trade Centre in New York contains four times as much space in only one of its two towers.

By providing office space in large units the development companies can achieve important economies of scale in relation to both demand and supply. On the supply side, the larger the site area the more floorspace can be provided for rent on each floor of the building. This normally makes the office more attractive to tenants. It is also possible to provide a wider range of services to tenants in large buildings, including car parking facilities, as an integral part of the structure. The unit costs of servicing a building with heating or lighting, for example, will also decrease as building size increases. But large buildings can also create diseconomies of scale as a result of site assembly costs, planning regulations on height and density or the need to incorporate other activities such as shops or open spaces as a requirement of permission to proceed. The latter may, however, represent the 'planning gain' from allowing large scale office development. Many small tenants, seeking office units of less than 5000 ft^2 are disadvantaged by large office buildings. Apart from the higher rents which large new buildings can command, some developers are not prepared to sub-divide buildings between several tenants. If possible, they prefer to let a building to a single tenant; this reduces

TABLE 15
ESTIMATED BUILDING SIZE OF COMPLETED
OFFICE SPACE IN CENTRAL LONDON[1] — 1951–66

Year	Estimated amount of office space completed (m. ft^2)	Average building size (000s ft^2)	Number of buildings
1951	0·6	45·6	14
1952	1·1	54·2	20
1953	0·9	46·8	19
1954	0·7	31·4	21
1955	1·9	41·6	47
1956	4·1	34·8	117
1957	4·2	40·2	105
1958	5·9	45·7	129
1959	4·6	32·2	142
1960	4·2	35·7	119
1961	3·0	30·1	100
1962	4·7	52·7	89
1963	3·2	30·6	106
1964	3·9	46·0	86
1965	2·2	34·0	66
1966	4·4	55·3	79
Total completed	49·4	41·1	1259

Note: 1. Central London is defined by the 'central block quadrats', each quadrat is 500 m square. The central block does not coincide exactly with the census definition of the conurbation centre.
Source: P. Cowan *et al. The Office: A Facet of Urban Growth* (London: Heinemann, 1969), Table VII. 3, p. 183.

administrative and other costs to a minimum.[57] This procedure clearly favours large office organizations which can either afford the high rents or are able to take a complete building. Even where sub-division is allowed, attempts are always made to encourage the largest tenants. These may sub-let some space in small units, if the terms of the main agreement allow, but this is often unattractive to small tenants because of the short-term character of most sub-leases. This problem seems most acute in British cities. It is far less important in the United States where office buildings frequently house a wide range of tenants from the smallest to the very largest. This may also reflect the larger scale of many office buildings in the United States and the absolute inability of any one company to lease all the space offered.

PLANNING CONTROLS

Planning controls instigated by central and local government also influence the supply of office floorspace. Central government is particularly important at the regional and national level and the relevant legislation will be discussed later. But individual local authorities possess a wide range of powers, vested in them and monitored by central government, which may directly or in- directly influence office space provision. The most important is development control.[58] Any office development proposal which involves a change of use, building extension with or without change of use, or alteration/adaptation of a building without change of use requires planning permission. Whether planning permission is re- fused or granted will depend upon whether the proposed office building conforms with the zoning, development programme, and policy given in the development plan for the local authority.[59] The development plan has been approved by central government so that the proposed office development must, to some extent, fit in with national, as well as local, objectives for office floorspace. The planning permissions given by a local authority may be one of three kinds; unconditional permission, permission subject to conditions given by the local authority, or refusal. In the event of refusal or conditional permission the applicant has the right of appeal to the Secretary of State. It is also possible for applications which raise planning issues of major importance to be 'called in' for Ministerial decision. Large office development proposals in areas such as central London or important suburban locations are often in this category.

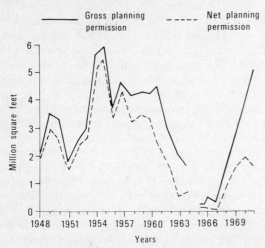

Fig. 15   Total Floorspace of Office Planning Permissions Granted Annually — London, 1954–70 (Data: Greater London Council)

Planning permissions for office development therefore fluctuate annually, reflecting national and local policies as expressed in development plans which should be revised every five years (Fig. 15).[60] A low level of permissions in any one year will be reflected in the supply of floorspace several years later although the amount of floorspace actually coming on to the market cannot be accurately predicted because long standing permissions which developers have been slow to

utilize or have saved will be acted upon when new permissions become difficult to obtain. The trough in approved planning permissions for central London office development between 1950 and 1954 is a product of building licence restrictions. This was followed by a period of relaxation between 1954 and 1962 when demand for offices was very high. This subsequently gave rise to a policy of stringent control of office location in central London, particularly between 1962 and 1968. This period is still affecting the supply of office space in central London and has resulted in a general increase in the amount of floorspace given planning permission since 1969. The office problem in central London will be discussed more fully in a later chapter.

The conditions attached to planning permissions often relate to daylighting codes, building height regulations, and plot ratios. These three factors can effectively control the amount of office floorspace constructed at any one site. Daylighting codes and height regulations have already been discussed in relation to skyscraper office building but plot ratios are also important. Plot ratio controls were introduced in 1948 following recommendations made by Holford, who devised the system.[61] Plot ratio is the relationship between the area of a site and the gross floor area of office building permitted on that site (Fig. 16). This replaced the control of buildings by

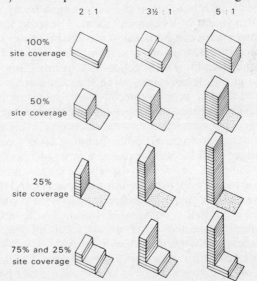

Fig. 16   Plot Ratios and Alternative Site Coverage

height zoning, angular limits, and a system of percentage of site covered by buildings at different levels of the building.[62] Hence, a site with a ground area of 10,000 ft^2 and allocated a plot ratio of 3:1 could be covered by 30,000 ft^2 gross of office space. There are a number of ways in which the space can be distributed over the site. Complete coverage of the site is not necessarily the most satisfactory; it excludes ancillary uses such as parking or access to underground parking; nor does it produce tall buildings of the type produced by 25 per cent cover, for example. By zoning development plans with various plot ratios it is possible to control the supply of office floorspace and, in turn, the density of office workers in particular areas of the city. Holford assumed that developers would not build the maximum space permitted by the plot ratio. But by 1957, when office development in the major cities was proceeding apace, plot ratios were regarded as the minimum rather than the maximum amount of space allowed on a site.[63]

In theory, plot ratios seemed an excellent way of controlling office development. There was, however, a major obstacle to their success which was not removed until 1963. The Third Schedule of the *Town and Country Planning Act 1947* was a notorious loophole utilized by most developers to obtain more floorspace. The Schedule specified that a building could be enlarged by up to 10 per cent of its cubic content. The main problems were caused when new office buildings replaced old, existing structures. Because older office buildings were generous in terms of room height, wide corridors, large staircases, etc. and had thicker, more numerous walls enclosing individual offices, the 10 per cent increase in cubic capacity claimed by owners/developers meant much more than an office building 10 per cent larger than before. It created a large increase in floorspace, and consequently employment, because of improved building techniques and the increase in open plan office designs evident since the mid 1950s. New office buildings therefore often contained floor areas substantially in excess of the permitted plot ratio.[64]

Local authorities, in particular the London County Council, knew at an early stage that plot ratios could be abused in practice. But they were almost powerless to prevent the contraventions because although they had powers to refuse planning permission they had, from 1954, to pay compensation. This covered the development value and profits lost by the refusal and it was clearly abortively expensive for most local authorities to pay the large sums involved, especially in London. Planners were therefore faced with a dilemma from which there was no escape until the Third Schedule was revoked in 1963. It then became unnecessary to pay compensation for refusing an addition of 10 per cent to the cube of an office building. A 10 per cent increase in the gross floor area of existing office buildings was still allowed, as distinct from new buildings on cleared sites. This controlled the net supply and increases in office floorspace but good architects could still add substantially to the amount of space available in a building.

Floor/area ratios are used to control the amount of office floorspace on individual sites in the United States. This is the ratio of gross floorspace of an office building to the area of the site.[65] The legal zoning limit in Manhattan is 18 although this can be varied by individual negotiation between developers and the planners. Hence, office buildings completed in Manhattan in 1969 had an average floor/area ratio of 20, i.e. each building contained 20 times its site area in office floorspace. The way in which the space is distributed over the site is left to the developer. In some cities such as Chicago or San Francisco the height of the building will be controlled and this restricts the way in which sites can be utilized. In New York the ratio can be fitted to any building height. From an American standpoint the disadvantage of the floor/area ratio is that it artificially controls the growth of office floorspace in city centres, which in turn discourages business activities from locating in the centre. It also makes it almost impossible to construct office buildings which are large enough to accommodate some of the larger companies. This can partly be overcome by allowing space bonuses in development set back from the building line. Similar allowances have been made in some of the planning permissions granted for London office blocks in return for parts of sites required for essential roadworks, e.g. Euston Tower, Centre Point.

OVER-SUPPLY PROBLEMS

Supply and demand for office space are rarely in equilibrium and under certain circumstances it is possible for parts of a city to be over-supplied with office floorspace. Nowhere is this better illustrated than in Manhattan.[66] In 1969 the stock of office floorspace increased by 16·2 m. ft² in 18 new buildings; this almost doubled the previous largest-ever increases of 7·7 m ft² in 1961 and 1963. In 1970 a further 14·8 m. ft² was added in 22 new buildings, to be followed in 1971 by a record 26·7 m. ft². These figures exclude the World Trade Centre, some of which was already completed in 1971. By the end of 1972 Carruth has estimated that Manhattan's office space had increased by 40 per cent in only four years, or an increase almost equivalent to the total for the period since 1945. This phenomenal growth of new office space in one central area represents the estimates of demand made by developers, despite rising costs of land and construction. It was already apparent in 1969 that the supply of new space was more than adequate and almost 50 per cent of the 26·7 m. ft² completed in 1971 would have no tenants.

Fluctuations in the building cycle gave rise to the clearly over-optimistic supply of office floorspace between 1969 and 1971 (Fig. 17). Allowing for demolition, the supply of floorspace up to 1963 was able to keep pace with the growth of office employment although it was not adequate if an increasing employee/floorspace ratio was taken into account. During the next two years construction slowed down until the very low figure of 1·2 m. ft² was added in 1966. This coincided with a crucial period in the supply/demand situation because annual office employment growth was increasing from 1·0 to 2·7 per cent in 1966, 4·3 per cent in 1967, and 6·0 per cent in 1968. This resulted in an acute space shortage. The amount of space immediately required was at least 12 m. ft² but allowing for demolition and a vacancy rate of 5 per cent, the actual demand was nearer 17 m. ft². This, plus an annual requirement due to natural growth of 10 m. ft² gave office builders scope for escalating supply, but not to the extent which has actually taken place. The headquarters' offices of some major corporations, insurance companies and others were already beginning to leave Manhattan for suburban areas and locations further afield, making the estimation of demand even more hazardous.

The New York City Planning Commission has estimated that in 1972 Manhattan had a surplus of 23·4 m. ft² of office floorspace (Table 16). This is the equivalent of at least two years supply without including space available for sub-letting in older buildings. The City Planning Commission maintains that the demand was predictable and the developers could have avoided over-supply by careful monitoring of the growth of office employment in the late 1960s and early 1970s, as well as noting the effect of decentralization of office activities from Manhattan.[67] In early 1973 the vacancy rate in Manhattan was 12·3 per cent which was still lower than Los Angeles (13 per cent) or Houston (17·6 per cent).[68] It might be expected that over-supply would lead to an easing of rents in order to attract tenants, but for the letting of buildings to be economic, especially new buildings, the minimum rent remains at its highest point ever of $8·50–$10·00 per ft². This reflects construction and other costs and developers cannot afford to rent for lower figures even if the market is over-supplied.

Dallas is another example of a city with a

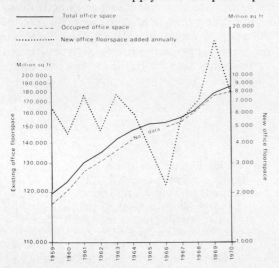

Fig. 17   Supply of Office Floorspace in Manhattan—1959–70 (Data: New York City Planning Commission)

TABLE 16
THE OVER-SUPPLY OF OFFICE SPACE
IN MANHATTAN—1970–4

Year (March)	Actual employment (000s)	Employment assuming no recession	Floorspace (m. ft^2)		
			Demand[3]	Inventory	Surplus
1970	1008[1]	1008	185·4	186·4	1·0
1971	1018[2]	1043	193·7	213·9	20·2
1972	—	1080	202·6	226·0	23·4
1973	—	1118	211·8	226·0	14·2
1974	—	1157	221·4	226·0	4·6

Notes: 1. Estimated growth of 3·5 per cent, March 1969–March 1970.
2. Estimated growth of 1·0 per cent, March 1970–March 1971.
3. Including an allowance for vacancy rate at 4·5 per cent.
Source: New York City Planning Commission, *The Demand for Office Space in Manhattan* (New York: City Planning Commission, 1971), p. 25. Derived from data in *Fortune,* 1971.

general over-supply problem.[69] With the exception of Manhattan, Dallas built more office space between 1950 and 1960, some 7 m. ft^2, than any other American city. The momentum continued into the 1960s and spread from the C.B.D. to the suburbs but the economic depression of the second half of the decade saw few buildings added to existing stock. Hence, vacancy rates in 1969 were lowe. than 2 per cent in the C.B.D. and 6 per cent in the suburbs. In anticipation of an upsurge in demand, developers have recently begun to fill the vacuum; during 1971, 52 office complexes were under construction and 33 were completed by the end of the year. By the end of 1972 this would add 6·5 m. ft^2 to suburban office space and 3·8 m. ft^2 to the C.B.D. Competitive office space coming on to the market in 1970 had an 8·7 per cent vacancy rate, 46·6 per cent for

1971 buildings and 80·7 per cent for 1972. Local developers remain optimistic, however, and estimate that the market for office space in Dallas will be much nearer equilibrium in 6–7 years when large corporations from the Mid-West and the Eastern seaboard begin to appreciate Dallas's locational attributes. It is already the major administrative and distributive centre for the South-West Region and should benefit from the opening of the new Dallas–Fort Worth International Airport.

In this chapter an attempt has been made to review the factors which influence, directly or indirectly, the supply and consequent growth of office floorspace in cities. But it is very difficult to discuss supply without reference to demand for offices and this will be the subject of the next chapter.

REFERENCES

1 Ministry of Housing and Local Government, *Statistics for Town and Country Planning, Series II, No. 1, Floorspace* (London: Her Majesty's Stationery Office, 1969).

2 Department of the Environment, *Statistics for Town and Country Planning, Series II, No. 2, Floorspace* (London: Her Majesty's Stationery Office, 1972).

3 Department of the Environment, *Notes for Guidance in Interpreting Inland Revenue Floorspace Data for England and Wales* (London: Department of the Environment, 1972).

4 A hereditament is generally regarded as including all land, buildings, and rights within one curtilage (ignoring internal roads) for which there is a single, rateable occupier, *ibid.,* p. 1.

5 *Ibid.,* p. 5.

6 The administrative offices of the General Post Office were counted as central government floorspace prior to November 1969. It has since

become a public corporation and its main office uses will be recorded as commercial office floorspace. But this does not apply to some departments not transferred into the corporation, *ibid.*, p. 7.

7 As late as 1969 many local authorities in Britain could not provide floorspace statistics for offices within their administrative areas. P. W. Daniels, 'Office decentralization from London: The journey to work consequences' (University of London, unpublished Ph.D. Thesis, 1972), pp. 67–8.

8 L. F. Gebbett, *The Land Use Survey, 1966* (London: Greater London Council, Department of Planning and Transportation, Research Report, no. 8, 1972), pp. 66–7.

9 Department of the Environment, *op. cit.* (1972), p. 1.

10 This is based only on a sample of 30 large office buildings in London. The E.F.A./R.C.A. ratio may be different for medium or small buildings.

11 Greater London Development Plan Inquiry, *Industrial and Office Floorspace Targets, 1972–76* (London: Greater London Council, Background Paper, no. B.452, 1971), p. 92.

12 E. M. Horwood and R. R. Boyce, *Studies of the Central Business District and Urban Freeway Development* (Seattle: University of Washington Press, 1959), p. 46.

13 R. M. Fisher, *The Boom in Office Buildings: An Economic Study of the Past Two Decades* (Washington: The Urban Land Institute, Technical Bulletin, no. 58, 1967), p. 5.

14 R. B. Armstrong, *The Office Industry: Patterns of Growth and Location* (Cambridge, Mass.: The M.I.T. Press, 1972), p. 119.

15 *Ibid.*, pp. 119–20.

16 G. Manners, *The Office in Metropolis: An Opportunity for Shaping Metropolitan America* (Harvard: Joint Centre for Urban Studies, Working Paper 22, 1973), pp. 2–3.

17 J. H. Dunning and E. V. Morgan (eds), *An Economic Study of the City of London* (London: Allen & Unwin, 1971), p. 32.

18 *Control of Office and Industrial Development Act 1965* (London: Her Majesty's Stationery Office, 1965).

19 Pilkington Research Unit, *Office Design: A Study in Environment* (University of Liverpool: Department of Building Science, 1965), p. 36. The figures quoted are approximate and based on a survey of local authorities in England and Wales.

20 R. M. Fisher, *op. cit.*, p. 6.

21 *Idem.*

22 R. B. Armstrong, *op. cit.*, Table 5.7, p. 120.

23 P. Cowan *et al.*, *The Office: A Facet of Urban Growth* (London: Heinemann, 1969), pp. 110–111.

24 *Ibid.*, pp. 121–6.

25 E. Carruth, 'Manhattan's office building binge', *Fortune*, vol. 83 (1969), p. 178.

26 O. Marriott, *The Property Boom* (London: Hamish Hamilton, 1967), pp. 159–65.

27 P. Cowan *et al.*, *op. cit.*, pp. 122–4.

28 *Ibid.*, p. 123.

29 O. Marriott, *op. cit.*, pp. 38–40. A history and analysis of the provision of institutional finance for property development, including offices, is given in B. P. Whitehouse, *Partners in Property* (London: Birn, Shaw, 1964).

30 P. Cowan *et al.*, *op. cit.*, pp. 123–4.

31 E. J. W. Buckler, *Bank Finance for Property Development* (London: Institute of Bankers, 1966). O. Marriott, *op. cit.*, pp. 34–6.

32 E. Carruth, *op. cit.*, pp. 176, 178, 183. E. Carruth, 'New York hangs out the For-Rent sign', *Fortune*, vol. 85 (1971), pp. 86, 88, 114.

33 R. M. Fisher, *op. cit.*, pp. 4–5.

34 The author is grateful to David Gransby and Ian Rowberry of Wates Developments Limited for a most useful interview on the role of the developer in the supply of office floorspace.

35 O. Marriott, *op. cit.*, pp. 138–41.

36 P. Cowan *et al.*, *op. cit.*, p. 114.

37 *Ibid.*, pp. 116–17.

38 E. Carruth, *op. cit.* (1971), p. 118.

39 H. B. Schechter, 'An analysis of commercial construction', *Land Economics*, vol. 26 (1950), pp. 115–35.

40 The top prevailing rent is defined as the highest rent currently being received for comparable office space facilities.

41 H. B. Schechter, *op. cit.*, p. 127.

42 E. Carruth, *op. cit.* (1969), p. 176.

43 R. M. Fisher, *op. cit.*, p. 9.

44 O. Marriott, *op. cit.*, p. 42.

45 Based on unpublished data kindly made available by the Property Services Agency, Department of the Environment.

46 H. B. Schechter, *op. cit.*, p. 128.

47 Greater London Development Plan Inquiry, *op. cit.*, pp. 94–6.

48 'Developers' Cautious Welcome to Threat on Empty Offices', *The Times*, 28 June 1972.

49 Greater London Development Plan Inquiry, *op. cit.*, p. 93.

50 R. M. Fisher, *op. cit.*, p. 15.

51 City of Manchester, *Central Manchester Office Survey, 1971* (Manchester: City Planning Department, 1972), p. 7.

52 M. V. Facey and G. B. Smith, *Offices in a Regional*

Centre: A Study of Office Location in Leeds (London: Location of Offices Bureau, Research Paper, no. 2, 1968), pp. 38–41.

53 'British and European Property', *The Times* (Supplement), 13 April 1973. Similar trends are apparent in the United States, see, for example, Dallas Chamber of Commerce, *A Guide to Dallas Office Buildings* (Dallas: Chamber of Commerce, 1973), pp. 34–5.

54 R. B. Armstrong, *op. cit.*, Table 5.18 and p. 141.

55 R. M. Fisher, *op. cit.*, p. 13.

56 The 'central area' comprises the area contained by the central block quadrats used by Cowan for the purpose of data collection and analysis.

57 It is often suggested that Centre Point and similar buildings in London have been held vacant because it has not been possible to obtain a tenant to lease the complete office block. It may be, however, that the organization of floorspace in such buildings does not meet the requirements of large tenants.

58 Details of the operation of development control and the powers of local authorities are discussed more fully in L. Keeble, *Principles and Practice of Town Planning* (London: Estates Gazette, 1969), pp. 297–313. J. B. Cullingworth, *Town and Country Planning in Britain* (London: Allen & Unwin, 1972), pp. 47–116. R. N. D. Hamilton, *A Guide to Development and Planning* (London: Oyez Publications, 1970).

59 These powers were initially provided by the *Town and Country Planning Act 1947*. As a result of the *Town and Country Planning Act 1968* development plans are now being replaced by a two-tier system of structure and local plans with the latter serving a similar role to development plans.

60 The curve for 'gross planning permissions' shows the amount of new and converted office space given town planning approval in central London year by year. Floorspace of new offices and extensions has been measured from the plans submitted to the G.L.C. in support of application. Prior to 1964 the figures exclude canteens, cafeterias, storage accommodation, showrooms, caretakers' and other flats, and car parking space. After 1964 these figures were included. Up to 1964, where the details of a proposal had been altered after permission has been granted, the variation in total floorspace approved has been included for the year of alteration, but only if it was an upward variation. From 1965 all sources of double-counting are eliminated. Up to 1964, permissions granted in outline only, and Crown buildings, have been excluded but since 1965 these categories have been included when known, subject to the double-counting proviso.

The curve for 'net planning permissions' is based on gross planning permissions less property demolished to make way for new development or subject to a change away from office use. Up to 1964, demolitions only have been taken into account if replaced by new offices. From 1965, they are taken into account if replaced by any type of use. Based on information kindly provided by D. R. W. Knight, Department of Planning and Transportation, Greater London Council (personal communication).

61 Ministry of Town and Country Planning, *The Redevelopment of Central Areas* (London: His Majesty's Stationery Office, 1947). Plot ratio is called the 'Floor Space Index' in this report.

62 J. B. Cullingworth, *op. cit.*, p. 108.

63 London County Council, *A Plan to Combat Congestion in Central London* (London: London County Council, 1957).

64 For examples see O. Marriott, *op. cit.*, pp. 170–1.

65 R. B. Armstrong, *op. cit.*, p. 107. E. Schultz and W. Simmons, *Offices in the Sky* (New York: Bobbs-Merrill, 1959), pp. 280–2.

66 Based on statistics in E. Carruth, *op. cit.* (1969), pp. 114–17, 176, 178, 183–4, 186. E. Carruth, *op. cit.* (1971), pp. 86–90, 114–15, 118, 120. See also G. D. McDonald, *Office Building Construction in Manhattan, 1947–67* (New York: Real Estate Board, 1964). 'Manhattan's empty spaces', *The Economist*, vol. 239 (1971), p. 92.

67 New York City Planning Commission, *The Demand for Office Space in Manhattan* (New York: City Planning Commission, 1971), p. 25.

68 W. McQuade, 'A daring new generation of skyscrapers', *Fortune*, vol. 87 (1973), p. 78.

69 C. Barta, 'New office space construction', in Dallas Chamber of Commerce, *op. cit.*, pp. 23–36.

CHAPTER 5

The Demand for Office Floorspace

In theoretical terms, the demand for office space can take three forms. Firstly, expressed demand through applications for planning permission for office development or change of use for office purposes. This can lead to an overstatement of demand because some developers make successive applications for the same site or several speculative applications on a variety of sites. It requires very detailed analysis of planning permission and refusals for a reasonably accurate estimate of expressed demand to be obtained.[1] The second measure of demand is total demand. This comprises expressed demand plus 'hidden' demand which is caused by controls operated by the planning system which discourage development on sites which developers may consider most desirable. Thirdly, satisfied demand is simply the total amount of occupied floorspace at one point in time. It is independent of either present supply or present demand for office floorspace. These three types of demand, provided they can be measured with some accuracy, are a useful aid to planners and others responsible for guiding the growth and location of office activities in urban areas towards desirable goals. The development companies are much less likely to utilize such theoretical definitions of demand, particularly in Britain's larger cities, because supply of suitable space is usually below total demand.

Three main factors influence the demand for office space: the growth of office employment; changes in the amount of floorspace per office worker; and the need to replace old, obsolescent offices. Demand derived from employment growth is by far the most important of these three factors (Table 17). Over 87 per cent of the demand for office space in Manhattan between 1959 and 1969 was due to employment growth. Unlike most other forms of urban development, the demand for office buildings is not a direct function of city population. Demand for space will partly depend on the employment mix of the local economy, such as the ratio of manufacturing to service employment, and its consequences for the occupational composition of the community. The role of the three demand factors will be considered individually although they are by no means mutually exclusive in their effects on floorspace demand.

TABLE 17

THE STRUCTURE OF DEMAND FOR OFFICE SPACE IN MANHATTAN—1959–69

	Total floorspace (m. ft² net)	% of total
Employment growth (288,000 jobs at 170·6 ft² per worker)	49·0	87·1
Floorspace increase per worker	1·9	3·4
Replacement of existing stock	5·3	9·5
Total demand	56·2	100·0

Source: New York City Planning Commission, *The Demand for Office Space in Manhattan* (New York: City Planning Commission, 1971), Table V, p. 4.

FLOORSPACE DEMAND AND EMPLOYMENT GROWTH

The unprecedented growth of office employment since 1945 in almost all sectors of economic activity has already been discussed. Such growth has generated substantial demands for office space which have been met by the sources of supply discussed in Chapter 4. As each firm expands its office labour force it can either attempt to accommodate it in the existing building or move to new, larger accommodation. Some firms will have vacant space to occupy in their existing building or buildings while the departure of tenants on sub-leases may make additional space available. Most firms are reluctant to move unless absolutely necessary because of the transitional costs this may involve, both fiscally and in terms of the effect on contacts and customers. Overcrowding, inadequate working facilities, and possible staffing problems may, however, make it compulsory for the office to move elsewhere. Such a move may involve decanting some employees into new space or a total move of the organization.

Most offices appear to pass through a cycle of employment growth which affects their demand for floorspace. Consolidation takes place during the early years of growth, normally at a single location and this may eventually lead to overcrowding, etc. As they grow, office organizations tend to fragment and disperse; employees and departments become scattered throughout the city centre. The final stage is marked by a return to concentration in one office building or a number of buildings at one location. As organizations become more fragmented efficiency is impaired and grouping of activities, at one or a limited number of locations, becomes necessary. Most estate agents would therefore suggest consolidation of the workforce as the main reason for office firms occupying new buildings.

Four case studies of a computer firm, the head office of a mechanical engineering firm, an advertising agency, and the offices of an insurance company have been used by Cowan to illustrate the growth of the office function and the new demands for office floorspace.[2] The case history of the computer firm illustrates the cyclical process in the expansion of office activities and employment (Fig. 18).[3] The study only included

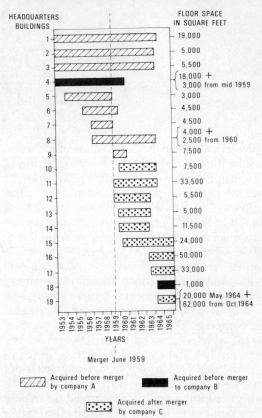

Fig. 18 Influence of Company Growth on the Demand for Office Space and Buildings (After P. Cowan et al., *The Office: A Facet of Urban Growth*, 1969, with the permission of Heinemann Educational Books Ltd.)

buildings used as headquarters premises between 1952 and 1965 by two large computer companies which merged in 1959 (Companies A and B) to form one new company (Company C). Between 1952 and 1958 the expansion of Company A caused it to increase its floorspace by 50 per cent, while after the merger the headquarters floorspace of Company C had increased by more than 100 per cent. Few of the buildings used as headquarters premises prior to 1959 were still used for this purpose in 1964. Company A occupied buildings 1, 2, and 3 which were in close proximity but the buildings occupied by Company B were smaller and a considerable distance away. At the time of the merger, therefore, Company C inherited a scattered collection of buildings but after discarding buildings 5, 7, and 9 it acquired buildings 10, 11, and 12. These three buildings were near to the remaining buildings in the Hyde Park Corner area of central London. The number of office employees continued to increase during the post-merger period, especially computer personnel. These were scattered in several buildings but were eventually centralized into one building in Putney (building 15). This choice was forced upon the company because of the shortage of suitable alternatives in central London. Subsequent attempts to build a central London headquarters for the 17 per cent of the staff needing to be located there proved unsuccessful and by 1965 the entire headquarters staff were located in four buildings in Putney which provided 169,000 ft^2 of floorspace. Not only had Company C grown, it had also shifted its floorspace demands from central to inner suburban London.

Brought together the four case studies reveal the extent to which organizations are prepared to move, and thus create demand for floorspace, because of dissatisfaction with buildings. This is not always connected with expansion difficulties. It was found that most office organizations seem to lack resources or foresight to plan space requirements for the future and are unable to reconcile idealistic priorities with the real world practicalities.[4] Consequently, most organizations are constantly reviewing their space requirements but they rarely look far enough ahead in relation to the expansion in numbers of employees. All four companies would have liked to consolidate their premises in central London rather than accept any other solution forced upon them by the supply of office space at any point in time. Spatially, there is no doubt where demand for office space would be focused if planning controls, which influence the supply/demand equation, were not enforced.

DEMAND PROJECTIONS

An ability to project the aggregated growth of industries and related office employment is vital when attempting to calculate the demand for floorspace. Once employment projections are made and floorspace/worker ratios are known, it is possible to calculate the demand for specified time periods. Demand is defined as actual employment plus unfilled vacancies. The first step involves forecasting labour demand on an industry basis and this can be illustrated by reference to some of the work undertaken for the Greater London Development Plan.[5] The techniques used are exploratory and certainly require further refinement but they are satisfactory for the present discussion.[6]

Techniques for forecasting labour demand at national levels are well established but are much more difficult to apply at the level of individual cities. This again arises from the shortage of adequate data at the local level and the G.L.C. found it necessary to extrapolate a ten-year trend in the demand for labour, measured by employment plus unfilled vacancies.[7] The industry-by-industry projection of labour demand was made to 1976 based on trends between 1959 and 1968. The employment data were provided by the Department of Employment and these reflect both supply and demand conditions and the unfilled vacancies.[8] Unfortunately, therefore, they are of restricted value as an independent measure of demand but there are no better statistics available.

Forecasts of labour demand on the basis of extrapolation from past trends can be made at a number of levels. The most straightforward involves projection of the trends revealed by the employment figures for each industry over the defined period for which data are available.[9] But this does not take account of the large number of other factors which affect trends in labour demand. It is more satisfactory to make forecasts which take these other factors into account but data limitations again make this difficult. It therefore proved necessary to rely on simple extrapolation of the observed trend for each industry. Two methods were used: least squares equations and a shift sub-model. Nine types of least squares equation were fitted to the observed

trends in order to establish best fit in terms of
the maximum amount of variation in the dependent variable (labour demand in industry i)
explained by the independent variable(s) (coefficient of determination) and the best standard
error of the estimate.[10] Almost without exception, the best fit for each industry was provided
by the equation:

$$L_D = a + CT,$$

where L_D is the labour demand in the G.L.C. in
an industry; T is the time (31 December
$1963 = 0$); and a and C are coefficients estimated
by least squares. This is the least satisfactory of
the nine possibilities because demand is considered to depend purely on the time factor. No
account is taken of other explanatory factors
such as changes in activity rates, the effects of
demographic changes on the supply of labour,
or changes in demand for particular types of output. The coefficients of determination for the industries to which the equation was applied
ranged between 0.70 and 0.98 and were generally
superior to the values obtained from the other
equations used. There is clearly considerable
room for improvement in the predictive power
of the equation and the variables incorporated.

The shift sub-model attempts to utilize the
relationship between labour demand in Greater
London and in Great Britain for each industry.
If the factors which control the labour demand
for any industry are of national rather than local
orientation, the relationship between the
national and 'regional' industry (taken as the
G.L.C.) can be used to forecast the G.L.C.
demand once the national level has been deter-
mined.[11] The shift sub-model projection equation takes the form:

$$D_{L(1976)}^i = a_i \frac{D_{L(T)}^i}{D_{N(T)}^i} D_{N(1976)}^i,$$

where $D_{L(T)}^i$ is the proportion of total Greater
London labour demand in industry i in year (T);
$D_{N(T)}^i$ is the proportion of total national labour
demand in industry i at year (T); $D_{N(1976)}^i$
assumes that there exists an independent estimate of labour demand for each industry at the
national level; and $D_{L(1976)}^i$ can be estimated, if
$D_{N(1976)}^i$ is known, assuming a consistent
$D_{L(T)}^i / D_{N(T)}^i$ ratio over the years.

Unfortunately, this model was not found to be
very successful in the Greater London context.
The ratio of $D_{L(T)}^i / D_{N(T)}^i$ varied widely from year
to year while the model assumed it would be constant. It would also have been better to have control data projections at the South-East, rather
than national, level but there are still no projections available of the demand for labour in individual industries for this region. Both models
also fail to incorporate the effects of cyclical
variations in vacancies and unemployment levels
on the projections.[12]

Where neither of these equations proved satisfactory, projections were made on the basis of
judgement. This was necessary for male labour
demand in 6 out of 24 industry orders and for
females in 4 industry orders. This underlines that
the above techniques are the first very tentative
attempts to project labour demand as a prerequisite for estimating office floorspace demand. The
detailed results for each industry order need not
concern us here but in order to relate the industry labour demand to the occupation group
projections which can then be made, a summary
of the results, by industry group, is given in Table
18. Note that the projections indicate a decrease
in total labour demand in every industrial group,
with the smallest decreases in services (Orders
XVIII–XXIV). Such aggregate changes hide
variations between the industries which are contained in the four groups. In the service sector,
for example, insurance, banking and finance
(XXI) and professional, scientific services (XXII)
have projected increases in labour demand by
1976. This has important implications for the
occupational structure of demand because these
are the industries in which office work is important (see Chapter 3).

Sources used for the occupation group projections in each industry were the employment
figures contained in the 1961 and 1966 Census
of Population. Four occupation groups were
identified: operatives; professional and administrative workers (office); clerical workers (office);
others. The 1961–6 rate of change in each occupation group's share of each industry's
employment was projected to 1971 and to 1976.
This method clearly depends heavily on past
trends and takes no account of variations in
future rates of change. But, again, there are no

TABLE 18
LABOUR DEMAND IN GREATER LONDON, BY INDUSTRY
GROUP—1966–76

Industry group	Actual demand 1966	Actual demand 1969	Projected demand 1976	Change (%) 1966–9	Change (%) 1966–76
Primary	12700	11400	10800	−11·2	−15·0
Manufacturing	1456800	1315600	1093600	−9·7	−24·9
Construction	292900	260900	275500	−10·9	−5·9
Services	2976400	2902500	2829400	−2·5	−4·9
Total	4738800	4490400	4209300	−5·2	−11·2

Source: Greater London Development Plan Inquiry, *Industrial and Office Floorspace Targets, 1972–76* (London: Greater London Council, Background Paper, B.452, 1971), Tables B.3 and B.4, pp. 81–2.

TABLE 19
PROJECTIONS OF LABOUR DEMAND, BY OCCUPATION GROUP AND
INDUSTRIAL SECTOR, GREATER LONDON—1966–76

Industry group	Operatives	Office Administrative and professional	Office Clerical	Other	Total
Primary, Manufacturing and Construction:					
1966	1092[1]	225	274	172	1763
1976	831	210	204	135	1380
Change 1966–76 (%)	−23·9	−6·7	−25·5	−21·4	−21·8
Services:					
1966	421	317	837	1401	2976
1976	352	395	846	1236	2829
Change 1966–76 (%)	−16·4	+24·6	+1·1	−11·8	−4·9
Total:					
1966	1513	542	1111	1573	4739
1976	1183	605	1050	1371	4209
Change 1966–76 (%)	−21·8	+11·6	−5·5	−12·9	−11·2
Change in employment[2] 1961–6 (%)	−5·9	+18·5	+5·5	0·0	+1·0

Notes: 1. All values are in thousands.
2. From 1961 Census, G.L.C. special tabulations corrected for bias and 1966 Census, County Leaflet corrected for under-enumeration.
Source: Greater London Development Plan Inquiry, *Industrial and Office Floorspace Targets, 1972–76* (London: Greater London Council, Background Paper, B.452, 1971), Table B.6, p. 85.

alternative methods which can be used, in the absence of any other information and data, which allow more accurate projections to be produced. The results are summarized in Table 19 which shows that there will be an increase in the demand for administrative and professional office workers up to 1976 but at a lower rate than between 1961 and 1966.[13] The demand for clerical workers is also projected to continue increasing but at a lower level than in 1961–6. All the projected increases in demand are concentrated in the service industries.

Once the office component of occupation demand has been isolated it is possible to make estimates of floorspace demand, in this case for 1976 (Table 20). If the floorspace/worker ratio is known for 1966 and the trend in the ratio is assumed to be upwards, the appropriate ratio is applied to the occupation demand figures for the relevant year. Increases in the floorspace/worker ratio can lead to an increased demand for floorspace despite a decrease in occupation demand.

This is illustrated for administrative and professional workers in primary, manufacturing, and construction industries. Similarly, the overall decline in the demand for clerical workers between 1966 and 1976 does not reduce the demand for office floorspace because it is anticipated that each worker will consume more space in 1976. Therefore, estimates of this type rely on satisfactory calculation of the floorspace/worker ratio which is only one of the factors influencing demand. No account has been taken of vacancy rates through time, of the trends in supply of floorspace which may not satisfy projected demand, or of the extra demand created by demolition of older office buildings. It may also be necessary to fit projected floorspace demand into planning objectives for the city or region and therefore an allowance will be necessary for future labour supply and population change. The demand model which has been outlined also discounts the location of projected demand although this could be incorporated as the next

TABLE 20

ESTIMATED DEMAND FOR OFFICE FLOORSPACE IN GREATER LONDON, BY PROJECTED OCCUPATION DEMAND—1966 AND 1976

Industry group	Administrative and professional		Clerical		Total office	
	L_D*	F_D†	L_D	F_D	L_D	F_D
Primary, Manufacturing and Construction:						
1966	225[1]	38·3	274	46·6	499	84·9
1976	210	40·5	204	38·8	414	79·3
Change 1966–76 (%)	−6·7	+5·7	−25·5	−16·7	−17·0	−6·6
Services:						
1966	317	53·9	837	142·3	1154	196·2
1976	395	75·1	846	160·7	1241	235·8
Change 1966–76 (%)	+24·6	+39·3	+1·1	+12·9	+7·5	+20·2
Total:						
1966	542	92·2	1111	188·9	1653	281·1
1976	605	115·6	1050	199·5	1655	315·1
Change 1966–76 (%)	+11·6	+25·4	−5·5	+5·6	+0·1	+12·1

Notes: *L_D = Labour demand in occupation group.
    †F_D = Floorspace demand calculated from L_D × floorspace/worker ratio. The ratios used in the calculations are hypothetical in view of the illustrative purpose of the table. For 1966, a ratio of 170 ft²/worker has been used, and 190 ft²/worker for 1976.
    1. L_D statistics obtained from Table 19.
Source: Table 19 and author's calculations.

stage using some kind of allocation procedure.[14] It is also apparent that office floorspace demand derived from employment and occupation figures will only be as accurate as the base statistics allow and the more steps there are in the procedure, the higher the risk of substantial error.

One of the problems of using employment projections is that they can vary according to the different assumptions used. There were four sets of office employment projections available to the New York City Planning Commission for their study of floorspace demand.[15] Two were made by the City Planning Commission, the first assuming no growth of productivity, a 4 per cent growth of the gross national product, and a complete halt to the suburbanization of office activities. This yields an annual growth rate for office employment of 3 per cent. Alternatively, the first two assumptions can be held constant but the suburbanization trends of 1959–69 assumed to continue. This reduces the annual growth rate of office employment in New York City to 2·6 per cent. This is likely to be an underestimate because large moves by major organizations in recent years are not taken into consideration. The New York State Department of Labour has made a third projection using 1980 employment estimates. This assumes the national productivity gains calculated by the Bureau of Labour

Statistics, a 4·3 per cent growth of the gross national product, and a slower rate of suburbanization than during the 1958–68 period. A 2·6 per cent annual growth rate results and this corresponds well with the second City Planning Commission projection. A fourth projection has been made by the Regional Plan Association.[16] Office employment is derived from the estimated population of the New York Region in the year 2000, with the main assumption that there will be no in-migration of population as a result of office job growth. The annual growth then varies between 1·7 and 1·9 per cent, depending on the definition of office employment used.

The major point to emerge from all these projections is that only one of them utilizes the concept of range in annual growth rates. Longer projection periods imply less accurate figures and an upper and lower limit would seem desirable. It is easy enough to convert a 2·5 per cent annual growth rate into new floorspace requirements but much more difficult to weight the result according to the other variables which are operating. Estimates based on a range of expected outcomes are both more realistic and less subjective than they appear because they are more in line with the market for office space which can fluctuate widely over relatively short periods of time.[17]

ROLE OF THE FLOORSPACE/WORKER RATIO

The amount of floorspace occupied by each office worker has increased steadily through time. This trend has been encouraged by the disproportionate growth of administrative and professional occupations during the last decade (see Table 19 and Chapter 3). Office workers in these occupations are normally allocated more space than clerical staff. Large office organizations have also been growing faster than smaller units and the latter are less generous with space provision, for cost reasons, than their larger counterparts. The increasing scale of office machines, especially computers, which have become an integral part of office infrastructure has also helped to inflate floorspace ratios. Legislation in Britain also specifies minimum standards of floorspace provision for office workers.[18]

The floorspace/worker ratio in Greater London did not change between 1961 and 1966 because office employment grew faster than floorspace (Table 21). Between 1966 and 1969 the ratio increased by 6·2 per cent from 193 to 205 ft^2 and it is expected to continue increasing to 216 ft^2 (5·6 per cent) by 1976. In New York, there has been a 63 per cent increase, from 109 ft^2 in 1948–9 to 178 ft^2 in 1967.[19] These are average figures; there are wide variations between different types of office ranging from 60 ft^2 in older, overcrowded offices to more than 300 ft^2 per employee in offices with a large proportion of administrative and executive staff. Increase in the floorspace ratio is one of the major factors accounting for the demand for office construction; 77 per cent of the increase in stock in

TABLE 21

ESTIMATED OFFICE FLOORSPACE/
WORKER RATIOS FOR GREATER
LONDON – 1961–76

Year	Total office floorspace (m. ft^2)	Total office workers (000s)	Floorspace/ worker ratio (ft^2)	Change (%)
1961	271	1404	193	—
1966	296	1535	193	0·0
1969	310	1512	205	+6·2
1976	348	1610	216	+5·4

Source: Greater London Development Plan Inquiry, *Industrial and Office Floorspace Targets, 1972–76* (London: Greater London Council, Background Paper, B.452, 1971), Table II.5, p. 27 and Table II.6, p. 28.

Manhattan between 1950 and 1969 can be attributed to the ratio alone.[20]

It is possible, however, that the role of the ratio in the demand equation has been overstated.[21] Increases in the ratio have been caused by improving ancillary, rather than work, spaces in office buildings; restaurants, staff lounges, reception rooms, and large foyers. These features are common amongst the larger organizations, particularly if they commission purpose-built accommodation in which prestige factors are important. The most frequently quoted source of increase in the floorspace/worker ratio takes place when firms move to new accommodation. Here, however, the 'increase' is simply an adjustment to contemporary space standards which overcomes overcrowding and lower than average space provision at the previous location. In some cases such changes represent a return to the *status quo* prior to overcrowding. Of the 500 occupants in a survey of new buildings in Downtown Manhattan, 57 per cent had apparently increased the floorspace per worker, but 86 per cent of these were overcrowded in their previous offices.[22]

Any absolute increases in demand are only generated by small organizations involved in major expansion due to the success of the activity. The New York survey estimates the median size of such offices to be 10,000 ft^2. Since 85 per cent of the office space in Manhattan is occupied by firms with more than this figure, or approximately 50 employees, it seems unlikely that this source of growth will have much effect on floorspace demand in the medium or long term.[23]

The future rate of change of the floorspace ratio will therefore depend largely on the degree to which élite office activities continue to increase their share of total office employment. Aggregation of élite activities in selected locations such as the central area will also create variations in floorspace ratio between different parts of a city.[24] Areas with a high proportion of routine clerical work will have lower ratios. Alternatively, the general increase of the floorspace ratio may cease as better use is made of new office space. With more efficient office layouts, improved design of office machines, and structural improvements to office buildings, this is certainly possible. Intensive use of the modern office building is now commonplace because structural features such as the interior core and supporting skeleton represent a much smaller proportion of the total space available. By using 'bürolandschaft' and modular principles a high density of workers can be achieved, while giving the impression of space. Consequently, it is now quite possible for tenants moving from old, pre-1950, buildings to actually decrease the floorspace/worker ratio and this will certainly have some effect on demand. The figures for Greater London (Table 21) suggest that this might already be happening; the ratio increasing at only 0·8 per cent per annum in the period 1969–76 compared with 2·1 per annum in 1966–9. The floorspace ratio in Manhattan is only expected to increase by 5 per cent (0·35 per cent per annum) between 1969 and 1985, or even to remain unchanged in Minneapolis C.B.D. during the period 1970–2000.[25]

REPLACEMENT OF EXISTING STOCK

The replacement of existing office buildings by new development or rehabilitation of existing, but obsolete, unrentable and uneconomic buildings represents about 10 per cent of the demand for new floorspace (see Table 17). In most central business districts replacement of office buildings involves direct exchange with more office space, while at non-C.B.D. locations office space may be replaced by other uses such as retailing or even residential development. In view of lack of data for British cities, it is again necessary to turn to Manhattan for some examples. In the period 1957–69, 82·6 per cent of the office space demolished was replaced by new offices (Table 22). Other replacement uses are much less important because, in a high land value area such as

TABLE 22
REPLACEMENT USE OF DEMOLISHED OFFICE SPACE IN MANHATTAN—1957–69

Replacement use	Floorspace (000s ft^2)	% of total
New offices	7165	82·6
Urban renewal	587	6·8
Institutional	561	6·5
Residential	127	1·5
Parking and vacant	153	1·8
Other	77	0·8
Total	8670	100·0

Source: New York City Planning Commission, *The Demand for Office Space in Manhattan* (New York: City Planning Commission, 1971), Table XII, p. 21.

Manhattan, other uses cannot compete for the land or lead to an economic development.

Physical obsolescence of office buildings is the main cause of replacement. But modern techniques of rehabilitation often make it economic to retain such buildings. They are particularly attractive to the smaller office organizations unable to afford the high rents demanded in the newer buildings.[26] Provided that vacant space in newer, but less prestigious buildings, does not attract tenants away from older buildings, it is likely that they will continue to have a major role

in the overall demand for office space. This is important because over 25 per cent of Manhattan's office buildings, for example, date from before 1920 and amount to some 50 m. ft^2. Over 35 per cent of the office buildings in Dallas C.B.D. were built before 1930 and account for 25 per cent of the floorspace in 1972.[27] Rehabilitation is cheaper than providing new office buildings and the high turnover of tenants which characterizes older buildings means that expansion for successful organizations is not difficult.

New office construction in the C.B.D. will also result in replacement of some non-office uses. All the demand cannot normally be accommodated by replacement of existing office land use. Non-office land use will be most affected around the fringes of the C.B.D. in areas where office clusters are expanding horizontally as well as vertically. British examples, by way of statistics, are difficult to obtain although the visual evidence is clear enough. The northward expansion of new office buildings in Liverpool involves encroachment into warehouses and some residential uses which formerly abutted the office area of the core. The proposals for the Albert Dock, adjacent to the C.B.D., will involve infilling of the area and a large new office development in association with a smaller proportion of retailing and residential uses. In areas of rapid office growth such as Downtown and Mid-town Manhattan, replacement affects large areas of other C.B.D. and non-C.B.D. uses (Table 23). Office buildings replaced 1·7 m. ft^2 of manufacturing industry floorspace in Downtown Manhattan between 1963 and 1971 alone. The expansion and migration of office activity from Downtown to Mid-town Manhattan is reflected in the replacement of 3·1 m. ft^2 of residential land use and over 6 m. ft^2 of other commercial uses such as retailing. Between them, these two categories of land use amounted to over 63 per cent of the floorspace replaced by office activities in Mid-town during the period 1963–71. Some 5200 houses were replaced by offices and 8600 manufacturing and wholesaling jobs were displaced.

These three factors of demand can be brought together into a model which can be used to calculate annual and period totals for a specified

TABLE 23
REPLACEMENT OF OTHER C.B.D. USES BY
OFFICE BUILDING IN MANHATTAN—1963–71

Uses replaced	Downtown		Mid-town	
	Floorspace (000s ft²)	% of total	Floorspace (000s ft²)	% of total
Residential	62·2	0·6	3112·2	21·6
Manufacturing	1653·6	16·3	952·5	6·6
Warehousing	310·9	3·1	19·1	0·1
Office	7198·9	72·4	2780·4	19·4
Other Commercial	560·6	5·6	6016·3	41·9
Other	210·4	2·0	1495·1	10·4
Total	9996·6	100·0	14375·6	100·0

Source: New York City Planning Commission, *The Demand for Office Space in Manhattan* (New York: City Planning Commission, 1971), Table XIV, p. 24.

number of years (Table 24). The range of outcomes depends on the weight given to each of the three factors. The Real Estate Research Corporation estimates of floorspace demand in Manhattan allow for an annual rate of replacement which accounts for 39 and 36 per cent of the high and low estimates, respectively. The

City Planning Commission consider the role of replacement to be negligible, however, and give employment growth and the floorspace/worker ratio a major role in all three of their projections.[28] The implications of varying the initial assumptions are clearly shown in Table 24. Annual demand ranges from a maximum of 8·2

TABLE 24
ESTIMATED ANNUAL DEMAND FOR OFFICE SPACE IN
MANHATTAN—1970–85

Source of demand	City Planning Commission			R.P.A.[2]	Real Estate Research	
	2% growth	2·5% growth	3% growth	1·7% growth	1·9% growth	1·0% growth
Employment growth	4·3[1]	5·6	7·0	4·2	3·8	1·8
	(85)[3]	(87)	(89)	(63)	(55)	(51)
Floorspace/worker ratio	0·6	0·6	0·6	1·1	0·4	0·4
	(12)	(10)	(8)	(16)	(6)	(13)
Replacement	0·2	0·9	0·3	1·4	2·7	1·3
	(3)	(3)	(3)	(21)	(39)	(36)
Sub-total	5·1	6·4	7·8	6·6	6·9	3·5
Vacancy rate (4·5%)	0·2	0·3	0·4	0·3	0·3	0·2
Annual demand	5·3	6·7	8·2	6·9	7·2	3·7
Demand 1970–85	79·6	101·0	123·0	104·2	108·3	55·0

Notes: 1. Million ft² net. Figures have been rounded to the nearest 100,000 ft².
2. Regional Plan Association.
3. Percentage of total demand derived from employment growth, floorspace/worker ratio and replacement.
Source: New York City Planning Commission, *The Demand for Office Space in Manhattan* (New York: City Planning Commission, 1971), Table IV.

m. ft^2 by the City Planning Commission to 5·7 m. ft^2 in Real Estate Research's low estimate. If this minimum estimate is excluded, the annual demand projections are fairly close to each other, particularly if the 3 per cent growth assumption is excluded. The latter is considered unlikely by the City Planning Commission. Estimates of demand are a useful way of monitoring anticipated growth or decline of office activities but are difficult to utilize in practice. The limited powers available to Planning Commissions provide only the minimum of control on the rate of office building construction and its location.

Most zoning ordinances allow buildings to be constructed as of right if they meet the requirements of the ordinance. Only cases which do not conform with the zoning ordinance need to be referred to the Planning Commission. It is therefore much more difficult either to channel demand to selected areas of growth in metropolitan areas, or to ensure that the supply of office floorspace does not exceed demand. Most office developers seem prepared to construct buildings for which there are no foreseeable tenants and to take the losses over a period of time.

A MARKET VIEW OF DEMAND

It may be more fruitful to consider the demand for office floorspace within the framework of office space markets.[29] This approach is particularly useful when attempting to identify gaps in city, or local, office space supply and for which there is expressed demand. Information of this type is useful to both the development companies and the organizations responsible for controlling office development. The market for office space is not homogeneous but consists of several strata, or sub-markets, which have varying space requirements.[30] The office sub-markets in a typical medium-sized city might be as follows:

1. Major institutional—offices occupied by banks and other financial institutions, often in the most prestigious locations, at the core of the city's office system. This sub-market comprises organizations seeking the best possible accommodation and location and they are prepared to out-bid other office activities, via the market mechanism, to obtain the facilities they depend upon.

2. General commercial—numerically, the largest sub-market in most cities. Includes a wide range of office activities which require accessible central area locations but not the most prestigious locations for successful operation. Most of these offices will be leasing space, possibly owned by the major institutional activities, at lower cost and with a lower standard of supporting services.

3. Semi-industrial—office space attached to

service activities outside the major office areas of a city. Often attached to research and development establishments or found in the better industrial parks of the United States.

4. Pure-industrial—office space attached to manufacturing plants, mainly for the purpose of plant administration. The demand for this office floorspace is linked to the locational and space

TABLE 25
SUB-MARKETS FOR GENERAL
COMMERCIAL OFFICE SPACE IN
SAN FRANCISCO C.B.D.

Building type	Rent range ($)
Buildings under construction	9·00–11·00
Post-war established buildings with full amenities	7·50–9·00
Pre-war buildings with central air-conditioning and self-service lifts	5·00–7·50
Pre-war buildings that are well maintained and well located	3·50–5·00
Buildings with marginal maintenance and location	varies considerably
Wholly owner-occupied buildings	no open market price

Note: War is Second World War.
Source: C. L. Detoy and S. L. Rabin, 'Office space — Calculating the demand', *Urban Land*, Vol. 31 (1972), p. 6.

requirements of the parent industry rather than to the office market in general.

The main source of demand for office space in new, free-standing buildings, comes from the major institutional and general commercial sub-markets. But each sub-market will also have different categories of space requirement depending on the space standards, types of amenities, and supporting services which tenants require or can afford to pay for (Table 25). The sub-markets for general commercial office space in San Francisco C.B.D. can be identified by reference to rents and types of buildings. Once these levels have been identified, the task facing any parties interested in estimating demand will be the origins of tenants for existing office space or buildings under construction. Some of the tenants for the $7.50–$9.00 sub-market will be exogenous to the San Francisco general commercial office market but the majority will be endogenous. These will consist of tenants moving between sub-markets, for the reasons already discussed. Most of the

movement will be upwards through the system and as offices leave one sub-market they will be replaced by others from below. Consequently, any one sub-market can only be understood by reference to all sub-markets relevant, in this example, to general commercial office space demand.

One of the main problems with this approach is the difficulty of classifying sub-markets which can be identified in the way illustrated here. Sub-markets can also be classified by reference to an industry classification of office activities or according to location within the city; central area, inner suburban, outer suburban, etc. but each sub-market cannot be considered in total isolation from the operation of other markets. Heavy demand for office space in the institutional group of activities combined with a space shortage may result in encroachment on the general commercial market with associated implications for rent levels. All the sub-markets are therefore closely interdependent.

PUBLIC SECTOR DEMAND

Although the private sector is the major source of demand for office floorspace, the public sector activities of local and central government also require office space. Public bodies are more likely to be tenants of office space than other types of income-producing properties such as factories or warehouses. Public sector demand is particularly evident in the administrative centres for local government and in most of the large cities where central government departments are located (Table 26). In 1967, almost 17 per cent of the total stock of floorspace in England and Wales was occupied by central government offices. The proportions for individual regions are closely clustered around this average but there are cities within the regions where there is a much heavier demand from the public sector. Hence, 27·6 per cent of the office floorspace in Newcastle is occupied by central government and this represents almost 80 per cent of all central government space in Northumberland. Although Manchester and Liverpool contain a lower proportion of central government floorspace than the regional average (17·2 per cent), they still contain 29·5 per cent of the total in the

region. The London Borough of Westminster, which contains the Whitehall complex of government offices, has over 21 per cent of its office floorspace in public sector use. This represents 9·4 m. ft^2 and it exceeds the total for all the local authorities in the North West Economic Planning Region.

Localized demand for public sector office floorspace also occurs in the United States.[31] The extreme example is Washington D.C. where the Federal Government probably owns as much floorspace as private landlords while it also leases one-fifth of all floorspace in privately-owned office buildings in the city. This also allows the Federal Government to exert considerable influence on the local office market in Washington. The local government activities of the City of New York owned and occupied some 8·5 m. ft^2 of office space at the end of 1965 and leased a further 5·3 m. ft^2 from private landlords.[32] Between 1960 and 1965 the amount of floorspace leased from private developers increased by 50 per cent while the total floorspace owned by the City remained constant.

TABLE 26

CENTRAL GOVERNMENT FLOORSPACE AS A PROPORTION OF TOTAL
OFFICE FLOORSPACE IN ENGLAND AND WALES—ECONOMIC PLANNING
REGIONS AND SELECTED CITIES, 1967

(million ft²)

Region or city	Total office floorspace	Central government floorspace	% of total
NORTHERN	17·5	3·3	18·9
Newcastle	4·7	1·3	27·6
YORKS AND HUMBERSIDE	26·3	3·9	14·8
Leeds	4·5	0·8	17·8
NORTH WEST	52·3	9·0	17·2
Manchester	14·4	1·7	11·8
Liverpool	9·6	0·9	9·4
Chester	0·9	0·2	22·2
EAST MIDLANDS	15·3	2·4	15·7
Nottingham	3·1	0·8	25·8
WEST MIDLANDS	26·4	3·1	11·7
Birmingham	9·2	1·1	11·9
EAST ANGLIA	8·3	1·3	15·7
Cambridge	1·1	0·3	27·6
SOUTH EAST	193·6	32·5	16·8
Greater London	151·7	24·8	16·3
Westminster	44·5	9·4	21·3
Kingston upon Thames	1·7	0·9	52·9
Harrow	1·9	0·9	47·2
Outer Metropolitan Area	29·3	4·6	15·7
Outer South East	19·8	2·3	11·6
SOUTH WEST	21·4	4·3	20·1
Bristol	4·8	0·8	16·6
WALES	13·6	3·0	22·1
Cardiff	3·4	0·9	26·5
ENGLAND AND WALES	374·4	62·8	16·8

Source: Department of the Environment, *Statistics for Town and Country Planning, Series II — Floorspace* (London: Her Majesty's Stationery Office, 1972), Tables 1 and 38.

Public sector demand is therefore an important element in the equation. The public sector prefers, as far as possible, to provide its own accommodation but at the end of 1972, 58·4 per cent of office floorspace occupied by Government departments in Britain was in leased property (Table 27). The Government is often referred to in the property world as the 'developer's friend' because of its propensity to lease rather than construct its own buildings.[33] During the early post-war years, developers could only have building licences for offices constructed for Government use. This system no longer operates but Government departments continue to lease

space when it would be more economic to invest in custom-built structures. The cost of borrowing money for land purchase, construction, etc. could be as much as 50 per cent less per year as the rents paid for leasing property. There might also be opportunities for sub-letting Government offices with long leases at constant rent in order to finance the move to custom-built offices.[34] Some Government offices are occupying space which could be let at ten times the market value at the time the long lease was agreed. With 69 per cent of the Government floorspace in central London located in leased office buildings, the public sector is clearly a major source

TABLE 27

DISTRIBUTION OF CROWN AND LEASED GOVERNMENT
OFFICE FLOORSPACE—GREAT BRITAIN, DECEMBER 1972

Region	Floorspace (ft^2 net)			Leased as % total
	Crown	Leased	Total	
London (central)	4415492	9938760	14354252	69·2
London (other)	2276118	3913446	6189564	63·2
Scotland	2362011	1941539	4303550	45·1
North East (Leeds)	2915506	3008239	5923745	50·8
North West (Manchester)	2229822	4056597	6286419	64·5
East (Cambridge)	762101	1590701	2352802	67·6
South (Reading)	1395532	1246538	2642070	47·2
South West (Bristol)	2422586	1356961	3769547	36·0
Wales	1030878	1309103	2339981	55·9
Midlands (Birmingham)	1654852	2096878	3751730	55·9
South East (Hastings)	1060498	1186145	2246643	52·8
Total (excluding all London)	15823786	17792701	33616487	52·9
Grand total	22515396	31644907	54160303	58·4

Note: The Regions listed are not Economic Planning Regions but relate to areas controlled by the listed Regional Offices of the Property Services Agency.
Source: Department of the Environment (Property Services Agency), unpublished data.

of demand in some cities. Outside London, the proportion of leased space is lower but, with the exception of the South West, it is still near or considerably in excess of 50 per cent. If these regional figures could be analysed at city level, they would probably reveal a pattern similar to London and the South East, i.e. a higher than average level of demand for Government office floorspace in leasehold buildings in the major provincial cities.

A SUPPLY/DEMAND MODEL

Detoy and Rabin have formulated a method for calculating the office space requirements of a city using a supply/demand model.[35] They suggest that the vital factor influencing office floorspace requirements is the difference between supply and demand, the 'absorption rate'.[36] When the absorption rate is positive, i.e. demand is greater than supply, there is scope for additional office space and the reverse is true when the rate is negative. Since it takes 3–5 years to produce space in a new office building, the future absorption rate is much more important than the present one. A basic office space absorption rate model can therefore be expressed as follows:

$$D - S = G + U + O_r - O_a - O_v,$$

where D is demand; S is supply; and G is the net real growth from new employment derived from the equation

$$G = a(d_1 + d_2 + d_3) - a(s_1 + s_2 + s_3),$$

where a is the floorspace/worker ratio; d_1 is the existing tenants' expanding space requirements; d_2 is the in-migration of firms from elsewhere in the city or from other cities; d_3 are the new tenants created by seed bed growth of new activities in the city; s_1 are the existing office tenants going out of business; s_2 are existing tenants reducing their space requirements; s_3 are existing tenants moving to other cities; U is the office space for upgrading tenants, i.e. increasing their space requirements; O_r are the forced relocations as a result of demolition of old space or as a result of partly owner-occupied buildings becoming wholly owner-occupied; O_a is the new office space added to the existing inventory (including space which has been rehabilitated or renovated); and O_v is the vacant space available from previous year (sometimes referred to as 'space overhang').

This is therefore an accounting equation for the absorption rate based on the subtraction of all the supply from all the demand factors.[37] The three demand factors d_1 to d_3 are the result of economic growth of the city and the supply factors s_1 to s_3 a product of economic decline. The equation is complete except for a built-in vacancy allowance which can be included as follows:

$$D - S = \frac{1}{(1 - V_n)}(G + U + O_r) - (O_a + O_v),$$

where V_n is the vacancy factor. In its operational form, the model depends upon estimates for the six input factors. The most difficult to estimate is U (number of tenants increasing their space requirements). Detoy and Rabin suggest that this is best calculated as a factor of net real growth from office employment, G. U could be expressed

as a percentage of G, using historical data or informed judgement. Therefore:

$$U = \beta G$$

and

$$D - S = \frac{1}{(1 - V_n)}(\beta G + G + O_r) - (O_a + O_v),$$

where β is the multiplier for demand caused by increasing space requirements. U could also be calculated by detailed field surveys of existing office tenants to establish when leases expire and whether they intend to seek more space in other accommodation. An important characteristic of U is that it fluctuates quickly, even on a quarter year basis (Fig. 19). The expiry of leases for office premises in a major West Coast city between 1970 and 1975 illustrates the way in which the demand for upgraded space can be estimated. Thus, in the first quarter of 1971, tenants occupying 208,000 ft^2 of 'second class' office space faced expiry of their leases and some, although not all, will be requiring new space. In the second quarter of 1971 only 5300 ft^2 of office space was affected by expiry of leases so that demand from

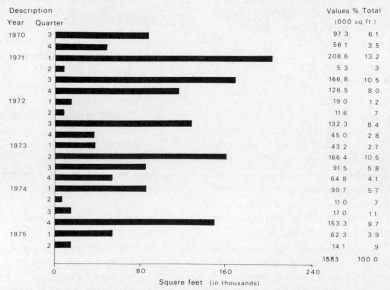

Description		Values	% Total
Year	Quarter	(000 sq. ft.)	
1970	3	97.3	6.1
	4	56.1	3.5
1971	1	208.6	13.2
	2	5.3	.3
	3	166.8	10.5
	4	126.5	8.0
1972	1	19.0	1.2
	2	11.6	.7
	3	132.3	8.4
	4	45.0	2.8
1973	1	43.2	2.7
	2	166.4	10.5
	3	91.5	5.8
	4	64.8	4.1
1974	1	90.7	5.7
	2	11.0	.7
	3	17.0	1.1
	4	153.3	9.7
1975	1	62.3	3.9
	2	14.1	.9
		1583	100.0

Square feet (in thousands)

Fig. 19 Fluctuations in Lease Expiry Rates — West Coast City, U.S.A. (After C. L. Detoy and S. L. Rabin, 'Office space: calculating the demand', *Urban Land*, 1972. Reprinted from *Urban Land* magazine with permission from ULI — the Urban Land Institute, 1200 18th Street, N.W., Washington, D.C. 20036. Copyright 1972)

this source becomes negligible. The wide differences between quarters can be smoothed out and the average demand from increased space requirements of office tenants calculated over the required period of years.

Estimates of net real growth from office employment, G, can be obtained by forecasting employment growth for each industry in the Standard Industrial Classification (S.I.C.). The office space requirements of different industries will vary according to the proportion of office employees in the total workforce. The wide divergence between agriculture and insurance, banking and finance, for example, has already been illustrated. An office employee coefficient is derived for each S.I.C. category.[38] G can then be calculated from:

$$G = aE_\phi,$$

where E is the forecasted increase in employment by S.I.C. sector; a is the average floorspace per employee; and ϕ is the office employee coefficient. The remaining variables, V_n, O_r, O_a, O_v can be estimated from either published data or special field surveys.

The use of the model can be illustrated with a hypothetical example. If the values of the six factors included in the model are as follows:

G = 500,000 ft^2 p.a. O_v = 275,000 ft^2
U = 350,000 ft^2 O_a = 150,000 ft^2
O_r = 75,000 ft^2 V_n = 4 per cent,

then:

$$D - S = \frac{1}{(1 - 0.04)}(500{,}000 + 350{,}000 + 75{,}000) - (150{,}000 + 275{,}000),$$
$$D - S = 538{,}478 \text{ ft}^2.$$

Therefore, over 500,000 ft^2 could be built and absorbed in our hypothetical city before demand for office floorspace exceeds supply. This is a city with high net real growth of office employment; it might be found to be negative in some cities or over-supply, such as the situation in New York might already be occurring. The relative roles of the various factors will also depend on the age of the city. An older city, in an area of economic decline, may be experiencing low net real growth but because it has a high proportion of old office buildings the absorption rate may be higher than in some newer cities. The model can also be applied iteratively, accumulating the values over any specified period $t + n$. The results can then be compared with the real world situation. Detoy and Rabin applied the model to a 14-year period (1961–75) for a major city in the western United States and found that during the decade 1961–71 it correctly identified one year of undersupply (1970) and consistently recognized the years of over-supply prior to 1970.[39] The model also forecasted major over-supply of office floorspace during the years after 1971.

The Detoy and Rabin model is very dependent on accurate floorspace data, particularly in relation to trends in the recent past. Many cities only have very limited historical office space data and Minneapolis/St Paul, for example, has attempted to make long range forecasts of office space growth with reference to forecasted employment growth.[40] The main premise is that employment growth is more regular than office space construction so that extrapolating office growth (supply) trends is more difficult than forecasting employment (demand). Assuming that employment forecasts of reasonable accuracy can be made, the following methodology was used for forecasting C.B.D., regional and sectional (local) office space:

1. *C.B.D. office space forecasts*
   (a) Convert employment forecasts to office employment.
   (b) Convert office employment to office space demand.
   (c) Relate demand to supply—including historic office space construction trends.

2. *Regional office space forecasts*
   (a), (b), and (c) repeated as above.

3. *Sectional office space forecasts*
   (a) Forecast population-related industrial and commercial office space.
   (b) Forecast employment-related industrial and commercial office space.
   (c) Forecast major industrial and commercial firms' office space.
   (d) Prepare office space forecasts of concentrations within each sector (allocate regional residual).

(e) Total above to obtain sectional forecast.

Various assumptions regarding floorspace/worker ratio and the ratio of office to non-office employment are part of the forecasting procedure. There are also different assumptions adopted for each level of forecast.

The absorption rate model can be applied to any office market or sub-market at levels of analysis ranging from the C.B.D. to suburban areas and the entire city. It is a market-orientated model which is well suited to the comparatively 'free' market for office space in the United States. It is more likely to be useful to American planners and developers because in Britain the influence of planning controls on the operation of the market for office space is a severe constraint on the value of the model as a method for forecasting the absorption rate. To most office developers a demand model of any kind in Britain is 'Utopian' but this model, or derivatives of it, could certainly be used by others interested in charting the demand for office space in British cities.[41]

A SIMULATION MODEL OF OFFICE CONSTRUCTION

A supply-orientated model, but with important implications for the location of demand, has been developed by Cowan *et al.*[42] Using land use and planning permissions data for central London, Monte Carlo simulation has been used to predict office development between 1957 and 1962. Land use surveys were available for the years 1957 and 1962 and were arranged in a network of 500 m squares. Planning permission data were also available on an annual basis but for irregularly shaped areas and were recorded in various ways.[43] This information was therefore standardized to the 500 m grid system which eliminates problems of aggregation over irregular areas, and achieves a uniform expression of the distance and density relations between units over the total area. The central area of London is covered by about 750 grid cells.

The available data was far from satisfactory and imposed a number of limitations on the operation of the model:

1. Different possible forms of offices required by users were ignored.
2. Office units differed only in size.
3. Users and developers were not explicitly specified as decision-makers.
4. General economic considerations were neglected.
5. Locations were stated only in terms of cells.
6. All other land uses were ignored.

These limitations are symptomatic of the data problems which have already been outlined. Fortunately, the situation in London is generally more satisfactory than in other cities. Clearly, other land uses will influence either the level of new office construction by demolition of other types of land use, or replacement of office space by other uses. The other types of land use in a cell will also determine the likelihood of office development being permitted adjacent to any of them. Temporary use of buildings for office purposes is also excluded.

The aim of the model is, given the position in 1957, to generate the situation in each cell in 1962. The latter can then be compared with the actual situation revealed by the Land Use Survey data. Simulation was undertaken for a time period, t, taken as one year and applied recursively in the following main steps:

1. Given the total number of approvals for each of three types of input (change of use, new buildings, extensions), for the current period t (1957), estimate the respective values of time $(t+1)$ (1958).
2. Derive lists of actual units from the size distributions of the three types.
3. Allocate each unit in turn to some cell in the central London region. Update the value of each cell's stock.
4. Repeat stages 1–3 for period $(t+2)$, $(t+3)$, etc. until the position for 1962 has been generated.
5. Repeat until a distribution of outcomes for 1962 has been constructed.

6. Compare the most likely outcome with the 1962 position revealed by actual data.

For any cell ij the amount of office stock at period t can be derived from:

$$O_{i,j,t} = O_{i,j,1} + \Sigma N_{i,j,t(p)} \\ + \Sigma E_{i,j,t(q)} + \Sigma U_{i,j,t(r)} - \Sigma D_{i,j,t(s)} \qquad (1)$$

and for the whole of central London:[44]

$$O_t = O_{i,j,t} \\ = O_{t-1} + \Sigma\Sigma N_{i,j,t(p)} + \Sigma\Sigma E_{i,j,t(q)} \\ + \Sigma\Sigma U_{i,j,t(r)} - \Sigma\Sigma D_{i,j,t(s)}, \qquad (2)$$

where $O_{i,j,t}$ is the amount of office stock existing in cell ij in period t; $N_{i,j,t(p)}$ is the pth new building completed in cell ij in period t; $E_{i,j,t(q)}$ is the qth extension completed in cell ij in period t; $U_{i,j,t(r)}$ is the rth change of use completed in cell ij in period t; and $D_{i,j,t(s)}$ is the amount of office stock demolished in cell ij in period t to permit insertion of new building and/or extension. Other notations utilized in the development of model relate to the number of approvals for central London in time for new buildings, extensions, and changes of use (n_t, e_t, and u_t). The order of these approvals over the whole of central London in period t is also used $\{N_t(x), E_t(y)$ and $U_t(z)\}$.

The detailed operation of the model along the various steps outlined above and utilizing the listed variables need not concern us here.[45] It is useful, however, to refer briefly to the third stage which involves allocating each unit of stock to a cell and updating its stock total. This is achieved by using eqn (1). When stage 2 has been reached each unit of stock, e.g. a new building is ready to be allocated to a cell in central London. This is accomplished by giving every cell an index of attraction ($I_{i,j,t}$) which specifies the relative probability that it will attract any unit. Three forms of the index were used:

$^1I_{i,j,t}$ as the amount of completed stock in each cell as proportion of that existing in the whole of central London.

$^2I_{i,j}$ as a measure of accessibility to the twelve main railway termini. The measure is based on the reciprocals of the distances $1_{i,j,u,v}$ to each of the main railway termini where the stations are located in cells u, v. The sum of the reciprocals gives the index for each cell.

$^3I_{i,j,t}$ as the arithmetic mean of $^1I_{i,j,t} + ^2I_{i,j}$

The second index does not vary through the period 1957–62 but the other two will clearly change according to the increase or decrease in office stock. They are therefore monitored for each year of the period for spatial allocation of any unit so that the index can be modified to take it into account. The relative strengths of these indices were assessed by comparing the percentage of simulated cell stock to the actual amount in each cell. A fourth index, $rI_{i,j}$, which gives every cell an equal probability of attracting any unit was used as a control for the other three indices.

Each of the three indices produced very similar results (Table 28). The index derived from accessibility of each cell to the main railway termini gives marginally better results while the percentage of cells with simulated values within 50 per cent of actuality is increased by the use of large cells (4×500 m cells). This underlines the importance of accessibility, for office workers and clients, as a factor in the demand for office floorspace which is reflected in the pattern of planning applications and subsequent approvals. Other indices of attraction on the basis of land use structure, existing services, and land values, for example, could also be built into the simulation process.

The value of this simulation model is apparent from Fig. 20 in which the spatial distribution of approvals actually occurring is compared with

TABLE 28

SIMULATED AND ACTUAL CELL STOCK OF OFFICE FLOORSPACE IN 1962—CENTRAL LONDON

	Small cells		Large cells[1]	
	Percentage of cells within		Percentage of cells within	
Index	$\pm 30\%$	$\pm 50\%$ of actuality	$\pm 30\%$	$\pm 50\%$ of actuality
$^1I_{i,j,t}$	46	70	63	78
$^2I_{i,j}$	49	69	63	76
$^3I_{i,j,t}$	46	69	58	78
$rI_{i,j}$	25	28	28	38

Note: 1. Large cells comprise 4×500 m cells.

Source: P. Cowan et al., The Office: A Facet of Urban Growth (London: Heinemann, 1969), Table IX.3, p. 247.

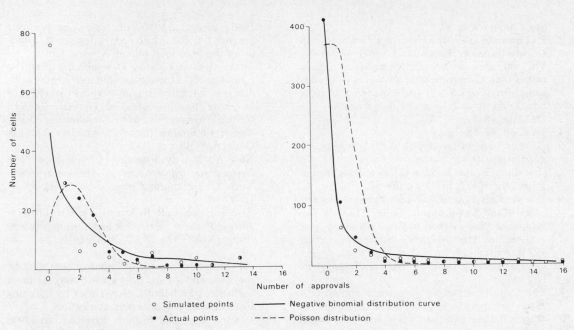

Fig. 20 Actual and Simulated Planning Approvals for Large and Small Cells—Central London, 1962 (After P. Cowan *et al.*, *The Office: A Facet of Urban Growth*, 1969, with the permission of Heinemann Educational Books Ltd.)

one of the simulated patterns for large and small cells. These are related to the Poisson and negative binomial distributions which, if the distribution is random over an area, express the probability of finding x events in any cell placed at random in the area. Cowan concludes that the spread of permissions for office development in an urban area is not a random process but appears to be due to a mechanism which makes it behave in a way similar to that described by the negative binomial distribution. This means that the initial permissions for office development trigger clusters of other events, and these clusters then grow regularly over time.

Models of office growth which uses simulation techniques are heavily dependent on the link between empirical observations of office activity and the mathematical techniques used to examine hypotheses. The hypotheses cannot be devised without reference to empirical studies and, conversely, the success and modification of the models cannot be achieved without referring back to empirical sources. Good data sources therefore have a vital part to play in this type of model building but the inadequacies of the empirical sources used by Cowan leaves much to be desired. It certainly limits the opportunities for more sophisticated modelling of office growth in response to the new hypotheses generated by some of the early stages in model-building. Because of these problems, the model which has been outlined is essentially short term. It would be more useful if it could simulate office development over 10 or 15 year periods. It should also be remembered that the model demonstrates patterns, but does not provide any explanations. Behavioural models may provide some of the answers but have yet to be developed.

REFERENCES

1   See Chapter 4, n. 60.
2   P. Cowan *et al.*, *The Office: A Facet of Urban Growth* (London: Heinemann, 1969), pp. 48–88. The four case studies are 'commercial' offices rather than Government departments or professional firms which will also experience change, but conditioned by special circumstances.
3   *Ibid.*, pp. 48–54.
4   *Ibid.*, pp. 87–88.
5   Greater London Development Plan Inquiry, *Industrial and Office Floorspace Targets, 1972–76* (London: Greater London Council, Background Paper, no. B.452, 1971), pp. 70–90.
6   The weaknesses are discussed in detail in Department of the Environment, *Greater London Development Plan—Report of Panel of Inquiry, Vol. I* (London: Her Majesty's Stationery Office, 1973), Annexe 5.2, pp. 161–6.
7   Greater London Development Plan Inquiry, *op. cit.*, p. 69.
8   The Department of Employment's annual estimates are based on a 25 per cent sample of National Insurance cards with an adjustment made for employees whose cards are not exchanged. Self-employed workers are excluded while numbers of part-time workers, based on quarterly counts of cards, tend to be overstated.
9   Major adjustments to the Standard Industrial Classification made it impossible to use a time series which pre-dated 1959.
10 The variables used in various combinations in the nine equations were:

L_D = labour demand in the G.L.C. in an industry (the dependent variable);

X = U.K. labour demand in an industry;

X_2 = dummy 'shift' variable;

X_3 = total labour demand less Distributive Trade labour demand;

T = time (31 December 1963 = 0); and

a, B, C, C_2 = coefficients estimated by least squares.

11 Greater London Development Plan Inquiry, *op. cit.*, pp. 71–2.
12 Department of the Environment, *op. cit.*, pp. 162–163.
13 The projection of the occupational structure of labour demand in each industry is based on the proportion of each of four occupation groups in 1966 projected to 1976. The resulting proportions are then translated into occupation group values using the 1976 total labour demand figure.
14 In the Greater London Development Plan the estimates of floorspace demand for Greater London were allocated to nine sectors in an effort to be more location specific. Greater London Council, *Greater London Development Plan: Report of Studies* (London: Greater London Council, 1970), pp. 91–2.
15 New York City Planning Commission, *The Demand for Office Space in Manhattan* (New York: City Planning Commission, 1971), pp. 6–12.
16 Also discussed in R. B. Armstrong, *The Office Industry: Patterns of Growth and Location* (Cambridge, Mass: The M.I.T. Press, 1972), pp. 114–19.
17 All the employment projections quoted may be too high and a 1 per cent growth may be more realistic. H. W. Schultz, New York City Planning Commission, personal communication.
18 *Offices, Shops and Railway Premises Act, 1963* (London: Her Majesty's Stationery Office, 1963).
19 R. B. Armstrong, *op. cit.*, p. 46.
20 This figure is derived from data collected by the Building Owners and Managers Association and it relates only to buildings owned or managed by the Association. These may not be wholly representative of all the office buildings in Manhattan, *ibid.*, Table 2.16, p. 47.
21 New York City Planning Commission, *op. cit.*, p. 15.
22 The survey was deficient in that average instead of median ratios were used and there was no adjustment for non-response. The findings compared favourably, however, with the City Planning Commission's own observations, *ibid.*, p. 60.
23 *Ibid.*, p. 16.
24 E. Hoover and A. Vernon, *Anatomy of a Metropolis* (Cambridge, Mass.: Harvard University Press, 1960), p. 112.
25 Twin Cities Metropolitan Council, *Office Space: An Inventory and Forecast for the Twin Cities Metropolitan Area* (St Paul: Twin Cities Metropolitan Council, 1973), Table 10, p. 28.
26 Some additional considerations are discussed in Chapter 4.
27 Dallas Chamber of Commerce, *A Guide to Dallas Office Buildings* (Dallas: Chamber of Commerce, 1973), p. 62.

28 The City Planning Commission estimates of the demand for office space in Manhattan are based on (*a*) calculation of the average amount of space each worker occupied in 1971; (*b*) projection of the number of office workers in 1985; and (*c*) judgement of the average amount of space each office worker will occupy in 1985.

29 C. L. Detoy and S. L. Rabin, 'Office space: Calculating the demand', *Urban Land*, vol. 31 (1972), pp. 4–13.

30 *Ibid.*, p. 5.

31 R. M. Fisher, *The Boom in Office Buildings: An Economic Study of the Past Two Decades* (Washington: The Urban Land Institute, Technical Bulletin, no. 58, 1967), p. 29.

32 *Idem.*

33 O. Marriott, *The Property Boom* (London: Hamish Hamilton, 1967), pp. 41–2. See also Appendix 7, p. 276.

34 *Ibid.*, p. 42.

35 C. L. Detoy and S. L. Rabin, *op. cit.*, pp. 7–13.

36 The term 'absorption rate' is not used consistently in the literature. It is often used to describe demand, supply, and demand–supply differences, as well as city absorption rates and historical, current, normal or target absorption rates. The demand–supply definition is used here.

37 Note the important distinction between space *added* to the market (supply factor 4) and total space *placed* on the market (all five supply factors). Total supply refers to the total placed space, rather than to the smaller item of added space, *ibid.*, p. 7.

38 The office employee coefficient (ϕ) is the proportion of employment in each S.I.C. category generating office space tenants.

39 *Ibid.*, p. 13.

40 Twin Cities Metropolitan Council, *op. cit.*, pp. 21–40.

41 See C. R. Jennings, 'Predicting demand for office space', *Appraisal Journal*, vol. 33 (1965), pp. 377–82.

42 P. Cowan *et al.*, *op. cit.*, pp. 223–56. P. Cowan, J. Ireland and D. Fine, 'Approaches to urban model-building', *Regional Studies*, vol. 1 (1967), pp. 163–72.

43 The planning applications and permissions were concerned with new office buildings, extensions, and change of use. The cell and year of approval of application was known in nearly every case but the size of unit, in thousands of square feet, is only complete for new buildings and extensions.

44 The double sigmas in eqn (2) indicate summation not only over all *p*, *q*, *r* and *s* but also over cells *ij*.

45 P. Cowan *et al.*, *op. cit.* (1969), pp. 229–45.

CHAPTER 6

Regional Patterns of Office Location

It is useful to consider the location of office activities at two levels: regional and urban. In many ways these two levels of analysis are interdependent in that characteristics such as population size, industrial structure, economic diversity, and centrality are as important to the location of offices at the regional scale as they are at the urban scale. To some extent, patterns of office location within urban areas can be viewed as a microcosm of distributions observed at the regional scale. It is therefore useful to begin this section on office location by identifying some of the major characteristics of regional distribution within countries by reference to employment, floorspace, and the location of individual office establishments. Most of the examples, in common with the preceding chapters, are taken from Britain and the United States.

REGIONAL DISTRIBUTION OF OFFICE EMPLOYMENT IN BRITAIN

It might be expected that the distribution of office employment would closely parallel the location pattern of other components of economic structure such as manufacturing industry or population. But one of the most important characteristics of office employment is the marked inequality of its regional distribution (Fig. 21). The average administrative county (excluding county boroughs and London boroughs) had 17·7 per cent of its economically active population in office occupations in 1966.[1] The distribution about this average ranges from a high of 26·0 per cent in Hertfordshire to a low of 8·8 per cent in Montgomeryshire. These two counties contrast sharply in location and industrial structure. The former is immediately adjacent to Greater London, which has a large proportion of its workforce in office work, and has a diversified, active industrial base. The latter is a predominantly agricultural county with only a limited range of manufacturing industry and a small population. These are not conditions which encourage high levels of office activity. Fig. 21 clearly shows that these two counties fall within contiguous regions of high and low levels of office employment. The counties with more than 15 per cent of the workforce in office work form a continuous, linear region from Lancashire, through the Midlands into Southern and South-East England. These are the areas of greatest population concentration and expanding economic activity, particularly growth industries. Northern England, every county in Wales, except Denbighshire, and Devon and Cornwall in the South-West Peninsula are the regions with less than 15 per cent office employment. These areas have a more limited economic base, often comprised of declining industries, and are losing economically active population through out-migration. Settlement density is low in many of these counties, particularly in Wales, and most higher order central places are small and not major generators of office-type employment.

Hence, of the 5·4 m. office workers in Great Britain in 1966, 43·4 per cent worked in the South East Economic Planning Region compared with only 33·6 per cent of the workers in all occupations (Table 29). Elsewhere, only the North West Economic Planning Region had more than 10 per cent of the national total of office employment while East Anglia had only 2·2 per cent. More significant, however, is the fact that both East Anglia and the North West also had a smaller proportion of office than total employment in Britain and this is characteristic of every region except the South East. Consequently, the latter

92

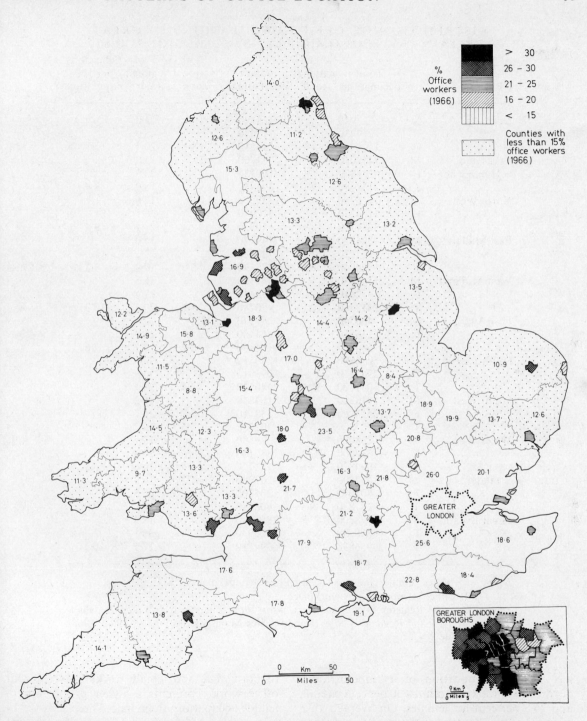

Fig. 21   Distribution of Office Employment in England and Wales—By Administrative Counties and County Boroughs, 1966 (Data: General Register Office, *Sample Census 1966, England and Wales*, 1968)

TABLE 29
DISTRIBUTION OF OFFICE OCCUPATIONS IN GREAT
BRITAIN – BY ECONOMIC PLANNING REGIONS, 1966

Region		Total occupations	% of national total	Office occupations[2]	% of national total	% of regional total	Office jobs per 100 population
Northern	M[1]	928920		128180		13·8	
	F	247430		111430		45·0	
	T	1176350	4·9	239610	4·4	20·4	7·3
Yorks and	M	1412010		211700		15·0	
Humberside	F	754770		180130		23·9	
	T	2177780	9·1	391830	7·3	18·0	8·4
North West	M	1926950		339260		17·6	
	F	1154230		310970		26·9	
	T	3081180	12·9	650230	12·1	21·1	9·8
East Midland	M	996820		149170		15·0	
	F	527220		123020		23·3	
	T	1524040	6·4	272190	5·0	17·9	8·3
West Midland	M	1561130		257320		16·5	
	F	852610		233460		27·4	
	T	2413740	10·1	490780	9·1	20·3	10·0
East Anglia	M	466340		62340		13·4	
	F	218510		54460		24·9	
	T	684850	2·9	116800	2·2	17·1	7·6
South East	M	5076890		1250510		24·6	
	F	2964810		1090010		36·8	
	T	8041700	33·6	2340520	43·4	29·1	14·1
South West	M	1018320		164640		16·2	
	F	517180		138110		26·7	
	T	1535500	6·4	302750	5·6	19·7	8·5
Wales	M	758020		99580		13·1	
	F	336800		82140		24·4	
	T	1094820	4·6	181720	3·4	16·6	6·8
Scotland	M	1432800		203080		14·2	
	F	805070		205200		25·5	
	T	2237870	9·3	408280	7·6	18·2	7·9
Great Britain	M	15578200		2865780		18·4	
	F	8378630		2528930		30·1	
	T	23956830	100·0	5394710	100·0	22·5	10·3

Notes: 1. Males, females and total occupations by workplace.
          2. Office occupations by workplace.
Source: General Register Office, *Sample Census 1966, England and Wales, Economic
          Activity Sub-Regional Tables* (London: Her Majesty's Stationery Office, 1968),
          Table 2.

has a higher proportion of its labour force devoted to office work; almost 30 per cent overall and 36·8 per cent for females. On average, this region has 10 per cent more of its workers in office occupations than any other region. This applies to both male and female workers except that office work represents a higher proportion of female occupations than male. There are over 14 office jobs per 100 population in the South East compared with an average of 10·3 for Great

Britain. This ratio is lowest in the peripheral regions such as Wales (6·8) and the Northern Region (7·3).

Office employment therefore has a distinctive centre-periphery distribution.[2] The periphery comprises Scotland, Wales, Yorkshire and Humberside, Northern and North West Planning Regions. These areas contained 44 per cent of national employment in 1951 but this had

growth was unevenly distributed (Table 30). The rate of growth in the peripheral regions was some 74 per cent of the rate in the centre for the 15-year period but this had decreased to 73 per cent in 1961–6. Hence, the employment sector which is growing fastest nationally is making its major contribution in regions where office employment is already concentrated and relatively more important in the overall employment structure.[4]

TABLE 30
GROWTH OF OFFICE EMPLOYMENT (PER CENT)
IN THE CENTRE AND THE PERIPHERY – GREAT
BRITAIN, 1951–66

Period	Great Britain	Centre	Periphery	Periphery as percentage of centre
1951–61 Growth of:				
Total employment	6·2	8·5	1·5	—
Office employment	38·2	41·8	32·2	77·0
males	37·4	41·4	30·5	73·6
females	39·3	42·2	34·3	81·4
1961–66 Growth of:				
Total employment	3·5	5·1	1·5	—
Office employment	12·3	13·6	9·9	73·0
males	8·6	10·2	5·7	55·9
females	16·7	17·8	14·9	83·6
1951–66 Growth of:				
Total employment	9·9	14·0	3·0	—
Office employment	55·2	61·1	45·3	74·0
males	49·2	55·8	37·9	67·9
females	62·6	67·5	54·3	80·4

Note: Derived from Census of Population data for 1951, 1961, and 1966.
Source: E. M. Burrows, 'Office employment and the regional problem', *Regional Studies*, vol. 7 (1973), Table 2, p. 20, Tables A.1 and A.2, pp. 29–30.

decreased to 41 per cent in 1966. This reflects differentials in growth rates between the centre and the periphery; the former increased its total employment by 14 per cent and the latter by only 3 per cent between 1951 and 1966.[3] Office occupations increased by 55·2 per cent in Great Britain in 1951–66 but as the above figures suggest, the

There is no evidence to suggest that this trend will be reversed.

The differential growth and distribution of office employment between the regions can be related to several factors. Clearly, industrial structure will be an important influence but there are no published statistics on the distribution of office employment by industry in the regions. The distribution of service industries is also important in this context and regions with an above average proportion of service activities will also have a larger share of national office employment. The size distribution of industrial establishments must also be considered; bigger units are more likely to require a large number of office workers for administrative and other purposes. The extent of regional control of industrial activities is also relevant.[5] Many of the offices which control large sections of manufacturing and service industry are concentrated in the South East and West Midlands, and their control extends to plants and branches located outside these 'centre' regions in the periphery. Burrows and Town found that in the East Midlands the location of control had a marked effect on the consumption of the region's office services and on the relative size of the office labour force compared with other regions. They note that the larger an industrial unit, the more likely it is that it will be controlled from another region, with consequent effects upon the growth of office employment in that region. Hence, centralized or national head offices tend to control the larger industrial units in the East Midlands from the South East or West Midlands. As companies get larger and more complex they attempt to achieve scale economies by centralizing both internal and external office functions.[6] The East Midlands is part of the 'centre' group

of regions and the impact of centralization of control is not as accentuated as in the peripheral regions. Here, branch plants of manufacturing industry form a large element of the industrial structure and these will invariably be controlled from the centre. Many of these units do not, therefore, generate office employment growth concomitant with their size.

The county statistics illustrated in Fig. 21 understate the level of office employment within individual urban areas. The proportion of office workers in individual county boroughs is consistently above the figure for the administrative county.[7] Thus, office activities are more likely to locate in urban areas and will not be widely distributed in accordance with population distribution. Although Northumberland county had only 14 per cent of its workers in office occupations in 1966, Newcastle upon Tyne had an equivalent figure of 30·4 per cent. The same is true of Manchester in the North West Region and of other smaller, but important administrative centres, such as Chester and Lincoln. In Greater London there are eleven boroughs with more than 30 per cent of the employees working there in office occupations. The figure for the City of London is 72 per cent and for Westminster, 53·6 per cent. Therefore, inequalities in the distribution of office occupations at the national and regional scale are also evident at the sub-regional level.[8] Over 65 per cent of all office employment

TABLE 31

OFFICE OCCUPATIONS IN THE CONURBATION CENTRES – ENGLAND AND WALES, 1966

Conurbation centre	All occupations	Office occupations	% of total	Males	Females
Greater London	1305940	775260	59·4	424680	350580
South East Lancashire	139740	67410	48·2	33050	34360
Merseyside	138550	57860	41·8	29500	28360
West Midland	108570	50000	46·1	22180	27820
Tyneside	76650	30200	39·4	14390	15810

Note: There is no central area delimited for the West Yorkshire conurbation and it is therefore excluded from the table.

Source: General Register Office, *Sample Census 1966, England and Wales, Economic Activity Tables, County Leaflets* (London: Her Majesty's Stationery Office, 1968), Table 2.

in England and Wales in 1966 was located in the county boroughs and London boroughs (approximately 3·3 m. jobs). Almost 50 per cent of these jobs are located in the Greater London boroughs which account for 30·6 per cent of the total for England and Wales.

The urban concentration of office activities within the Economic Planning Regions does not complete the picture. Within these urban areas, office location reveals a propensity towards concentration in the central area (Table 31). This is well illustrated by reference to the employment structure of the centres of the major British conurbations.[9] Over 59 per cent of the workers

in the centre of the Greater London conurbation are in office occupations. The other four conurbation centres have proportions between 39·4 (Tyneside) and 48·2 per cent (South East Lancashire). Unfortunately the Census does not provide statistics on office occupations in the total area of these conurbations but in Greater London, for example, approximately 50 per cent of all office jobs are located in the conurbation centre.[10] Similar, or even higher, proportions are likely for the remaining conurbations, some of which are in the peripheral areas defined by Burrows.

REGIONAL DISTRIBUTION OF OFFICE EMPLOYMENT IN THE UNITED STATES

The regional distribution of office activities in the United States is best analysed by using the Standard Metropolitan Statistical Areas (S.M.S.A.s) as a base. Of the 24 m. workers in office-type occupations in the United States in 1960, 9·3 m. were located in the 24 S.M.S.A.s with over 1 m. population (Fig. 22). Some 39 per cent of the country's office workers were located in these S.M.S.A.s but 8·6 per cent (1·9 m.), 4·8 per

cent (1·1 m.) and 4·3 per cent (0·9 m.) were concentrated into New York, Los Angeles, and Chicago S.M.S.A.s respectively (Table 32). Other S.M.S.A.s with a large share of United States office-type occupations were Detroit, Philadelphia, and Boston, all of which are located on the heavily industrialized North Eastern Seaboard or in the Great Lakes industrial region. A large proportion of the office activity, as in

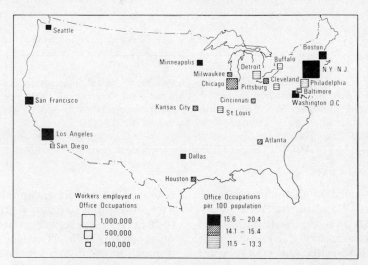

Fig. 22   Office Employment in Metropolitan Areas with Over 1 Million Population, United States—1960 (After R. B. Armstrong, *The Office Industry: Patterns of Growth and Location*, 1972, with the permission of the Regional Plan Association, New York)

TABLE 32
DISTRIBUTION OF OFFICE OCCUPATIONS IN S.M.S.A.s WITH
OVER 1 MILLION POPULATION – UNITED STATES, 1960

S.M.S.A.	Total non-agricultural employment (000s)	% of national total	Employment in office occupations (000s)	%	% of national total	Office jobs per 100 population
New York	4755·4	7·8	1884·2	39·6	8·6	17·6
Newark	733·4	1·2	254·7	34·7	1·2	15·1
Paterson	406·0	0·7	136·8	33·7	0·6	11·5
Chicago	2745·9	4·5	942·3	34·3	4·3	15·1
Los Angeles	2613·0	4·3	1050·8	40·2	4·8	15·6
Philadelphia	1697·6	2·8	579·5	34·1	2·6	13·3
Detroit	1322·2	2·2	454·3	34·4	2·1	12·1
San Francisco	1100·7	1·8	452·2	41·1	2·1	16·2
Boston	1140·5	1·9	430·4	37·7	2·0	16·6
Pittsburgh	852·6	1·4	282·2	33·1	1·3	11·7
St Louis	805·6	1·3	270·2	33·5	1·2	13·1
Washington	832·1	1·4	408·7	49·1	1·9	20·4
Cleveland	776·0	1·3	255·8	33·0	1·2	14·2
Baltimore	675·6	1·1	227·6	33·7	1·0	13·2
Minneapolis–St Paul	620·7	1·0	241·5	38·9	1·1	16·3
Buffalo	469·9	0·8	161·3	34·3	0·7	12·3
Houston	500·4	0·8	176·7	35·3	0·8	14·2
Milwaukee	499·2	0·8	168·1	33·7	0·8	14·1
Seattle	409·7	0·7	178·6	43·6	0·8	16·1
Dallas	436·1	0·7	181·0	41·5	0·8	16·7
Cincinnati	449·4	0·7	151·3	33·7	0·7	14·1
Kansas City	418·4	0·7	160·6	38·4	0·7	15·4
San Diego	295·7	0·5	127·1	42·9	0·6	12·3
Atlanta	420·7	0·7	155·8	37·0	0·7	15·3
Total S.M.S.A.s	24976·8	41·0	9331·7	37·4	39·0	15·2
United States	60877·7	100·0	21948·8	36·0	100·0	12·2

Notes: Office-type occupations include professional, technical, managerial, and clerical workers. Because of the nature of published data, farmers and farm managers are included in the S.M.S.A. figures but not in the national total. Standard Metropolitan Statistical Areas are defined by the Bureau of the Budget.

Source: R. B. Armstrong, *The Office Industry: Patterns of Growth and Location* (Cambridge, Mass.: The M.I.T. Press, 1972), derived from data included in Tables 2.1 and 2.2, pp. 25–6.

Britain, is concentrated in distinctive regions, primarily the North East and the West Coast. Armstrong suggests that this distribution can best be understood by reference to the economic base concept.[11] Historically, the major export base of urban areas was derived from location relative to raw materials and the production and distribution of a wide range of industrial products. Export success of an urban area en-

couraged the import of capital and this acted as a major stimulus to regional growth, particularly to locally based service industries and related office employment. This, in turn, stimulated population expansion, improved the viability of the export function, and firmly supported the continued growth and diversification of the local service functions. In the most prosperous and largest urban areas the process of service diversification began not only to satisfy immediate local requirements but also those of adjacent, but smaller, urban areas, the surrounding region and in some cases, the nation.

The export component of office activities is therefore a vital factor affecting their distribution. The number of office-type occupations per 100 population of each S.M.S.A. provides a crude measure of its export office component (see Table 32). At the national level, 12·2 office occupations service every 100 people but the average for S.M.S.A.s with over 1 m. population is 15·2, leaving all other areas with an average of 10·2. S.M.S.A.s with strong orientation towards export-orientated office jobs have values above 15·2 and include Washington, New York, Boston, Minneapolis–St Paul, and San Francisco. Production-dominated centres such as Chicago, Philadelphia, Detroit, and Pittsburgh are weak exporters of office services even though they contain a relatively large proportion of the nation's office-type occupations. A similar exercise can be undertaken for the British Economic Planning Regions in which the South East, with 14·1 office

jobs per 100 population, emerges as the most export-orientated office region (Table 29).

The S.M.S.A. statistics also conceal considerable concentration of office activities in downtown areas.[12] New York, Houston, Dallas, and Washington all had more than 60 per cent of their office employment in 1960 in downtown. These are also the cities with a high proportion of office workers per 100 population and an emphasis on export-orientated office activities. Other S.M.S.A.s have between 35 and 50 per cent of their office employment downtown and this compares favourably with the statistics for the British conurbation centres (Table 31). Not all S.M.S.A.s are dominated by a single downtown area, however, and in dispersed S.M.S.A.s such as Los Angeles, Wilmington, Detroit, St Louis, and Kansas City, less than 30 per cent of the office employment is in the downtown area. S.M.S.A.s dominated by a major centre, such as Newark and Paterson in the case of New York, also have low levels of office employment concentration in their downtown areas.

A REGIONAL OCCUPATION FACTOR

Regional disparities in the distribution of office occupations can be measured by calculating an occupation factor (R).[13] The factor is calculated as follows:

$$R = 100 \left[\frac{L_i - \{(N_i L)/N\}}{L_i} \right] \%$$

where R is the occupation factor; L_i is the regional office employment in all industries; N_i is national office employment in all industries; N is national employment in all industries; and L is the regional employment in all industries. Assuming that a region has x per cent of all national employment, the same percentage might be regarded as the norm for office employment in the region. The R factor therefore expresses the surplus or deficiency of a region's office employment compared with the national distribution.

The South East Region is the only area with surplus office occupations (Table 33). An R-value of 22·6 per cent shows it is clearly over-supplied compared with the peripheral regions such as

Wales ($-35·7$) or Yorkshire and Humberside ($-24·5$). Large deficits are not characteristic of all the peripheral regions, however, and the North West and Northern Regions do not have R-values concomitant with their position relative to the centre. This general picture does not change significantly if office occupations are subdivided into clerical and administrative/professional groups. Of note, however, are the large deficits in administrative and professional office jobs in the peripheral regions, particularly Scotland ($-40·0$), Wales ($-37·6$), and Yorkshire and Humberside ($-22·9$). Other regions with large overall deficits in office occupations do not have such large deficits in administrative/professional work. Examples are the East and West Midlands with $-19·1$ and $-1·0$ respectively. This reflects the managerial and administrative expertise required by the major national industries located in these regions. Regional deficits in office occupations affect male rather than female employment so that the South East has a smaller surplus

Universitas
BIBLIOTHECA
Ottaviensis

TABLE 33
REGIONAL OCCUPATION FACTORS
FOR OFFICE, CLERICAL AND
ADMINISTRATIVE/PROFESSIONAL
OCCUPATIONS – GREAT BRITAIN, 1966

Region		All office occupations	Clerical	Administrative/ professional
Northern	M	− 33·3	− 26·7	− 33·9
	F	− 32·9	− 34·4	− 42·0
	T	− 10·6	− 7·4	− 8·9
Yorkshire and	M	− 22·7	− 20·9	− 21·9
Humberside	F	− 26·5	− 24·8	− 38·4
	T	− 24·5	− 23·8	− 22·9
North West	M	− 4·5	− 0·7	− 5·5
	F	− 12·0	− 11·1	− 11·1
	T	− 6·7	− 4·0	− 9·1
East Midland	M	− 22·9	− 26·9	− 18·7
	F	− 29·4	− 28·0	− 30·5
	T	− 26·1	− 28·4	− 19·1
West Midland	M	− 11·6	− 33·4	1·2
	F	− 10·2	− 8·5	− 23·8
	T	− 10·7	− 14·9	− 1·0
East Anglia	M	− 37·6	− 33·4	− 39·4
	F	− 21·1	− 20·1	− 40·9
	T	− 32·0	− 30·1	− 34·8
South East	M	25·3	25·3	24·0
	F	17·9	16·5	26·2
	T	22·6	21·5	22·5
South West	M	− 13·7	− 12·9	− 14·1
	F	− 13·0	− 12·8	− 22·2
	T	− 14·2	− 15·0	− 13·1
Wales	M	− 40·0	− 29·4	− 45·3
	F	− 23·8	− 23·1	− 26·4
	T	− 35·7	− 33·3	− 37·6
Scotland	M	− 29·8	− 22·0	− 35·7
	F	− 18·4	− 15·7	− 72·2
	T	− 23·4	− 16·0	− 40·0

Note: R factors are given for males, females, and total workers.
Office occupations as defined by the Registrar General
in the Census are used. The administrative/professional
group are an amalgamation of the relevant sub-groups
in Orders XXIV and XXV of the Census.

Source: Calculated from data in: General Register Office, *Sample Census 1966, Great Britain, Economic Activity Sub-Regional Tables* (London: Her Majesty's Stationery Office, 1968), Table 2.

of female office occupations.[14] Female administrative and professional office workers are over-represented in the South East but there are heavy deficits in every other Region compared with males in the same category. The reverse occurs for clerical workers and this is an indication of the differences in employment opportunities for males and females in these two basic sub-divisions of office occupations. Between 1961 and 1966 internal migration of economically active managerial and professional migrants to the regions which generate high status office employment in major urban centres, particularly the South East, has helped to accentuate the regional imbalance indicated by the R factors.[15]

A recent analysis by Westaway, using Metropolitan Economic Labour Areas (M.E.L.A.s), shows that the pattern of gains and losses of professional and managerial jobs confirms the broad regional trends analysed by Waugh.[16] M.E.L.A.s in the South East and Midlands gained while many of the M.E.L.A.s in the other regions recorded absolute losses. Significantly, however, the large M.E.L.A.s, irrespective of location, have a higher probability of achieving absolute increases in professional and managerial functions. This has implications for the regional policies discussed later.

REGIONAL DISTRIBUTION OF OFFICE FLOORSPACE

It is reasonable to expect that the regional distribution of office floorspace will match the pattern shown for employment (Table 34). Over 53 per cent of the total stock of office floorspace in England and Wales in 1967 was located in the South East Region; 40·5 per cent in Greater

London alone. Central government floorspace has a similar distribution with only the North West Region having more than 10 per cent of both commercial and central government space. It is worth noting that in 1967 the South East had only 35·2 per cent of the estimated

TABLE 34

REGIONAL DISTRIBUTION OF COMMERCIAL AND CENTRAL GOVERNMENT OFFICE FLOORSPACE – ENGLAND AND WALES, 1967

Region	% Estimated population[1]	Floorspace (m. ft²) Commercial	Central government	Floorspace per capita Commercial	Central government	% all regions Commercial	Central government
Northern	6·9	12·1	3·3	3·6	1·0	4·3	5·2
Yorkshire and Humberside	9·9	19·8	3·9	4·1	0·8	7·0	6·2
North West	13·9	39·4	9·0	5·8	1·3	14·0	14·4
East Midlands	6·8	11·1	2·4	3·4	0·7	3·9	3·9
West Midlands	10·4	20·2	3·1	4·0	0·6	7·2	4·9
East Anglia	3·3	6·1	1·3	3·9	0·8	2·2	2·1
South East	35·2	150·2	32·5	8·8	1·9	53·4	51·8
Greater London	16·2	113·9	24·8	14·6	3·2	40·5	39·5
South West	7·8	14·1	4·3	3·7	1·1	5·0	6·9
Wales	5·6	8·6	3·0	3·2	1·1	3·0	4·7
England and Wales	100·0	281·5	62·8	5·8	1·3	100·0	100·0

Note: 1. Regional population as percentage of national total.

Source: Department of the Environment, *Statistics for Town and Country Planning, Series II — Floorspace* (London: Her Majesty's Stationery Office, 1972), Tables 1 and 3.

population of England and Wales while the North West had 13·9 per cent. Outside the South East there is a reasonable association between the proportion of total population in a region and the proportion of commercial and central government office floorspace. The South East is in a superior position because of its lower than average proportion of industrial floorspace. Hence, 48·9 per cent of all the floorspace in the region in 1967 was industrial compared with 69·3 per cent in Yorkshire and Humberside and 67·1 per cent in the North West. Commercial offices accounted for 12·8 per cent of all floorspace in the South East but only between 4 and 6 per cent in the other regions.

The distribution of floorspace *per capita* ranges between 3·2 and 5·8 ft^2 for commercial offices outside the South East. The South East is the only region with more commercial floorspace *per capita* than the average of 5·8 ft^2 for all regions. This provides a further crude measure of the important export function of office activities in the region. The pattern is similar for central government offices except that floorspace *per capita* is only 25 per cent of that for commercial offices. The North West is again the only region with a *per capita* distribution of government floorspace equal to the national average. Every other region is under-represented; the West Midlands has only 0·6 ft^2 *per capita*. It should be noted, however, that the peripheral regions have a larger share of the national total of central government floorspace than commercial space. Wales, for example, has 4·7 per cent of the former and only 3·0 per cent of the latter; the Northern Region 5·2 and 4·3 per cent respectively and the South West 6·9 and 5·0 per cent. Regions in the core area for office occupations have a larger share of commercial office floorspace and in this respect they resemble the South East.

Most of the office floorspace in England and Wales is concentrated in local authorities with more than 500,000 ft^2 of commercial space (Fig. 23). If the central government floorspace in these centres is also included then 70·3 per cent of all office space is located in 87 local authorities; 39·4 per cent in 28 London boroughs, and 30·9 per cent in 59 'provincial' centres. But as with office employment, this again understates the extent of floorspace concentration. Over 44 per cent of the

Fig. 23   Distribution of Office Floorspace in England and Wales—By Local Authorities with More than 500,000 ft^2 of Commercial Floorspace, 1967 (Data: Department of the Environment, *Statistics for Town and Country Planning, Series II No. 2, Floorspace,* 1972)

space in 'provincial' centres is found in just six major cities which, ranked according to total office floorspace, are Manchester, Liverpool, Birmingham, Bristol, Newcastle, and Leeds.[17] A similar situation exists in Greater London where 65·3 per cent of the floorspace, in rank order, is located in Westminster, the City of London, and

Camden. These local authorities could be labelled 'office centres' and almost all are the foci of regional administration, commercial activities, industrial expansion, and communications networks. All six major provincial centres are over 100 miles from London which dominates the distribution of office activity within the South East. With the exception of Manchester and Liverpool, the provincial 'office centres' command distinct regions to which they can export their services and perpetuate the growth of office activities. The close proximity of Liverpool and Manchester largely reflects the role of historical inertia; Liverpool being Britain's second port and supporting considerable indigenous office activity. Manchester is better placed relative to the North West Region as a whole and already has a more important function as an exporter of regional office services.[18]

CITY SIZE AND TOTAL OFFICE FLOORSPACE

Analysis of the location of office activities at the regional level is a useful preliminary exercise, but urban areas have been shown to possess the largest proportion of all office floorspace. It has also been noted that office activities are disproportionately concentrated in the larger cities, either within an individual region or for the nation. There seems to be a relationship, therefore, between city size and the amount of office floorspace.

A study of the relationship between C.B.D. office space and urbanized area population for 60 cities in the United States has revealed a direct and exponential relationship between the two variables.[19] Therefore, as cities become larger office space *per capita* increases at a higher rate. The urbanized area population in 1950 was related to reported office space in 1946 and 1956 and for each unit increase in population, office space increased by at least two units in the distribution for each year. There is also a significant correlation between total office space and urbanized area population with an r of 0·90 for 1946 and 0·89 for 1956. The amount by which cities deviate from the least square line ranges from one-fifth of the expected to five times the expected office space. Cities with large deviations from the least squares line were the higher order central places in 1946 and 1956, such as Denver, Atlanta, San Francisco, and Seattle. All are regional capitals and are not part of large conurbations. Cities with less office space than expected are those in regions which had a declining economic base, were located within the area of economic dominance of a much larger city, or were predominantly manufacturing cities. The study therefore shows that 'as a city becomes larger it accumulates office space at a greater rate than it acquires population'.[20]

A similar exercise for British cities with more than 500,000 ft² of commercial office floorspace exhibits similar relationships (Fig. 24).[21] The least squares line shows that as population increases, the stock of office floorspace also increases and the equation can be used to calculate that a city of 100,000 population should have approximately 852,000 ft² of office space, while a city of

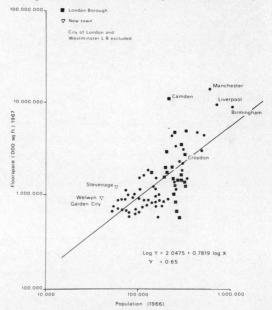

Fig. 24 Relationship Between City Population and Total Office Floorspace, England and Wales—1966 (Data: General Register Office, *Sample Census 1966, England and Wales*, 1968 and as for Fig. 23)

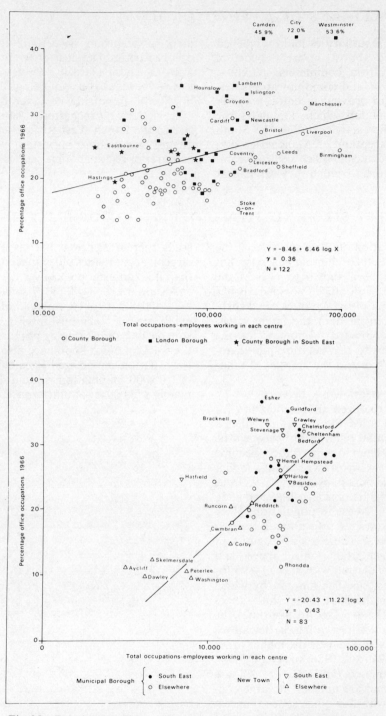

Fig. 25   Relationship Between Total Employment in a City and Proportion of Office Occupations, England and Wales—By A) County and London Boroughs and B) New Towns and Municipal Boroughs, 1966 (Data: General Register Office, *Sample Census 1966, England and Wales*, 1968)

104

1 m. population should have approximately 2·9 m. ft^2. As expected, several cities deviate substantially from the average. Manchester has between four and five times more office space than expected for its population of 597,870 in 1966 and Liverpool and Birmingham three times more space. Because of the regional dominance of Manchester and Liverpool other cities in the North West Region, such as Blackburn, Bolton, and Blackpool have less office space than would be expected in relation to population size. A similar process operates in Greater London where the central boroughs such as Camden, Islington, and Lambeth contain an above average share of office space; Camden contains five and a half times more. The suburban boroughs, except Croydon, are under-provided.

There is also a positive relationship between the total number of workers with workplaces in a city and the proportion of office occupations in 1966 (Fig. 25). Separate graphs have been prepared for county and London boroughs, and for municipal boroughs and new towns, in England and Wales. Three London boroughs have been excluded from Fig. 25 because of their extreme values for proportion of office occupations; this would distort unnecessarily the regression equation and the correlation coefficient. With r values of 0·36 and 0·43 respectively, the two sets of data reveal considerable variability in office occupation levels relative to total occupations but a number of important points emerge. Some of the major provincial cities such as Leeds, Birmingham, and Sheffield have below average levels of office employees working there; only Manchester, Bristol, Newcastle, and Cardiff have a higher level of office occupations than expected. Well over half the London boroughs and almost all the county boroughs in South East England have an above average level of office work. By comparison, apart from the major cities, provincial county boroughs with similar sized working populations as their counterparts in the South East are under-provided with office occupations.

At the lower level of municipal boroughs and new towns, almost all of which have working populations of less than 90,000, the proportion of office occupations increases sharply with size (Fig. 25). Apart from this, the main observation here is the major discrepancy between the proportion of office work in the South East compared with provincial new towns of approximately similar size. Bracknell or Hatfield have two or three times more office work than expected (20–30 per cent of all employees working there) while Peterlee and Washington have less than expected (9–10 per cent). Size is clearly an important consideration and is directly related to levels of office work, but cities and towns in the South East consistently do better than provincial centres. This is important in the context of regional development policies (see Chapter 9).

The strength of the relationship between city population and office space distribution or working population and proportion of office occupations should not be exaggerated. Least squares analysis illustrates the direction of the relationship but does not provide any explanations for the observed distribution. Other variables such as regional population, employment in service industries, proportion of clerical workers, or rateable value of office floorspace could have been used with equal success.

Armstrong has also illustrated a significant relationship between S.M.S.A. office employment and C.B.D. office floorspace and finds that, on average, the higher the office worker/population ratio, the higher the proportion of office workers concentrated in C.B.D. offices.[22] All these results indicate that some cities are more attractive than others for office location and that there is a moderate to strong statistical relationship between pairs of variables used to illustrate the dominance of these cities. But why should some cities be more attractive than others? This can best be answered by more detailed reference to the location of office activities within urban areas. Before moving on to this theme, however, it is useful to look at one other index of the regional pattern of office activities; the location of major headquarters offices.

LOCATION OF HEADQUARTERS OFFICES

The locations chosen by the headquarters offices of major industrial and non-industrial companies provide a good insight to the relative merits of various regions for office activity. Such companies have vast financial power and resources, employ large labour forces, and their locational preferences for head offices is a vital stimulus to the growth and attraction of other office activities. There are two main sources of data; for Britain, *The Times 1000* lists the top 1000 companies with a turnover exceeding £7·6 m.[23] The headquarters office location of each company is given, along with a list of principal activities, turnover (for manufacturing companies), and number of employees. The latter covers the complete firm and does not distinguish headquarters office employees from other workers. The major ranked list refers to manufacturing companies, quoted and unquoted, but there are also smaller lists of the top 50 life and non-life insurance companies, finance companies, and nationalized industries including location of head offices. Similar statistics for the United States can be traced via the top 500 list published by *Fortune* magazine.[24] The top industrial corporations are ranked by sales but corporate assets, net profits, invested capital, and number of employees are also given. *Fortune* also publishes a list of the 50 largest life insurance companies, diversified financial companies, commercial banks, utility, transportation, and merchandising companies. Both lists are published annually and therefore permit analysis of the changing characteristics of headquarters location, as well as the influence of the companies listed on the national and regional economy. Although both these sources only cover approximately 5 and 1 per cent respectively of all possible companies they account for a large proportion of total sales and employment. *Fortune*'s 500 industrial companies, for example, are responsible for more than 50 per cent of total sales and over 70 per cent of total profits each year.

Central London dominates the location pattern of the headquarters offices of Britain's top 500 manufacturing companies (Fig. 26).[25] Hence, the larger the firm, the more likely it is to have its head office in London.[26] It contains 57 per

Fig. 26   Location of Headquarters Offices of the Top 500 Manufacturing Companies, Great Britain—1971–1972 (Data: *The Times 1000 Leading Companies in Britain and Overseas 1971–72*, 1972)

cent (285) of the headquarters offices in this category and, more important, 16·2 per cent (81) are offices of the top 100 companies. These are the headquarters which control and administer companies with total turnover of £44 m. in 1971, or 77 per cent of the total turnover of the top 500 manufacturing companies. They also employ some 4·6 m. workers although this slightly overstates the significance for the British economy because overseas workers are also included where relevant. This concentration of headquarters offices of manufacturing companies in London has increased since 1955.[27] Of the 393 manufacturing companies with more than £2·5 m. assets in 1955, only 29 per cent (113) had headquarters offices in central London although they did represent companies with 44·1 per cent of total assets. Compared to central London, other British cities are only minor centres for the head-quarters offices of manufacturing companies. The next nine centres, ranked in order of total head-quarters, are Glasgow (10), Birmingham (9), Liverpool and Sheffield (8 each), Manchester (7), Leeds (5), Brentford (Hounslow L.B.) (5), Brad-ford and Slough (4 each). Therefore, 68·8 per cent (344) of the top headquarters offices are located in just ten cities. Only the Glasgow offices control companies with a turnover exceeding 1 per cent of total turnover for the 500 firms listed.[28] The location pattern of headquarters outside London largely coincides with the list of major cities with above average office floorspace *per capita* (Fig. 24). Westaway has noted, however, that between 1969/70 and 1970/1 four major provincial office centres lost 17 head offices between them (Man-chester, Birmingham, Leeds, and Sheffield).[29] This does not necessarily mean increasing centralization but wider dispersal outside Lon-don. There is no evidence for increasing centralization during the period covered by *The Times* Guides.[30]

Classification of the headquarters offices in the ten major centres by S.I.C.s shows that, outside London, they are closely associated with major industrial activities in the respective regions. Hence, Birmingham has four head offices of engineering and electrical goods (VI) firms and there are three in Sheffield. Of the four offices in Bradford, two are headquarters of textile com-panies (X), while five offices in Liverpool can be classified as transport and communication (XIX) and reflect its port functions.[31] Central London contains a wide diversity of headquarters offices which comprehensively reflect the nation's in-dustrial structure and the role of London as the national 'office centre'. Its position is enhanced if the offices in the London boroughs (Fig. 26) are added to the total for the centre. Locations with single headquarters offices are widely dis-tributed and usually represent lower order com-panies connected with local industry; clothing and footwear companies in Leicester and Not-tingham or engineering and metal manufacture in the West Midlands.

Regional disparities in headquarters office

TABLE 35
DISTRIBUTION OF THE HEADQUARTERS OFFICES OF A SAMPLE OF 1000 FIRMS IN GREAT BRITAIN—1971–2

	South East[1]	Prosperous areas[2]	Less Prosperous areas[3]
10 per cent Systematic Sample:			
observed	61	15	24
expected	34	25	41
Size Categories:[4] observed:			
large	88	6	6
medium	58	19	23
small	43	19	38
expected	34	25	41

Notes: 1. South East, including London.
2. South West, West Midlands, East Mid-lands, East Anglia.
3. Wales, North West, Yorkshire and Hum-berside, Northern, Scotland, Northern Ireland.
4. The size categories were derived from three new data sets:
(a) largest 100 firms (turnover > £132 m.)— large.
(b) middle 100 firms (turnover £17–22 m.)— medium.
(c) smallest 100 firms (turnover £7–9 m.)— small.

Source: H. D. Watts, 'Giant manufacturing corpora-tions: Further observations on regional growth and large corporations', *Area*, vol. 4 (1972), Table 1 and Table 3, pp. 270–1.

location have been measured by Watts and Par-sons.[32] Using a sample of headquarters from *The Times 1000* there is a significant difference at the 0·1 per cent level between the observed and expected distribution in the South East, Prosperous and Less Prosperous Areas (Table 35).[33] The distribution in the South East is clearly underestimated in the expected calculations with the reverse occurring in the Prosperous and Less Prosperous Areas. The discrepancy is most marked in the latter, a situation which is even less satisfactory if the observed distribution is analysed in respect of corporate size and headquarters location. The observed distribution of the headquarters of the smallest firms (turnover £7–9 m.) in the Less Prosperous Areas is only 3 points less than expected but medium and large firms are far less important than expected (Table 35). Indeed, 88 per cent of the headquarters offices of large firms (turnover > £132 m.) are located in the South East, particularly in central London. Hence, the larger the firm, the greater the probability that its location will contribute to deviations from the expected distribution of headquarters at the aggregate level. Watts tentatively suggests that firms with a turnover in excess of £10 m. are more likely to have headquarters control located in the South East than elsewhere. Parsons notes that apart from Group head offices; central services, divisional head offices, and research and development units also reveal disproportionate concentration in London and the South East.[34]

The characteristics of manufacturing headquarters location are paralleled by finance, life insurance, and nationalized industry headquarters (Fig. 27). Of the top 50 life insurance companies (ranked by funds), 68 per cent have their headquarters in central London, almost exclusively within the City of London's financial core. Most of the companies with headquarters offices located outside London appear in both the life and non-life lists. Therefore, although they appear as separate offices in Fig. 27 many are the headquarters of the same company, e.g. the Royal Insurance Group in Liverpool. The headquarters of financial offices are more widely distributed amongst individual locations although 76 per cent are still located in the City of London. All the accepting and issuing houses (30 headquarters) are located in central London and all the offices outside London are the headquarters of finance houses with strong regional or local orientation and origin, e.g. the Hodge Group in Cardiff. With only some exceptions, these offices are located in cities which possess, or are very accessible to, the regional stock exchanges such as the Midlands and Western, while they will also have close links with London. Nationalized industries are almost exclusively controlled from central and suburban London, only Edin-

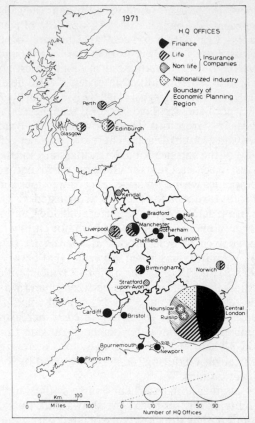

Fig. 27   Location of Headquarters Offices of Finance, Life Insurance and Nationalized Industry, Great Britain—1971–72 (Data: as for Fig. 26)

burgh and Glasgow possessing headquarters of Scottish-based activities. Hence, only 22 cities in Britain are utilized as headquarters locations by finance and related offices with all the largest companies concentrating their control in London, Manchester, Liverpool, Cardiff, and Edinburgh. Regional imbalance is even more evident than that shown for industrial headquarters.

Most of the ideas on 'élite' headquarters location have been derived from work on the long-standing *Fortune* lists in the United States. Goodwin has proposed the term 'management centre' for any city in which there is a 'concentration of headquarters offices of nationally important companies'.[35] This is based on an observation, made some years earlier by Vernon, that the growth of the office function 'may well occur to a disproportionate extent in the office districts of the larger central cities, at the expense of regional centres'.[36] Functional classifications of cities have completely ignored the management function, rather they incorporate these activities with the employment figures for transport, retailing or manufacturing in the classification.[37] In the early work of Harris, Nelson, or Moser and Scott management may not have been considered one of the most important urban functions when measured by employment because it

Just under 50 per cent of the top 500 industrial corporations in the United States have headquarters locations in ten major cities (Fig. 28). The 242 companies involved represent 57·9 per cent of the sales revenue, 59·1 per cent of the assets, and 56·4 per cent of the employees in the top 500. Ranked in order of total sales, the top ten cities in 1971 are New York, Detroit, Chicago, Pittsburgh, Los Angeles, St Louis, Cleveland, Minneapolis/St Paul, Philadelphia, and Milwaukee. New York, Chicago, and Detroit

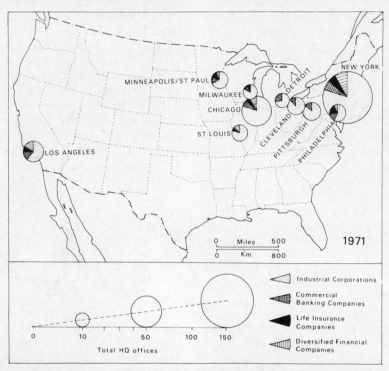

Fig. 28   Location of Headquarters Offices of Industrial Corporations, Commercial Banking, Life Insurance, and Diversified Financial Companies, United States—1971 (Data: *Fortune: The Fortune Directory (Annual Supplement)*, 1972)

was, and still is, difficult to extract from census data. Clearly, management activities and their supporting employment in offices have become much more important in our major urban areas during the last 10–15 years. Some cities may therefore merit description as 'management', 'office' or even 'quaternary' centres in contemporary functional classifications. The *Fortune* list and other sources are well suited to such a task.

have 161 headquarters offices or 66·5 per cent of the total in the top ten centres. Detroit has the smallest number of headquarters in the list, Pittsburgh, Los Angeles, and Cleveland have almost twice as many but sales of the Detroit car companies in particular are much higher than for any other centre outside New York. But on any of the measures, New York is four times as large as any of the other cities and has 116 headquarters offices. This still represents a deterioration from its position in 1963 when it had 163, although the smaller number of head offices in 1971 had almost double the sales of the companies represented in 1963.[38] Goodwin's listing of the ten major management centres in 1963 is also rather different to the above list. He used three arbitrarily chosen criteria to define a management centre, which were (a) at least ten headquarters offices; (b) at least $2 m. in assets or sales in 1962; and (c) at least 100,000 employees.[39] Several cities satisfied at least two of these criteria but failed to have at least ten headquarters offices of industrial corporations. Using these criteria, only seven cities in 1971 had more than ten industrial corporation headquarters. Excluded from Goodwin's list are Detroit, Philadelphia, and Milwaukee; the latter would also be excluded because its head offices control less than 100,000 employees. Dispersal of headquarters activities has changed the pattern noted by Goodwin and this is best expressed by the appearance of Min-

neapolis/St Paul in the 1971 list of management centres.[40]

By including the offices of the top 50 commercial banking, life insurance, and diversified financial companies listed in *Fortune* in 1971, the status of the top ten centres is enhanced (Fig. 28) and they all satisfy Goodwin's first and third criteria. The second criterion cannot be tested because assets rather than sales are used as the ranking criterion. It should be noted that Detroit, Cleveland, and Pittsburgh have no life insurance or diversified financial companies in the top 50. This underlines the fact that the bulk of control exerted by the headquarters offices in these cities is industrially-orientated and these are classified by Goodwin as secondary centres. The total assets controlled by the headquarters in the top ten centres adds support to this classification (Fig. 29). In terms of diversity of headquarters and total assets only New York and Chicago can be classified as national management or quaternary centres. Los Angeles, Philadelphia,

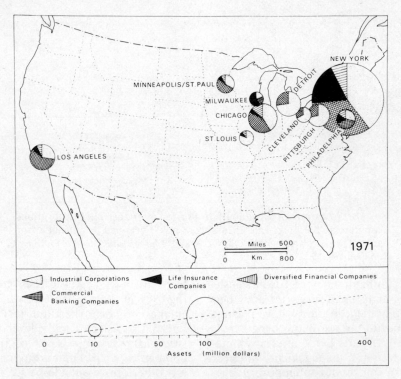

Fig. 29   Assets Controlled by Headquarters Offices Located in Top Ten 'Headquarters' Cities, United States—1971 (Data: as for Fig. 28)

TABLE 36
LOCATION OF MAJOR HEADQUARTERS OFFICES IN THE
UNITED STATES—1971

City	Total H.Q. offices	Industrial corporations[1]	Commercial banking companies[2]	Life insurance companies[3]	Diversified financial companies[4]	% National sales[5]	% National assets	% National employees
New York	147	116	10	7	14	31·1	36·2	31·1
Chicago	46	37	3	2	4	5·4	5·5	5·2
Los Angeles	23	14	3	2	4	2·4	4·5	2·0
Pittsburgh	17	15	2	—	—	3·7	3·1	3·3
Cleveland	16	14	2	—	—	1·9	1·4	2·1
Philadelphia	16	9	3	3	1	1·1	2·2	1·3
Minneapolis/St Paul	15	10	2	2	1	1·6	2·0	2·0
St Louis	13	10	—	1	2	2·3	1·0	3·7
Detroit	11	8	3	—	—	7·9	3·7	7·3
Milwaukee	11	9	1	1	—	0·5	1·1	0·6
Total	315	242	29	18	26	57·9	60·7	58·6

Notes: 1. Industrial corporations (top 500).
2. Commercial Banking Companies (top 50).
3. Life Insurance Companies (top 50).
4. Diversified Financial Companies (top 50).
5. Percentage of total sales of industrial corporations only. The proportion of assets and employees includes all four types of headquarters office in each city. It is therefore expressed as a percentage of total assets and employees controlled by the top 650 companies.

Source: Fortune, vol. 86 (1972).

and Minneapolis/St Paul can be classified as regional management centres.

Closer scrutiny of the non-industrial headquarters shows that only 36 per cent of the life insurance companies have offices located in the ten major cities. This is also true of the diversified financial companies with 50 per cent of their headquarters outside the major centres. Hence, the classification excludes tertiary centres, or cities with important regional or national financial activities excluded from the above list.[41] San Francisco, Hartford or Dallas contain the headquarters of some of the largest non-industrial companies, particularly insurance offices.[42] Milwaukee is probably the only city in the top ten which could be classified as a tertiary centre. The statistics for the major office centres are summarized in Table 36.[43] More extensive analysis could be made on the basis of S.M.S.A.s or larger regions which probably provide a better measure of the relative status of cities as office centres. Semple has attempted this by using a dispersion statistic to calculate the changes in spatial concentration of headquarters at the regional level between 1956–71.[44]

Few British cities meet Goodwin's criteria for management centres. London is clearly a quaternary centre of national significance while Manchester and Glasgow are the major regional quaternary centres. In terms of number and diversity of headquarters offices, Birmingham would also be included. The secondary centres are Liverpool, Sheffield, and Leeds and these are mainly important at the regional level of headquarters control. The only tertiary centre is Norwich which, although it is the location of only one insurance company headquarters, commands a very large share of the life and non-life funds of Britain's insurance companies. Unlike the United States, there are no other published sources which can be used to analyse headquarters office location in Britain. The above classification is not totally satisfactory because of the restricted analysis which can be used to derive it and the absence of a good time series. The changing status of London, for example, as a management centre is not clear and can only be deduced from office relocation data. These will be discussed in a later section. Government offices have also been excluded from the classification. Some 62 per cent of the headquarters office staff of the Civil Service were located in London at the end of September 1972.[45] Other centres for Civil Service headquarters are Cardiff and Edinburgh and this certainly adds to the diversity of office activities in these cities, perhaps making them eligible for classification as management centres.

Although this has been a brief review of the attributes of regional patterns of office location and employment, it suggests that there is much more we need to know about the disparities in distribution. In some cases the right type of data is not available but that which can be obtained could usefully be utilized in closer examination of the relationship between regional attributes, such as industrial structure, female activity rates, the ratio of growth to declining industries, investment in regional infra-structure or attitudes to environment, and the location pattern of office activities on an intra- and inter-regional basis. Concentration of office functions in a limited number of cities which are over-provided in relation to their own, or even regional, needs suggests that offices have location requirements which only urban areas can best provide. It is therefore vital to discuss office location at the micro-scale, i.e. within urban areas in order to understand the importance of spatial aggregation to many sectors of office activity.

REFERENCES

1 'Office occupations' are used as defined in Chapter 3, n. 12.

2 E. M. Burrows, 'Office employment and the regional problem', *Regional Studies*, vol. 7 (1973), pp. 17–31. J. Rhodes and A. Kan, *Office Dispersal and Regional Policy* (London: Cambridge University Press, Department of Applied Economics Occasional Papers; no. 30, 1971), pp. 7–13. See also M. J. Bannon, 'Office location and regional development in Ireland', in M. J. Bannon (ed.), *Office Location and Regional Development* (Dublin: An Foras Forbartha, 1973), pp. 9–19.

3 E. M. Burrows, *op. cit.*, Table A.1, p. 29.

4 *Ibid.*, p. 20.

5 E. M. Burrows and S. Town, *Office Services in the East Midlands* (Nottingham: East Midlands Economic Planning Council, 1971).

6 E. M. Burrows, *op. cit.*, pp. 22–3.

7 The statistics for administrative counties cover all other administrative areas within their boundaries, e.g. municipal boroughs, except the county boroughs.

8 This is briefly illustrated in Yorkshire and Humberside Economic Planning Board, *The Service Industries: Prospects in Yorkshire and Humberside* (Leeds: Department of the Environment, 1972).

9 The conurbation centres are defined as that area containing the principal concentration of administrative and commercial offices, major shopping streets, theatres, cinemas and dance halls, public buildings, hotels, special areas and precincts, and main railway and coach termini. General Register Office, *Sample Census 1966, England and Wales, Economic Activity County Leaflets, General Explanatory Notes* (London: Her Majesty's Stationery Office, 1968), p. xxi. See also G. C. Cameron and A. W. Evans, 'The British conurbation centres', *Regional Studies*, vol. 7 (1973), pp. 47–55.

10 These figures can be calculated by aggregating the totals for each appropriate occupation order given in the occupation tables for the conurbations in the Census.

11 R. B. Armstrong, *The Office Industry: Patterns of Growth and Location* (Cambridge, Mass.: The M.I.T. Press, 1972), pp. 23–6.

12 *Ibid.*, p. 49 and Table 2.17.

13 The R factor is derived from the regional employment factor used by G. Manners, 'Service industries and regional economic growth', *Town Planning Review*, vol. 33 (1963), pp. 293–303. Other techniques for comparing regional employment structures are fully discussed in M. Chisholm and J. Oeppen, *The Changing Pattern of Employment: Regional Specialization and Industrial Localization in Britain* (London: Croom Helm, 1973), pp. 11–41.

14 For a more detailed background to regional differences in the R factor see E. M. Burrows, *op. cit.*, pp. 20–2.

15 A detailed analysis is given in M. Waugh, 'The changing distribution of professional and managerial manpower in England and Wales between

1961 and 1966', *Regional Studies*, vol. 3 (1969), pp. 157–69. C. B. Hall and R. A. Smith, 'Socio-economic patterns of England and Wales', *Urban Studies*, vol. 5 (1968), pp. 59–66. E. Hammond, *An Analysis of Regional Economic and Social Statistics* (Durham: University of Durham, 1968).

16 J. Westaway, *Contact Potential and the Occupational Structure of the British Urban System 1961–1966: An Empirical Study* (London: London School of Economics and Political Science, Geography Department Discussion Paper, no. 45, 1973), pp. 7–13. Metropolitan Economic Labour Areas (M.E.L.A.s) were first defined by Political and Economic Planning using 1961 Census information, see P. Hall, 'Spatial structure of metropolitan England and Wales', in M. Chisholm and G. Manners (eds.), *Spatial Policy Problems of the British Economy* (London: Cambridge University Press, 1971).

17 Using rateable value and floorspace data, Wright produced a similar list in 1967 with only one addition, Cardiff. See M. W. Wright, 'Provincial office development', *Urban Studies*, vol. 4 (1967), pp. 219–23.

18 Over 40 per cent of the offices in central Manchester service North West and Northern England, see City of Manchester, *Central Manchester Office Survey 1971* (Manchester: City Planning Department, 1972), Table 8, p. 13.

19 E. Horwood and R. Boyce, *Studies of the Central Business District and Urban Freeway Development* (Seattle: University of Washington Press, 1959), pp. 46–57.

20 *Ibid.*, p. 57. R. B. Armstrong, *op. cit.*, p. 23.

21 Data for commercial and central government floorspace are represented but each city must have at least 500,000 ft² of commercial office floorspace for inclusion in the analysis. Westminster and the City of London represent extreme deviations from the least squares line and, if included, would produce an unrepresentative relationship.

22 R. B. Armstrong, *op. cit.*, pp. 49–51.

23 *The Times 1000 Leading Companies in Britain and Overseas 1971–72* (London: Times Newspapers Ltd, 1972). *The Times* has published lists for the top 300 industrial companies for 1965, 1966, and 1967; the top 500 in 1968–9, 1969–70, and 1970–1971; and the top 1000 in 1971–2 and 1972–3.

24 *Fortune: The Fortune Directory* (*Annual Supplement*) (New York: Time, Inc.). Published in July of each year since 1956. For a more detailed discussion of the merits of the *Fortune* data see W. Goodwin, 'The management centre in the United States', *Geographical Review*, vol. 55 (1965), pp. 5–6. R. B. Armstrong, *op. cit.*, pp. 37–9.

25 Companies are ranked according to turnover (sales).

26 This has also been noted by J. Westaway, *op. cit.*, p. 14. See also, A. W. Evans, 'The location of the headquarters of industrial companies', *Urban Studies*, vol. 10 (1973), pp. 388–9.

27 W. T. W. Morgan, 'The geographical concentration of big business in Great Britain', *Town and Country Planning*, vol. 30 (1962), pp. 122–4.

28 It is possible that urban areas with a single headquarters office may represent a larger proportion of the total turnover of the top 500 companies, depending on the rank of the company compared to the groups in cities such as Glasgow and Manchester.

29 J. Westaway, *op. cit.*, p. 15.

30 A. W. Evans, *op. cit.*, p. 394.

31 A similar relationship has been noted by W. T. W. Morgan, *op. cit.*, p. 124.

32 H. D. Watts, 'Giant manufacturing corporations: Further observations on regional growth and large corporations', *Area*, vol. 4 (1972), pp. 269–273. See also G. F. Parsons, 'The giant manufacturing corporations and balanced regional growth in Britain', *Area*, vol. 4 (1972), pp. 99–103.

33 The three units for analysis are derived by aggregating the relevant Economic Planning Regions (shown in Table 35). The expected distribution of headquarters is based on the assumption that the proportion of employees in each unit reflects the number of offices in that unit.

34 See also, J. M. Hall, 'Industry grows where the grass is greener', *Area*, vol. 2 (1970), pp. 40–6.

35 W. Goodwin, *op. cit.*, p. 3.

36 R. Vernon, *The Changing Economic Function of the Central City* (New York: Committee for Economic Development, Supplementary Paper, no. 1, 1959), p. 60.

37 See, for examples, C. D. Harris, 'A functional classification of cities in the United States', *Geographical Review*, vol. 33 (1943), pp. 86–99. H. J. Nelson, 'A service classification of American cities', *Economic Geography*, vol. 31 (1955), pp. 189–210. C. A. Moser and W. Scott, *British Towns: A Statistical Study of their Social and Economic Differences* (Edinburgh: Oliver & Boyd, 1961).

38 W. Goodwin, *op. cit.*, Table 1, p. 7.

39 *Ibid.*, pp. 7–8.

40 Goodwin also suggests that apart from concentration of offices, they should also undertake widespread control, both spatially and in industrial groups, as well as separation from production facilities. He has plotted maps of the plants controlled by industrial headquarters in the major cities and finds that in 1963 only New York and

Chicago offices had plants in all 48 of the co-
terminous United States and Canada. A city
whose control did not extend to at least 24 states
and Canada is not regarded by Goodwin as
having the status of management centre.

41   *Ibid.*, pp. 15–16.

42   R. B. Armstrong, *op. cit.*, pp. 40–2.

43   It must be remembered that the *Fortune* or *Times
1000* lists provide an incomplete guide to the true
status of any city because only a fraction of all
industrial and non-industrial companies in each
country are included. There are other sources
such as the U.S. Census *Enterprise Statistics*
(1963), the *Census of Business: Selected Services*
(1958 and 1963), unpublished Factories Inspectorate data for Britain, or various other miscellaneous sources.

44   R. K. Semple, 'Recent trends in the spatial concentration of corporate headquarters', *Economic
Geography*, Vol. 49 (1973), pp. 309–18.

45   *Dispersal of Government Work from London* (The
Hardman Report) (London: Her Majesty's Stationery Office, Cmd 5322, 1973), Table 1(2), p. 20.

CHAPTER 7

Intra-Urban Office Location

At first sight the wide range of office activities which occupy space in urban areas do not appear to share common location factors. But the actual range of work taking place within offices is broadly similar, irrespective of the type of industry or service which they represent. Record-keeping or negotiation is just as important in the headquarters office of a chemical company as it is in the office of a life insurance group. Given this standardization, on a general basis, of intra-office activities, it becomes much easier to seek common locational controls on offices of all types of economic activity.

PARALLELS WITH LOCATION OF MANUFACTURING INDUSTRY

As a starting point in the study of office location it is worthwhile attempting to establish whether there are any analogies with industrial location theory. Compared with office location, the study of industrial location is well advanced and is based on well developed models and theories which have been extensively tested and improved.[1] The literature on industrial location is extensive and reflects a long history of continuous interest in adequate explanation of observed and future patterns. Interest in office location is much more recent, despite the pioneering efforts of Haig in 1927,[2] and past references to it have been both spasmodic and largely attributable to the same source area. This area is New York and data on the location of office functions in the New York Metropolitan Region led Hoover and Vernon to suggest that 'common locational forces have been operating to create the distribution of (office) jobs, and that most of these are forces already encountered in our analysis of manufacturing'.[3]

The optimum location for a manufacturing plant is that which minimizes the cost of inputs such as labour or transport and maximizes profits within the framework of a general equilibrium system made up of producers and consumers.[4] The decision to select any particular site is based upon anticipated costs and revenues for several alternatives. Transport costs, comprising the assembly of the raw materials or semi-manufactured goods at the location and distribution of the finished goods to the market, are a major factor when choosing a location for a manufacturing plant. Because the raw materials used by offices are less tangible than the materials used by manufacturing plants and the finished product is equally difficult to define, transport costs are much more difficult to relate to office location. They not only represent the costs of physically gathering and distributing material on paper but also involve transmission and exchange of information along telecommunications channels. The influence of the distance factor, which is so important for the transport costs of manufacturing plants, can generally be said to be less important for offices. It costs the same to send a 2 oz letter to a destination 500 miles away as it does to send it to an address in the same street as its origin. Telephone charges are scaled according to distance zones from the origin of the call but they become uniform for calls to destinations over 50 miles in Britain. The regularity of production requirements and distribution patterns for manufacturing plants also makes it relatively easier to estimate cost differentials between locations. It is much more difficult for offices, with their highly variable demands for daily telephone links for example, to estimate transport cost differences of alternative locations.

The influence of the market adds an important

second dimension to industrial location theory. In many cases the need to have access to a large market will outweigh transport cost factors so that manufacturing industry has increasingly gravitated towards major concentrations of population or to areas where the industries which they supply with components are located. A market-orientated location with a large population will also possess a large and varied supply of labour, will promote economies in processing costs, and will give access to a wide range of supporting services. Although often separate from the manufacturing plant, an office will certainly require a location giving good access to its market. Much of the work of an office involves promotion of its company's goods or services as efficiently and competitively as possible. This is best achieved at the centre of population and communications appropriate to the national, regional or local market within which the office operates. Clients may also require to use an office for negotiations or demonstrations of a product or service and location close to the market again becomes relevant. It has also been suggested in Chapter 3 that office activities are demanding a wider range of employees with increasingly specialized skills. A market-based location invariably narrows the choice to the larger cities for most offices because the larger the population, the wider the range of office skills likely to be available. Availability of the right kind of labour is at least as important in office location choice as it is for industrial location. But as we shall see later, the precise role of market factors in office location depends on the type of office and the size of the market which it serves.

Manufacturing industry may also be attracted to a market location because of the benefits derived from agglomeration economies.[5] The three major economies are: economies of scale, localization economies, and urbanization economies.[6] Hence, some firms process the products of other industries and therefore benefit from close association with their suppliers. Others use waste products, such as various types of scrap from steel manufacture, to produce new goods, while some plants require specialist services at infrequent intervals. The latter will only be supplied where the demand is high enough to justify locating in an area. Economies of scale derived

from close spatial association are also important to offices, either because they require rapid communication and exchange of information, as in the case of financial offices, or because of the knowledge and expertise provided by adjacent office activities are essential to the operation of certain types of office, such as the headquarters of multi-divisional or multi-national corporations. It must be stressed, however, that the consequences of these agglomerative forces are very different for factory and office location. Manufacturing industries are not concentrated in particular urban areas and the agglomerations which have formed may cover very large areas such as the textile industries of North West England or the chemical industries of the Mersey estuary. Most office activities, on the other hand, are almost exclusively agglomerated in a limited number of urban areas and within very small areas within individual cities.

Therefore, transport and communication costs, markets, labour availability, and scale economies all have a role to play in the location of office activities. The major difference between industrial and office location rests with the role of raw material availability and transfer costs. Office raw materials, primarily information of various kinds, can be exchanged in a variety of ways with almost equal success from any location. In this way the relative advantages of alternative locations for office activity are, in theory at least, smoothed out. Offices should be less locationally constrained than manufacturing plants, yet all the evidence shows that they are more concentrated than all other types of economic activity.

The analogy between industrial and office location within urban areas can be taken a stage further. Using material from work by Martin on the industrial areas of London,[7] Hamilton suggests three types of industry occupying distinctive locations in a large metropolis.[8] The first group are the industries in central locations because of their dependence on high levels of access by skilled labour from the city as a whole, e.g. the printing industry; to the central business district which provides the main outlet for their goods, e.g. the bespoke clothing industry; or to the regional and national market for the distribution of the goods, e.g. newspapers. Most of the industries in this group are small scale. They are not large consumers of space and therefore they can just afford to remain in and around the C.B.D. Certain types of office parallel these location requirements. The headquarters of major corporations, banks, and other financial services require 'élite' and skilled personnel as well as accessibility to their markets and to other offices in the centre. A central location is therefore vital to offices of this type.

Industries in the second group depend less on skilled labour but rely more on ease of material assembly and efficient production methods. Consequently, they are often large scale and require more land than the first group and are found along arterial routes out of the city, particularly major highways, railways, and port or river frontages. These industries will be grouped because they seek similar transport advantages to their competitiors within the urban area. It is more difficult to identify offices which mirror this industrial group. It may be noted, however, that all offices cannot obtain, or indeed do not require, a C.B.D. location and offices of smaller firms with city or sub-regional markets are more likely to be located outside the centre. Offices performing purely administrative functions could be classified in this group but they will not follow the pattern of location shown by industry; they will tend to locate in suburban commercial nuclei where basic supporting services are available. These suburban nodes will also have good transport links with the centre as well as with areas outside the city.

The third group are large scale industries which, although often dependent on skilled labour and good distribution facilities, either create environmental conflicts or are very large space consumers. Therefore, they are unable to obtain locations anywhere other than the fringe areas of the city, e.g. the iron and steel industry or oil refining. There are no offices which directly parallel the location attributes of this group of industries, mainly because the criteria determining location are not relevant except where office activities are attached to the industries concerned.

Generalized industrial location models of this type provide a useful framework for identifying some aspects of office location in urban areas. Clearly, they can only provide partial answers because outside the C.B.D. offices tend to seek locations which resemble, at a smaller scale, the characteristics of the central area. Industrial location does not follow this pattern of behaviour. It is also apparent that, although some industries require C.B.D. locations, offices occupy a much larger proportion of the total floorspace or the land area of a metropolitan C.B.D. The reverse occurs in the suburbs which still satisfy the space requirements of industry rather than offices.

INTRA-URBAN OFFICE LOCATION: SOME EMPIRICAL EVIDENCE

The C.B.D. dominates office location patterns in urban areas (Fig. 30). Its role has already been outlined in Chapter 6 (Table 31) in the context of the conurbation centres and the statistics for 21 S.M.S.A.s in the United States further illustrates this point.[9] Some 40 per cent of the office employment in all 21 areas is located in the C.B.D. but New York S.M.S.A. has 63 per cent in Manhattan, Washington S.M.S.A. has 63 per cent, and Houston S.M.S.A., 68 per cent. If the central cities are included, approximately two-thirds of the 6 m. office workers are employed there and more than one-third of the C.B.D. office jobs are located in Manhattan. The amount of office floorspace in the 21 C.B.D.s has also increased between 1960 and 1970, particularly in New York, Washington, Los Angeles, and Chicago S.M.S.A.s. The dominance of Manhattan is again apparent; its floorspace increased by the equivalent total for the next largest downtown areas, Chicago, Washington, Philadelphia, Boston, and Los Angeles.[10] Although 20 per cent of the national increase in floorspace between 1960 and 1970 was concentrated in the 21 C.B.D.s, their total share of national inventory decreased by 1 per cent from 24 to 23 per cent in 1970.

It is not surprising, therefore, that empirical studies designed to establish reasons for office location have focused attention on the C.B.D.

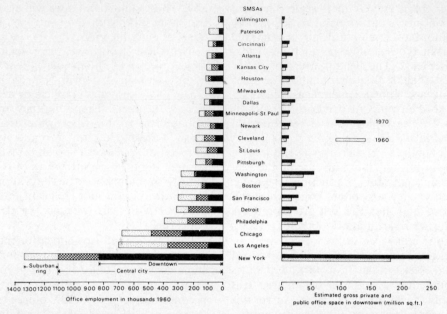

Fig. 30   Office Employment in Downtown, Central City and Suburban Ring, 1960, and Gross Public and Private Office Floorspace in Downtown, 1960–70, United States—Selected S.M.S.A.s (Data: R. B. Armstrong, *The Office Industry: Patterns of Growth and Location*, 1972)

Such studies aid our understanding and explanation of office location, at least in the context of the central area, and provide some material for developing hypotheses.

In a survey of 571 offices in central and outer Greater London, Cowan found that the largest proportion (24 per cent) mentioned proximity to clients as a factor which made their address a suitable location.[11] A further 16 per cent listed 'near to a specified place' as an important reason and this is associated with proximity to clients. Offices outside central London mentioned rather different reasons, particularly 'reasonably central' (13 per cent), 'good communications' (12 per cent), and 'suitable rent' (8 per cent). Almost all the firms which needed proximity to clients or to be near a specific place were in central London and mentioned either the money, commodity and other markets of the City or the central government ministries in the Whitehall area. Cowan notes that over 50 per cent of the central London respondents mentioned only one reason while nearly 80 per cent of the non-central firms gave more than one. The latter have probably

given more thought to the suitability of their location than the former, particularly if they have moved out from central London. It is also notable that the seven reasons most frequently mentioned by firms were all communications orientated. It is only after these initial 'transport' considerations that the costs of 'suitable locations' begin to be considered, particularly by central London firms.

The results of an earlier survey of central London offices by the Economist Intelligence Unit (E.I.U.) are broadly similar although the analysis is more detailed.[12] Firms were asked to rank the four main reasons for having their offices in central London (Table 37). When the first choices were taken and expressed as a proportion of all reasons (there were nine reasons in the list of location factors given to respondents), contact with external organizations accounted for 54·1 per cent of the prime (first) reasons, tradition, 9·8 per cent, communications with the rest of the United Kingdom, 6·7 per cent, and prestige 5·9 per cent. Prestige was most frequently mentioned as a subsidiary reason, while 'tradi-

TABLE 37
REASONS FOR LOCATION OF OFFICES
IN CENTRAL LONDON

Locational factors	Reasons in order of priority (%)			
	1st	2nd	3rd	4th
Contact with external organizations	54·1	20·7	10·0	5·4
Contact with internal departments	5·1	14·9	5·7	7·8
Contact with parent/associate companies	3·1	3·7	7·1	5·4
Communications with rest of U.K.	6·7	14·9	15·6	13·9
Internal communications	5·1	12·4	10·9	8·4
Supply of staff	2·8	6·2	17·1	12·1
Tradition	9·8	10·3	6·6	20·5
Prestige	5·9	12·0	22·8	22·3
Central location for international firm	3·1	1·7	0·5	2·4
Central position for convenience of overseas customers	—	0·8	0·8	0·6
Contact with government, quasi government and national institutions	3·5	1·6	1·9	1·2
Central position in area of operations	0·8	0·8	1·0	—
Total	100·0	100·0	100·0	100·0
Number of respondents	255	242	211	166

Source: Economist Intelligence Unit, *A Survey of Factors Governing the Location of Offices in the London Area,* A Report prepared for the Location of Offices Bureau (London: E.I.U., 1964), Table CI 4, p. 6.

tion' declined quickly after its inclusion as a first choice. The prestige factor was the most frequently mentioned third and fourth reason given by firms. Factors such as the supply of staff or internal communications were infrequently listed and account for only 7·9 per cent of the prime reasons. Contact with government, quasi-government and national institutions is also much less important than indicated by the firms in Cowan's survey.

The E.I.U. survey also asked 130 firms outside central London to indicate the four most important reasons for choosing their present location (Table 38). The principal first reason was availability of suitable office space which was listed by 20·8 per cent of the respondents, followed by good communications with London, 10 per cent. In contrast to the central London offices, a good labour supply was important to the non-central firms, particularly as a second or third order reason for choice of location. But however good the labour supply at a particular location, firms cannot utilize it until office space becomes avail-

able. Consequently, labour supply becomes a secondary factor unless vacant space becomes available at the right location at the right time for each firm. Communications again form a large proportion of the reasons given for location choice and are clearly important to most offices, whether in central area or suburban locations. One of the difficulties with assessing these statistics is that the location factors listed in Tables 37 and 38 are not mutually exclusive. Unless they are carefully defined, 'close to London' and 'good communications with London' (Table 38), or 'internal communications' and 'contact with internal departments' (Table 37) could be interpreted by respondents as meaning the same thing. The relative roles of some of the factors listed could therefore be understated.

There is one important difference between the findings of the E.I.U. survey and the results of Cowan's work. This concerns the role of prestige as a location factor. Most studies of office activity refer to prestige as a major consideration in location choice and the E.I.U. survey showed

TABLE 38
REASONS FOR LOCATION OF OFFICES
OUTSIDE CENTRAL LONDON

Locational factors	Reasons in order of priority (%)			
	1st	2nd	3rd	4th
Close to London	6·9	23·1	12·4	13·9
Good communications with London	10·0	14·3	20·6	4·2
Good international communications	—	—	3·1	11·1
Good communications with rest of U.K.	3·1	5·4	1·0	6·9
Good labour supply	0·8	11·6	18·6	8·3
Cheap labour supply	—	—	5·2	2·8
Low office rent	10·0	10·7	8·2	8·3
Suitable office available	20·8	8·9	11·3	15·2
Suitable site available	4·6	0·9	—	—
Near factory/warehouse	10·0	2·7	1·0	1·4
Near suitable housing	0·8	3·6	5·2	4·2
Good educational facilities	—	—	—	2·8
Close to home of director(s)	6·1	—	1·0	1·4
Staff live nearby	2·3	0·9	—	1·4
Low total cost	0·8	1·8	1·0	2·8
Near distribution centre	0·8	0·9	—	—
Space available for expansion	1·5	0·9	—	1·9
Ease of local travel	0·8	1·8	—	2·8
Good amenities/pleasant surroundings	0·8	0·9	5·2	2·8
Always located there/tradition	7·7	2·7	—	—
Other	12·2	8·9	6·2	8·3
Total	100·0	100·0	100·0	100·0
Number of respondents	130	112	97	72

Source: Economist Intelligence Unit, *A Survey of Factors Governing the Location of Offices in the London Area*, A Report prepared for the Location of Offices Bureau (London. E.I.U., 1964), Table I 10, p. 115.

it to be 'important' or 'very important' for 68·3 per cent of the respondents.[13] Cowan's survey produced a figure of just 4 per cent (23 firms). Such a large discrepancy could hardly have arisen by chance. It underlines the influence of questionnaire design and survey technique on survey conclusions. In the E.I.U. survey, prestige was explicitly listed as a location variable, while Cowan did not prompt respondents on any location factors; each firm was simply asked to indicate the factors which influenced its location. In the absence of a 'reminder' or 'prompt' in a list of possible factors, prestige seems less likely to be evaluated as a location variable by many office organizations.

The E.I.U. survey does concede, however, that the general importance of the prestige factor in office location is uncertain. It seems that the size of the office may be a pertinent consideration.[14] Prestige was considered 'important' or 'very important' by 75 per cent (61) of the offices in central London employing less than 500 staff. For firms employing more than 500 staff the equivalent figure was 70 per cent (54) and if offices employing over 5000 staff are excluded, the figure becomes 68 per cent. Over 81 per cent of the respondents considering prestige to be 'important' or 'very important' (142 out of 174 respondents) related it to clients, with 80 of them also indicating its 'public' relevance. Certain manufacturing companies therefore consider a central London address prestigious because of its affect on the image of the company and, possibly, its products. Some firms also related prestige to their links with the financial institutions from which they obtained loans, etc. reasoning that it increased their credibility and chances of obtaining funds. In the case of smaller firms, the prestige derived from a central area location may also reflect their dependence upon larger organizations for business, rather than on prestige in the broader, national sense.

Prestige may not, therefore, be as important as is so often assumed in most office location studies. Its precise role will always be difficult to quantify because, like 'tradition' in office location, it is not a tangible variable. The truth may lie somewhere between the E.I.U. figures and Cowan's extremely low values. A survey of offices which had moved, or been newly established in central Manchester, during the last ten years produced a rating of 42 for prestige, on a scale of 0–100.[15] The study also showed that there is no clear relationship between office function and the role of location factors such as prestige. Banks, insurance companies, and professional services, however, do stand out in terms of the emphasis placed on prestige and accessibility, while professional services offices also stress the importance of locational prestige for staff recruitment. The offices of manufacturing companies gave below average ratings for most location factors, including prestige, at least in relation to central Manchester but Armstrong suggests that these companies do derive benefits from a central area location of the order of those experienced by other offices.[16] In central Manchester, manufacturing company offices were mainly interested in

staff and customer parking and the availability of hotels for clients. Compared to central London or Manhattan, there is greater intermixing of industrial and office land uses in central Manchester, so that some manufacturing offices may have emphasized reasons which are related to the factories to which some are attached.

The above conclusions are corroborated by the findings of a survey in Wellington, New Zealand.[17] Prestige was a factor only considered by 3 out of 50 firms interviewed while access to contacts was a major influence on the location of 82 per cent of the firms, including all the offices in transport and finance. Staffing was a major locational influence for less than 50 per cent of the firms and almost 40 per cent considered that it had no effect on location choice. Parking, staffing, and access to contacts were, however, mentioned specifically at interview while prestige was not. Hence, discrepancies in survey methodology lead to wide differences in the role attributed to the various factors affecting office location. It is clear, however, that although the details vary, the relative importance of the main location factors is consistently expressed in the findings of different surveys.[18] In order of importance the major location factors are therefore: communications (both inside and outside the central area), staffing, rents and related costs, and prestige/tradition. Communications take on several forms and influence office activities in various ways; this theme will therefore be considered in greater detail in the next chapter.

HAIG'S CONTRIBUTION TO OFFICE LOCATION STUDIES

Haig's contribution to the analysis of office location rests on his discussion of the role of accessibility and the costs of friction on the location of economic activity in the city.[19] He uses the term accessibility in the sense of the ease or difficulty of contact which it permits between activities; this contact being provided by transport which overcomes the friction of distance necessary for contact to be made. Activities organize themselves in urban space according to the degree with which they can afford to turn accessibility into profits.[20] Some activities will be able

to outbid others for particular sites at any given level of accessibility. Because some sites are afforded better accessibility by superior transportation there is more competitive bidding for them, so that their value, and subsequently rents, will be higher than less accessible points in the urban area.[21] The centre of the city is the point where transportation costs for an activity serving the entire city and/or region can be reduced to a minimum. Office activities clearly fall into this category and have much to gain from location at the centre. Site rents and transportation costs, the 'costs of friction', are closely interlinked so that 'while transportation overcomes friction, site rentals plus transportation costs represent the social cost of what friction remains' and 'an economic activity in seeking a location finds that, as it approaches the centre, site rents increase and transportation costs decline. As it retreats from the centre, site rents decline and transportation costs increase.'[22] The theoretically perfect site for any office is that which involves the lowest costs of friction.

The financial district of Manhattan in the Wall Street and 42nd Street areas is used by Haig to illustrate his ideas. Finance is almost exclusively an office-based activity and includes insurance offices, banks, stock and foreign exchanges, unit trust companies, and various other types of finance house.[23] But why should offices of this kind be so highly clustered in the centre: they do not appear to rely heavily on good transportation facilities? Such offices deal almost exclusively in information which is exchanged via telecommunications channels and face-to-face meetings. The New York Region's telephone, cable, and other facilities all converge upon the C.B.D. and permit information to move inwards and outwards with great ease. Face-to-face meetings in the form of conferences, meetings with lawyers, solicitors, accountants or directors, for example, do not form part of Haig's theory but they are a vital part of the communications network which leads to close spatial association of financial offices. The men involved in these meetings are normally of managerial status and above and the ability to have meetings arranged quickly and problems resolved expediously leads to efficient use of their valuable time.

Haig suggests that the financial district in Manhattan can be viewed as 'one big structure' and the 'geometrical proposition that the contents of two spheres are to each other as the cubes of their diameters has sent skyscrapers into the air'.[24] Skyscrapers are described as the economical way to produce space in the centre of the city. The need for close linkages between financial offices means that they are prepared to outbid all others for the site they require. This, of course, assumes that the scale of the financial transactions being undertaken and the speed necessary for making decisions outweighs the disadvantages of less accessible locations at lower cost where the same decisions could, in theory at least, be made.

Some empirical evidence cited by Haig underlines the interdependence of financial offices. In 1926, 40 of the 95 main offices of commercial banks in Manhattan were located south of Fulton Street and these included all the really large banks.[25] More than 60 per cent of the local depositors were also located south of Fulton Street, i.e. other firms, and in a sample of four large banks, 50 per cent of the accounts were with customers outside New York. This stresses the benefits arising from a location at the nub of communications. In addition, the Clearing House, the Federal Reserve Bank, the Sub-Treasury, and the Custom House were all in the Wall Street section. Such a concentration of banking activities has subsequently led to the attraction of other activities. The headquarters offices of investment bankers are found in the Wall Street area and the head offices of insurance companies. The latter place a high premium on the convenience of being near to the large sources of finance required to underwrite the numerous range of risks which they try to accommodate. Whilst this factor binds the insurance companies to the banks, the fact that insurance companies often spread the risks on large policies amongst each other binds the insurance activities of a particular type together. Hence, the life insurance companies were located north of Fulton Street, the marine interests in William Street, and the fire insurance companies in Maiden Lane and Fulton Street.

MORE RECENT CONTRIBUTIONS

Haig's references to office activities were brief but succinct and they undoubtedly laid the foundations for later work. Most of the reasons he advanced for concentration, particularly with reference to financial offices, still hold true today. The emphasis on location studies of financial offices was continued by Robbins and Terleckyj who have written at length on the role of these activities in the New York Region.[26] At about the same time, Lichtenberg adopted a wider approach, dividing offices into financial and other office work.[27] The latter includes central administrative offices of corporations; the offices of supporting activities such as advertising, engineering, public relations, employment agencies; the offices of central and local government, unions and business associations; and numerous other businesses. The reasons put forward for the location of office activities in Manhattan by Robbins and Terleckyj and by Lichtenberg bear a marked resemblance to those propounded 30 years earlier by Haig, except that they are examined in greater detail and illustrated by more sophisticated examples. A visiting corporate official, for example, would 'visit' the financial institutions and 'shop around' and inspect the intangible opportunities for financing or investing, while negotiations in the money market require face-to-face communications.[28] It is also pointed out that not all the transfer of products or information is intangible in the financial area; stock certificates pass by hand between brokerage houses and the stock clearing companies of the two New York exchanges. Speed is all important and one of the rules of the stock clearing operation of New York Stock Exchange is that a member firm must keep an office in downtown Manhattan.[29]

The main point emerging from the two analyses is the role of markets as a factor in intra-urban office location. This was alluded to by Haig but not stressed in his argument. Lichtenberg suggests that the 'key to the whole complex of *non-financial* offices is that portion which most directly serves the nation'.[30] He is referring, in particular, to the headquarters offices of the manufacturing corporations which, as already shown, are most highly concentrated in Manhattan and the New York Region generally. These offices contain the decision-making élite, 'producing' the solutions to a range of 'atypical' problems which need to be solved by synthesizing large volumes of up-to-date information and by seeking the advice of the appropriate expertise surrounding them in the city centre. As with financial offices, the need for speed and efficiency

in the decision-making process makes it unsatisfactory for executives to move between plant(s) and head office to obtain information, while the nature of the problems encountered often precludes use of the telephone but depends on face-to-face contact.

Hoover and Vernon also cover much of the same ground as Lichtenberg.[31] They refer to the common centralizing force of the 'money market' on financial offices. This is just one of the internal markets of the financial core of a major city; others include the bill market, the stock market, the bullion market, the foreign exchange market, the Euro-dollar market, the inter-bank call loan market, and the local authority loans market.[32] The various types of financial offices have links with some of all of these internal markets. Hence, British overseas banks have connections with all of them, while discount houses are only connected to the stock, bill, and money markets. It is important, therefore, to distinguish between those markets which largely operate within the central area and those which also operate externally. The latter particularly influence the location of manufacturing offices which are not directly connected to the internal money and other markets.

A further dimension to the dominance of the central area in office location is added by the requirement for large numbers of support workers. The decision-making élite in the merchant banks or major manufacturing company headquarters require extensive clerical and other support, both to collect and to provide them with pertinent information, and to ensure proper control and monitoring of the company's affairs. Supporting office staff outnumber higher management and the decision-makers by 50 or even 100 to 1 and there are therefore obvious advantages in locating within areas where public transport and other facilities converge. It is also likely, however, that the City of London or Manhattan could not exist as foci for office activities if the cost of office space was very much higher than elsewhere. The rents for premium buildings are always well above the local level, they have reached over £25/ft^2 for a few buildings at prime locations in the City, but older and more standard office stock in the same area can be rented at levels only slightly higher than elsewhere in

TABLE 39
LOCATION OF HEADQUARTERS, MIDDLE MARKET, AND
LOCAL OFFICE EMPLOYMENT — NEW YORK REGION, 1965

Area	Jobs in office buildings					
	Head-quarters	% of total	Middle market	% of total	Local market	% of total
Manhattan C.B.D.	368090	80·1	404420	55·5	31910	8·7
Rest of core	27860	6·1	148590	20·4	166080	45·0
Inner ring	29580	6·4	87550	12·0	86800	23·5
Intermediate ring	28670	6·2	75600	10·4	59350	16·1
Outer ring	5110	1·1	13100	1·8	24870	6·7
Total	459310	100·0	729260	100·0	369010	100·0
% of all jobs in office buildings	29·5		46·8		23·7	

Note: Detail may not add up because of rounding.
Source: Regional Plan Association data in R. B. Armstrong, *The Office Industry: Patterns of Growth and Location* (Cambridge, Mass.: The M.I.T. Press, 1972), Table 4.6, p. 97.

central London. If this was not the case, many of the supporting office activities and staff could not be accommodated at a cost most companies could afford.

The most recent work by Armstrong on office location in the New York Metropolitan Region builds upon the market-orientated approach advocated by Lichtenberg and others. He suggests that there are three categories of office jobs, each related to the economic-base concept and the export of office services. These are headquarters, middle market, and local market office jobs.[33] It should be stressed that Armstrong views these markets as external rather than internal to the office system and they influence the location of a much wider range of activity.

The headquarters market comprises office jobs which primarily export their services to national or international areas. These offices are involved in the most complex operations and are well represented in the manufacturing and non-manufacturing sectors as well as by central government offices of national importance. The requirements of these offices are many and varied so that the benefits of concentration will only be reaped in the largest urban centres. Numerically, the number of headquarters jobs in the New York Region is exceeded by the middle market offices but headquarters are usually the largest office units in a city and certainly the most

important influence on regional growth and stability (Table 39). It is not surprising that in 1965, over 80 per cent of the headquarters office jobs in the New York Region were located in Manhattan.

Middle market office jobs are ubiquitous to most regions and provide services for areas within their regions. They account for 47 per cent of the office jobs in the New York Region, for example, and include branch offices serving regional needs as well as offices which service headquarters offices at the core of a region, such as market research, public relations or advertising. The location of middle market offices is guided by population distribution and/or the location of headquarters offices, so that 50 per cent of the middle market jobs are in Manhattan and the remainder distributed throughout the Region. Because they represent such a large proportion of total employment, middle market offices depend heavily on the availability of a suitable labour force. This constrains location choice to central city areas accessible by office workers. Armstrong therefore suggests that these offices will rarely operate in regions with a population of less than 150,000.

Areas of under 150,000 population are served by local market offices. These are offices which benefit from locations close to the population which they serve; solicitors, branches of various financial offices, local government offices or estate agents would be examples. The figure of 150,000 or less was arrived at by establishing the minimum requirements for office jobs in small groups of primarily residential municipalities in the New York Region. Armstrong calculates the figure to be two office jobs for every 100 residents; if the ratio is higher than this it is assumed that the offices belong to the middle market or headquarters category. Table 39 shows that local market jobs are therefore poorly represented in Manhatten but become proportionally more important at locations further from the centre. In the outer ring they represent more than 55 per cent of the total office jobs. Some 23 per cent of these jobs are in the inner ring which had 25 per cent of the population of the Region in 1965.

OFFICE CENTRALITY AND TYPE OF INDUSTRY

It should be apparent from the preceeding discussion that the offices of different industries are not uniformly represented in the central area. This has led Armstrong to conclude that 'the more consumer oriented and/or non-durable is a firm's product, the stronger is the need or desire to be headquartered in a central location'.[34] Although this conclusion is made with reference to manufacturing headquarters, it might equally be applied to non-manufacturing offices which deal in their own kind of non-durable product. One would therefore expect the proportion of office workers in certain industries to be over-represented, compared with the national distribution, in central areas (Table 40). It is not possible to identify headquarters from other office workers in the statistics for the City, central London (excluding the City), and England and Wales, but the results provide a rough guide to the variations in the centrality tendencies of different industries.

Of the service industries, insurance, banking, and finance offices reveal particularly high concentrations in the City of London. While 2·3 per cent of all office workers in England and Wales in 1961 were in these activities, they employed 28·7 per cent of the office workers in the City. A similar pattern is shown by other service industries, although the discrepancy between the City or central London and the national distribution is not as large. Hence, professional and scientific services accounted for 5·9 per cent of

TABLE 40
LOCATION OF OFFICE WORKERS BY INDUSTRY
IN THE CITY, CENTRAL LONDON (EXCLUDING CITY),
AND ENGLAND AND WALES, 1961

Industry	Percentage of employment 1961		
	City	Central London (ex. City)	England and Wales
Manufacturing and extractive	9·5	10·7	7·6
Transport and communication	9·0	4·7	1·7
Distributive trades	7·3	5·2	2·2
Insurance, banking and finance	28·7	4·2	2·3
Professional and scientific services	6·9	5·9	2·0
Other services	6·2	17·9	5·1
All services	58·0	38·0	13·2
Total	67·6	48·6	20·9

Source: *Census of Population 1961*, after J. H. Dunning and E. V. Morgan (eds), *An Economic Study of the City of London* (London: Allen & Unwin, 1971), Table 2.3, pp. 60–1.

the office workers in central London compared with 2 per cent for England and Wales. There is also evidence of specialization in office location as indicated by the important role of other services for office employment in central London (excluding the City) and the dominance of insurance, banking, and finance in the City.

Office workers in manufacturing and extractive offices are only over-represented in the City and central London by approximately 2 and 3 percentage points respectively. But this conceals important variations between industry groups. Table 40 does not allow these differences to be identified but the point can be illustrated with reference to manufacturing offices in the New York Region.[35] Hence, over 94 per cent of the headquarters offices of the leather industry are located in Manhattan compared with 25 per cent for the lumber and wood industries. Conversely, 21·9 per cent of the headquarters of printing and publishing are located in the inner ring with 64·1 per cent in Manhattan. The mean for all manufacturing industry headquarters is 72·1 per cent in Manhattan and the remainder distributed between the various rings around the centre. Industries producing non-durable goods dominate the headquarters with above average concentration and these are activities which depend on access to consumer markets. Some examples are transportation, textiles, petroleum and coal, and leather. Industries producing durable goods are twice as numerous amongst the headquarters with below average concentration in Manhattan. They produce goods for the intermediate consumer market, i.e. other industries, and are therefore less in need of locations requiring access to consumer markets in the broadest sense. Indeed, the headquarters offices of electrical machinery or fabricated metals industries are more likely to be influenced by the location of the industries they serve than by the trend towards a central area location amongst headquarters in general.

Variations in the centrality tendencies of manufacturing offices can be further related to the character of inter-industry office relationships. The first of these are links with purchasing establishments which range from individual households to multi-product corporations and government establishments. Depending on the types of purchasing establishment and their numbers, industries will utilize a number of communications methods to reach their market. If the purchasers are few in number, contact with the market is probably best achieved by face-to-face meetings. This encourages location near to the offices of purchasers. If the market is large and diffuse, perhaps almost exclusively made up of individual households, advertising is likely to be the means of communication used to influence the market. Therefore industries depending on households as their main purchasers, such as leather, apparel, and tobacco, have strong central preferences because the concentration of marketing, advertising, and media services in the C.B.D. exerts a powerful pull on their headquarters offices. But the bulk of manufacturing industries are geared towards other producing industries as purchasers so that advertising is far less important. For these industries, offices which exhibit a stronger than average preference for central locations reflect dependence for income upon other sectors which tend to locate in the centre themselves or are strongly identified with it. Headquarters offices which are least dependent upon a central area location are those which are not subject to centralizing forces from their purchasing sectors, e.g. the leading purchasers from chemical industries are other industries within the chemical group.

The second group of links are those with production establishments. Headquarters location patterns will be influenced to some degree by factory distributions. There is some relationship between the distribution of factory employment in an industry and office employment in the various rings of the New York Region for example. But the effect of these links should not be overstated. Headquarters offices which have decentralized from Manhattan will invariably move to non-industrial sites such as office parks, rather than near their major production plants. Only 11 out of 28 major industry headquarters in the New York suburbs are in the same county as the production facilities which they control and represent. For some firms, however, there are certainly benefits to be derived from close spatial association of office and production facilities, particularly durable goods industries.

The pull of the production function of a company on the location of its offices assumes that separation of factory and office has in fact occurred. In cases where separation is about to take place, the choice of location for the office is likely to be influenced by at least two considerations.[36] First, to what extent is there a need for continual communication between the office and its plant(s)? The closer the juxtaposition of the two, the quicker this communication will be facilitated, but this might be at the expense of a location close to a pool of skilled labour and sources of information. Secondly, to what extent do the multiple duties of senior personnel, which include reference to production units and office

whether the location of a head office is right or wrong. Even if it is wrong, its effect on the company may not be revealed in a way which impairs its efficiency. Any response to a 'wrong' location will invariably be sluggish and not as catastrophic in economic terms as it would be for a manufacturing plant.

Some of the main points to emerge from this analysis of intra-urban office location are brought together in Fig. 31. It presents a simplified model of the relationship between types of office, the markets they serve, and location. The strength of the links between types of office and

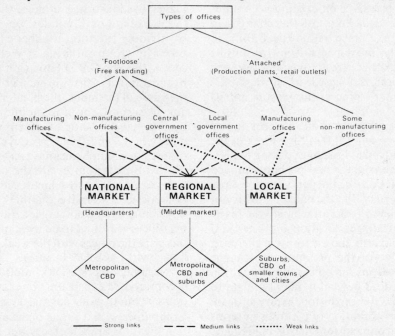

Fig. 31   Relationship Between Types of Office, Markets Served, and Location

operations, control the choice of location? There is no single answer to either of these problems but separation of office from production functions becomes essential when 'the economic benefits of obtaining and comparing information within the market become greater for the detached office than the cost–savings of directing production from a plant-attached site'.[37] Patterns of office location could perhaps be considered as a product of compromise, at least for manufacturing offices. It is difficult to know

external markets are also indicated in order to point to the relative dominance of different offices in the intra-urban locations specified. Clearly, many variables have been excluded from the model such as detailed inter-industry differences in location patterns; the influence of office size; or the effect of urban area size (population) on intra-urban office location. In addition, 'footloose' or free-standing office buildings which contain a large proportion of office space in cities are often associated with other uses, particularly retail uses in suburban centres and smaller towns and cities. Permission to provide office space is often granted on condition that a number of shop units are provided on the ground floor.

Such detailed influences on office location in urban areas must clearly be taken into account but would make generalized models of the type outlined in Fig. 31 unnecessarily complex.

INTRA-C.B.D. OFFICE LOCATION DYNAMICS

Office location cannot be viewed as a static component of the urban system. The location requirements of individual offices, or of groups of related office activities, will change through time in response to the changing distribution of other activities or to pressures on existing accommodation and facilities. Many of the changes in office location take place within the C.B.D., in addition to any movements from within its boundaries to other areas outside. For the present, attention is focused on intra-C.B.D. office mobility and some of the reasons for its occurrence.

In a study of office location in Leeds it was found that 57 per cent (217) of the offices in the core area had moved at least once during the last 20 years.[38] Some of these had probably moved two or three times during the period but 66·8 per cent had remained within the core.[39] This is not surprising in view of the attachment of many offices to a central area location but one-third of the offices had still chosen to leave the core. This is indicative of the pressures for change within it. The reasons for offices moving within the core, and indeed beyond it, mainly relate to insufficient space for expansion, expiry of lease or unsatisfactory condition of premises in terms of working environment for staff or inadequate facilities. Firms anticipating moves in Leeds placed more emphasis, however, on car parking problems than insufficient floorspace although it is likely that in the final analysis, the latter will be more likely to initiate a move. Facey and Smith were unable to identify any significant differences between the reasons for moving given by different types of office. But Merriman, working in Christchurch, found that floorspace and related problems were particularly important to government offices, insurance, and oil companies while parking problems were considered extremely important by land agents, surveyors, and manufacturers' agents.[40] Parking problems

will always be important in the central area but floorspace difficulties will vary according to the success and growth of a firm.

Office mobility varies according to size, function, status, and age of present premises.[41] Davey has illustrated some of the variations by the use of a mobility index which is calculated by dividing the total number of moves undertaken by groups of firms in Wellington (84 per cent within the C.B.D.) during a ten-year period by the number of firms in each group. The higher the value of the index, the greater the mobility of an office group. The most mobile offices, grouped by size, have 6–10 or 11–20 employees with indices of 0·72 and 0·74 respectively. Offices with more than 20 employees have an average mobility of 0·51. Smaller offices are the ones most likely to be expanding and which need to achieve the best possible external economies. These are often best achieved by changing location. Manufacturing offices are found to be most mobile (0·84) and these are the offices with the weakest 'traditional' links with C.B.D. locations. Financial and wholesaling offices are less mobile and prefer to accommodate expansion, for example, by development on, or adjacent to, their present site.[42] Companies with a single office are more mobile than head or branch offices but this reflects the likely size categories of these offices rather than any other attribute. Finally, mobility varies inversely with the age of office building at present occupied. The older the building occupied, the less likely it is that firms have moved during the last ten years. This excludes firms which have moved into space becoming available during the ten-year period and which must, therefore, have moved at least once.

This is an unexpected conclusion because many of the older office premises will be occupied by small firms with expansion prospects and which have been shown to be most mobile. This probably reflects the low cost of older space or the fact that small units of space cannot be obtained in the larger, newer office buildings in the C.B.D. Hence, of the 65 activities which had moved into the nineteenth-century Fitzroy Square area of central London, between 1950 and 1965, over half (35) stayed less than two years.[43] Many of these offices were small with each unit of office accommodation providing space for an average of 5·7 activities during the 15-year period. Financial companies, societies and associations, and professional and individual services were the activities which moved on after less than two years. The importance of the size factor in office mobility is suggested by the view that 'it

various postal districts between 1951 and 1966. The statistics for publishers are given in Table 41 and include the number of immigrant and emigrant firms for each postal district. These are firms listed in the 1951 and 1966 *Directories* but at different addresses. Firms listed in 1966 but not in 1951 are regarded as births and vice-versa for deaths. Goddard finds that most of the changes between 1951 and 1966 have not been caused by migration of existing offices between different parts of central London but by the appearance of new firms in one area and extinctions elsewhere. In the W.1 postal district, which had the largest total increase in publishers, some 80

TABLE 41

CHANGES IN THE NUMBER OF PUBLISHERS IN CENTRAL LONDON POSTAL DISTRICTS, 1951–66

| Postal district | Deaths | Births | Sources of Change | | Natural change | Migration change | Total |
			In-migration	Out-migration			
W.1	81	122	29	17	+41	+12	+53
S.W.1	37	28	4	14	−9	−10	−19
W.C.1	67	45	16	24	−22	−8	−30
W.C.2	76	49	21	26	−27	−5	−32
E.C.1	11	23	10	9	+12	+1	+13
E.C.2	12	7	3	8	−5	−5	−10
E.C.3	11	2	—	3	−9	−3	−12
E.C.4	88	62	19	23	−26	−4	−30
S.E.1	7	10	—	1	+3	−1	+2

Source: J. B. Goddard, 'Changing office location patterns within central London', *Urban Studies*, vol. 4 (1967), Table IV, p. 281.

does seem likely ... that short stay activities tend to be those occupying least space'.[44] But Cowan also found that in the longstanding office area of Threadneedle Street (City of London) 42 per cent of 1936 occupants were still there in 1963. This supports Davey's observations but suggests that age and location of an 'office area' must also be considered when evaluating existing and potential mobility of offices in the C.B.D.

Migration by existing office establishments only partially contributes to processes of change in the C.B.D., or elsewhere in a city. 'Births' of new and 'deaths' of existing establishments must also be considered.[45] By using *Kelly's Post Office Directories* for central London, Goddard was able to establish the number of births and deaths of publishers and advertising agencies in

per cent was caused by natural rather than migration change. In E.C.4, which lost 30 publishers during the study period, natural change was the major factor. Because many of the publishers are small firms, high turnover rates can be expected and this helps to explain the importance of natural change as opposed to migration.

Births, deaths, and migration of offices also contribute to shifts in the centre of gravity of office activities in the central area. Since 1918, book publishers' offices have migrated westwards in central London, initially from the City to Covent Garden because of the effects of bombing on the former, and subsequently to more scattered locations away from the established grouping in Covent Garden.[46]

Bannon has demonstrated the south-eastward migration of office establishments in central Dublin between 1940 and 1970 by calculating the 'mean centre' or 'centre of gravity' of office activity in each year.[47] In 1940 the centre of gravity of the aggregate total of office establishments was College Green but by 1970 it had migrated 600 m to the south. Of the 20 office categories identified in the study, 17 had shifted their centre of gravity by 1970. This migration is largely a response to changes in space demands which the core area has been unable to sustain. Changing relationships between office groups has also accelerated the process and it could well be that offices are becoming less tied to particular types of location than they were in the past, particularly before the war.[48] Improvements in telecommunications have undoubtedly helped to bring about this relaxation on some of the location constraints (see next chapter). There have also been significant changes in the overall pattern of office location in the central areas of Wellington and Christchurch.[49] Here, the movement has largely been from the core to the 'frame' surrounding the C.B.D.[50] Merriman suggests that office mobility of this type follows a cyclical pattern which reflects availability of accommodation in vacant space and from new construction.[51] Movement from core to fringe leaves space in the core for expansion of firms which remain but once this space is filled the rate of movement to the fringe will again increase.

Shifts in the centre of gravity or outward expansion of C.B.D. office activities often takes the forms of 'colonization' of predominantly residential areas. Residential property is easier to convert to office use than wholesale or manufacturing property, while it is also likely to be located in a congenial environment of the type attractive to office tenants. Many of the early colonizers will be small firms pushed out of the higher value locations by excessive costs or pressure on space and it is relatively easy for these firms to fit into the small office units initially provided by residential conversion. New firms will also tend to seek this kind of accommodation which, in the early stages, will be less prestigious and therefore cheaper to rent. As the area develops it becomes attractive to more, and possibly larger, firms who may move in to embryonic concentrations of similar, but smaller-scale, activities. Their larger space requirements can be accommodated by converting residences at present used by several small firms into single units of accommodation. This may cause movement of the small firms to other premises in the area or into new areas on the fringe. Finally, the colonized area may provide sufficient attractions to encourage large organizations to move in and this may involve construction of purpose-built office space by demolition and clearance of the converted residential properties. Hence, in 1886 over 50 per cent of the houses in Fitzroy Square were residential but by 1925 only two houses remained in this use and this had been reduced to one in 1965.[52] All the former residential façades have been retained and modern office buildings have not replaced them as yet. It remains to be seen whether the final stage in the office colonization process will be achieved.

The location of office activities within urban areas therefore consists of static and dynamic elements. The static elements are the factors which make various parts of an urban area attractive to different types of office activity. These elements also account for the clustering of interdependent office activities at separate locations within the C.B.D. or suburban office nuclei. Time and technological developments, particularly in the field of telecommunications, have perhaps made the static elements in office location less important but they still underlie location decision-making by most firms. The dynamic elements are the factors producing reorganization and realignment of office location patterns. So far, their effects have only been discussed in the context of the C.B.D. and its frame, but they have also been responsible for movement to other parts of cities and beyond. In some cities the C.B.D. has lost more offices through emigration than it has gained through immigration and the causes and consequences of this are discussed in more detail in a later chapter. Changes in office location at the intra-C.B.D. level are primarily over very short distances and it may take several decades for them to emerge as a definite spatial change or extension to existing functional groups of offices. In contrast, extra-C.B.D. migration has had more immediate consequences for office location patterns.

REFERENCES

1 See for example W. Isard, *Location and Space Economy* (Cambridge, Mass.: The M.I.T. Press, 1956). M. L. Greenhut, *Plant Location in Theory and Practice* (Chapel Hill: University of North Carolina Press, 1956). F. E. I. Hamilton, 'Models of industrial location', in R. J. Chorley and P. Haggett (eds), *Models in Geography* (London: Methuen, 1967). D. M. Smith, *Industrial Location: An Economic Geographical Analysis* (London: Wiley, 1971).

2 R. M. Haig, *Major Economic Factors in Metropolitan Growth and Arrangement* (New York: Committee on Regional Plan of New York and its Environs, Regional Survey, vol. 1, 1927).

3 E. M. Hoover and R. Vernon, *Anatomy of a Metropolis* (Cambridge, Mass.: Harvard University Press, 1959), p. 78.

4 For a full discussion of transport and other industrial location factors see D. M. Smith, *op. cit.*, pp. 23–94.

5 W. Isard, *Methods of Regional Analysis* (New York: Wiley, 1960), pp. 404–5.

6 W. L. Henderson and L. C. Lederbur, *Urban Economics: Processes and Problems* (New York: Wiley, 1972), pp. 48–57. W. Isard, *op. cit.*, pp. 68–75.

7 J. E. Martin, *Greater London: An Industrial Geography* (London: Bell, 1963).

8 F. E. I. Hamilton, *op. cit.*, pp. 408–10.

9 R. B. Armstrong, *The Office Industry: Patterns of Growth and Location* (Cambridge, Mass.: The M.I.T. Press, 1972), pp. 48–9.

10 *Ibid.*, p. 49.

11 P. Cowan *et al.*, *The Office: A Facet of Urban Growth* (London: Heinemann, 1969), pp. 104–6 and Table IV.14.

12 Economist Intelligence Unit, *A Survey of Factors Governing the Location of Offices in the London Area* (London: Economist Intelligence Unit, 1964), pp. 6–9. See also Interscan Ltd., *Survey of Offices in the Central Area* (London: Location of Offices Bureau, 1970).

13 *Ibid.*, Table C.I.8, p. 13.

14 *Ibid.*, Tables C.I.9 and C.I.10, pp. 14–15. See also M. J. Croft, *Offices in a Regional Centre: Follow-up Studies on Infra-Structure and Linkage* (London: Location of Offices Bureau, Research Paper, no. 3, 1969), pp. 65–70.

15 City of Manchester, *Central Manchester Office Survey 1971* (Manchester: City Planning Department, 1972), pp. 16–19 and Table 12.

16 R. B. Armstrong, *op. cit.*, pp. 69–70.

17 J. A. Davey, *The Office Industry in Wellington: A Study of Contact Patterns, Location and Employment* (Wellington: Ministry of Works, 1972), pp. 74–5 and Table 22. J. A. Davey, 'Wellington's office industry', *Pacific Viewpoint*, vol. 14 (1973), pp. 45–60.

18 For another example see M. J. Bannon, *Office Location in Ireland: The Role of Central Dublin* (Dublin: An Foras Forbartha, 1973), pp. 67–76.

19 R. M. Haig, *op. cit.*, pp. 38–42.

20 Profits include site rent.

21 For a fuller discussion of the theoretical bases of the urban real property market see B. Goodall, *The Economics of Urban Areas* (Oxford: Pergamon Press, 1972), pp. 48–79. R. Turvey, *The Economics of Real Property* (London: Allen & Unwin, 1957).

22 R. M. Haig, *op. cit.*, p. 39.

23 A more detailed discussion of the activities represented by the banking, finance and insurance sector is given in J. H. Dunning and E. V. Morgan (eds), *An Economic Study of the City of London* (London: Allen & Unwin, 1971), pp. 271–334.

24 R. M. Haig, *op. cit.*, p. 41.

25 *Ibid.*, pp. 101–3.

26 S. M. Robbins and N. E. Terleckyj, *Money Metropolis* (Cambridge, Mass.: Harvard University Press, 1960), pp. 25–147.

27 R. M. Lichtenberg, *One-Tenth of a Nation* (Cambridge, Mass.: Harvard University Press, 1960), pp. 144–77.

28 *Ibid.*, p. 151.

29 *Ibid.*, p. 152.

30 *Ibid.*, pp. 154–5.

31 E. M. Hoover and R. Vernon, *op. cit.*, pp. 88–112.

32 For a description of the 'markets' see J. H. Dunning and E. V. Morgan, *op. cit.*, pp. 156–9.

33 R. B. Armstrong, *op. cit.*, pp. 18–20 and 97–9.

34 *Ibid.*, p. 70.

35 *Ibid.*, Table 3.5 and pp. 69–75.

36 R. M. Lichtenberg, *op. cit.*, p. 156.

37 R. B. Armstrong, *op. cit.*, p. 18.

38 M. V. Facey and G. B. Smith, *Offices in a Regional Centre: A Study of Office Location in Leeds* (London: Location of Offices Bureau, Research Paper, no. 2, 1968), pp. 47–60.

39 Bannon has noted that of the 473 traceable migrations between 1960 and 1970 in central Dublin, 18 per cent were relocations within the same quadrats and therefore unlikely to exceed 400 m in length.

40 R. H. Merriman, 'Office movement in central

Christchurch, 1955–65', *New Zealand Geographer*, vol. 23 (1967), p. 123.

41   J. A. Davey, *op. cit.* (1972), pp. 82–7. S. M. Robbins and N. E. Terleckyj, *op. cit.*, pp. 100–3. See also J. A. Davey, 'Office location and mobility in Wellington', *New Zealand Geographer*, vol. 29 (1973), pp. 120–33.

42   Bannon has shown, however, that 25 per cent of the internal moves in central Dublin between 1960 and 1970 were made by financial offices. M. J. Bannon, *op. cit.*, p. 37.

43   P. Cowan *et al.*, *op. cit.*, pp. 94–5.

44   *Ibid.*, p. 96.

45   J. B. Goddard, 'Changing office location patterns within central London', *Urban Studies*, vol. 4 (1967), pp. 280–1.

46   *Ibid.*, pp. 282–3.

47   M. J. Bannon, *op. cit.*, pp. 31–7. See also M. J. Bannon, 'The changing centre of gravity of office establishments within central Dublin, 1940 to 1970', *Irish Geography*, vol. 6 (1972), pp. 480–4.

48   This has also been suggested by R. M. Pierce, 'Towards an optimum policy for office location' (University of Wales, unpublished M.Sc. Thesis, 1972).

49   J. A. Davey, *op. cit.* (1972), pp. 87–96. R. H. Merriman, *op. cit.*, pp. 129–30.

50   See E. M. Horwood and R. Boyce, *Studies of the Central Business District and Urban Freeway Development* (Seattle: University of Washington Press, 1959), p. 20.

51   The important role of the availability of accommodation has also been stressed by J. Rannells, 'Approaches to the analysis of the city centre', *Journal, American Institute of Planners*, vol. 27 (1961), pp. 17–25.

52   P. Cowan *et al.*, *op. cit.*, p. 91.

CHAPTER 8

Communications and Office Location

It has been suggested earlier that most office activity involves the collection, storage, recording, and transmission of information. These are essentially secondary office tasks which support the primary activities of generation, development, and implementation of ideas. Office location is much more a product of information flows than the movement of goods. It can therefore be reasoned that a better understanding of the way in which flows of information between offices are generated and accommodated by communications systems will add to our comprehension of the location of these activities. It will also allow better control of the contemporary location patterns exhibited by offices and reinforce predictions of future trends.

Whether communication is interpersonal or intermachine its aim, in the broadest sense, is the resolution of uncertainty.[1] Some, although by no means all, office work is concerned with resolving problems arising from uncertainty about markets, competitors, durability of products, sources of finance for new projects or legal matters. Hence, in an administrative sense, communication is 'the process of transmitting ideas or thoughts from one person to another, or within a single person, for the purpose of creating understanding in the thinking of the person receiving the communication'.[2] To 'create understanding' could be changed to 'resolving uncertainties' or 'solving problems'. Communication is a system involving a sender and a receiver which can utilize a number of channels which permit links to be achieved.

The urban system as a whole comprises a complex range of adapted space activities which require and generate the movement of information, goods, and people. Various forms of communication provide the linkages for fulfilling these requirements and have come to be recognized as a major influence on the location pattern of office and other urban activities. As the range

and degree of specialization of activities which fit into the urban system has widened, the volume and diversity of information flows through the system has increased and generated new communications channels to meet the new demands. Indeed, this process has been used by Meier to explain the growth of urban society in which cities have developed essentially to facilitate human communication at all levels of activity.[3] By schematically and empirically tracing the connections or linkages between establishments or individuals it becomes possible to describe the entire complex of urban activities.[4] Törnqvist has also hypothesized that one of the most important factors explaining the concentration of certain activities, among them offices, in large urban regions is the requirement for contacts and exchange of information between increasingly specialized functions in the community.[5]

Communication between any level of office activity, either endogenously or exogenously is achieved, either along physical channels such as railways, roads or airlines, or by means of a growing range of telecommunications (non-physical communications). The former are largely responsible for moving people and items such as correspondence while the latter permit rapid transfer of signals in the form of audio, visual or printed form over virtually any distance. At the higher levels of office activity, human/human communications are also considered particularly important because many of the contacts involve problem solving, reconnaissance or negotiation, for example.[6] Personal involvement and effort is very important and at present this can only usually be achieved by utilizing physical communication channels to bring the interested parties to a common location. Non-physical communication may eventually permit such contacts to be made without the participants leaving their offices but developments in this area are mainly in the experimental stage. Some substitution of non-physical for physical communications already takes place in the form of letters, telephones or telex but high order or important contacts cannot be maintained satisfactorily in this way. The bulk of routine contacts which can be maintained by telecommunications or correspondence could, in theory, make some office activities 'footloose' but the other 'personal contact activities' within the same businesses are often a major control on location.

The split between the physical and non-physical communications used by offices varies for different activities. As a general rule, the higher the proportion of personal contact required, the more central will the location of an office need to be if costs are to be minimized. The most important cost factor is the value of executive time; the more time spent travelling to meetings the higher the cost of maintaining personal contacts. Executive efficiency is achieved by maximizing the amount of time in meetings and minimizing time devoted to travel. This undoubtedly contributes to the central location tendency of offices, a feature which might only change when the substitution of telecommunications for transportation becomes an effective alternative.[7]

SOME EMPIRICAL EVIDENCE

Despite the acknowledged role of communications in office location, it is only in recent years that their actual significance and precise influence has been closely scrutinized quantitatively. Prior to this, an idea of the possible importance of communications, or linkages, was provided by empirical studies in which the distribution of office establishments was mapped.[8] Morgan has mapped the location of office establishments in the West End of London on a door-to-door basis, using a classification which permitted easy placement of each establishment in an appropriate category. By plotting the distribution of each type of establishment, such as accountants or insurance offices, he shows the existence of distinct functional clusters characterized by a large proportion of the total establishments in any one category (Fig. 32). Even so, some categories are more widely distributed than others; accountants are more widely dispersed throughout the West End than embassies or insurance offices while patent agents or film and cinema offices are highly clustered with only a minority at more scattered locations. Morgan suggests that the observed distributions are largely attributable to prestige and functional interrelationship, the latter reflecting a need for communication of some kind between establishments in the same group or with those in other groups. This is best illustrated by a localizing function such as Parliament which requires that ministers and civil servants be as close as possible to each other and to the House. Because of the concentration of Government departments, other office functions which require extensive consultation with or are dependent upon them for their business activities, are located close by, e.g. the offices of consulting engineers. Conclusions derived from an empirical investigation of this type assume that communications are a fundamental component of office functional interrelationships. Morgan does not measure the degree of association which is observed nor the extent to which communications operate as a locational factor. The same is true of the 11 functional regions differentiated by the types, or combination of types, of offices found in each. These range from the Government centre in and around Whitehall which includes Government offices, Church of England administration, and Commonwealth government offices, to Mayfair with its intermixing of high-class residential areas and embassies, advertising agencies, and United States Government offices and associated institutions.[9]

Evidence of functional grouping created by strong linkages between offices is also provided in Davies's study of Cape Town C.B.D.[10] Using land use and floorspace data, financial and general office groups were identified and their location characteristics illustrated by cluster analysis and maps of the distribution of buildings containing floorspace in each category (Fig. 33). The general office cluster has a centre of gravity which is marginally nearer to the peak land value intersection than that of the financial group, but it covers a much larger area of the

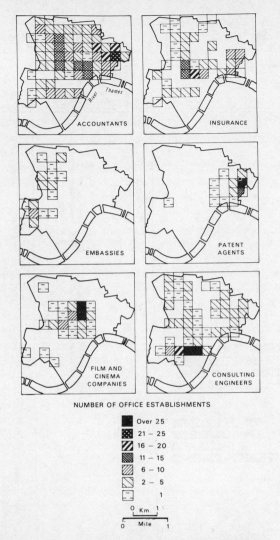

NUMBER OF OFFICE ESTABLISHMENTS

■	Over 25
▓	21 — 25
▨	16 — 20
▨	11 — 15
▨	6 — 10
▨	2 — 5
□	1

0   Km   1

0   Mile   1

Fig. 32   Location of Specific Types of Office Establishments in London's West End (After W. T. W. Morgan, 'A functional approach to the study of office distributions', *Tijdschrift voor Economische en Sociale Geografie*, 1961, with the permission of the Editor)

C.B.D. and is distributed amongst a much larger number of buildings. It is also more heterogeneous than the financial group because of the general classification adopted. A simple index of concentration is provided by identifying the location of buildings which contain 50 per cent of the floorspace in each cluster. The radial graphs for each cluster, which show the propor-

tion of floorspace in each land use category in relation to the proportion of total floorspace of each land use group in the entire study area, show that buildings in the financial cluster are almost exclusively devoted to financial and general office space. This is illustrated in more detail in the bar diagrams showing the proportional distribution of floorspace for all use categories within a cluster. In the financial area the strength of the links between the activities, most of which are accommodated in offices, are clearly strong enough to cause exclusion of most other uses.

Other measures of concentration which illustrate the localization of office employment have been used by Goddard.[11] The coefficient of localization, or example, measures the concentration of employment in a statistical unit, e.g. a grid square, relative to all employment. Each unit's share of employment in a particular category is subtracted from its percentage share of all office employment and the sum of the positive differences divided by 100 leads to an index in which 1·0 represents maximum concentration and 0·0 complete dispersion. This shows that industrial office categories, such as clothing, leather, and textiles, are highly concentrated while financial categories are moderately dispersed. When a concentration index based on the Lorenz curve is used the situation is reversed. This method does not depend on comparison with the total employment base and it more closely represents the absolute concentration of financial office categories. An index of 'relative dominance' has been suggested by Pierce.[12] If D_r is much greater than 1·0 an office type is very 'relatively dominant', but if D_r is slightly less or only slightly greater than unity, low relative dominance is indicated and this represents dispersal. The propensity of office types to be relatively concentrated or dispersed is obtained by totalling the indices of relative dominance for each unit of the study area and calculating the average for each activity. Finally, the standard distance allows for spatial arrangement of employment which is not included in the other indices. The standard distance measures the dispersion of employment about the mean centre, or centre of gravity, of the distribution.[13] Not surprisingly, insurance and banking emerge

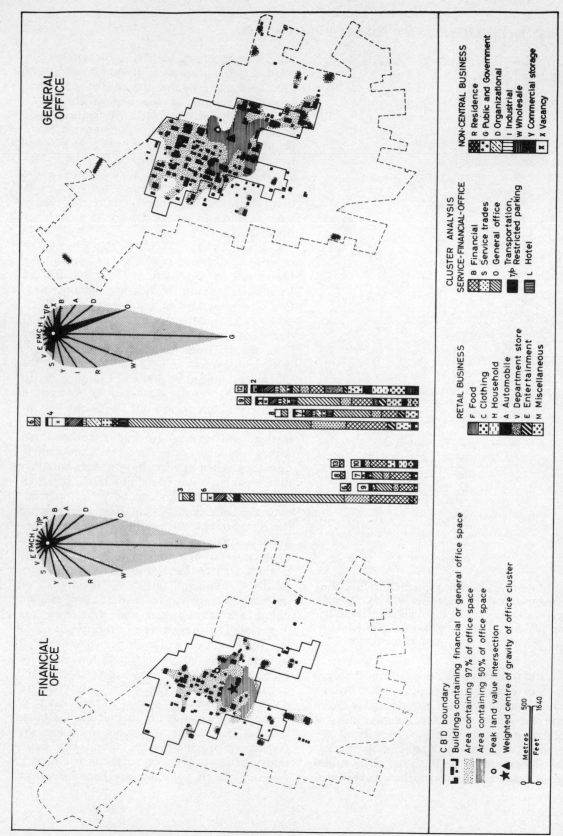

Fig. 33 General and Financial Office Clusters in Cape Town C.B.D. (After D. H. Davies, *Land Use in Central Cape Town: A Study of Urban Geography*, 1965, with the permission of the Longman Group Limited)

as highly concentrated when using this measure while some industrial offices, which form their own individual clusters, are shown to be much less concentrated. All these measures produce values which can be mapped.

More detailed work on the functional grouping of office activities in the City of London has been undertaken by Goddard.[14] In common with Davies and Morgan, the importance of communications links between and within

The first stage of the analysis involved correlation of each office activity with every other office activity. Significance at the 99·9 per cent confidence level occurs for 206 out of 3160 inter-relationships considered and these are the pairs of activities which can be considered to be spatially linked within the City.[15] The highly significant correlation bonds between pairs of activities are shown in Fig. 34 according to their distribution in relation to nine major groups of

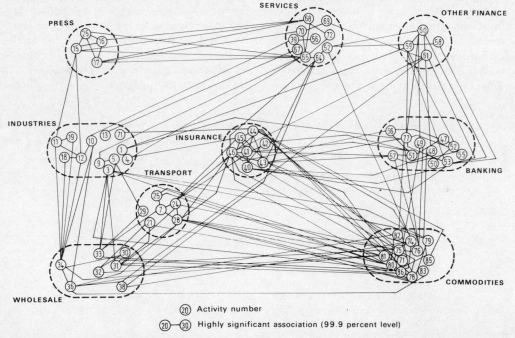

Fig. 34   Correlation Bonds Between Activities in the City of London (After J. B. Goddard, 'Multivariate analysis of office location patterns in the city centre: A London example', *Regional Studies*, 1968, with the permission of the Editor)

functional groups is inferred from their locational association, but the conclusions are arrived at by applying more rigorous multivariate techniques to a classification of 80 types of office activity. Davies recognized that his office clusters contained more than one type of activity but, without using multi-variate techniques, it was not possible to establish more than the basic locational attributes of activities within each functional cluster. Goddard endeavours to incorporate the contribution of as many different types of office as possible to the identification of functional clusters.

activities which can be recognized in the City. Most of the offices in the major functional groups have strong within-group spatial linkages, e.g. insurance, commodities or banking, but between-group spatial linkages are also shown to be of considerable importance. The major example of this is the pattern of linkage between commodities (75, 80 and 81), shipping (24 and 28) and insurance (40–46). Another, less obvious example, is the spatial linkage between commodities, banking, and insurance. Only industries and wholesaling do not reveal strong within-group bonds and are heavily dependent upon their between-group linkages with other office activities such as those concerned with commodities.

Correlation analysis identifies the pattern of association between office activities in the City in relation to a subjective categorization of nine major functional groups. It is also worth noting that the analysis is based on a view of the City as a closed system and no account is taken of links extending outside its boundaries. The City depends for its existence on its operation as an open system and this may affect the location of office activities within it.

The most important groups of interrelated activities are not identified by correlation analysis and Goddard achieves this by applying factor analysis to the large number of relationships in the original correlation matrix. The office activi-

ties (primary variable) which form the five main factors underlying the spatial variation of employment in the City are shown in Table 42.[16] They contain 50 of the 80 original office activities classified, the balance being made up of variables excluded because of their lack of linearity. The trading factor (Factor 1) includes the interdependent office activities of shipping, commodity trading, and risk insurance. These occupy a similar area within the City and represent one of its best known functions. Publishing and professional services (Factor 3) is made up of activities associated with the Press in the Fleet Street area and includes offices from several of the subjective groups illustrated in Fig. 34. Most of the activities in Factor 1 are associated with the international trading function of City offices while

TABLE 42

BASIC FACTORS UNDERLYING THE SPATIAL
VARIATION OF EMPLOYMENT IN THE CITY

Primary variable (no.)	Factor loading
THE TRADING FACTOR (FACTOR 1)	
General produce merchants (81)	−0·65
Transport services (28)	−0·63
Grain dealers (75)	−0·61
Tea and coffee merchants (78)	−0·60
Dealers in other Plantation House commodities (80)	−0·58
Miscellaneous commodity dealers (86)	−0·55
Lloyds insurance brokers (33)	−0·52
Food, drink, and tobacco manufacturers (3)	−0·47
Port and inland water transport (25)	−0·47
Wholesale distribution—grocery and provision (31)	−0·47
Rubber merchants (79)	−0·47
Shipping companies, airlines (24)	−0·45
Other insurance brokers (44)	−0·45
Other insurance—reinsurance (46)	−0·45
Shipbuilding (7)	−0·42
Wholesale distribution—tobacco (33)	−0·39
Metal dealers (76)	−0·39
Import and export merchants (74)	−0·38
Underwriters and underwriters' agents (45)	−0·38
Non-life insurance (41)	−0·37
THE FINANCIAL RING FACTOR (FACTOR 2)	
Stockbrokers and jobbers (59)	0·60
Other finance—building societies, etc. (61)	0·55
Other banks (77)	0·53
Foreign banks (53)	0·53
Investment and Unit Trusts (60)	0·52
Accountants (62)	0·49
Finance houses (58)	0·48
Mining companies (1)	0·47

the textile trading and other manufacturing factor (Factor 4) is largely comprised of office activities with regional or national ties within Britain. The only exception are the wool dealers which are found in similar areas because of their association with some textile manufacturers. Factors 2 and 5 represent the finance functions of the City. The financial core factor (Factor 5) almost exclusively includes offices closely involved in the daily operations of the City's money market. The financial ring factor (Factor 2), on the other hand, comprises offices active in the investment and capital sector such as finance houses or foreign banks.[17]

Spatial distribution of the office activities in the factor groups can then be examined to see whether distinct areas of the City are occupied by each. The standard scores of each street block on all 80 variables are used to estimate each block's score. Although much of the original detail is lost as a result, a plot of the first and second octiles of the factor scores shows that areas with distinctive groupings of offices can be identified (Fig. 35). The distribution of office activities contributing to Factors, 1, 2, 3, and 5 clearly suggest spatial independence within the City, although clearly there is overlap in this small and extremely complex part of central London. Factor scores in the first octile dominate street blocks in the Fleet Street area where publishing and professional services are located, while trading activities in both octiles are closely

TABLE 42—*continued*

Primary variable (no.)	Factor loading
THE PUBLISHING AND PROFESSIONAL SERVICES FACTOR (FACTOR 3)	
Printing and publishing of newspapers and periodicals (16)	−0·60
Advertising and public relations (68)	−0·59
Other professional services—consultancy (65)	−0·58
Paper and board manufacturers (15)	−0·45
Other business services (70)	−0·41
Wholesale distribution—paper, stationery, books (35)	−0·41
Miscellaneous services (72)	−0·37
THE TEXTILE TRADING AND OTHER MANUFACTURING FACTOR (FACTOR 4)	
Wholesale distribution—clothing footwear (34)	0·71
Leather, leather goods, and fur (11)	0·60
Textile manufacturers (10)	0·58
Clothing and footwear manufacturers (12)	0·51
Wool dealers (82)	0·43
Other manufacturing industries (18)	0·43
Construction (19)	0·43
Wholesale distribution—other non-food goods (36)	0·39
THE FINANCIAL CORE FACTOR (FACTOR 5)	
British Overseas and Commonwealth banks (52)	0·74
Scottish and Northern Irish banks (51)	0·68
Members of the discount market (56)	0·68
Life and non-life insurance companies (42)	0·50
London clearing banks—headquarters offices (47)	0·42
Non-life insurance (41)	0·41
Other banks (77)	0·41
Life insurance (40)	0·34

Source: J. B. Goddard, 'Multivariate analysis of office location patterns in the city centre: A London example', *Regional Studies*, vol. 2 (1968), Table 2, p. 75.

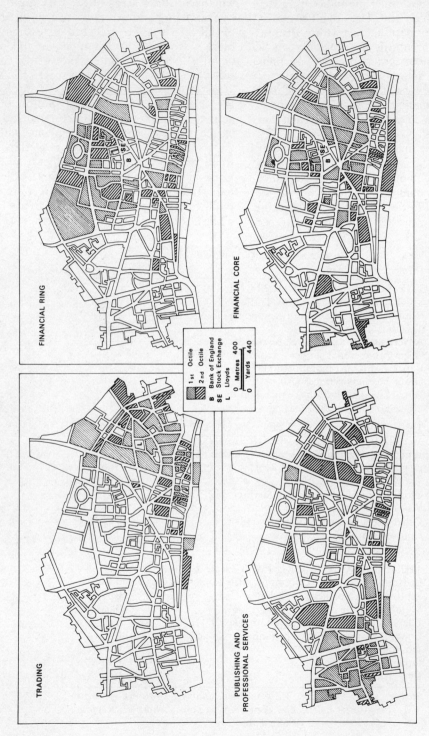

FINANCIAL RING

FINANCIAL CORE

TRADING

PUBLISHING AND
PROFESSIONAL SERVICES

1st Octile
2nd Octile
B   Bank of England
SE   Stock Exchange
L   Lloyds

0   Metres   400
0   Yards   440

Fig. 35 Distribution of Blocks with High Factor Scores for Four Major Factor Groupings of Office Activities in the City of London
(After J. B. Goddard, see Fig. 34)

grouped around Lloyds and to the east of a line down Bishopsgate to London Bridge. Similarly, the financial core offices are clustered around the Bank of England with the ring activities forming a crescent to the north west of the Stock Exchange.

Multi-variate analysis is therefore a powerful tool for studying some aspects of the locational attributes of office activities. The pattern of these activities in the City is partly a product of historical factors, particularly the growth of London as the centre for Britain's financial and trading activities, and partly due to simple inertia. The latter may be causing some office activities to remain in the City even though they no longer derive many direct or indirect benefits from remaining there. But much more important than

either of these variables, are the strong economic linkages between office activities which bind them together and to the City. Goddard's conclusions are still based on inferred linkages, however, and only incorporate the spatial element. Linkages between offices which are independent of distance between them are not evaluated, i.e. those linkages based on non-physical communications. Movement of goods and people along physical channels of communication must also be considered in any attempt to identify linked groups of office activities. Indeed, the flow of information and people within the city centre does not seem to be random, but consists of a number of sub-systems which form part of the master system of linkages within the office sector and between offices and other urban activities.[18]

CONTACT STUDIES

Many of the deficiencies of the above studies can be remedied by contact studies of office workers. The precise importance of interperson contact for office location can only be established by detailed analysis of its characteristics for various types of office activity and at different levels within an office organization. Information flows through personal contact, particularly at face-to-face meetings, take place at a high cost to company resources and time. The significance of these costs for office location may only change when techniques of telecommunication will reduce the cost–benefit of face-to-face meetings to a level which will make information flow by either method unimportant in the office location equation. By collecting information on the characteristics of personal communications within and between offices it becomes possible to assess the implications of telecommunications for present and future information flows. The question then arises as to whether the patterns of interperson communications for existing offices take a form which implies major locational constraints or whether some proportion of the personal contacts could be transferred to future telecommunications systems without any detrimental consequences for office opera-

tions.[19] It is also possible that better knowledge of office contact systems could be used to guide and change office location in the interests of regional development.[20]

The earliest examples of this approach to communications and office location have come from Sweden.[21] Interest has largely centred on the significance of business contacts for regional development using information collected from businessmen about destination, purpose, duration, and types of contact used to arrange and participate in meetings. Törnqvist has studied the contact modes and patterns of 14 separate Stockholm-based organizations over a week-long period, using logs or diaries of contact completed by each individual employee.[22] Thorngren has also collected records of over 1500 contacts by 3000 businessmen. This work has stimulated a growing volume of research in Britain, particularly by Goddard, in studies commissioned by the Location of Offices Bureau and at the Communications Study Group of the Joint Unit for Planning Research, London.[23] A Government report on the dispersal of civil service offices from London has also referred in some detail to contact patterns and their effects on location.[24]

TYPES OF CONTACT

There are three main types of personal contact: face-to-face, by telephone or by post. Postal communications are the least important of the three, partly because the individuals concerned do not have audio-visual contact, and because for most types of correspondence the cost is the same, irrespective of distance. Delivery time may, however, vary according to the distance between locations and postal communication is most likely to be used where precision rather than speed of information exchange is important.

The telephone provides the main alternative to face-to-face meetings. It has the advantage of providing virtually immediate contact but only between two individuals at a time. Where large distances separate the two speakers and there are pressing problems to be resolved, the telephone has obvious advantages over a face-to-face meeting. Some of the disadvantages of the telephone can now be overcome by the 'Confra-Phone' system which permits several people to hold a meeting through linked telephone circuits, but this is not a facility which is generally available as yet.[25] But 'Confra-Phone' does not permit participants to see each other which is an important benefit of face-to-face meetings. Psychological factors such as seating position, facial expression, emotional intent, gestures, and the ability to display information in the form of duplicated sheets and visual material make up the visual feedback of meetings.[26] These considerations are especially relevant in 'non-programmed' decision-making in which the participants are often unfamiliar with each other but dealing with a wide range of subject matter.[27] 'Programmed' decision-making involves routine operations using a well structured system in which the participants are usually well known to each other. Many of these decisions are made within office organizations while the 'non-programmed' types are the product of between-organization contacts. The former are well suited to telephone contacts.

A compromise between telephone and face-to-face contact is provided by 'Confra-Vision', the 'Picturephone', and 'Viewphone'.[28] The former is a product of the Post Office which links together with vision and sound two distant studios which are equipped to resemble a company boardroom. The Viewphone incorporates a small picture into the structure of the conventional telephone. The Picturephone, developed by Bell Laboratories in America, is a version of this and incorporates a display unit with a loud-speaker and a microphone contained in a separate control unit. Both Bell Laboratories and the Post Office are still experimenting with the 'Picturephone' and 'Viewphone' respectively. Post Office research suggests that the head and shoulders view provided by both systems should be supplemented by a facility to scan documents and other recorded information for an additional visual display which can be used by participants.

Although personal contact appears to be a pre-eminent influence on office location, it must be remembered that a substantial proportion of contacts between office activities involve non-personal information flows. The simplest of these involve physical transfer of records or other documents from one location to another but the most important rely on telecommunications to facilitate rapid transfer of information between headquarters and branch offices, for example. The systems available are wide ranging and are constantly being improved and may be exclusively used by individual organizations or may form part of a public network. Computers, microfilm, and facsimile facilities are particularly important in this context. They permit efficient storage, as well as exchange of information, and a stage has now been reached where it is possible to get letters dictated onto recording tape, typed from the tape record, simultaneously producing a punched tape duplicate, and sent to the originator for checking and signature. Any corrections are made manually with the remainder of the letter produced automatically at high speed. It is also possible to transfer letters, by facsimile, without using the conventional postal system. Although cost factors make many such systems uneconomic at the present time, the long-term consequences of such non-personal communications will undoubtedly be to liberalize office location. It remains to be seen whether telecommunications substitution for personal contact will parallel this trend.

Personal, face-to-face contact takes up a large proportion of an office executive's time. In a study of 76 top managers in seven different companies it was found that between 42 and 80 per cent of their time was devoted to spoken communication; between 12 and 29 per cent to written communication; and 8 to 29 per cent on interpretation.[29] The amount of time devoted to each form of contact is related to job status, so that it has been estimated that middle management spend 57 per cent of their time on internal contacts, and only 11 per cent on external personal contacts.[30] Only 6 per cent of the managers' time recorded by Stewart was spent on the telephone compared with 43 per cent in face-to-face meetings. Executives concerned with sales and promotion at upper management levels would probably spend most of their personal contact time on external contacts. Burns also notes that the volume of personal contacts increases at the same rate as the growth of a firm and, proportionally, they command a larger share of office time.

RELATIVE ROLES OF TYPES OF CONTACT

A guide to the relative importance of the types of contact utilized by offices is given in Table 43. Offices in Leeds were asked to state their main method of contact with customers, clients, other firms as well as other departments within the same office organization. The latter does not necessarily mean contact within the same building. Despite reservations about the reliability of the data provided by respondents to this part of the questionnaire, Facey and Smith clearly demonstrate that face-to-face contact is the principal mode of communication amongst Leeds offices.[31] Meetings at the office or elsewhere are almost evenly balanced although, surprisingly, 52 per cent stated that personal contact with customers or clients at other locations was more important than at their own office. More specialist forms of communication were not extensively used by Leeds offices at the time of the survey and the few systems in use were mainly for

TABLE 43
METHODS OF CONTACT USED BY OFFICES IN LEEDS

Method of contact	Customers/ clients	Other firms	Other departments of organization
Personal contact at office	544	350	238
Personal contact elsewhere	620	291	167
Post[1]	698	573	387
Private messenger	85	114	83
Railway parcel service	86	65	87
Public telephone[1]	512	450	321
Direct telephone[1]	309	236	247
Telegraph	32	18	13
Teleprinter	10	5	41
Telex	24	20	33
Radio	1	0	5
Datel	1	1	0
Other	6	4	4

Note: 1. These figures may not be entirely representative because of problems arising in the questionnaire. See f. 24.

Source: M. V. Facey and G. B. Smith, *Offices in a Regional Centre: A Study of Office Location in Leeds* (London: Location of Offices Bureau, Research Report, no. 2, 1968), Table 6.A, p. 79.

intra-firm contacts. Similar statistics for London would probably show a higher propensity to use telecommunications channels.

Some other characteristics of telephone and meeting contacts have been noted by Goddard for central London offices.[32] Both contact modes have common characteristics, i.e. length, pre-arrangement, frequency, purpose, range of subject matter discussed, concern with sales or purchases, number of participants and the media involved. On the basis of these characteristics there are some clear distinctions between the two types of contact. Some 87 per cent of telephone contacts take between 2 and 10 min while meetings, which generally take more time to arrange, usually last longer; 52 per cent lasting more than 30 min. Most telephone contacts are not pre-arranged compared with 27 per cent of meetings which are arranged more than a week in advance. The frequency of contact and range of subject matter discussed do not differ widely between the two modes although a higher proportion of the face-to-face contacts (35 per cent) involve discussion of several subjects. The most important role of telephone contacts is to receive information, while meetings serve mainly to exchange it and

for general discussion. Approximately 33 per cent of the meetings took place outside the respondents' office. Correlation analysis between contact characteristics of telephone and face-to-face meetings combined reveals that the type of medium used is closely associated with length of contact, the extent of pre-arrangement, and the number of participants ($r = 0.70$, 0.65, and 0.52 respectively). The more time the contacts take the more likely they are to be arranged a long time in advance, to involve a large number of participants and to involve a moderate range of subject matter ($r = 0.61$, 0.66, and 0.33 respectively). Any lengthy contacts in terms of time taken are made infrequently and the larger the number of participants the further in advance the meeting has to be arranged.

Use of the three main types of personal contact varies according to office function (Table 44). Manufacturing, physical services, and other professional offices in Leeds made above average use of face-to-face meetings, mainly because they have products to sell or services to offer which involve negotiations or documentation which can only be made successfully on that basis. Offices of insurance, other finance, and legal activities

TABLE 44

RELATIVE IMPORTANCE OF THREE MAIN FORMS OF CONTACT BY DECISION-MAKERS IN OFFICES IN LEEDS AND WELLINGTON

Average ranking of the three forms of contact

Form of contact	Manufac-turing	Physical services	Insurance	Other financial	Legal	Other Profes-sional	Miscellaneous	All forms
Face-to-face								
Leeds	1·7	1·5	2·2	2·4	2·2	1·8	2·0	1·9
Wellington	2·0	1·1	—[1]	—	—	—	1·8	2·0
Telephone								
Leeds	1·8	1·8	1·6	2·1	2·1	2·4	1·8	1·8
Wellington	1·8	1·9	—	—	—	—	1·5	1·7
Post								
Leeds	2·5	2·7	2·2	1·5	1·7	1·8	2·3	2·3
Wellington	2·2	2·8	—	—	—	—	2·3	2·2

Note: 1. Difficult to make direct comparison between Leeds and Wellington functional classification.

Sources: M. J. Croft, *Offices in a Regional Centre: Follow-up Studies of Infra-structure and Linkages* (London: Location of Offices Bureau, Research Report, no. 3, 1969), Table 1, p. 4. J. A. Davey, *The Office Industry in Wellington: A Study of Contact Patterns, Location and Employment* (Wellington: Ministry of Works, 1972), Table 9, p. 46.

made more use of telephones and the postal system. Many of their customers and clients are individual households scattered throughout Northern England and it is necessary for them to visit the offices personally to complete transactions. Postal contacts were, however, used at above average levels in legal offices and this suggests that an element of caution is required when interpreting Table 44. Although the relative importance of each type of personal contact is ranked, this does not take into account their value to a business. There is also no account

taken of the level within a business at which each type of contact is used; infrequent face-to-face meetings at managerial level in a legal office may be more vital to the company's success than the high frequency of communication by letter.

Davey has used a similar method of analysis for offices in Wellington and finds that there is reasonable agreement, allowing for some differences in functional classification, between the two surveys.[33] It is worth noting, however, that when Davey compares the statistics produced by structured interviews (see Table 44) with those

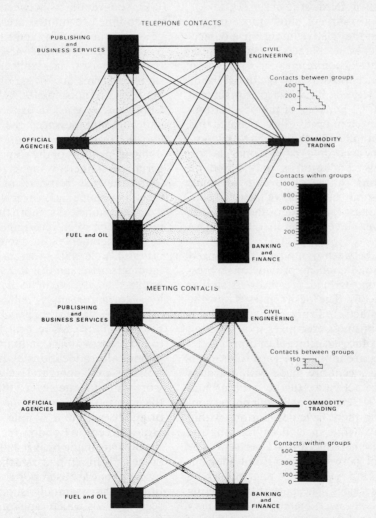

Fig. 36   Spatial Pattern of Telephone and Meeting Contacts in Central London (After J. B. Goddard, *Office Linkages and Location*, 1973, with the permission of Pergamon Press Ltd.)

produced by a postal questionnaire, some discrepancies emerge. The postal questionnaire results show that telephone contacts are very important to finance offices but the interviews showed them only to have equal status with face-to-face meetings.[34] This kind of discrepancy suggests that it is necessary to rigorously state the definition of types of contact listed in postal or interview-based questionnaires. This is important if the relative roles of the major forms of personal contact are to be accurately assessed. Similar difficulties were encountered by Facey and Smith in their Leeds study.

Although both surveys show that the difference between the relative importance of face-to-face and telephone contacts is marginal, the value of face-to-face meetings becomes clear when the distance factor is also included. Faced with a choice between face-to-face contact and other methods, 82 per cent of the 55 decision-makers interviewed in Leeds offices claimed that distance did not influence choice.[35] The proportion did not vary according to functional classification. But this conclusion is only based on contact decisions by the office élite; distance will almost certainly be a negative factor in contact choice amongst lower order office staff, and some may never have to consider face-to-face meetings.

Within- and between-group patterns of meeting and telephone contacts provide an expression of the linkages binding offices to similar locations (Fig. 36). The desire lines show the volume of contacts utilizing each mode by a sample of 705 business executives in a selection of commercial offices in central London.[36] Telephone contacts are more numerous than meetings but 54·2 per cent are made within groups of similar office activities. In the banking and finance sector, 71·2 per cent of the telephone contacts originating there have destinations within the same group, while in civil engineering the equivalent figure is reduced to 43 per cent. The latter has major between-group telephone contacts with banking and finance and publishing and business services. The pattern of meeting contacts reveals a lower degree of connectivity between functional groups with the number of meetings taking place within groups averaging 60 per cent. The between-contacts are particu-

larly weak for commodity trading and official agencies and these groups are also categorized by a very low number of meetings compared with other office groups. Therefore, although meetings are fewer in number than telephone contacts, the fact that more of them take place within functional groups (established by factor analysis) has clear implications for the location of the offices concerned. Telecommunications substitution then becomes crucial if location changes outside the existing contact network can be considered.

Personal contacts between office activities are not confined to limited areas of a city, as suggested in the data for central London (see Fig. 36). Important outside links also take place, this is illustrated by data collected from a random sample of firms occupying office premises in the City of London in 1967.[37] Individual office employees were asked to record both incoming and outgoing messages, the method of contact, and the origin or destination of each contact. Some 65 per cent of the respondents were managerial personnel or higher order staff. It was found that 526 respondents made 28,292 contacts in a single day. Over 45 per cent of them were telephone calls; more than 50 per cent taking place between locations within the City, to or from members of the same firm or to or from others (Table 45). Most of the calls between members of the same firm, 72 per cent, took place within the City, the majority in the same building. Not surprisingly, calls to or from others extended beyond the City's boundaries but 82·1 per cent of the calls recorded were still confined to locations within London. Long distance telephone calls to locations elsewhere in Britain or overseas were comparatively unimportant. It is worth noting, however, that 70 per cent of the international telephone calls from Britain originate within a 4 mile radius of Faraday House in central London, including the City, and the bulk are made by just 400 international companies.[38] This emphasizes that external contacts by telephone are as important to some organizations as the essentially, short distance, local or regional calls which typify most of the offices in the City sample.

Long distance contacts beyond London are the perogative of the postal system, although

TABLE 45
SPATIAL PATTERN OF TELEPHONE AND
POSTAL CONTACTS OF SAMPLE OFFICE
EMPLOYEES IN THE CITY OF LONDON—1967

Origin or destination	To or from members of same firm	To or from others	Total
In same building:			
telephone calls	2870	159	3029
letters	—	—	—
Elsewhere in City:			
telephone calls	990	3374	4364
letters	363	1790	2153
Elsewhere in London:			
telephone calls	947	1794	2741
letters	565	1893	2458
Elsewhere in U.K.:			
telephone calls	484	745	1229
letters	1142	3075	4217
Overseas:			
telephone calls	15	222	237
letters	390	1175	1565
Totals	5306	6294	11600
	2460	7933	10393

Source: J. H. Dunning and E. V. Morgan, *An Economic Study of the City of London* (London: Allen & Unwin, 1971), p. 162.

some 44 per cent of postal contacts were between locations in London (see Table 45). As a method for intra-business contact, the public postal system is much less important mainly because many large companies operate their own postal system or it is often much easier to contact colleagues by telephone in circumstances where they are known to the individual concerned. Only 22·6 per cent of the letters to or from other businesses were exchanged within the City, a much lower proportion than for telephone calls. The respondents also recorded 3997 meetings and 90 per cent were held in their own buildings. Meetings outside their own buildings were attended by 388 respondents and 70 per cent of these took place in the City. A further 19 per cent took place within the Greater London area. Therefore, 89 per cent of the face-to-face contacts were made within 15–20 miles of the City, the majority much nearer, and this provides a crude measure of the benefits of offices clustering as close together as possible.

Offices also generate 'social' contacts. In an analysis of trips generated by Leeds offices, Croft found that only 19 per cent were to destinations in other offices; 69 per cent of the trips were entirely divorced from the economic activities of the offices generating them, i.e. for personal/domestic reasons. There are therefore linkages produced by office workers which have no direct connection with either their own offices or other offices. Croft suggests that if linkage or communications surveys confine attention to decision-makers, for example, with particular reference to economic contacts, they will only provide a partial picture of the influence of contacts and linkage on office location. Therefore, the 'social infrastructure of office development tends to be more geographically concentrated than its economic infrastructure' and is a

product of short distance linkages with restaurants, hotels, public houses, and shops.[39]
The widest range of these 'support' activities are
found in the C.B.D. where they serve both the
daily requirements of office and other workers,
as well as consumers throughout the city
and its region. It would therefore be unwise to
underestimate the role of these factors in office
location decisions.

The general importance of a wide range of
'support' activities to centrally located offices is

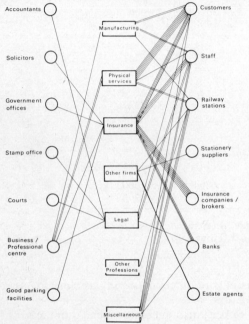

Fig. 37 The Influence of 'Support' Activities on
Office Location in Leeds (Data: M. J. Croft, *Offices
in a Regional Centre: Follow-up Studies on Infra-
structure and Linkage*, 1969)

outlined in Fig. 37. Although based on the responses of 64 decision-makers in the Leeds survey, and therefore excluding the bulk of office
workers, it provides a basic guide to the contact
requirements of various office functions. Each
line denotes a response by a decision-maker.
Over one-fifth of them, as expected from earlier
discussions in this chapter, mentioned accessibility by or to customers. Almost the same proportion (19 per cent) listed staff factors, which included easy recruiting, transport convenience,
and availability of restaurants. Proximity to railway stations was the third most frequently
mentioned linkage used by decision-makers, customers and staff. The offices fall into two main
groups. First, offices with a wide diversity of contacts, particularly the legal and insurance offices,
and secondly, offices with 'limited range' but still
very important contacts; mainly manufacturing
services and physical services offices. The decision-makers in these offices considered a central area location essential largely on the basis
of customer accessibility and staff availability.
This suggests that these offices are potentially
less dependent on a highly central location, but
less tangible linkages, derived from prestige and
tradition, must not be overlooked. In earlier
time periods, many manufacturing offices
administered production plants very close to, if
not within, the central areas now dominated by
office activities. Indeed, the Economist Intelligence Unit's survey of offices in London showed
that 37 per cent of the 83 firms interviewed
quoted tradition as an important locational
determinant for departments which were not
considered essential to keep in central London
for contact purposes.[40]

INDICES OF CONTACT

An objective expression of the significance of
communications for different types of office
activity is an essential prerequisite for the study
of location as well as the potential for change.
Until very recently, most of the measures used
to classify contacts have been subjectively derived from survey questions. One of the earliest
examples classified contact as essential or not
essential from the point of view of offices having

communication with and access to other firms
and institutions.[41] This kind of approach is open
to bias according to the attitudes of respondents
and rationalization of their locational preferences. A survey of offices in central Manchester has graded contacts as strong linkage,
weak linkage or no linkage, leaving respondents
to interpret the difference between strong and
weak.[42] The strength of linkages between office

groups is expressed on a scale of 0–100 for each type of linkage and converted to a linkage rating. This is calculated by multiplying the number of firms with strong links by 100, the number with weak links by 40, and dividing the sum by the total number of offices in the group. The higher the value of the rating, the stronger the link between office groups. Hence, insurance offices have strong links with each other, rating 85, but very weak with national and local government offices, 10.[43]

Three contact indices have been used by Davey.[44] The most straightforward is 'contact level' which is the percentage of respondents within any group, e.g. clerical staff, who record any contact with other specified office groups or employees. The 'contact frequency' index allows for variations in the number of contacts recorded by respondents by weighting them on a scale from 1 for contacts of less than once a year to 1000 for those taking place several times a day. The weighted figures for all respondents in any group are then summed and divided by the number of respondents. Finally, the 'personal contact' index is the percentage of contact with any category of activity which takes place on a face-to-face basis, whether in the respondent's office, the contact's office or elsewhere. Face-to-face meetings are used to calculate the index because of their contribution towards keeping offices in the C.B.D.

The total values of each index for every respondent in relation to contact categories

defined by function or status, for example, can then be plotted and divided into median, upper, and lower quartiles. This provides a relative measure of strength of contact and values above the upper quartile are considered high and conversely for values below the lower quartile. Values between the median and upper quartile are moderately high and between the median and lower quartile, moderately low. Although these terms may appear just as subjective as those used in the Manchester or London studies, they have been produced by a more objective attempt to measure the actual contacts taking place. The three indices combined give a 'contact intensity' index.[45] Davey takes all high values for each index in relation to a particular function as 1·0 and all moderately high values as 0·5. The actual values used can be varied to suit the needs of individual studies. Hence, in order to identify distinct differences in contact patterns between functional groups the contact intensity index provides a useful summary measure (Table 46).

Croft has also attempted an objective assessment of the relationship between contacts and office location.[46] Visual analysis of data may suggest an apparent relationship between contacts and location but this may be the indirect result of offices in particular locations having particular attributes such as status, size or function. If it is assumed that offices can be categorized according to three variables which influence communications patterns—function, location, and status—then holding two variables constant

TABLE 46
CONTACT INTENSITY INDICES FOR MAJOR OFFICE
FUNCTIONS IN WELLINGTON

Office function	Score for contact level	Score for contact frequency index	Score for personal contact index	Total score for contact intensity index	Rank in contact intensity
Manufacturers	10·5	6·5	8·5	25·5	5
Wholesalers	10·5	7·5	8·5	26·5	3
Import/export	11·0	8·5	11·0	30·5	1
Transport	9·0	7·0	7·0	23·0	6
Finance	10·0	12·0	4·0	26·0	4
Professional	12·0	8·5	9·0	29·5	2
Miscellaneous	6·5	5·0	6·0	17·5	7

Source: J. A. Davey, *The Office Industry in Wellington: A Study of Contact Patterns, Location and Employment* (Wellington: Ministry of Works, 1972), part of Table 8, p. 38.

allows the other to vary and it becomes possible to establish its relative importance.[47] An example would be an analysis of the main method of contact with customers or clients by offices with a different location in Leeds but similar in status and function. Croft found that 26 pairs of contacts were significantly different at the 25 per cent level (38 per cent of the total contacts analysed). A further 18 contacts were significant at the 1 per cent level (26 per cent). Even allowing for sampling errors, this suggests that the main method used by offices for contact-

ing customers or clients does vary according to location of the source office. With function and status held constant, it can also be concluded that there is likely to be a relationship between office location and patterns of contact.[48]

The main problem with this technique is that it is cumbersome to produce a large number of test statistics. If there are several methods of contact being examined using a detailed office classification the task becomes almost impossible because several hundred significance tests would be required.

MULTI-VARIATE CLASSIFICATION OF CONTACT PATTERNS

Using the eight contact characteristics already described, Goddard has developed a classification of office contacts in terms of the strength of communication links to central London.[49] The data for the multi-variate classification was collected by the use of 'contact sheets' or 'contact diaries' in which office employees recorded every meeting and telephone call undertaken during a three-day period. The meeting record included, amongst other things, the frequency and purpose of individual meetings, the subject matter discussed, the location of the meeting, and the mode of travel and time taken to get there. A similar range of information was obtained for telephone contacts. The contact sheets were general enough to apply to any type of office organization and were designed to 'measure the strength of the existing communication linkages of different office sectors and job types to central London'.[50] Cross-tabulation or simple correlation analysis of the contact characteristics obtained from the contact sheets does not, however, take account of all possible inter-relationships. This difficulty can be resolved by using latent profile analysis.[51]

Three distinct classes of contact emerge when latent profile analysis is applied to 6680 contacts made up of meetings and telephone contacts (Fig. 38). The class means for each of the eight variables are expressed as standard scores which can therefore take on both positive and negative values. The axes of the profile are scaled in terms of positive and negative standard scores and the class variables plotted accordingly. Contacts in

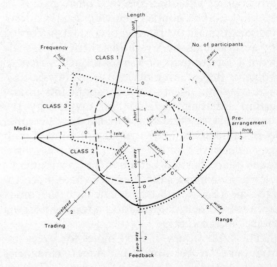

Fig. 38 Latent Profile Analysis of Meeting and Telephone Contacts in Central London (After J. B. Goddard, 'Office communications and office location: A review of current research', *Regional Studies*, 1971, with the permission of the Editor)

Class 1 (orientation contacts) are generally meetings of above average length, arrangement, and number of people involved.[52] These meetings deal with an above average range of subject matter and of feedback and they take place with below average frequency; 971 contacts, or 14·5 per cent, are grouped in Class 1 while by far the largest group, 5429 (81·2 per cent) are in Class 2. The former are mainly face-to-face meetings but the latter involve a large proportion of telephone contacts which take place with above average frequency and below average length, arrangement and number of people involved. Class 2 can be described as programmed contacts.[53] Contacts which are generally short, very infrequent, involve only two participants but which are arranged a long time in advance characterize Class 3 (4·2 per cent of the total). Goddard suggests that this group represents regularized transactions on the financial markets of the City of London. Once the classes have been identified their detailed characteristics in relation to each of the categories of the original variables can be examined. Hence, 99·8 per cent of the contacts in Class 1 are face-to-face and only 23·6 per cent take less than 30 min; in Class 2, 93·8 per cent of the contacts are by telephone and 85·2 per cent last between 2 and 10 min.[54]

Because almost all the contacts in Class 1 are meetings, it is possible to conduct a separate, latent profile analysis on them. Meeting Class 2 contacts are shorter, take place more frequently and are not arranged as far in advance as the contacts in Meeting Class 1. The meetings in Class 2 therefore possess some of the characteristics of the majority of telephone contacts in the combined meeting/telephone classification and it is possible that many of them could be transferred to telecommunications.

The contact classification can also be interpreted with reference to types of office, occupation of 'respondents or types of departments within organizations.[55] For telephone and meeting contacts combined; banking, chemicals, professional services and paper, printing and publishing offices have an above average share of orientation contacts (Class 1) while programmed contacts are proportionally more important in insurance, business services or construction industry offices. But within individual organizations, the ratio of programmed to orientation contacts will also vary according to departmental functions. Market research, long range planning or organization and methods departments generate a much higher proportion of orientation contacts compared with company records or accounts departments. The relative importance of orientation contacts increases with occupation status; over 19 per cent of managing directors' contacts involve orientation compared to almost 9 per cent for executives. If meetings only are considered, orientation contacts characterize 63·6 per cent of managing directors' meetings and only 31·5 per cent of the meetings recorded by executives. Similarly, if meetings only are examined in the context of types of office and departments the rankings suggested by the combined analysis of meetings and telephone contacts are changed. Planning, market research or organization and methods departments ranked high on orientation contacts (Class 1) in the combined analysis but many of the meetings are in Meeting Class 2. Although a relatively small proportion of all the contacts in marketing or export departments are of the orientation type, almost all the meetings are well above average in length and therefore in Meeting Class 1. At the level of aggregated data for individual offices, Goddard notes distinctive contrasts between the head office of a London clearing bank and the head office of an international oil company. The latter had a lower intensity but wider geographical spread of contacts than the former but proportionally more were of the orientation type. Many of the bank's contacts were of a routine programmed nature and telecommunications substitution, already taking place to some degree, would be even more feasible if fewer contacts were concerned with 'bargaining' and exchange of documents.

Identification of the relative weights of orientation and programmed contacts in different types of office could be used by office organizations, planners, and others to guide them on office location requirements within urban areas and the possibilities for redistribution both within large cities and between regions (see Chapter 9). Intra-firm analysis also provides guidance on which departments or individuals most need to occupy central office locations and which do not. The opportunities for communications substitution can also be demonstrated and the implications for office location assessed within a more objective framework.[56]

EFFECT OF LOCATION CHANGE ON OFFICE COMMUNICATIONS

Data on the communications patterns of central London civil servants have been used to assess the possibilities for continued Government office dispersal from London.[57] Each Government Department included in the study was divided into 'blocks of work', i.e. groups of staff with an identifiable responsibility and who are in day-to-day contact with each other. Over 1500 blocks were identified and contact information from the staff within them was collected using methods similar to those employed by Goddard. However, only face-to-face contacts were recorded in terms of typical frequency, typical periods of peak contact outside the 'normal' frequency, and a revised frequency, assuming a preferred pattern, of contacts inhibited by separation or fragmentation of Departments.[58]

'Link strength' is then used as a measure of the importance of face-to-face contact and is calculated from the following:[59]

Link strength = sum of contact frequency × salary weighting.

$$L_{xr} = \left\{ \sum_{i/i \in x} \right\} P_{ir} \times £\,i,$$

where L_{xr} is the link strength from block x to block r; P_{ir} is respondent i's preferred monthly frequency of face-to-face contact with people designated as members of block r; and $£i$ is the salary weighting proportional to the mean of the scale for respondent i's grade at the time of the study. The link strength of all the respondents in a block of work are summed and expressed as percentage link strength of contact with other blocks of work.[60] Salary weighting is obtained by taking the ratio of mean salary for a grade to the mean salary of an executive officer.

An important contribution of the study is its attempt to measure the 'communications damage' caused by separating linked blocks of work. The damage is only considered for face-to-face meetings and in the event of dispersal from central London there are two courses of action open to would-be participants: abandon the meeting or one or more participants must travel. The latter gives rise to penalties in the form of fares and expenses and the time during which participants are away from their own offices. Time is the most important penalty incurred by separation and 'damage' is defined as the time spent in travel or 'separation' time. The damage incurred each month, assuming that meetings are not abandoned, in separating a block of work from one of its contacts is then calculated as follows:

Damage (without abandonment) =
        separation × average link strength.

$$D_{xr} = k \times S_{xr}(L_{xr} + L_{rx})/2,$$

where D_{xr} is the damage incurred by separating from each other two blocks of work, x and r, which are currently co-located assuming that participants travel to every meeting irrespective of separation; S_{xr} is the separation (estimated return travel time by the quickest economically acceptable means of transport) of the proposed locations of blocks x and r; and k is a constant (intended to convert monthly figures to appropriate 'total future discounted' values).

The effects of abandoning meetings on communications damage are more complex. The above measure of damage is probably an overestimate of the true disruption to face-to-face communications because many of the preferred contacts will not be considered so essential as to warrant travelling the long distances necessary to maintain them. Indeed, it was found by comparing the preferred frequency of contact with what actually took place at the time of the study, that even very short distances between the buildings in which two respondents were housed considerably reduced the number of times they met, compared with what they thought desirable. As separation increases the higher the chance of abandoning a meeting and this allows the proportion of meetings having a certain value to be calculated. Using this information, derived from existing observations, the damage caused by a given separation can be calculated. It consists of two parts: damage from travelling to a certain proportion of meetings and damage resulting from abandonment of the remainder. At the maximum distance for which any particular contact would be maintained, the damage caused by abandoning the meeting must be equal to that caused by travelling to it. The total damage resultant upon given separation of all contacts for all blocks of work is somewhat less than the communications damage if one or more participants must travel. This is termed 'effective separation' and is derived from:

$$S^1_{xr} = \int S_o{}^{xr} a(s) \times s \times ds + S_{xr}\int_{Sxr} a(s) \times ds,$$

where S^1_{xr} is the effective separation between the locations of blocks x and r; $\int S_o^{xr} a(s) \times s \times ds$ is the cost of meetings abandoned at distances less than the separation considered (the sum of the products of the distances at which meetings are abandoned multiplied by the proportion of meetings nearly· abandoned at that distance); $S_{xr}\int S_{xr} a(s) \times ds$ is the cost of meetings still held at that distance (the separation multiplied by the probability of maintaining contact at that distance); and $a(s)$ is the density function of the probability that a meeting would be abandoned at separation s (i.e. the proportion of meetings to which respondents are assumed likely to travel at this separation, additional to the proportion still attended at a marginally greater separation). $a(s)$ was obtained from results of the survey questionaire. It then follows that the 'effective damage' of separating two blocks of work is:

$$D^1_{xr} = k \times S^1_{xr} \times [L_{xr} + L_{rx}]/2.$$

This can then be summed over all blocks of work at given separation S_o to express 'effective separation':

$$\text{Effective separation} = \frac{\text{total damage}}{\text{total link strength}}$$

$$S_o = \frac{\left(\sum_{vx_1 r/S_{xr}} = S_o \right) D^1_{xr}}{k \left(\sum_{vx_1 r/S_{xr}} = S_o \right) L_{xr}}.$$

The idea behind effective separation is best illustrated with an example. If it is assumed that abandonment of meetings is not considered and participants, at least one of them, travel to make contact, then if:

no. of contacts = 100, separation = 4 hr,
average link strength = L,
then *communications*
damage = $4 \times 100 \times L = 400 \times L$.

Let us then assume that at the 4 hr separation level, the observed chance of abandonment of contacts is 35 out of 100. The value of the 35 abandoned contacts will vary but observations show that most of the values are small, perhaps an average of three-quarters of an hour. Then if:

no. of contacts = 100,
no. of abandoned meetings = 35,
no. of meetings held = 65,
separation = 4 hr,
average value of abandoned meetings = $\frac{3}{4}$ hr,

then:

$$\begin{aligned}
\textit{effective separation} &= (4 \times 65 \times L) + (\tfrac{3}{4} \times 35 \times L) \\
&= (260 \times L) + (26{\cdot}3 \times L) \\
&= 286{\cdot}3 \times L.
\end{aligned}$$

Hence for separation of 4 hr there is an effective separation of 2·9 hr for each contact. *Probable communications damage* is then:

$2{\cdot}9 \times 100 \times L$
(or link strength × effective separation).

The amount of communications damage increases in direct proportion to the distance which offices are moved from their location in central London. The above calculations relate to communications damage for 1 month, larger terms can easily be calculated by multiplying by the appropriate number of months. If large numbers are to be avoided it is useful to scale down the values obtained by 100 or 1000.

In Goddard's work on office communications, office location is held constant; the value of the communications damage approach is that account is taken of possible changes in location. Any changes in the present, highly centralized location of Government headquarters offices must have implications for efficiency. By attempting to measure the communications damage for different blocks of work within Departments, the possibilities for relocating parts of, or complete, units without impairing efficiency can be examined more objectively. Conclusions based on communications requirements alone, however, would need to consider the possibility that communications damage may be over-estimated. It may well be unreasonable to assume that only one meeting per trip is undertaken for it is possible to arrange several meetings on the same day. This cuts down unnecessary journeys and reduces effective separation to a much lower level than actual separation if trips are made to each meeting separately. The number of contacts between blocks of work in each month is an average figure which does not allow for within-block variations caused by the different contact requirements of staff, or of staff in different blocks but doing similar jobs. It is also important to make allowance for changes in communications requirements through time in response to changing office organization, function, and structure. This could mean that communications damage produced by changing the location of existing offices could become communications gain in future.

COMPARABILITY OF OFFICE COMMUNICATION STUDIES

One of the most encouraging features of the communications studies undertaken to date is the similarity between results for different cities. This suggests that if communications media and the tasks they have to perform are similar at different locations, there are certain underlying regularities in office contact patterns. Davey notes the remarkable level of similarity between contact patterns of offices in Leeds and Wellington.[61] The basis for comparison is the ranking of contact categories using the contact frequency index in Wellington and the ranking of office contacts weighted for frequency in Leeds. Although not all the contact categories in the two surveys are directly comparable, it was necessary to group some of the office functions identified in Wellington to correspond with the physical services category used in Leeds, broad comparison can justifiably be made. Using Spearman's rank correlation coefficient, Davey shows a statistically significant correlation between each of the major office sectors in each city. The values of r range from 0·59 for manufacturing offices to 0·81 for finance. Perhaps not surpris-

ingly, only offices in the miscellaneous group fail to reach a correlation which is statistically significant. This reflects the wide diversity of office activities within this category and the differences between the office structure of Wellington and Leeds. If central and local government contacts are removed from the data, the values of r increase further to 0·87 for finance offices and 0·96 for all contacts. Leeds and Wellington are cities of similar size and, in some respects, function and it is encouraging to find common patterns of contact amongst their office sectors.

It remains to be seen whether such comparisons can be extended to larger metropolitan centres such as New York and London. The complexity of their office systems may defy attempts to identify common patterns of office communications. But Goddard and Thorngren have also demonstrated similarities in office contact patterns in London, Stockholm, Gothenburg, and Malmö and it may be that the basic structure of office communications is similar both within and between cities in different countries.[62]

COMMUNICATIONS AND THE FUTURE LOCATION OF OFFICE ACTIVITY

Substitution of inter- and intra-urban travel with telecommunications make office activities potentially more footloose than at present. During recent years the development of telecommunications devices suitable for substitution and faster exchange of information has proceeded apace but their value for individual office employees and offices generally has not been investigated to any large degree. It is still not clear whether communications substitutes will be acceptable and economically viable for existing urban business trips. It is probable that the evolution of physical transport modes will take place more slowly than the development of communications technology. Consequently, it is not unreasonable to expect telecommunications substitution to become more important in future. The amount of substitution which takes place will depend on costs. Narrow-band systems which utilize similar transmission systems to the telephone are much cheaper than wide-band systems which use circuits similar to those used by television. Probably about 50 per cent of the meetings between office workers could be transferred to narrowband systems.

Some evaluation of possible communications substitutes for face-to-face meetings has been undertaken at the Joint Unit for Planning Research.[63] Laboratory and field experiments on different types of communications media have been used to test their effectiveness in decision-making, problem solving or bargaining. In the laboratory experiments, for example, the participants were allowed to communicate about the same problem using, initially, notes to each other and then moving up through the telephone, closed circuit television, microphones or loudspeakers and ending with face-to-face contact. The resolutions to the problem, using different media, were then analysed statistically for differences arising from the type of medium used. For face-to-face contacts, television produced better results than audio channels but it remains to be seen whether this would also be true for group communications. The field experiments involved an assessment of user experience of different types of equipment. Two of the most interesting are the use of closed circuit television and the 'remote meeting table' which overcomes the identification problem of group audio devices. The system provides for remote conferences by two groups of participants in which speakers are automatically identified to the listeners. The early results are encouraging and at least two Government Departments are installing the 'remote meeting table'.[64]

Widespread adoption by offices of 'Confravision', 'Picturephone', 'Videophone', 'Viewphone' or the 'remote meeting table' will ultimately depend on the economic trade-off between their adoption and travel costs. The major problem for most of these systems is the massive investment required to produce even a limited public network and the wide band width used in their operation.[65] It is also important to consider the 'psychological acceptability of a television presentation in place of face-to-face contact, the loss of social amenities such as handshakes, and the possible loss of orientation and perspective caused when everyone from corporate president to file clerk appear on the same screen. There would be no building to identify the man's image with, no office to reflect his personality or position, and no possibility of being invited to lunch. Instead, he would be just another face on the same old screen.'[66] If problems of this type persist, it is unlikely that the role of person-to-person meetings in office communications will be completely usurped. Certain types of face-to-face meeting will have to take place irrespective of the alternative methods available so that constraints on the location of some office activities will remain.

Developments in audio-visual office communications systems also need to be paralleled by the improvement of facsimile devices which can transmit printed, diagrammatic, and photographic information along the same channels. The main difficulty is the time factor; facsimile reproduction is relatively slow, approximately 5 min/page, for direct copies of material. Coding schemes could reduce the time by a factor of five or more and consequently allow quick reproduction of necessary information for use during a tele-conference.[67] Microfilm systems are also being used increasingly for their space saving and quick retrieval characteristics. The National Westminster Bank retains more than 9 m. sheets of computer output on microfilm which can be called into use by 800 bank branches linked by Post Office private lines.

The actual impact of these, and other developments, on office location patterns was already becoming apparent in 1960. Vernon observed that the 'introduction of electronic data processing may also speed the separation of routine office functions from the élite activities' on the basis of empirical observations of offices in the New York Region.[68] Improvements in telecommunications have certainly encouraged functional separation of offices although they are not the only factors operating (see Chapter 9). The best expression of the effects of these improvements are the growing number of office blocks located outside the C.B.D.s of major cities which are occupied by some departments of organizations with headquarters remaining in the centre. Not all these departments rely on telecommunications substitution; some are self-contained and do not require a central area location. Complete headquarters offices have also moved out of 'traditional' C.B.D. locations during the last decade in London, New York, Chicago, and other major cities. The success and encouragement for such locational change can be partially attributed to the opportunities for efficient telecommunications substitution for travel to face-to-face meetings, particularly for short inter-office contacts.

Present day and future short- and medium-term changes in office location patterns may eventually become outmoded. 'Office workers' may eventually be home based, using telex terminals, facsimile equipment, computer terminals and telephones to fulfil their job functions for employers.[69] The firm or company and its associated offices and/or production establishments could cease to exist as we know them if telecommunications were taken to their logical conclusion. Yet, the human element remains important in most higher level transactional activities and this may be sufficient to retain an élite core of office establishments at the centre of major cities. They would be linked by public and private telecommunications networks to satellite offices located near to, or at, the homes of employees. But even at the lower levels, staff attitudes to remote work will depend on its impact on job satisfaction and the balance between work and leisure time. Remote working also introduces problems of staff control and efficient allocation of tasks to individual workers. There are therefore many social or economic consequences of telecommunications for office work which might affect location trends. But whatever the future distribution of office activities, it is unlikely that the central location tendency, which has grown in significance during the last 100 years, will ever be as strong again.

REFERENCES

1   J. K. Pierce, *Symbols, Signals and Noise: The Nature and Process of Communication* (New York: Harper & Row, 1961), p. 79.

2   G. E. Browne, 'Communication is understanding', in K. Davies and W. G. Scott (eds), *Readings in Human Relations* (New York: McGraw-Hill, 1959), p. 331.

3   R. L. Meier, *A Communications Theory of Urban Growth* (Cambridge, Mass.: The M.I.T. Press, 1962), pp. 1–14. See also M. Webber, 'The urban place and nonplace urban realm', in M. Webber *et al.* (eds), *Explorations into Urban Structure* (Philadelphia: University of Pennsylvania Press, 1968). K. W. Deutsch, 'On social communications and the metropolis', in L. Rodwin (ed.) *The Future Metropolis* (London: Constable, 1962).

4   J. Rannells, *The Core of the City* (New York: Columbia University Press, 1956), pp. 19–21. A classification of functional linkages is given on pp. 29–32.

5   G. E. Törnqvist, 'Flows of information and the location of economic activities', *Geografiska Annaler*, vol. 50 (1968), p. 101. The interweaving of quaternary activities in Nantes has also been examined in the context of the city and its region, see A. Meonard and A. Vigarie, 'Les interrelations dans la tertiaire superieur Nantais', *Cahiers Nantais*, no. 7 (1973), pp. 5–120.

6   A. Custerson, 'Telecommunications: The key to the non-city?', *Built Environment*, vol. 2 (1973), p. 406.

7   R. C. Harkness, *Communication Innovations, Urban Form and Travel Demand: Some Hypotheses and a Bibliography* (Seattle: University of Washington, Department of Urban Planning and Civil Engineering, Research Report no. 71–2, (1972), pp. 2–3. D. W. Jones, *Must We Travel? The Potential of Communication as a Substitute for Urban Travel* (Stanford: Stanford University, 1973). M. Elton and R. Pye, *Travel or Telecommunicate? The Comparative Costs* (London: Communications Study Group, Joint Unit for Planning Research (University College London), 1974).

8   W. T. W. Morgan, 'Office regions in the West End of London', *Town and Country Planning*, vol. 29 (1961a), pp. 257–9. W. T. W. Morgan, 'A functional approach to the study of office distributions', *Tijdschrift voor Economische en Sociale Geografie*, vol. 52 (1961b), pp. 207–10. D. H. Davies, *Land Use in Central Capetown: A Study of Urban Geography* (Cape Town: Longmans, 1965). J. Rannells, *op. cit.*, pp. 118–82.

9   W. T. W. Morgan, *op. cit.* (1961b), pp. 209–10.

10 D. H. Davies, *op. cit.*

11 J. B. Goddard, *Office Linkages and Location* (Oxford: Pergamon, 1973), pp. 129–36.

12 R. M. Pierce, 'Towards an optimum policy for

office location' (University of Wales, unpublished M.Sc. Thesis, 1972), pp. 72–4. The index is based only on office employment statistics.

13 Derivation of standard distance is fully described in J. B. Goddard, *op. cit.*, p. 130.

14 J. B. Goddard, 'Multivariate analysis of office location patterns in the city centre: A London example', *Regional Studies*, vol. 2 (1968), pp. 69–85.

15 The application of correlation analysis to spatially arranged data violates the independence assumption and the problem of auto-correlation arises. The observed correlations therefore underestimate the true amount of spatial association, *ibid.*, p. 72.

16 For a full discussion of the derivation of Factors see J. B. Goddard, *op. cit.* (1968), pp. 74–5.

17 This distribution of financial activities is also suggested in S. M. Robbins and N. E. Terleckyj, *Money Metropolis* (Cambridge, Mass.: Harvard University Press, 1960), pp. 29–33.

18 J. B. Goddard, 'Functional regions within the city centre: A study by factor analysis of taxi flows in central London', *Transactions, Institute of British Geographers*, vol. 49 (1970), pp. 161–82.

19 J. B. Goddard, 'Office communications and office location: A review of current research', *Regional Studies*, vol. 5 (1971), p. 264. R. Pye, *A Cost Minimization Model for Choosing Office Location* (London: Communications Study Group, Joint Unit for Planning Research (University College London), 1973).

20 B. Thorngren, 'How do contact systems affect regional development?', *Environment and Planning*, vol. 2 (1970), pp. 409–27. See also B. Thorngren, 'Communication studies for Government office dispersal in Sweden', in M. J. Bannon (ed.) *Office Location and Regional Development* (Dublin: An Foras Forbartha, 1973), pp. 48–55.

21 B. Thorngren, 'Regional economic interaction and flows of information', in *Proceedings of the Second Poland-Norden Science Seminar* (Warsaw, 1967). G. E. Törnqvist, *op. cit.*, pp. 99–107. G. E. Törnqvist, *Contact Systems and Regional Development* (Lund: Gleerup, Lund Studies in Geography, Series B, no. 35, 1970).

22 G. E. Törnqvist, 'Contact requirements and travel facilities: Contact models of Sweden and regional development alternatives in the future', in A. R. Pred and G. E. Törnqvist, *Systems of Cities and Information Flows* (Lund: Gleerup, Lund Studies in Geography, Series B, 1973), pp. 81–121.

23 M. V. Facey and G. B. Smith, *Offices in a Regional Centre: A Study of Office Location in Leeds* (London: Location of Offices Bureau, Research Paper, no. 2, 1968). M. J. Croft, *Offices in a Regional Centre: Follow-up Studies on Infra-structure and Linkage* (London: Location of Offices Bureau, Research Paper, no. 3, 1969). J. B. Goddard, *op. cit.* (1970). J. B. Goddard, *op. cit.* (1973). A. Reid, *Face-to-Face contacts in Government Departments* (London: Joint Unit for Planning Research, 1971). City of Manchester, *Central Manchester Office Survey 1971* (Manchester: City Planning Department, 1972). See also M. J. Bannon, *Office Location in Ireland: The Role of Central Dublin* (Dublin: An Foras Forbartha, 1973).

24 *Dispersal of Government Work from London* (The Hardman Report) (London: Her Majesty's Stationery Office, Cmd 5322, 1973), pp. 75–84.

25 J. B. Goddard, *op. cit.* (1971), p. 266.

26 Some examples are F. Williams and J. Tolch, 'Communication by facial expression', *Journal of Communications*, vol. 2 (1965), pp. 17–27. H. J. Leavitt, 'Some effect of certain communication patterns on group performance', *Journal of Abnormal Psychology*, vol. 46 (1951), pp. 38–50. A. Kendon, 'Some functions of gaze-direction on social interaction', *Acta Psychologica*, vol. 26 (1967), pp. 22–63. J. D. Croxton and H. B. Goulding, 'The effectiveness of communication at meetings: A case study', *Operational Research Quarterly*, vol. 17 (1967), pp. 45–7.

27 H. A. Simon, *The Shape of Automation for Men and Management* (New York: Harper & Row, 1960).

28 A. Custerson, *op. cit.*, pp. 404–5. L. J. Hardman, 'When will Picturephone break out', *Electronics* (1971), pp. 97–8. I. Donos, 'Picturephone', *Bell Laboratory Record*, vol. 47 (1969).

29 T. Burns, 'Management in action', *Operational Research Quarterly*, vol. 8 (1957), pp. 45–60.

30 R. Stewart, *Managers and Their Jobs* (London: Macmillan, 1967), pp. 29–69.

31 Some respondents only completed the less obvious sections in this part of the questionnaire, ignoring use of the post for example. The technically fine dividing line between telephone, telegraph, teleprinter, telex, and datel also caused problems. M. V. Facey and G. B. Smith, *op. cit.*, pp. 76–7.

32 J. B. Goddard, *op. cit.* (1971), pp. 269–71. For a more detailed analysis of meetings and other communications activities of office workers (including an analysis of some regional differences in Britain) see S. Connell, *The 1973 Office Communications Survey* (London: Communications Study Group, Joint Unit for Planning Research (University College, London), 1974), pp. 34–60.

33 J. A. Davey, *The Office Industry in Wellington: A Study of Contact Patterns, Location and Employment* (Wellington: Ministry of Works, 1972), pp. 43–7.

34 *Ibid.*, p. 47.

35 M. J. Croft, *op. cit.*, Table 3, p. 9.

36 J. B. Goddard, *op. cit.* (1973), pp. 172–82. L. L. H. Baker and J. B. Goddard, 'Inter-sectoral contact flows and office location in central London', in A. G. Wilson (ed.), *London Studies in Regional Science, Vol. 3* (London: Pion, 1972). S. Connell, *op. cit.*, pp. 37–41.

37 J. H. Dunning and E. V. Morgan (eds), *An Economic Study of the City of London* (London: Allen & Unwin, 1971), pp. 161–3. M. J. Croft, *op. cit.*, pp. 16–26.

38 *The Sunday Times*, 12 August 1973.

39 M. J. Croft, *op. cit.*, p. 17.

40 Economist Intelligence Unit, *A Survey of Factors Governing the Location of Offices in the London Area* (London: Economist Intelligence Unit, 1964), Table C.I.7, p. 12.

41 *Ibid.*, Table C.I.5, p. 9.

42 City of Manchester, *op. cit.*, pp. 9–12 and Appendix 14, pp. 44–5.

43 *Ibid.*, Appendix 14, pp. 44–5.

44 J. A. Davey, *op. cit.*, pp. 14–42.

45 *Ibid.*, p. 37.

46 M. J. Croft, *op. cit.*, pp. 70–84.

47 Disaggregated data for 50 groups of offices defined by location, function, and status are used as a base. There were three possible responses to the question 'What is your main method of contact with your customers/clients?' (*a*) By their visiting your firm in your own offices. (*b*) By you or your staff visiting them in their office/home/elsewhere. (*c*) By other than face-to-face contacts. The Student's *t* test is used to compare pairs of contact figures for offices similar in function and location, but different in status, or similar in status and function, but different in location, *ibid.*, pp. 70–1.

48 Similar tests were applied to pairs of figures (relating to main method of contact with customers/clients) for offices similar in status and location but different in function, and to offices similar in function and location, but different in status. The results, in terms of the proportional distribution of pairs of contacts at given significance levels, proved remarkably similar. The relationships between function, location, and status and main method of contact attain approximately the same magnitude.

49 J. B. Goddard, *op. cit.* (1971), pp. 271–6.

50 *Ibid.*, p. 269.

51 Unlike factor analysis, latent profile analysis does not reduce data into a minimum number of independent factors but it seeks to identify within a scatter of observations (or points on a graph) those which form a perfect circle, i.e. in which two characteristics are locally uncorrelated, for example. The characteristics making such a group distinctive can be compared by comparing the means and standard deviations of the observations in a group with the equivalent values for all the data in the sample. Any number of variables can be used to search for groupings and Goddard uses eight contact characteristics. J. B. Goddard, *op. cit.* (1973), pp. 192–3 and Appendix D, pp. 229–30. W. A. Gibson, 'Three multi-variate models: Factor analysis, latent structure analysis and latent profile analysis', *Psychometrika*, vol. 24 (1959), pp. 54–77.

52 J. B. Goddard, *op. cit.* (1971), Table 6, p. 275. For an alternative classification see S. Connell, *op. cit.*, pp. 61–72.

53 'Orientation contacts' involve scanning the development space for new alternatives.

54 'Programmed contacts' utilize existing alternatives and take place at proximal locations.

55 J. B. Goddard, *op. cit.* (1973), pp. 204–10.

56 It should be stressed that one of the difficulties with using contact records is the possible lack of objectivity in the context of actual contacts. Goddard deliberately avoids subjective sub-divisions in the answers to each question on the contact sheets but contacts indicated as 'frequent' by respondents may not reflect objective frequency because they like having the contacts for personal reasons. It is also difficult to check for bias in the contact records caused by the attitudes and memories of respondents, so that the proportion of all contacts recorded is also unknown. These are not major problems but they become important when attempting to compare results of office communication studies in different cities and contact environments. See also S. Connell, *Report on the Pilot Communications Survey Contract* (London: Communications Study Group, Joint Unit for Planning Research, (University College London), 1972), pp. 5–41. S. Connell and R. Pye, *Survey Methods in Applied Telecommunications Research* (London: Communications Study Group, Joint Unit for Planning Research, (University College London), 1973).

57 Only staff down to Higher Executive Officer Level were included. *Dispersal of Government Work from London, op. cit.*, pp. 49–54.

58 *Ibid.*, p. 52.

59 I am indebted to T. P. Turner of the Civil Service

Department for his help and advice in the formulation of the equations included in this section.

60 Link strength was only expressed as a percentage during the initial stages of the study for the purposes of identifying the major contacts of each block of work and presentation of results to heads of departments.

61 J. A. Davey, *op. cit.*, pp. 36–7.

62 J. B. Goddard, *op. cit.* (1973), pp. 198–9. B. Thorngren, *op. cit.* (1973), pp. 50–1.

63 A. Reid, *Needs, Technology, Effectiveness and Impact* (London: Communications Study Group, Joint Unit for Planning Research, (University College, London), 1971). Communications Study Group, *The Scope for Person-to-Person Telecommunication Systems in Government and Business* (London: Communications Study Group, Joint Unit for Planning Research (University College London), 1973). *Dispersal of Government Work from London, op. cit.*, pp. 77–80. R. C. Harkness, *op. cit.*, pp. 13–14. S. Connell and R. Pye, *op. cit.*, pp. 8–25.

64 *Dispersal of Government Work from London, op. cit.*, pp. 78–9.

65 'Tomorrow's office', *The Times*, 5 September 1973.

66 R. C. Harkness, 'Communications substitutes for intra-urban travel', *Transportation Engineering Journal*, vol. 98 (1972), p. 587.

67 *Ibid.*, p. 595.

68 R. Vernon, *Metropolis 1985* (Cambridge, Mass.: Harvard University Press, 1960), p. 126.

69 C. Cherry, 'Electronic communication: A force for dispersal', *Official Architecture and Planning*, vol. 33 (1970), pp. 773–6. A. Custerson, 'Telecommunications: The office node', *Built Environment*, vol. 2 (1973), pp. 647–9. R. Pye, *The End of the Journey to Work: Fact or Fiction* (London: Communications Study Group, Joint Unit for Planning Research (University College London), 1974).

CHAPTER 9

Office Location: Forces for Change

During the last 15 years the central location tendency so characteristic of office activity has been increasingly counterbalanced by decentralization to suburban areas and to regions well outside the major concentrations of office employment. Some of the regional attributes of office location in respect of employment and the distribution of headquarters activities have already been demonstrated and disparities between regions have been an important stimulus to office decentralization in Britain and in other countries.[1] The need to resolve regional planning problems can generally be considered as the 'pull' factors. Equally important are the 'push' factors, such as congestion or spiralling rents, which cause offices to leave traditional central area locations. The relative roles of the push and pull factors on highly centralized office activities and their effects upon office location patterns will be the subject of this and the following chapter.

DEFINING 'DECENTRALIZATION'

It is useful to begin by defining the term 'decentralization'. Terms such as 'dispersal', 're-location', 'out-movement', 'migration' or 'diffusion' are commonly used to describe the changing location of office or industrial activities, but they are rarely defined for the purposes of the particular study. The value of defining the term used has been discussed at length by Woodbury.[2] He refers to the ambiguous and confused use of terminology in most studies, particularly in urban development and planning. Woodbury defines decentralization as a process or procedure that results in the withdrawal or redistribution of something from a place or centre in which it has previously been concentrated'.[3] Using this definition, office decentralization therefore involves the physical redistribution of office buildings, office space or office employees from the city centre to other locations not characterized by similar levels of concentration. It is important to distinguish between physical and management decentralization; the latter involves the transfer of responsibility from central control to satellite departments or individuals, either within the same building or in buildings elsewhere. This can take place without changes in the location of personnel or office space.

Woodbury also distinguishes between 'general' and 'proper' industrial decentralization, terms which could be equally well applied to offices.[4] 'General' office decentralization refers to the redistribution of offices amongst states and geographic regions, including movement to and from non-urban places of concentration. 'Proper' decentralization refers to intra-city and inter-city redistribution. The latter qualification of decentralization will be the context in which it is used below, although there is some overlap with 'general' decentralization because some offices have moved from central London, for example, to non-urban localities.

SOURCES OF DATA

There are few published statistics which relate directly to office decentralization. Until 1964 it was necessary to make intelligent guesses about the extent of decentralization in Britain by examining Census statistics for central areas or by conducting surveys designed to identify decentralized establishments, or surveys of offices known to have decentralized.[5] These were largely deductive exercises which incorporated substantial margins of error. Since 1964, the Location of Offices Bureau (L.O.B.) has annually published statistics for offices which have decentralized from central London.[6] Offices are categorized according to direction and distance moved; according to size and industrial classification; and firms which have approached L.O.B. for information, but have decided not to decentralize, are also tabulated for comparison with the movers. Separate lists of the number of offices and jobs which have moved to individual towns and cities in Britain, organized on the basis of Economic Planning Regions, are also available and are updated annually. The names of some of the companies which have decentralized can also be obtained and utilized for the purposes of survey work. But the L.O.B. statistics only relate to central London; there are no equivalent data for other major cities where decentralization, even if on a much smaller scale, may also be taking place. A more fundamental problem is that L.O.B. statistics do not cover all the offices which have decentralized because some firms have not chosen to use the services it provides. Hence, 'there has been a considerable amount of decentralization independent of L.O.B., of which no record is obtained'.[7]

Directories can be used to fill the gaps in L.O.B. statistics but this is an arduous task if long time series are required. Both Goddard and Hall have used *Kelly's Post Office Directory* which lists firms alphabetically by street, business, and name.[8] By comparing the addresses of offices listed in the directory for any two years or sequence of years the firms which have not moved, which have moved within central London, or which have moved out of the central area can be identified. Firms already known to L.O.B. are then excluded and the remaining firms with addresses no longer in the central area assumed to have decentralized.

There are a few difficulties encountered when using *Kelly's Directory*. The most important is identification of firms which occupy office space. The description of a firm's business is not always accurate enough as a guide to the kind of premises it occupies. In the case of central London, it is fairly safe to assume that most of the firms selected as offices from the directory will in fact occupy office space, but in Liverpool or Manchester, for example, the intermixing of commercial, industrial and warehouse activities would invalidate such an assumption. The offices of large industrial or service industries in central London or elsewhere are easy to identify but the distinction between office and production premises of smaller firms is difficult. A further difficulty is that only complete office moves can be traced because partial office decentralization need not involve the vacation of existing premises. Even some of the complete moves may be missed, however, in cases where a continuous time series is not used. If decentralization between two base years, X and Y, is being traced, the following may be excluded: firms established after year X and decentralized before year Y; firms that have changed their name either prior to, or after, decentralizing; firms which have moved and decentralized before year Y; and firms not listed for some reason by *Kelly's*.[9]

Taking these problems into account, Hall found that the information obtained from *Kelly's Directory* for central London was accurate for approximately 75 per cent of the firms in a 6 per cent sample of 1729. It seems particularly effective for tracing firms which have moved out of London's central area without consulting L.O.B. It seems that L.O.B.'s records cover approximately 50 per cent of the jobs decentralized from London and they are biased towards larger offices which move further from London and involve more partial moves than those undertaken independently.[10]

The lists of manufacturing and non-manufacturing headquarters locations given in *Fortune* and the *Times 1000* are in a similar category to directories.[11] The techniques used to trace decentralized offices and the disadvantages are similar to those outlined above. In addition, both sources are biased towards the larger firms and only identify headquarters but this is counterbalanced to some extent by the large number of office jobs involved. For the U.S.A., the *Fortune* lists are particularly important because there are no other major sources similar to the L.O.B. Detailed statistics on office decentralization are much less satisfactory than in Britain because of the obvious bias in the *Fortune* data and its limited coverage of all office establishments in the United States.[12]

All the above sources provide rather unsatisfactory data on commercial sector offices. Because they are under central control, the decentralization of Government Departments is more fully recorded. Until recently, however, the published information was sporadic and mainly appeared in *Hansard* or in fragmentary references in departmental reports.[13] In 1969 the *Whitley Bulletin* published a complete list of offices decentralized from London since 1963 as well as plans for future moves.[14] In 1973, all the relevant statistics were brought together and published as part of a Government report on office dispersal.[15] This, and the other sources mentioned, only relate to the non-industrial Civil Service which is almost completely office-based. Excluded are offices of nationalized industries and other quasi-government organizations which do not belong to the Civil Service. The limited amount of published information makes it difficult to obtain decentralization statistics for these sectors.

Inadequate coverage of changes in office location by the commercial sector can be partially rectified by reference to local authority office surveys. But, office surveys are by no means universal and tend to be conducted infrequently.[16] At best, therefore, sources of information on office mobility are incomplete, except for offices of the non-industrial Civil Service. A single, comprehensive source of annual statistics is urgently required. Offices already have to provide certain information, such as present address, number of employees or description of main activities, each year to the Factories Inspectorate under the *Offices, Shops and Railway Premises Act 1963*. If a question on previous, as well as present, address could be included along with the total employment of male and female office staff, a comprehensive record of changes in office location and employment would be obtained.[17] As an alternative, Hall has suggested that the Department of Employment's records could be adapted to an occupational as well as industrial classification, but this would only permit net rather than gross movements of office workers to be traced.

PRESSURES AT THE CENTRE

Experience in metropolitan areas throughout the world shows that as the density and congestion of activities in the C.B.D. increases, some of the activities which least need to be there are forced to move out. Industrial and residential uses are normally the first to suffer from increasing competition for the limited supply of central area space, but the spiralling costs of central area locations have also caused office activities to decentralize. It has already been shown that there are many mutual benefits derived from centralization of offices in the C.B.D. but there are also disadvantages. Amongst the most important are traffic congestion, overcrowding on commuter railways and underground systems, unnecessarily long and arduous journeys to work, inadequate and expensive parking facilities, high rent levels compared with less congested locations, and many office premises are obsolescent and difficult to convert to modern office standards and requirements. Staff costs are also higher in the C.B.D. and there are often shortages of suitable recruits. Turnover rates of secretarial staff, in particular, are also high and this adds to total costs.

The reasons actually given by office firms considering decentralization reflect some of the disadvantages of a central area location. The need for more space to accommodate firms' expansion requirements was mentioned by 48 per cent (24) of a sample of 50 central London offices.[18] High rents was the second most frequently mentioned reason (30 per cent), followed by the opportunity to reduce costs (22 per cent). Almost one-third of the offices in the sample mentioned that they were decentralizing in order to conform with Government policy but L.O.B.'s involvement in the survey probably prompted firms to give this reason even though, in the final analysis, its actual influence on the decision to decentralize may have been minimal. These figures largely corroborate statistics relating to reasons for decentralization published each year by L.O.B.[19] It is interesting to note that offices only stress reasons which affect their operating economics directly; factors such as traffic congestion or staff travel problems which represent community-borne costs and which do not directly influence the operation of individual office establishments, are comparatively unimportant, even though offices are themselves making a major contribution to such problems.

Other reasons for decentralizing have been cited by offices in Manhattan.[20] The high crime rate has led to sizeable losses of property through thefts and bombings while companies are also concerned about the dangers to employees travelling to work in the city's streets and subways. City and State taxes, which maintain New York's growing welfare costs, are considered exorbitant and racial minority problems are also listed. Some firms also find difficulty in transferring staff to their Manhattan offices even if this means that the staff involved have to leave their companies as a result. This problem is particularly acute amongst middle management personnel who are increasingly prepared to provide their services elsewhere if it means they can avoid New York. Inadequate housing, living costs, unco-operative city officials and the unhealthy physical environment of Manhattan are other reasons for considering decentralization. Many of these reasons probably rank as secondary push factors and the weight they carry depends on the value which individual executives place on being in Manhattan.

Pressures within the C.B.D. have therefore generated 'voluntary' decentralization from central London, New York, Chicago, Paris, Sydney and other major cities. There are some common underlying causes which explain the movement taking place in all these cities but in Britain the situation is complicated by the adoption of official policies and legislation designed to encourage decentralization. These policies have their roots in two related problems; regional inequalities in economic structure and employment opportunities, and the problems created by excessive concentration of offices in central London. Before evaluating the pattern of office decentralization in Britain during the last decade it is necessary to look at the background to the formulation of policy and legislation.

REGIONAL BACKGROUND TO BRITISH DECENTRALIZATION POLICIES

It is now more than 30 years since the Barlow Report on the *Distribution of the Industrial Population* was published but it remains an important benchmark in the development of decentralization policies in Britain.[21] This was the first Government report to examine in depth 'the causes which have influenced the present geographical distribution of the industrial population, and the probable direction of any change in the future; to consider what social, economic or strategical disadvantages arise from the concentrations of industries in large towns or in particular areas of the country; and to report what remedial measures should be taken in the national interest'.[22] Essentially, the Report was concerned with national imbalances in the distribution of population and manufacturing industry and did not directly discuss office activities. It seems reasonable to suggest, however, that in some parts of the Report where factory workers are mentioned, office workers could also be included. The Commission noted that 'as the workshop industries in the centre became replaced by factories on the outskirts, commercial and business houses and administrative offices will increase and multiply at the centre, and use even more intensively the space formerly used industrially'.[23] The demand for centrality amongst office activities was therefore already recognized in the Barlow Report but the problems likely to arise from this were not evaluated.

The main value of the Report was that it drew attention to the uneven distribution of growth industries, such as vehicles or electrical goods, in the South East Region. At the same time, the declining industries, such as textiles or shipbuilding were not being replaced by growth industries in the depressed areas outside the Midlands and South East. It is unfortunate that these trends in the location of industry were not linked to the related growth of office employment, both in connection with growth industries and the tendency for centralization within the South East, particularly London. The main recommendations of the Barlow Report involved decentralization of industry from the 'congested' areas and the creation of more equitable distributions of population and industry. It even suggested that a central authority be established to assess the advantages and costs of different methods of decentralization but this recommendation was not implemented until more than 20 years had elapsed, and then only partially.

The decentralization policies recommended by Barlow were inter-regional but the congested South East Region had its own problems of intra-regional redistribution of economic activities. The dominance of London both within its own region and nationally was clearly recognized in the Barlow Report and one of the Commission's members, Sir Patrick Abercrombie, subsequently produced two plans solely devoted to metropolitan planning problems and their influence on development in the South East. These were the *County of London Plan* and the *Greater London Plan 1944* published in 1943 and 1945 respectively.[24] Both plans were designed to examine techniques for implementing the Barlow recommendations and Abercrombie clearly realized that 'the decentralization of population implies decentralization of certain types of business undertaking and of industry, some Departments of Government may also wish to remain outside the central area. Pre-war trends emphasized in War Time should be encouraged.'[25] The emergent 'office problem' was apparent to Abercrombie and he recognized that commerce should be decentralized to existing and new

towns in the South East alongside industry. Routine office work could be carried out in the suburbs and beyond where rents were lower and where office workers could live nearer to their place of work.

During the immediate post-war period, however, attention was exclusively given to the control and decentralization of industrial development in London, particularly to the new towns recommended by Abercrombie and largely implemented under the *New Towns Act 1946*. At the same time, central government was involved in various activities designed to encourage industrial movement to the Development Areas. The *Distribution of Industry Act 1945* gave the

TABLE 47

GROWTH OF OFFICE EMPLOYMENT IN BRITAIN'S ECONOMIC PLANNING REGIONS—1951–61 AND 1961–6

Region	1951–61 Growth (%)		1961–66 Growth (%)	
	Males	Females	Males	Females
Northern	35·3	37·3	7·2	20·7
Yorkshire and Humberside	30·0	41·9	8·7	15·8
North West	27·9	33·5	6·1	15·0
East Midlands	41·0	46·0	12·0	21·0
West Midlands	41·2	42·6	11·1	15·4
South East and East Anglia	40·8	41·8	10·2	17·7
South West	44·4	41·8	7·3	19·7
Wales	37·7	39·6	1·5	20·0
Scotland	29·2	26·9	3·2	9·1
Periphery	30·5	34·3	5·7	14·9
Centre	41·4	42·2	10·2	17·8
Development Areas	31·4	30·3	3·3	13·2
Non-Development Areas	38·7	41·4	9·7	17·5

Note: Office employment is based on the Registrar General's definition of office occupations (1966), adjusted where necessary to fit 1961 and 1951 Census data. Growth rates are derived from the *Census of Population* 1951, 1961, and 1966.

Source: E. M. Burrows, 'Office employment and the regional problem', *Regional Studies*, vol. 7 (1972), Tables A2 and A5, pp. 30–1.

Board of Trade powers to build advance factories, to provide capital loans for firms, to apply compulsory purchase orders, and to improve the infrastructure and services of the depressed areas. The initial powers provided by the 1945 Act were given teeth by the introduction of industrial development certificates (I.D.C.s) in the *Town and Country Planning Act 1947*. Any industrialist wanting to build a new factory or an extension to existing premises involving more than 5000 ft^2 or 10 per cent increase in floorspace had to apply for an I.D.C. from the Board of Trade. Development control powers were also vested in counties and county boroughs which enabled them to achieve the objectives of local development plans within the overall framework of industrial decentralization policy. There is no doubt that these controls, which have been subject to periodic changes since 1945, have been a powerful influence on the location of industry in Britain. Movement from London to locations in the South East and to Britain's other Economic Planning Regions and Development Districts has been substantial.[26]

Abercrombie's references to office activity remained submerged for almost 15 years by an obsession with manufacturing decentralization. Meanwhile, office work was growing faster than any other type of employment and office de-velopment remained unhindered by direct policies and controls of the type affecting manufacturing industry. Development control procedures used in planning were an ineffective influence on location, partly because there was no policy adopted to control or guide office development. The movement of manufacturing plants from London probably involved some redistribution of office work connected with day-to-day administration of the factories involved but the number of office employees was low compared with the number of industrial jobs moved. In the absence of restrictions, the office space lost as a result of the wartime bombing in central London was soon replaced when building restrictions were lifted. Central London was able to re-establish itself as Britain's major office centre and to strongly enhance its position until legislation directed at offices was finally introduced in 1965.[27] During the intervening period, growth of male and female office employment in regions outside the South East/East Anglia, West and East Midlands, and the South West generally lagged behind (Table 47). Comparison of growth rates between the Centre and the Periphery or Development and non-Development Areas reveals a continuing discrepancy in growth rates between 1951 and 1966.

LONDON'S OFFICE PROBLEMS

Concentration of office activities in central London has also been a catalyst for decentralization; yet a decade had elapsed after 1945 before the office problem was considered seriously. Symptomatic was the *City of London Plan 1944* which, although subsequently rejected, revealed no anxiety about the future rate of development in commerce and trade which formed much of its economic base.[28] It was keen to permit rapid reconstruction of offices and warehouses to immediately pre-war levels. It was not expected that building heights would exceed by very much the pre-war situation and therefore the number of daytime workers in the City, many of them employed in offices, was not considered likely to exceed the pre-war estimate of 500,000. Land behind commercial properties fronting onto main roads was to be made available for residential purposes, although conversion to commercial use would be possible later if demand exceeded anticipation. The first Development Plan for the County of London (1951) increased the amount of land zoned for offices from 795 to 925 acres while at the same time acknowledging that the central area, in particular, was already congested. The Plan recognized, however, that it was important 'to ensure by zoning and plot ratio control that the extent of offices and other commercial accommodation is not in conflict with the policy of decentralization'.[29] Offices utilize space at higher densities than most other activities, however, and because of this the 1951 proposals were consequently amended before the Plan was approved in 1955.

Decentralization of population and industry from the County of London was an overriding consideration in the Development Plan proposals and surrounding counties allocated land in their own development plans for the purpose. But allocation of land for office construction which would provide space for decentralized offices in these areas only took place on the initiative of the Ministry of Housing and Local Government. The *County of Middlesex Plan*, for example, was therefore amended to include specified areas for decentralized offices in the suburban areas beyond the North Circular Road.[30]

This marked the beginning of a more positive approach to office development in central London. The L.C.C. announced new policies which had four major objectives, two of which related to office development.[31] First, it was proposed to reduce the area in which large office buildings were permitted and to stem the tide of increasing employment in the centre. Secondly, with the co-operation of Government Departments and other local authorities such as Middlesex and Surrey, an attempt would be made to encourage office development nearer the areas where office workers lived. Many of these areas were outside the L.C.C.; the continuing concentration of office space in central London was causing office workers to make longer journeys to work than other workers in London. The congestion at the centre was defined in terms of crowded trains and the fatigue of a long journey to work; the queues at rush hours; the crawling buses; the traffic jams; and the cramped working conditions in office buildings.[32] There was approximately 77·5 m. ft^2 of office floorspace in the central area in 1948; by 1962 it had increased by approximately 34 per cent to 1·14·8 m. ft^2.

The office boom was therefore well under way by the time the L.C.C.'s policy document emerged. Development charges were withdrawn in 1953 and building licence controls in 1954 so that whereas planning permission was granted for only 2·4 m. ft^2 in central London in 1952, this increased rapidly to 5·7 and 5·9 m ft^2 in 1954 and 1955 respectively.[33] Such trends were partially countered by revising plot ratios and reducing the area allocated to office development but these were largely ineffective because of the loopholes

provided by the Third Schedule.[34] Consequently, offices continued to push other uses out of central London and continued to generate increased demand for housing within daily commuting distance, together with uneconomic and congested utilization of public transport facilities. It is not surprising, therefore, that concern about the growth of office activities in central London continued to gain momentum during the next few years.

A number of studies dealing in full or in part with the office problem emerged during the early 1960s.[35] One of the most influential was the *Paper Metropolis* which analysed the growth of office employment in London, reported on a survey of offices which had decentralized, and made a number of recommendations. The report uncompromisingly pointed to the fact that there was 'no office dispersal policy in terms of a clear programme of action' and 'the net result must appear as an almost complete failure to limit, much less reduce, office space and employment in central London'.[36] In a memorandum to the Government the report listed a number of policy objectives which relied heavily upon decentralization for their success. These would be achieved by encouraging office building in the suburbs and in selected towns between 25 and 40 miles from central London, combined with maximum dispersal to major provincial cities outside the South East. The new and expanded towns were seen as particularly suitable for receiving decentralized offices. But such objectives could not be achieved without more stringent planning controls. Office development certificates, similar to the industrial development certificates already in use, were considered to be unworkable on an equitable basis. 'Freezing' of planning permissions for a period was also considered but eventually rejected in favour of a mixture of strengthened conventional planning controls and new financial measures. The memorandum is vague about the form of these controls and measures although the floorspace levy payable to the Government by offices in central Paris was outlined. There was also a recommendation that the Third Schedule be rescinded as soon as possible.

Exhortation to decentralize and adopt stronger policies towards offices was, in some ways, rather late. There is evidence that decentralization was already taking place 'naturally' soon after the war and the trend increased as local authorities such as Middlesex and Essex attempted to attract decentralized offices after 1956.[37] Initial impetus was provided by firms building their own office premises which allowed them to avoid the rising land and rent costs of central London. Decentralization of this kind was enhanced by the office boom and speculative office development was common in suburban London well before the *Paper Metropolis* appeared. Its proposals simply involved articulation of an existing trend in favour of towns beyond suburban London. Various suburban centres and towns had been listed as suitable for receiving decentralized offices in the various reports appearing between 1957 and 1964. The centres recommended were rarely the same, however, and there was little co-ordination of the policies adopted by local authorities prepared to receive offices. Indeed, the initial enthusiasm for receiving offices shown by local authorities adjacent to the L.C.C. had already changed to doubt and eventual abandonment of the decentralization policy by 1962.

Expansion of the London conurbation encroached upon large parts of Middlesex and Surrey, for example, and office development there simply increased the floorspace total for the conurbation as a whole and did little to relieve London's problems. Suburban office blocks were generating local traffic problems and attracting firms moving from areas other than the L.C.C. Attempts were made to limit the occupation of new office buildings to firms from the L.C.C. or those already located in the particular county but these proved ineffective because they were difficult to apply once the first tenants had been replaced. Middlesex, Essex, Hertfordshire, and Surrey had all reversed their policies by 1962 and only Croydon, which was London's most rapidly growing suburban office centre, continued to actively attract new office construction and decentralized offices. It had become very clear that existing planning legislation was inadequate to encourage decentralization, particularly as the local authorities representing some of the most attractive locations for decentralized offices were no longer committed. In addition, the oppor-

tunities for promoting decentralization to centres in the South East, outside London, and as part of regional development policies, began to be reemphasized.[38]

In 1963 the Government published a White Paper which set out a broad strategy for an attack on London's office problems and this included a proposal to establish a bureau to promote decentralization.[39] In September 1963 the Location of Offices Bureau (L.O.B.) was created with a view to demonstrating to London businessmen the facts of the situation and to encourage decentralization; to provide free and impartial information to firms interested in decentralization and those seeking locations outside central London; and to carry out research on all aspects of the office problem.[40] The Bureau has continued to execute these terms of reference and has undoubtedly acted as an important information centre for actual and intending movers. It is important to appreciate, however, that it does not possess any executive powers and is not part of the formal machinery of land use planning. The Bureau cannot intervene in planning disputes affecting office development, neither does it act as an estate agent. The 1963 White Paper reiterated that new office centres should be established in the suburbs; that there should be greater dispersal of civil servants and that office centres should also be created well away from the London Region. This theme was continued in the *South East Study* (*1964*) and, later that year, by yet another White Paper.[41]

The latter introduced the first planning controls directly affecting office development. From 4 November 1964 there was to be a total ban on office development in specified areas and the proposals were implemented through the *Control of Offices and Industrial Development Act 1965*. The Act had retrospective effect, to 4 November 1964, on office development on land in the Metropolitan Region. In addition to normal planning permission, each development required an office development permit (O.D.P.) whether for a new building, change of use, or extension of existing buildings. Within the G.L.C., an O.D.P. was required even if planning permission had been given, unless a contract to build had been entered into before 5 November

1964.[42] Only office development of less than 3000 ft² gross was exempt. The Board of Trade, given the responsibility of granting or refusing O.D.P. applications, was given powers to attach conditions to them which had to be taken into account by local authorities receiving the subsequent applications for planning permission.

Although originally confined to the London Metropolitan Region, the controls were gradually extended to cover the remainder of the South East and West and East Midlands Planning Regions and, finally, East Anglia (Fig. 39). In response to the structure of demand for office space, the exemption limit was raised to 10,000 ft² in the areas outside the London Metropolitan Region in 1967. In March 1969 the controls were removed from East Anglia, Lincolnshire, Rutland, and Herefordshire and the exemption limit raised to 10,000 ft² in those parts of the London Metropolitan Region outside Greater London. Finally, in December 1970 the O.D.P. exemption limit was also raised from 3000 to 10,000 ft² in Greater London. The remaining parts of the East and West Midlands still subject to control were also given complete exemption.

The controls were originally to operate for seven years from 5 August 1965 but were extended for a further five years from 2 August 1972.[43] Apart from O.D.P.s, building licences were introduced in July 1965 for commercial projects of over £100,000 in all except the development areas. The value of contracts covered by this additional restriction was further reduced in 1966 to £50,000 but Parliament did not approve this system and it was removed in 1967. Only commercial office development by private developers, local authorities or statutory undertakers is covered by the 1965 Act. Until October 1971, Government Departments, particularly the Ministry of Public Building and Works, did not require O.D.P.s or planning permission for office development. This procedure, often referred to as Circular 100, has since been revised to make Government Departments at least consult local authorities about proposed development before proceeding.[44]

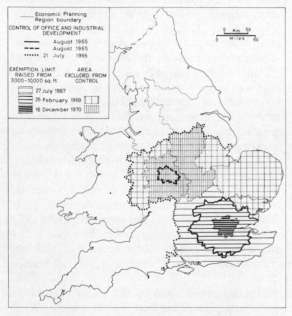

Fig. 39   Areas Covered by Office Development Controls—1965–73

INACCURATE ASSUMPTIONS?

By mid-1964, outstanding planning permissions, office zoning and Third Schedule liabilities suggested a potential increase of more than 170,000 office employees in central London. It therefore appeared sensible to introduce legislation which would influence the rate at which commitments and future proposals were implemented. In retrospect, however, it is doubtful whether the objectives of the 1965 Act were based on sound statistical evidence. There were two main assumptions; that office jobs in central London were increasing at 15,000 jobs per annum; and that the number of commuters travelling into central London would increase by 200,000 (including 50,000 non-office workers) between 1961 and 1971.

The first assumption was an estimate based on an increase of 150,000 office jobs in the central area between 1951 and 1961.[45] But the 1961 Census results were not available until 1965 and almost every official and unofficial source utilized the figure of 15,000 without qualification.[46]

At the end of 1966 it was shown that the actual increase between 1951 and 1961 had been 55,000,[47] an increase of roughly 6000 per annum. Indeed, between 1961 and 1966, total employment in the central area fell by 65,000 with only administrative and professional office occupations showing an absolute increase. This was balanced by a decline in the number of clerical workers, partly caused by decentralization already in progress before the Act became operational, so that the overall number of office workers stabilized during the inter-censal period. The fall in central area employment means that office employment could have increased by 13,000 per annum without resulting in an increase in total employment. Allowing for employment changes in other central area activities, it is unlikely that office employment increased at the maximum rate. The drift of employment into the South East Region from the remainder of the country has also not been as serious as expected. During the last decade employment in the Region has reached a peak of almost 8·1 m. in 1966 and has since decreased to less than 7·8 m. in 1971.[48]

The transport assumption was based on the view that 'it seems unlikely that the increasing load (of commuting into central London) could come to less than an annual average of 20,000 in the period up to 1971. This means that we must expect 200,000 more commuters, over and above the numbers travelling to central London in 1961.'[49] But total employment in central London had already begun to decrease between 1961 and 1966, making the estimated growth of commuting inaccurate by at least 140,000–150,000 trips. The number of peak period commuters into central London has shown a steady decline since 1962 (Table 48) although, because of the ever-widening residential distribution of office workers, there was an increase of 8000 trips from beyond Greater London in 1961–6 and this trend has continued. Hence, congestion of London's public transport system has probably increased during the last decade, particularly during the peak hours. It is also possible that the figures in Table 48 incorporate an element of double counting, particularly on the trains and underground; while not all the arrivals in the central area actually work there.[50]

TABLE 48

PEAK PERIOD COMMUTERS INTO CENTRAL LONDON — 1962–70

Year	By rail ('000)	Change	By road ('000)	Change
1962	883	—	338	—
1963	860	-23	311	-27
1964	860	—	312	1
1965	861	1	296	-16
1966	852	-7	290	-6
1967	860	8	283	-7
1970[1]	830	-30	263	-20
Total change 1962–70		-51		-75

Note: 1. No data published for 1968 and 1969. The count refers to the period 07.00–10.00 hr.
Source: London Transport.

The need for controls designed to promote decentralization and to prevent employment growth in central London has therefore been questioned in some quarters.[51] It is argued that the O.D.P. controls have interfered with the market system for office space to the detriment of central London and the other areas included at various times. By limiting the amount of new office space built annually in central London there has been a growing imbalance between supply and demand. It has been estimated that office rents in central London for old properties spiralled 380 per cent between 1965 and 1970 and 480 per cent for new buildings.[52] At the end of 1968 there was only 20,000–30,000 ft^2 of new space immediately available in the City. The boom in office building in the years after 1954 had led to a situation where new office buildings in central London could not be let in the early 1960s and demand was clearly declining. Once O.D.P.s were introduced the supply of office space immediately became artificially restricted, causing the empty buildings to be occupied, and eventually causing rapid rent increases. In addition, the spectacular growth of office buildings during the boom could not be equated with equally rapid increases in office employment because floorspace/employee ratios were also improving compared with older buildings. It has also been suggested that the controls were introduced at precisely the time when developers were actively engaged in evaluating decentralized locations in suburban London and the South East for new projects.[53] But O.D.P.s were also required in these areas and frustrated potential market trends.

The Layfield Report develops these arguments and suggests that O.D.P.s are ineffective as a method of controlling short- and medium-term growth of office employment and activity in central London.[54] They can only affect new premises; there is no attempt, because it is almost impossible, to distinguish between the needs of those offices which need to be in central London and those which do not; and, finally, because there is no fixed relationship between office floorspace and level of occupation the effect of O.D.P.s on employment is unpredictable. The Report suggests that O.D.P.s be removed and replaced by a system of taxes or charges which would raise the cost to firms of being in central London to levels well above those they presently support. This would encourage firms to decentralize on their own accord. Alternatively, it has been suggested elsewhere that planning permission, which must be obtained after an O.D.P. has been granted, should be awarded to the highest bidder.[55] This would be the developer prepared to pay that value for a site which would accrue to it as soon as planning permission is granted. This can be several times the price paid to the landowner for the site without planning permission. If a site really is worth several million pounds the property company would be willing to pay the sum to the local authority. Such a system will reduce excessive speculative development and lead to social as well as private gain.

POLICY CHANGES

Doubts and uncertainties about the need to control office development are reflected in more general changes in policy since 1965. Originally, the aim was to redistribute office jobs within South East England, using L.O.B.'s persuasion and some Civil Service office dispersal.[56] This made sense relative to the continuing outward movement of London's population at a faster rate than the dispersal of employment. Office workers have been in the forefront of such movement and the separation between homes and workplaces would have increased if no attempt had been made to move office jobs from central London. Greater London has been losing population at the rate of approximately 90,000 per year since 1961 while the Outer Metropolitan Region and the Outer South East have achieved substantial positive increases as a result. When the controls were extended to cover areas outside the South East (see Fig. 39) the policy changed to incorporate inter-regional objectives, i.e. decentralization to the 'depressed areas' in the north and west. As we shall see later, this initiative did not prove successful, and policy has again concentrated on redistribution within the context of the *Strategic Plan for the South East*.[57]

Finally, in 1973 a further variation of policy was introduced and involves the provision of grants to service industries (XVIII–XXIV) prepared to move to Areas for Expansion, i.e. the whole of Scotland, Wales, Northern and North-West England, Yorkshire and Humberside, some parts of the Midlands and much of South West England. Business and company offices such as those in insurance, banking and finance (XXI) are eligible provided they have a genuine choice of location between moving to the Areas of Expansion and the rest of the country and the move will provide at least 10 new jobs in the reception area. Aid consists of a removal grant of £800 for each employee moved with his work up to a limit of 50 per cent of the number of additional jobs created in an area and a grant to cover 100 per cent of the approved rent of premises in the new location.[58] Equivalent help is given where premises are bought rather than rented.

Since 1965 there has undoubtedly been a general relaxation of office controls, both spatially and in terms of the number of O.D.P.s granted. The percentage of declared demand permitted increased from 16 per cent in 1965–6 to 37·7 per cent in 1968–9 for central London, and from 29·2 to 53·5 per cent for the Outer Metropolitan Region.[59] But this has not made the task of

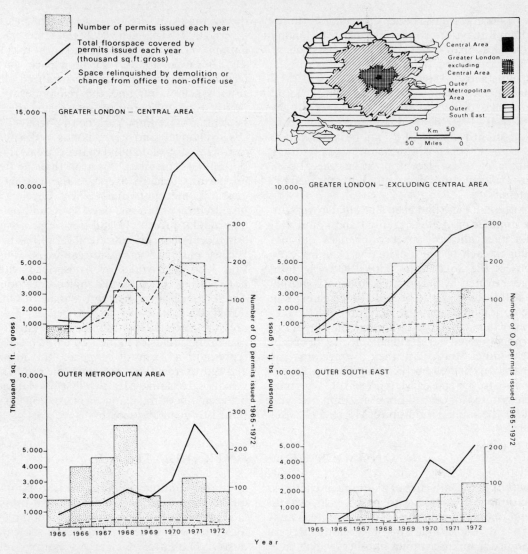

Fig. 40   O.D.P.'s Granted for Areas of the South East Planning Region—1965–72 (Data: *Trade and Industry*, 1973)

decentralization any easier. At the time the Act was passed there was approximately 25 m. ft^2 of office space already in the 'pipeline' for central London alone. The amount of space with outstanding permission or with approval subject to an O.D.P. was considerably less in the remainder of the Greater London area and in the Outer Metropolitan Region; approximately 13 m. ft^2 of new offices were complete or under construction.[60] This was the seed of a serious problem

in that as soon as the controls were applied very few O.D.P.s were granted (Fig. 40). The restrictions were particularly severe in the centre and remainder of the G.L.C. but were almost as tight elsewhere. Most of the space receiving permits (54 per cent in the G.L.C. in 1966) replaced that relinquished by demolition or change from office to non-office use. The amount of new space consistently formed less than 50 per cent of all O.D.P.s granted for the G.L.C. until 1969, and the position was little better in the Outer Metro-politan Region (55–60 per cent). Central London gained less than 600,000 ft^2 in 1966, 1·3 m. ft^2 in 1967 and 2·0 m. ft^2 in 1968. The space in the 'pipeline' satisfied some of the demand in central London but in outer London, for example, vacant space had decreased from 12 to 8 m. ft^2 by 1967.[61] By 1970 the total new and vacant space in the suburbs and O.M.R. had been reduced to just 3 m. ft^2 which is a measure not only of the volume of office decentralization but also of the artificial shortages caused by the O.D.P. system.[62]

Although there had been a gradual increase in the number of O.D.P.s granted and amount of floorspace allowed, marked changes did not occur in each of the four major planning divisions of the South East until 1969. The total space covered by permits has increased sharply since that time, partly because of the changes in exemption limits, but also in response to the realities of demand. Hence, although the number of permits granted has declined since 1970, except in the Outer South East, their average area has consistently increased (Fig. 40). During the 12 months to the end of March 1973, 131 permits were granted for central London, compared with 180 in the same period up to March 1972. But the average size of each development has risen from 66,000 to 69,000 ft^2.[63] At the same time, the amount of space relinquished has formed a smaller proportion of total floorspace, particularly in areas popular with decentralized offices; suburban London and the remainder of the South East. New office space has therefore become a more important component of floorspace changes and corresponds more to the characteristics of demand in these areas. It is important to remember, however, that the figures for permits tend to overstate the true level of existing and potential office development, because more than one developer can apply for a particular project. In addition, approximately 30 per cent of the permits are never utilized, often because planning permission cannot be obtained from local authorities oversubscribed with, or not wanting to encourage, office development. The less rigid approach to the issue of O.D.P.s during the last few years also reflects political pressures exerted by Members of Parliament questioning refusals in their constituencies. This represents a form of 'appeal', not normally allowed by the 1965 Act, and can result in reversal of decisions. Meanwhile, the relationship between offices and planning in London has continued to generate debate.[64]

ECONOMICS OF DECENTRALIZATION

Apart from the influence of planning restrictions, decisions to decentralize are based on an evaluation by companies of the costs and benefits arising from re-location. This information is best obtained from case studies of offices which have actually moved but there have been surprisingly few analyses of this kind.[65] The most comprehensive has been undertaken by Rhodes and Kan who have analysed data from a sample of 62 offices representing a cross-section of experience in office movement and a range of manufacturing and service industries. The main criteria determining choice of new location were found to be: (1) the need to retain communications with offices in London; (2) the location had to be acceptable to key staff actually moving with the office; (3) a good and reliable supply of secretarial and clerical staff; (4) the immediate avail-ability of suitable premises, i.e. the right size, quality, and location relative to local transport facilities; and (5) some organizations preferred locations with little existing manufacturing industry. The latter is clearly a prestige-related variable. Rhodes and Kan note that in 'the majority of cases there was no doubt that environmental and psychological factors play as important a part in the location decision with respect to offices as they do in the location of manufacturing plants'.[66] Indeed, 'the choice of headquarters location is far more subjective and value laden than any other business decision'.[67] Consequently, only 50 per cent of the offices in the sample claimed to have given close attention to the economic effects of their decentralization decision; only 1 in 10 of the companies interviewed had attempted detailed costing and these were for offices which had actually been moved. The situation was similar amongst firms which had not yet moved but were considering doing so.

The operating costs of office activities at different locations reflect variations in rents, rates, salaries and related items, and communications costs. There are problems of standardization when trying to compare rents for different localities but, in general, outside central London rents fall sharply so that new premises in the West End may let for an average of £7.50/ft^2 compared with £2.50/ft^2 for similar standard suburban office space. Beyond Greater London the rent gradient falls more slowly and begins to rise again as the larger provincial cities are approached. Rent levels then begin to parallel or even exceed those for similar premises in suburban London, particularly for new office space.[68] The differential in rateable values between areas of Britain is not as marked as for rents and Rhodes and Kan estimate the difference to be approximately £60–£90 per employee per annum assuming that the same space standards are employed at both locations. Staff costs, largely made up of salaries, can also be reduced by decentralization but the actual saving achieved depends on the proportion of staff moving with the office. The higher the proportion and the larger the inducements necessary to attract central London staff, the lower the initial reduction in staff costs; in certain circumstances they may even increase marginally, particularly for small office organizations. Offices decentralizing with a small proportion of their existing staff stand to gain from the lower salaries prevailing outside central London and the absence of 'London weighting'. The actual savings achieved would ultimately depend on location chosen because there are areas outside central London, such as Merseyside and Clydeside, where median salaries of clerical workers in some grades are higher.[69] A recent report based on nine case studies of offices which moved between 20 and 80 miles shows that rent and rates savings are almost non-existent and three firms had increased costs amounting to £300 per employee.[70] This is also starting to occur in the United States.[71]

Most offices place great stress on the communications difficulties which discourage them from decentralizing even part of their activities. Such problems need to be seen in perspective, however, in that although decentralization may lead to some increase in communication costs, reductions in the cost of other items will more than compensate.[72] Problems of transferring items such as data over long distances are retreating with the introduction of new facilities at reasonable cost. Most of the offices in the sample used by Rhodes and Kan noted that post-decentralization communications damage had not been serious and was less than expected. Indeed, there had been an actual improvement in intra-company communication because of the forced investment in modern, long distance, communications facilities.

In a model of the office location decision, suggested by Pye, the feasibility of maintaining desired levels of communication, as expressed by the value of time, at a decentralized location is examined in detail using data from an office which has moved.[73] It is assumed that desired levels of communication will continue to be held and that those who travelled short distances to meetings before decentralization will continue to travel. The additional costs of such communication are compared with the savings on rents, rates and salaries. Assuming that other factors such as executive preference or availability of suitable premises can be ignored, the model indicates that the use of narrow-band systems will usually make it cost-effective to decentralize to all locations if time is valued at £2·50 per hour or less. The additional use of wide-band systems only provides incentives for short distance decentralization unless time is valued at more than £10 per hour. Comparison of the model results with data from the departments in the case study office suggests, however, that the telecommunications encouragement to decentralization is actually relatively small at the present time and certainly not sufficient to make firms move beyond South East England. The pattern of decentralization discussed in the next chapter corroborates this observation.

Decentralization will also involve immediate 'once and for all' costs which Rhodes and Kan term 'transitional' costs. Such costs arise from occupation of the new premises, equipping it and preparing it for the organization's particular user

...uirements. There are also employee-derived costs such as disturbance allowances, legal fees, short-term bridging loans for house purchase and removal expenses. Transitional costs exclude the capital cost of purchasing new premises but if they are then modified some transitional costs are incurred and comprise the cost of alterations less the amount by which the value of the premises has increased to a potential buyer. The level of transitional costs, averaged at £474 per job created in the Rhodes and Kan study, will vary according to distance moved, the type of activities, and the efficiency of the exercise in management terms.

REFERENCES

1 M. J. Bannon, 'Office employment and regional development in Ireland', J. Toby, 'Regional development and Government office relocation in the Netherlands', in M. J. Bannon (ed.) *Office Location and Regional Development* (Dublin: An Foras Forbartha, 1973), pp. 9–20 and pp. 37–46.

2 L. Woodbury, *The Future of Cities and Urban Redevelopment* (Chicago: University of Chicago Press, 1953), pp. 207–11.

3 *Ibid.*, p. 207.

4 *Ibid.*, p. 208.

5 J. V. Aucott, 'Dispersal of offices from London', *Town Planning Review*, vol. 31 (1960), p. 39. Town and Country Planning Association, *The Paper Metropolis* (London: Town and Country Planning Association, 1962).

6 Location of Offices Bureau, *Annual Reports* (London: Location of Offices Bureau, 1964–74).

7 J. B. Goddard, 'Changing office location patterns within central London', *Urban Studies*, vol. 4 (1967), p. 284. Other, rather more specialized, statistics can be obtained from local authorities involved in overspill programmes. The best example is the G.L.C. which has records of firms moving to expanded towns throughout the South East. The New Town Corporations also keep records of offices and other activities which move in to their areas and these can usually be traced back to origin.

8 *Ibid.*, p. 277. R. K. Hall, 'The movement of offices from central London', *Regional Studies*, vol. 6 (1972), pp. 386–7. P. Cowan *et al.*, *The Office: A Facet of Urban Growth* (London: Heinemann, 1969), pp. 96–7.

9 R. K. Hall, *op. cit.*, p. 388.

10 *Ibid.*, p. 399.

11 *Fortune: The Fortune Directory* (*Annual Supplement*) (New York: Time Inc., 1956–74). *The Times 1000 Leading Companies in Britain and Overseas 1971–72* (London: Times Newspapers Ltd, 1972).

12 The Building Owners and Managers Association publish relevant statistics in *Skyscraper Management* as well as producing locally derived statistics for individual cities. The coverage, however, varies from city to city depending on membership of the Association and number of office building owners responding to its surveys.

13 See E. Hammond, 'Dispersal of Government offices: A survey', *Urban Studies*, vol. 3 (1967), p. 258.

14 'Dispersal', *The Whitley Bulletin*, February 1969.

15 *Dispersal of Government Work from London* (The Hardman Report) (London: Her Majesty's Stationery Office, Cmd 5322, 1973), pp. 21–30.

16 P. W. Daniels, 'Office decentralization from London: Policy and practice', *Regional Studies*, vol. 3 (1969), p. 172.

17 *Idem.* R. K. Hall, *op. cit.*, p. 392.

18 Economist Intelligence Unit, *A Survey of Factors Governing the Location of Offices in the London Area* (London: Economist Intelligence Unit, 1964), Table C.I.40 and 41, pp. 48–9.

19 Location of Offices Bureau, *Annual Report, 1972–73* (London: Location of Offices Bureau, 1973), Table 5, p. 35.

20 J. R. O'Meara, *Corporate Moves to the Suburbs: Problems and Opportunities* (New York: The Conference Board, 1972), pp. 11–12. New York City Planning Commission, *Headquarters Relocation in New York City and the Region* (New York: City Planning Commission, 1972), pp. 10–12.

21 *Report of the Royal Commission on the Distribution of the Industrial Population* (London: His Majesty's Stationery Office, Cmd 6153, 1940).

22 *Ibid.*, p. 1. For a full discussion of the Report see H. G. Lind, 'Location by guesswork', *Journal of Transport Economics and Policy*, vol. 1 (1967), pp. 154–61.

23 *Report of the Royal Commission on the Distribution of the Industrial Population, op. cit.*, para. 188.

24 J. H. Foreshaw and P. Abercrombie, *County of London Plan* (London: London County Council,

1943). P. Abercrombie, *Greater London Plan 1944* (London: His Majesty's Stationery Office, 1945). For a more detailed discussion of Abercrombie's proposals in the *Greater London Plan* see D. E. Keeble, 'The South East and East Anglia: The Metropolitan Region', in G. Manners *et al.*, *Regional Development in Britain* (London: Wiley, 1972), pp. 88–92.

25 P. Abercrombie, *op. cit.*, para. 101.

26 For examples see D. E. Keeble, 'Industrial decentralization and the metropolis: The North West London case', *Transactions, Institute of British Geographers*, vol. 44 (1968), pp. 1–54. R. S. Howard, *The Movement of Manufacturing Industry in the United Kingdom 1945–65* (London: Her Majesty's Stationery Office, 1968). D. J. Spooner, 'Industrial movement and the rural periphery: The case of Devon and Cornwall', *Regional Studies*, vol. 6 (1972), pp. 197–215.

27 *Control of Office and Industrial Development Act 1965* (London: Her Majesty's Stationery Office, 1965).

28 P. Abercrombie, *City of London Plan 1944* (London: Corporation of London, 1944).

29 Administrative County of London, *Development Plan 1951: Analysis* (London: London County Council, 1951), p. 4.

30 Middlesex County Council, *Development Plan* (Harrow: Middlesex County Council, 1956).

31 London County Council, *A Plan to Combat Congestion in Central London* (London: London County Council, 1957).

32 *Ibid.*, p. 2.

33 O. Marriott, *The Property Boom* (London: Hamish Hamilton, 1967), pp. 5–6.

34 London County Council, *op. cit.* (1957), pp. 10–12. London County Council, *Administrative County of London Development Plan: First Review, 1960* (London: London County Council, 1960) para. 555–67. The Third Schedule is discussed in Chapter 4.

35 Town and Country Planning Association, *op. cit. London. Employment: Housing: Land* (London: Her Majesty's Stationery Office, Cmd 1952, 1963). Ministry of Housing and Local Government, *The South East Study* (London: Her Majesty's Stationery Office, 1964), pp. 37–40.

36 Town and Country Planning Association, *op. cit.*, p. 33.

37 O. Marriott, *op. cit.*, pp. 178–9. W. F. Manthorpe, 'The limitation of employment in central London', *Journal of the Royal Institute of Chartered Surveyors*, vol. 34 (1954), pp. 389–99. E. J. C. Griffith, 'Moving industry from London', *Town Planning Review*, vol. 26 (1956), p. 62.

38 P. Cowan *et al.*, *op. cit.*, p. 170.

39 *London. Employment: Housing: Land*, *op. cit.*

40 Location of Offices Bureau, *Annual Report, 1963–1964* (London: Location of Offices Bureau, 1964), pp. 6–7.

41 Ministry of Housing and Local Government, *op. cit.*, pp. 76–7. *Offices: A Statement by Her Majesty's Government* (London: Her Majesty's Stationery Office, 1964).

42 The reactions of office developers to the announcement of controls in the White Paper are described in O. Marriott, *op. cit.*, pp. 182–3. Paris also uses an O.D.P.-type system known as 'agrement'.

43 *Town and Country Planning (Amendment) Act 1972* (London: Her Majesty's Stationery Office, 1972). Department of the Environment, *Control of Office Development* (London: Her Majesty's Stationery Office, Circular 80/72, 1972).

44 Department of the Environment, *Development by Government Departments* (London: Her Majesty's Stationery Office, Circular 80/71, 1971). J. B. Cullingworth, *Town and Country Planning in Britain* (London: Allen and Unwin, 1973), pp. 102–4.

45 A. W. Evans, 'Myths about employment in central London', *Journal of Transport Economics and Policy*, vol. 1 (1967), pp. 214–25.

46 *Ibid.*, p. 214. Some examples are listed in n. 1.

47 O. Marriott, *op. cit.*, p. 183.

48 Central Statistical Office, *Abstract of Regional Statistics* (London: Her Majesty's Stationery Office, 1971).

49 Ministry of Housing and Local Government, *op. cit.*, p. 43.

50 A. W. Evans, *op. cit.*, p. 218.

51 *Ibid.*, pp. 224–5. O. Marriott, *op. cit.*, pp. 183–4. P. R. Smethurst and R. U. Redpath, *Central London Workers: Changes in Distribution of Residence* (London: Greater London Council, Research Paper S.R.1 1966), pp. 1–27. Department of the Environment, *Greater London Development Plan—Report of Panel of Inquiry, Vol. 1* (London: Her Majesty's Stationery Office, 1973), pp. 114–118.

52 D. R. Denman, 'Frustrated development', *Westminster Bank Quarterly Review*, November (1970), p. 45. 'The office market: A commentary', *Estates Gazette*, vol. 225 (1973), pp. 53–4. *The Times*, 28 October 1968.

53 D. Gransby, 'The end of O.D.P.s' (London: Wates Limited, mimeo, 1972).

54 Department of the Environment, *op. cit.* (1973), p. 108.

55 'A case for auctioning office planning permits', *The Times*, 5 February 1974.

56 G. Manners, 'On the mezzanine floor: Some reflections on contemporary office location policy', *Town and Country Planning*, vol. 40 (1972), p. 210.

57 South East Joint Planning Team, *Strategic Plan for the South East* (London: Her Majesty's Stationery Office, 1971).

58 For a period of up to five years in a Development Area and up to three years in an Intermediate Area.

59 D. R. Denman, *op. cit.*, Table II, p. 45.

60 Location of Offices Bureau, *Annual Report, 1969–1970* (London: Location of Offices Bureau, 1970), p. 10.

61 These figures are based on statistics produced by Brecker, Grossmith and Company, published annually in the 'Market Review', *Estates Gazette*.

62 Location of Offices Bureau, *op. cit.* (1970) pp. 10–11.

63 Department of the Environment, *Town and Country Planning Act 1971, Control of Office Development: Annual Report* (London: Her Majesty's Stationery Office, 1973).

64 'Aspects of London office development', *Estates Gazette*, vol. 218 (1971), pp. 1171–2. O. Luder, 'Offices and planning in London', *Estates Gazette*, vol. 222 (1972), pp. 1595–1603.

65 J. Rhodes and A. Kan, *Office Dispersal and Regional Policy* (London: Cambridge University Press, Department of Applied Economics, Occasional Papers, no. 30, 1971), pp. 23–67. E. Hammond, *London to Durham: A Study of the Transfer of the Post Office Savings Certificate Division* (Durham: Rowntree Research Unit, 1968), pp. 4–25.

66 J. Rhodes and A. Kan, *op. cit.*, p. 27.

67 New York City Planning Commission, *op. cit.*, p. 13.

68 Location of Offices Bureau, *Office Rents (1)— Outside Central Area 1963–72* (London: Location of Offices Bureau, mimeo, 1972).

69 The Institute of Administrative Management, *Clerical Salaries Analysis, 1972* (London: Institute of Administrative Management, 1972).

70 British Institute of Management, *Office Relocation: A Report on a Series of Cost Studies of Firms which have Decentralized from London* (London: British Institute of Management, 1971).

71 G. Manners, *The Office in Metropolis: An Opportunity for Shaping Metropolitan America* (Harvard: Joint Center for Urban Studies, Working Paper, no. 22, 1973), pp. 12–13.

72 J. Rhodes and A. Kan, *op. cit.*, pp. 47–8.

73 R. Pye, *A Cost Minimization Model for Choosing Office Locations* (London: Communications Study Group, Joint Unit for Planning Research (University College London), 1973), pp. 27–48.

CHAPTER 10

The Pattern of Decentralization

The planning framework designed to control office development and to encourage office decentralization is best tested by reference to experience during the last decade. There have been a number of empirical studies of office decentralization, almost exclusively concerned with movement from central London, and certain underlying themes emerge in their conclusions.[1] These themes are best examined by using the most recently available data for, first, commercial offices, and second, for Government offices.[2]

COMMERCIAL OFFICE DECENTRALIZATION

Contrary to the broad policy objectives, 44·5 per cent (593) of the offices which have moved from central London between 1963 (October) and 1973 (March) have remained within Greater London, or less than 15 miles from their origin (Fig. 41). They represent 41·7 per cent (39,000) of the jobs which have been decentralized. The statistics quoted by L.O.B. are based on an estimate by each firm of the number of staff they expect to employ when they are fully operational at the new location. The actual number of jobs moved from central London to the decentralized location probably represents less than 50 per cent of the above total, and the proportion decreases as firms move further from the centre.[3]

Decentralization within Greater London contains strong directional and locational bias. Over 50 per cent of the jobs and 42 per cent of the offices have moved to the outer suburbs, particularly to Croydon which has received 19·4 per cent of the offices and 30·4 per cent of the jobs moved since 1963. Most of the offices are concentrated in a well-defined 'office centre' which has grown in response to Croydon's consistent policy of encouraging decentralized offices and their related development since 1956.[4] A similar pattern has emerged in West London which has received 28 per cent of the decentralized office jobs, largely concentrated in Hounslow (10·2 per cent) and Richmond (3·9 per cent). The eastern and northern suburbs have attracted far fewer offices and only Barking has attracted more than 1000 jobs (2·7 per cent). The inertia of Croydon, the attractions of London airport for offices moving west, and the existing distribution of office workers' residences have all exerted a strong pull on office developers and tenants/owner-occupiers.

The G.L.C. is a microcosm of the pattern of commercial office decentralization within the South East (Fig. 41). A further 43·0 per cent of all decentralized offices have moved to locations within the South East Planning Region, but outside the G.L.C. They account for 39·2 per cent of the office jobs so that the South East as a whole has received 87·5 per cent of the offices and 80·9 per cent of the jobs. Most of the centres receiving decentralized offices are therefore within 45 miles of central London or approximately 60 min journey time by rail and not much longer by road for centres adjacent to motorways. Put another way, 78 per cent of L.O.B. clients that have moved or are moving, go less than 40 miles. They represent 64 per cent of the jobs.[5]

These figures are often quoted as indicative of major constraints on the location choice of decentralized offices. But the pattern of decentralization to the O.M.R. and O.S.E. is widely dispersed and has so far involved no less than 156 different centres. By no means all of them are as accessible to London as the 60 min limit implies. In March 1973, only six centres, Bracknell, Basingstoke, Cosham, Harlow, Southend,

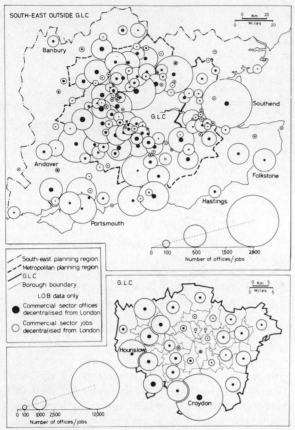

Fig. 41 Commercial Office Decentralization from London—Greater London and the South East, 1963–73 (Data: Location of Offices Bureau)

and Watford had accumulated more than 1000 decentralized office jobs and at least five office establishments.[6] Portsmouth, Hemel Hempstead, Brighton, and Horsham were also near this level with between 900 and 1000 jobs. By comparison, over one-third of the London boroughs had received more than 1000 jobs by March 1973. The Location of Offices Bureau has observed that commercial offices tend to select individual locations, which are often medium- or small-sized towns, where they often comprise the only decentralized office, rather than the embryonic 'office centres' such as Southend or Basingstoke.[7]

The emerging pattern has grown haphazardly, however, without an overall strategy for distributing decentralized office employment to desig-

nated towns or suburban areas. Croydon has grown to its present importance as an 'office centre' despite, rather than because of, the influence of unclear planning objectives. One of the difficulties has been that central London, Greater London, and the remainder of the South East are considered as separate sub-regions. The G.L.C. is isolated by its administrative boundary from the surrounding parts of the South East, with which it is intimately linked in an economic and social sense. This has led to inconsistencies in the planning strategies recommended for guiding the redistribution of population and employment in the region. Beginning with the *County of London Development Plan 1960* through the sequence of regional plans for the South East to the *Greater London Development Plan* (G.L.D.P.) the areas named as growth points for various types of development, including offices, have rarely coincided.[8] Clearly, the needs of different suburban areas and towns for office employment will change through time, with the older towns more balanced and less in need of office employment than those experiencing recent, rapid expansion of population. But it has already been shown that offices benefit from proximal economies, at least in the central areas of major cities, and it would seem equally important to duplicate these conditions in 'office centres' clearly defined and identified and not subject to periodic changes in designation through time. Concentration also makes it easier to provide an adequate range of shopping, restaurant, and other facilities for office workers, as well as permitting better returns from infrastructure investments such as transport facilities.

Commercial offices have been reluctant to move beyond the South East Region (Fig. 42). Less than 20 per cent of the jobs and 12 per cent of the offices which have moved during the last decade have done so, although they are usually larger scale moves than the average for the South East. Many small office organizations cannot afford to move far from their main source of business in London and they are also unable to support the transitional costs of moving, retaining key personnel or communications. Larger offices can often spread such costs amongst other activities included in the organization and indeed may be subsidized by other parts of the business.[9]

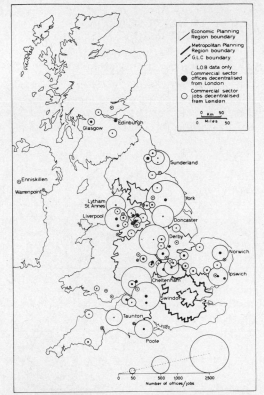

Fig. 42 Commercial Office Decentralization from London, excluding Greater London and South East— 1963–73 (Data: Location of Offices Bureau)

Moves to the provincial Planning Regions are often tied to the location of existing production plants or warehouses and may form part of a programme of company centralization, leaving 'front' offices in central London for important meetings and other business.

The South West, East Midlands, Yorkshire and Humberside, and the North West have received the majority of commercial decentralized offices (Table 49). The major provincial cities such as Manchester, Liverpool, Glasgow, and Bristol, have attracted a large number of offices but fewer jobs than some smaller urban areas which have received large offices.[10] Examples are the move of a large insurance company to Lytham St Annes, a major manufacturing company office to Taunton, or the decentralization of part of Barclays Bank's activities to Knutsford. The provincial cities, potentially excellent 'office centres' are largely geared to local and regional sources of demand for office space and most of them do not allow for demand from decentralized offices when allocating land for office development or granting planning permissions.[11] Consequently, apart from any difficulties of attracting key staff to move from London or the unsatisfactory image of the provinces seen from the centre, there may be no suitable space available when it is required.

The new and expanding towns should be major beneficiaries of office decentralization policies. One of the long-standing problems, particularly in the new towns, has been an excessive dependence on manufacturing employment.[12] Decentralized offices provide an ideal opportunity to redress the balance but the results, in the commercial sector, are not encouraging. New and expanding towns in the South East have done rather better than their provincial equivalents but there is considerable variation. Harlow and Bracknell have received more than 1000 jobs but Basildon or Hatfield, which belong to the same generation of post-war new towns, have received just over 100 jobs between them. Similar dichotomies occur amongst the expanding towns, e.g. Basingstoke (1496 jobs), Princes Risborough (40 jobs). All these centres have good access to London but variations in local authority policies, problems of obtaining O.D.P.s or the inertia started by decentralized offices selecting a new town such as Harlow at an early stage have operated to the disadvantage of some of the other new towns. During the early years of the O.D.P. controls, office development in the new and expanded towns tended to be looked upon more favourably than other places in the South East.[13] Since the acceptance by the Government of the recommendations in the *Strategic Plan for the South East*, most weight has been given to specified growth areas. A number of new towns lie within the growth areas and therefore continue to be in a more favoured category than those outside. Provincial new towns have been almost exclusively ignored by commercial decentralized offices. Much more needs to be done to attract commercial offices to these rapidly growing towns which are desperately in need of a better balanced employment structure. It remains to be seen whether the grants now

TABLE 49
COMMERCIAL OFFICE JOBS DECENTRALIZED FROM
LONDON BY PLANNING REGION, 1963–73

Region	No. of offices	(%)	No. of jobs	(%)	Mean size (jobs/offices)[1]
Northern	13	1·0	1656	1·8	127
Yorkshire and Humberside	12	0·8	3614	3·9	301
North West	34	2·6	2861	3·1	84
East Midlands	23	1·7	2901	3·1	126
West Midlands	11	0·8	169	0·2	15
East Anglia	25	1·9	1561	1·7	62
South East					
G.L.C.	593	44·5	39000	41·7	66
O.M.A. & O.S.E.	573	43·0	36685	39·2	64
South West	33	2·5	4718	5·0	143
Wales	5	0·4	93	0·1	19
Scotland	9	0·7	219	0·2	24
Northern Ireland	2	0·2	21	0·0	11
Totals	1333	100·0	93498	100·0	74

Note: 1. Rounded-up to the nearest whole number. Statistics to 31 March 1973.
Source: Data provided by the Location of Offices Bureau.

available to service industries will improve the situation.

The relative popularity of the four major zones shown in Figs 41 and 42 has changed only marginally since 1964 (Fig. 43). In terms of the proportion of moves, the provincial Planning Regions have received more offices in recent years, particularly between 1967 and 1970 when the full effects of the O.D.P. restrictions were causing severe shortages of space in the South East. A similar pattern is evident for office jobs although a small number of very large moves can distort the proportional distribution. The actual number of firms and jobs moved each year reflects fluctuations in the market for office space in central London. The largest number of moves and jobs took place in 1967/8 when there was insufficient space for expansion. Between 1967/8 and 1970/1 the number of offices moved fell to 109 and the number of jobs followed a similar trend. During this period office space remained at a premium in central London but it was also becoming difficult to obtain elsewhere in the suburbs and the rest of the South East as the last of the outstanding speculative developments came on to the market. Rather than move well

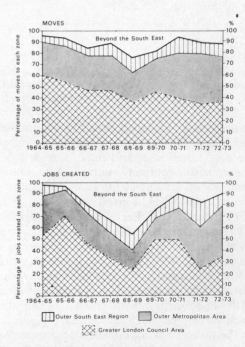

Fig. 43 Trends in the Number of Jobs and Offices Moved (After Location of Offices Bureau, *Annual Report, 1972–73*, 1973, with the permission of the Location of Offices Bureau)

away from the London area, many firms preferred to endure the increasing rents and congested working conditions in their central London offices. The fact that until Dec. 1970 O.D.P.s were required for developments of more than 3000 ft^2 also affectively prevented small firms, requiring 5000–10,000 ft^2 of office space, from moving the short distances they preferred.

Since 1971, however, there has been a further upsurge of commercial office decentralization. This has been caused by firms trying to economize on their space costs or capitalizing on favourable long leases, rather than simply a shortage of space for expansion.[14] Rent inflation arising from the development restrictions has been a constant difficulty in central London and office space is many times more expensive than elsewhere although the differential between the suburbs and the centre has narrowed slightly because of shortages of space in the latter. Apart

from the effects of O.D.P.s, there have also been major rent increases demanded for older office properties which, in normal circumstances, could not be justified. Such office space is predominantly occupied by the smaller office organizations and consequently, in 1972/3 the average size of decentralizing offices has decreased. In an attempt to slow down the rent spiral, the Government imposed controls on rent levels in central London and elsewhere in November 1972, but unfortunately these had the reverse effect to that intended. By June 1973 prime office space in the City was fetching £20/ft^2, 25 per cent more than just one month earlier.[15] Elsewhere in central London, office rents increased by more than half on 1972 levels. As more firms decentralize, suburban rents have also been pushed up to more than £5/ft^2 in some areas.[16] Because of this the controls on office rents were completely removed in March 1975.

GOVERNMENT OFFICE DECENTRALIZATION

Decentralization of Government offices since 1963 has corresponded more closely to the objectives of official policies (Fig. 44). Indeed, the Government has always been an active protagonist of decentralization by example, beginning with initiatives as far back as 1940 when decentralization of office work was necessary for strategic reasons.[17] Many offices were moved well away from central London to centres in the regions such as Bath, Blackpool or Harrogate. A second initiative was taken in 1963 following an unpublished report by Sir Gilbert Flemming on the possibilities for dispersal of headquarters work. The report reviewed approximately 95,000 Civil Service posts and recommended dispersal of 14,000 from the London area and 5500 to the suburbs of the city.[18] The Flemming proposals were accepted and formed the basis for Government office decentralization until the publication of a third initiative in 1973, which, if accepted and fully implemented, could result in a further 31,427 headquarters posts being moved from London.[19] In common with the earlier reviews, London is taken to include suburban as well as central locations. A further aspect of Government policy on the location of its own offices is

that since 1965 any new Department, for example the former Land Commission, should, if at all possible, be located outside London. In addition, since 1967 choice of location for the new offices has been governed by a policy of preference for assisted areas.

The volume of long distance decentralization to Scotland, the North East, North West, and Wales contrasts with the predominantly short distance moves by commercial offices (Table 50). But although more than 22,000 posts have been decentralized from London and over 9000 new posts have been established, headquarters jobs remain heavily concentrated in the South East (70·6 per cent). Non-headquarters staff are more widely distributed but almost 47 per cent of all non-industrial Civil Service jobs were still located in the South East in October 1972. There are therefore parallels, but less strongly developed, with the distribution of commercial office jobs, particularly for headquarters staff; 79 per cent of those in the South East work in inner London. Hammond has used an 'index of regional concentration' to assess the inequalities in the distribution of Civil Service non-headquarters jobs.[20] Between 1951 and 1965 the

Fig. 44   Government Office Decentralization from London—1963–72 (Data: *Hansard*, *Whitley Bulletin* and Location of Offices Bureau)

TABLE 50
DISTRIBUTION OF NON-INDUSTRIAL CIVIL SERVANTS, 1972 AND
DISPERSED STAFF 1963–72—BY ECONOMIC PLANNING REGION

Region	H.Q. Staff 1972		Non-H.Q. Staff 1972		Dispersed Staff[1] 1963–72		New Office Work[2] 1963–72		Total (1 + 2)	
	No.	%	No.	%	No.	%	No.	%	No.	%
Northern	13745	9·0	18025	5·4	3112	13·8	265	2·8	3377	10·5
Yorkshire and Humberside	2213	1·5	22201	6·7	783	3·5	—	—	783	2·4
North West	8430	5·5	37465	11·3	4176	18·5	1821	19·2	5997	18·7
East Midlands	189	0·1	17579	5·3	211	0·9	535	5·6	746	2·3
West Midlands	503	0·3	23463	7·1	279	1·2	—	—	279	0·9
East Anglia	1240	0·8	9281	2·8	1192	5·3	—	—	1192	3·7
South East	107448	70·6	117952	35·5	6222	27·6	2782	29·3	9004	28·1
Inner London	*85744*	*56·4*	—	—	—	—	—	—	—	—
South West	6574	4·3	35628	10·7	692	3·1	640	6·7	1332	4·2
Wales	1452	1·0	19392	5·8	1174	5·2	1652	17·4	2826	8·8
Scotland	10332	6·8	31566	9·5	4684	20·8	1797	18·9	6481	20·2
Total	152126	100·0	332552	100·0	22525	100·0	9492	100·0	32017	100·0

Notes: 1. Staff which have already been dispersed, the bulk of them in Headquarters offices, under decisions taken on or before 1 October 1972.
2. Work in new Government organizations which, on 1 October 1972 had been established or were to be established outside London under the policy initiative of 1965. In most cases these organizations are of national Headquarters character.
Source: Civil Service Department, *The Dispersal of Government Work from London* (London: Her Majesty's Stationery Office, Cmd 5322, 1973), Table 1.3, p. 20, Table 1.4, p. 21, Table 1.5, pp. 3–27.

index of concentration for the South East has changed only marginally; it had one and a half times the national average number of civil servants in 1965. By 1972 the index had been reduced to 143, or slightly less than one and a half times the national average, and this provides a crude measure of the effectiveness of Government decentralization from London and the South East to deficit areas such as Scotland and Wales.

Almost 30 per cent of the jobs decentralized since 1963 have remained in the South East but more than 50 per cent have been moved to deficit regions, particularly Scotland, the Northern Region, Wales, and the North West Planning Region. It may be significant, however, that many of the jobs decentralized to these regions are non-headquarters jobs or offices mainly concerned with regional or local areas. In the South East, just over 15 per cent of the decentralized jobs are in this category, the remainder are headquarters posts which still seem to depend on access and contact with the London concentra-tion. The regional distribution of new posts reveals a similar pattern but although the number of new offices located in the South East is only seven, the number of new jobs created is larger than for any other region (see Table 50).

Within the South East there is a measure of association between the individual towns and cities chosen by commercial and Government decentralized offices. Good examples are Basingstoke, Southend, and Reading. With the exception of Crawley, Government offices have also largely ignored the employment requirements of the new towns. Elsewhere there is less evidence of common locational choice. This may partly reflect the small number of commercial offices moving to the peripheral regions but those which have done so, have chosen centres other than the provincial 'capitals' such as Manchester, Leeds, Newcastle, and Cardiff. The reverse has happened with Government offices, whether decentralized or new office jobs are involved, particularly in the peripheral regions. This may reflect conflict between the needs suggested by broad regional strategies for employment distribution in the Planning Regions and the details of local requirements.[21]

Given the observations already made on the interdependence of office activities, particularly the links between Government and commercial offices at many levels, it would seem to be more fruitful to guide decentralized offices to regional centres or 'development poles' where scale and external economies can be generated and new economic activity stimulated.[22] These might also encourage other intending movers to more seriously consider moving well beyond London and the South East. Some of the differences in location choice by commercial and Government offices in the peripheral planning regions is complemented by a general 'boycott' of the East and West Midlands. The initial application of the O.D.P. controls to these areas may provide a partial explanation for the absence of decentralized commercial offices but Government offices have also missed these two regions. Both are dominated by industrial employment and office work is not excessively represented (see Table 29, Chapter 6). Preoccupation with the South East and the peripheral Regions may be at the

expense of providing a broader employment base in the Midlands.

The Hardman Report recommends continued decentralization of Civil Service headquarters work from London (Table 51). The proposals are based on a more thorough analysis of the possibilities and implications of removing work from the centre than either of the previous proposals. Some 78,000 posts were considered for dispersal in the review using empirical evidence of the communications and other requirements of 'blocks' of work within Departments to assess the damage, resource gain, and average trade off generated by various locations able to receive decentralized office work.[23] Over 31,000 posts are considered suitable for dispersal with a 'recommended' and two alternative solutions for their distribution (see Table 51). With commercial offices largely ignoring the possibilities for moving to the regions beyond the South East, the Hardman recommendations attempt to achieve a balance between regional requirements and efficient operation of Civil Service offices. In the event of either of these factors being given priority, the Report suggests a 'regional' and an 'efficient' solution. The latter reduces the share of decentralized office jobs to be received by the

TABLE 51

'RECOMMENDED', 'EFFICIENT', AND 'REGIONAL' ALTERNATIVES FOR FURTHER DECENTRALIZATION OF GOVERNMENT WORK FROM LONDON—BY ECONOMIC PLANNING REGIONS

Region	'Recommended'		'Efficient'		'Regional'	
	Jobs	%	Jobs	%	Jobs	%
Northern	2110	6·7	500	1·6	5742	18·3
Yorkshire and Humberside	—	—	1610	5·1	—	—
North West	6276	20·0	5217	16·6	5676	18·1
East Midlands	—	—	—	—	—	—
West Midlands	—	—	1390	4·4	—	—
East Anglia	737	2·3	737	2·3	737	2·3
South East	12098	38·5	13018	41·4	5880	18·7
South West	3487	11·1	2813	9·0	5097	16·2
Wales	5542	17·6	6142	19·5	6518	20·7
Scotland	1177	3·7	—	—	1777	5·7
Totals	31427	100·0	31427	100·0	31427	100·0

Source: The Dispersal of Government Work from London (London: Her Majesty's Stationery Office, Cmd 5322, 1973), pp. 98–103.

peripheral regions. The South East would receive 38·5 per cent of the jobs decentralized under the recommended solution and 41·4 per cent if the efficient solution were adopted. These proportions would be reduced by half for the regional solution but it is clear that certain Departments cannot, or are not prepared to, move beyond the South East and it is only by reducing the number of posts moved by the Ministry of Defence to Bletchley that the South East receives less than 20 per cent of the jobs.[24] Wales and the North West will receive almost 40 per cent of the dispersed jobs between them whichever solution is adopted while regions with similar requirements for new office work such as the Northern Region and Scotland are less fortunate. A notable feature of the proposals is that only 15–16 centres are recommended as reception areas. Most are major centres of communication or centres already possessing other headquarters offices and are therefore 'preferred' locations for some Departments.[25]

Despite the decentralization activities of Government offices, the dichotomy between the South East/London and the remainder of the country has continued to be strong. Office policies have been consistently criticized since their inception, mainly on the grounds that they have operated as a negative control on choice of location by offices; that in the absence of suitable inducements they have failed to achieve the regional policy objectives; that the excessive concern with the problems of London and the South East has generated unnecessary problems of supply and demand and office growth in general in that region.[26] It is undoubtedly necessary to operate some kind of office policy supported by appropriate controls in the South East but in practice it has proved difficult to achieve a balance between central London and the remainder of the region.[27] Changes in the O.D.P. requirements, the absence of consistent designation of suburban and other growth centres, uncertainties about the relationship between increases in office floorspace and employment, and the inaccuracies of projected growth and allocation of office activity to areas within the South East have contributed to the confusion. Manners has suggested that market forces should be allowed to operate without severe restriction for a short period in London and in the South East but, as most office development is speculative, the opportunities for decentralization may, as a result, be reduced as supply becomes re-focused on central London.

It may be unrealistic to attempt large-scale inter-regional movement of office activity. Certainly, in the absence of financial inducements to encourage decentralization to the Regions, success has been limited. Following the powerful case for financial aid made by Rhodes and Kan, some provision has been made but it is too early to evaluate the impact on commercial office decentralization. With the amount of manufacturing industry moving to the peripheral regions declining it has become crucial to stimulate as much movement of office work as possible. Alternatively, it may be more fruitful to stimulate growth of office activities indigenous to the problem regions.[28]

CHARACTERISTICS OF DECENTRALIZED OFFICES

Some of the problems confronting office decentralization policies as they relate to London arise from the characteristics of the offices which actually move. Over 48 per cent (678) of the commercial offices which have left central London during the period 1963–73 employ less than 25 staff. They also represent more than 50 per cent (582) of the offices which decided not to decentralize during the same period.[29] The number of jobs in these offices is only some 6 per cent of the total but with increasing suburban rents, an unwillingness on the part of the developers to let small units, and a reluctance to move further than absolutely necessary has discouraged movement by these, and larger office units of up to 100 staff, as the effects of the O.D.P. restrictions have materialized. The size characteristics of commercial decentralized offices partially explains the changes made in the exemption limits for O.D.P.s. By pushing the limit upwards, smaller office buildings suitable for the smaller firms have been encouraged. Large moves (over 500 jobs) amount to 4 per cent (54) of the total but 38 per cent of the jobs decentralized during the decade. But few of them are prepared to move outside South East England and in 1972/3 they comprised only 1 per cent of the moves and 21 per cent of the jobs decentralized. Not only are the controls on office development therefore affecting the lower end of the office market, but the curtailed supply of floorspace suitable for large office units has also caused their movement to be more restricted.

It is also necessary to consider two types of office movement, complete and partial. The former involves removing the entire organization from one location to another and is more frequent amongst small offices unable to support the costs of operating two premises. Complete moves reduce any internal communication problems for an organization but they might increase the difficulties of communicating with clients and competitors.[30] Research suggests, however, that these difficulties may be exaggerated, perhaps because of the absence of suitable empirical observations.

Partial moves involve separation of the office, usually on the basis of departments, in a way which minimizes interference with existing communications links with customers and others, but increases the efficiency of departments largely involved in routine tasks which can operate equally well at a non-central location. Rhodes and Kan have suggested a twofold division of partial office moves; those involving a small number of departments, usually routine functions, and leaving the largest part of the organization in the original location; and moves in which almost all the organization decentralizes but leaves a small 'front' office at the original location to maintain business contacts and to act as a meeting place. These are termed minority and majority decentralization respectively.[31] Large offices tend to engage in partial decentralization and on average a partial move from central London affects twice as many office jobs as a complete move.[32] The impact of decentralization on the source area will therefore reflect the ratio of complete to partial moves and the size characteristics of the offices involved.

A reason frequently quoted as a disincentive to office decentralization is the loss of business contact with other activities in central London. Goddard and Morris have used contact diaries to obtain data from 335 employees in 21 offices which have decentralized from London in order to test the significance of this hypothesis.[33] The methodology used and data collected was similar to that described in Chapter 8. Decentralized offices certainly have very different patterns of communication when compared with offices in central London. This seems to be a product of the role played by decentralized offices within their organizations; some 50 per cent more of the contacts of decentralized office workers are concerned with internal matters than is the case for their equivalents in central London prior to relocation. Distance moved also has an important influence on communications needs and the reduced role of external contacts is particularly evident at intermediate distance locations in the South East (outside Greater London). Over 90 per cent of the business contacts of such offices require journeys of more than 30 minutes while in central London 78 per cent of business trips last less than 30 minutes. The incentive to retain contacts with central London is therefore considerably reduced while the pattern of decentralization to South East locations provides limited opportunities for local replacement. If organizations decentralize in order to release time for internal matters the 'costs', in terms of lost external contacts, may not be excessive. But if administrative decentralization is the objective it seems that relocation, especially to intermediate distance locations generate 'costs', again linked to external contacts, which will make office operations inefficient and may well force some firms to return to central London. The best solution to this problem is long distance decentralization well outside the South East (beyond 80 miles) where Goddard and Morris have established that firms make more external links with reception areas and therefore reduce the costs of travel associated with the maintenance of external business contacts. If major provincial cities are chosen as locations these will provide adequate substitute external contacts for those which would have been used in central London.

Office decentralization is also industrially selective (Table 52). It has already been shown that office jobs are more important in the service

TABLE 52

OFFICES DECENTRALIZED FROM LONDON 1963–73
AND NON-MOVERS 1963–73—BY INDUSTRY

	Offices moved and moving			Non-movers		
Industry[1]	No. of firms	No. of jobs	Mean size (Jobs/ offices)	No. of firms	No. of jobs	Mean size (Jobs/ offices)
Food, drink, tobacco	361	4259	118	24	3145	131
Chemicals, allied industries	84	12311	147	54	5175	95
Engineering, electrical goods	153	10125	66	111	8203	74
Office machinery/furniture	33	6262	190	10	699	70
Textiles, leather goods, etc.	18	1115	62	17	717	42
Paper, printing, and publishing	72	8105	113	82	6658	81
Other manufacturing industries	92	5318	58	54	2421	45
Construction	36	4440	123	15	1613	107
Distributive trades	128	7631	60	100	6073	61
Insurance	146	20651	141	55	5513	100
Banking and finance	51	8361	164	32	3271	102
Professional/scientific services	177	9166	52	157	7626	49
Miscellaneous services	103	7253	70	112	6684	60
Trade associations	55	1101	20	43	2149	50
Transport and communications	88	10390	118	45	6634	147
Totals	1272	116488	92	911	66581	73

Note: 1. Industry groups do not coincide with the S.I.C. classification but have been devised to fit the requirements of L.O.B.

Source: Location of Offices Bureau, *Annual Report, 1972–73* London: Location of Offices Bureau, 1973), Table 7, p. 37.

industries and it is not surprising, therefore, that 25 per cent (29,012) of the jobs decentralized from central London since 1963 are in insurance, banking, and finance. To some extent this reflects the concentration of these activities in the City but, in addition, there are also many routine departmental functions incorporated in these offices which make them ideal for re-location. The average size of the movers exceeds 150 personnel, substantially larger than the non-movers, although most have been majority or minority partial moves. The smaller offices representing professional and scientific services have been the largest single group of movers (14 per cent) and reflect the impact of rising costs on the ability of small organizations to remain in central London. Service industries as a whole have moved

more office jobs than manufacturing industries; approximately two service for every manufacturing job. This contradicts the view that service industry office activities have strong links with central area locations which, if severed, will reduce their effective operation. Equally, however, almost half the jobs which organizations decided not to decentralize between 1963 and 1973 were in the service sector. Offices of chemical and allied industries, engineering and electrical goods, and paper, printing and publishing have been most prone to decentralize in the manufacturing sector and, on average, the movers are twice as large as the non-movers. Most of the long distance moves are made by offices in these industries and in insurance and professional/scientific services.[34]

Organizational structure will also influence the opportunities for decentralization. Small organizations with single, centralized head office activities are potentially more mobile than large organizations which have complex, tiered structures (Fig. 45). The local offices at the third level in the hypothetical hierarchy are the least mobile and are tied to the areas which they serve; these offices will often be controlled by divisional

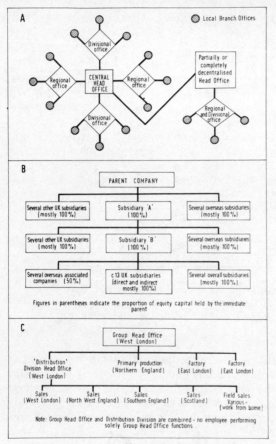

Fig. 45 Influence of Organizational Structure on Opportunities for Decentralization (Sections B and C after Economic Consultants Limited, *Office Classification* Systems, Report for L.O.B. 1974, with the permission of the Location of Offices Bureau)

or regional offices which are most likely to be candidates for intra-regional movement. This goes some way towards explaining the large proportion of short distance moves within the South East.

Inter-regional decentralization is therefore most likely to emanate from the upper levels of the organizational hierarchy; head offices which can move *en masse* or partially and perhaps establish their own hierarchy of satellites at the new location. The alternatives open to a large organization wanting to change the distribution of its office employees have been listed by Rhodes and Kan; (1) establish new branch offices in regions in which it is under-represented and the converse in regions in which it is over-represented; (2) establish new regional offices; (3) move office work previously undertaken at branch level into the regional office or vice-versa; (4) move work previously undertaken in regional offices to head office or vice-versa; (5) move head office completely within the region or from one region to another; and (6) undertake partial decentralization of head office activities into another location in the same region or into a completely new region.[35] Similar considerations apply in the Government sector, hence the Hardman Report's consideration of 'blocks' of work.

The actual legal and administrative structure of a company with group head office in the West End illustrates the difficulty, however, of generalizing about the influence of organizational structure on decentralization (Fig. 45).[36] The group operates activities in both the manufacturing and service sectors and Division 'A' is mainly concerned with the manufacture and distribution of a particular class of manufactured goods. The sub-divisions of Division 'A' are also product-based and responsible for producing goods in a limited territory. Face-to-face contacts between head office and divisions is fairly restricted but intra-divisional links are much more important, especially between central London and the new town offices. The latter establishment includes 240 office workers brought together from various pre-existing dispersed establishments. The new town office labour force has subsequently increased to 400. Structural reorganization of the division led to the moves into the new town in 1968. Recent mergers and other structural changes in the organization may lead to further office decentralization leaving a small West End 'front office'. Although the group head office has remained intact in central London, pressures on space as the group has expanded rapidly may also lead to decentralization of this part of the organization. It is clear, therefore, that decentralization of office activities may involve 'centralization' of dispersed departments or sub-divisions, redistribution of office staff within an existing set of office premises (central and decentralized), and the creation of completely new office establishments occupied by decentralized and other office staff.

OFFICE DECENTRALIZATION IN THE UNITED STATES

The redistribution of office activities between central cities and suburbs has taken place in the United States, in recurring cycles, since the turn of the century.[37] The changes are best documented for corporate headquarters, particularly those listed in the *Fortune* directory, which have been moving out of the central cities of most of the larger S.M.S.A.s in increasing numbers (Fig. 46). These location changes, in direct contrast to those taking place in Britain, are exclusively voluntary. They are a response to central city pressures and the attractions of the suburbs. Inter-regional redistribution of office activities has been less important in the United States and, with a number of exceptions, most corporate headquarters are moving to the suburbs of the same city. The suburbs provide adequate room for expansion or for recentralization of activities distributed amongst several buildings in the central city. This leads to better working conditions for employees and can make recruiting easier. Suburban locations also provide an element of convenience; to the existing residences of central city staff; to the residences of new recruits who might otherwise commute to the central area; to airport facilities used by senior personnel. They also make for better productivity which is linked to the superior working environment, lower absenteeism, lower staff turnover, and ease of recruiting. Individual office workers also stand to benefit from working in suburban locations; one study estimated that if two individuals on the same salary lived next to each other in the same county, one commuting to Manhattan and

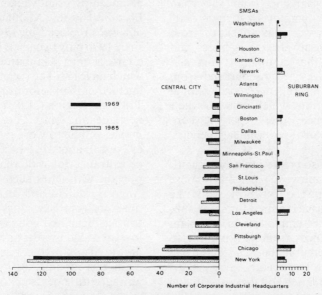

Fig. 46   Changes in the Number of Corporate Headquarters in the Central City and Suburban Ring, United States— Selected S.M.S.A.s, 1965–69 (Data: R. B. Armstrong, *The Office Industry: Patterns of Growth and Location,* 1972)

the other working at an office in the same county, the man working in the city office would be left with about 11 per cent less disposable income.[38] Most of the savings arise from differences in respective tax and transportation expenses.

Most companies which have moved their headquarters to the suburbs are satisfied with the outcome but there are some problems. The Conference Board cites the problem of accommodating manpower needs; even with generous relocation and other allowances, some companies lost more than 50 per cent of their labour force when leaving Manhattan including experienced secretaries and junior executives. These have proved difficult to replace at suburban locations while recruitment of other replacement staff has disappointed many companies. In order to overcome this difficulty some companies recruit staff to work in Manhattan or central Chicago before the office is decentralized.[39] The company pays their journey to work costs until the time of the move when they hope that the employees will continue to work for them in the suburbs. Inevitably, during the interim, some of them will have begun to like working in the C.B.D. and will leave the organization when it decentralizes. Other disadvantages arising from suburban locations concern key employees such as marketing staff who claim that they are cut off from effective contact with advertising agencies and with colleagues in other companies; financial or personnel executives are discouraged from attending evening meetings of professional societies and associations which influence their professional competence; others experience contact difficulties with banks, government agencies, and suppliers.[40]

Suburban offices also create journey to work problems for some employees, particularly those who must travel by public transport, while the amount of parking space required for some suburban buildings causes employees to complain about walking distances from parking lot to office. The cost differential between suburban and central city offices is gradually being eroded as suburban taxes are raised and the cost of living becomes comparable with the central city. Relocation costs also often considerably exceed the original estimates. As early as 1960, Vernon suggested that decentralized offices moving to sub-urban locations could not expect to benefit much from lower space costs because the provision of support facilities such as parking, restaurants, and recreation space would reduce the savings accruing from lower land costs.[41]

In 1965 approximately 1 in 7 of the headquarters offices located in the S.M.S.A.s shown in Fig. 46 were in the suburban ring; by 1969 the figure had increased to 1 in 6. The process of suburbanization seems confined to metropolitan areas with a population exceeding 2 m. Cities such as Atlanta, Pittsburgh, and Minneapolis have invested heavily in improving the facilities and the environment of their C.B.D. areas in order to retain corporate headquarters. In Minneapolis, of 384 companies which had left the central area by 1964, 25 per cent had returned since 1960 and others have continued to do so as their suburban leases have expired.[42] There is increasing evidence that this is now happening in other cities.[43] But in New York more than 50 headquarters have left or intend to leave Manhattan since 1969, 30 of them involving 11,400 jobs.[44] Decentralization from Manhattan has been characterized by growing imbalance. During the late 1950s and early 1960s, out-movement was balanced by in-movement; 12 companies in the *Fortune* 500 left Manhattan between 1956–66 but were replaced by 17 others moving in. But since 1970 only two firms have moved their headquarters into Manhattan compared with 15 which have left. The recent movers are also moving further than before, many of them outside the Tri-State Region (New York, New Jersey, Connecticut) and only 7 per cent of the post-1970 moves will be to Core or Inner Ring areas such as Nassau and Westchester. Inter-regional office decentralization is therefore becoming more important with cities such as San Francisco, Los Angeles, Dallas, and Houston attracting headquarters from New York and Chicago.[45] Houston has benefited considerably from this trend; low taxes, living costs and construction costs, the ability to annex 10 per cent of its area each year from surrounding territory and to carry over annual entitlements up to 30 per cent, in addition to the absence of land use controls, have all contributed to its phenomenal growth as an office centre during the last decade.[46]

Reference to the American experience of decentralization has been very brief but it is sufficient to suggest major differences compared with Britain.[47] The legislative and administrative framework used to influence the location of office activities in British cities and regions is far less acceptable in the U.S.A. where free enterprise and minimum intervention by planners in the location of activities is the norm. The need for decentralization of offices from major cities like London is partly a product of the methods used to encourage movement, i.e. the planning restraints have sharply increased the costs of being in the centre compared to suburban and other areas. The central areas of British cities also remain, in general, much more accessible than suburban centres and this also pushes up costs because of the competition for office space in these areas. In American metropolitan areas decentralization is more closely related to the social problems of the inner cities and the associated problems of obtaining satisfactory labour. With suburban expansion taking place at much lower densities than in most British cities and many potential and existing office workers in the forefront of the migration of population from the central cities, it is not surprising that some offices have followed the trend and reduced the problems of getting staff to travel to the C.B.D. With car-based travel dominating journey to work movements in all but the largest metropolitan areas such as New York or Chicago, it is easier to travel to suburban office centres. It is also apparent, however, that American cities are less concerned about existing levels of centralization of office employment in the C.B.D. Indeed, some are anxious to encourage office development because of its implications for the city tax base, employment balance, and social structure.[48] This raises the question of the impact of changing office location patterns on reception areas, the companies which have decentralized, and their employees. This forms the subject of the next chapter.

REFERENCES

1   J. V. Aucott, 'Dispersal of offices from London', *Town Planning Review*, vol. 31 (1960), pp. 39–50. J. S. Wabe, 'Office decentralization: An empirical study', *Urban Studies*, vol. 3 (1966), pp. 35–55. E. Hammond, 'Dispersal of Government offices: A survey', *Urban Studies*, vol. 4 (1967), pp. 258–75. K. B. Williams, 'The factual basis of office policy in South East England' (University of London, unpublished M.A. Thesis, 1965). P. W. Daniels, 'Office decentralization from London: Policy and practice', *Regional Studies*, vol. 3 (1969), pp. 171–178. J. Rhodes and A. Kan, *Office Dispersal and Regional Policy* (London: Cambridge University Press, Department of Applied Economics, Occasional Papers, no. 30, 1971).

2   'Locations to which L.O.B. clients have moved', Information sheet published annually by the Location of Offices Bureau. *Dispersal of Government Work from London* (The Hardman Report) (London: Her Majesty's Stationery Office, Cmd 5322, 1973), Table 1 (5), pp. 23–30.

3   Location of Offices Bureau, *Annual Report, 1972–1973* (London: Location of Offices Bureau, 1973), Table 9, p. 38.

4   London Borough of Croydon, *The Redevelopment of Central Croydon* (Croydon: Borough Engineer, Surveyor and Planning Officer's Department, 1971).

5   Location of Offices Bureau, *op. cit.*, Table 10, p. 39.

6   Cosham is an exception to this observation; a single office provides 1080 jobs.

7   Location of Offices Bureau, *Annual Report, 1967–1968* (London: Location of Offices Bureau, 1968), p. 7.

8   Greater London Council, *Greater London Development Plan: Report of Studies* (London: Greater London Council, 1970).

9   A good example of a large-scale move from central London by a commercial organization is Barclays Bank's decentralization to Knutsford, Cheshire. M. E. Green, 'Office decentralization from London: A case study', Paper read at Regional Studies Association Conference on Office Employment: The Regional Problem, Sheffield, 14 November 1973.

10 Bristol has recently emerged as an important provincial 'office centre' attracting a number of major insurance and banking offices such as NatWest, Sun Life, Clerical, Medical and General, and Phoenix Insurance. 'Setting up office Bristol-fashion', *The Times*, 15 September

1973. C. Sladen, 'Banks move head offices out of London', *Administrative Management*, vol. 27 (1973), pp. 23–5.

11 M. W. Wright, 'Provincial office development', *Urban Studies*, vol. 4 (1967), pp. 227–8.

12 For some examples see R. Thomas, *London's New Towns* (London: Political and Economic Planning, Broadsheet 510, 1969), pp. 448–62. R. Thomas, *Aycliffe to Cumbernauld: A Study of Seven New Towns in Their Regions* (London: Political and Economic Planning, Broadsheet 516, 1969), pp. 945–52. See also *Office Decentralization to the New Towns* (London: Location of Offices Bureau, mimeo 1974).

13 O.D.P. data are not kept separately for the new towns but in 1967, 36 permits (684,000 ft² gross) were granted for local authorities in the South East which include new towns. For the years 1969–73, the average number of permits granted had fallen to 13 but in 1973 this was equivalent to 1,389,000 ft² gross compared with 469,000 ft² gross for the 15 permits granted in 1969. Between 1965 and 1973, Basildon, Bracknell, and Hemel Hempstead received almost twice as many permits as Welwyn Garden City, Harlow or Hatfield new towns, for example. The average floorspace allowed with each permit for the former new towns is also larger. Based on unpublished statistics for O.D.P.s for local authorities in the South East which include new towns within their boundaries, kindly provided by G. J. Edwards, Department of the Environment (personal communication).

14 Location of Offices Bureau, *op. cit.* (1973), p. 11.

15 'Property in Britain and Europe', *The Times*, 3 October 1973. 'Sustained rise in London office rents forecast', *The Times*, 30 October 1973.

16 The office problems of the South East were further complicated in December 1973 by the introduction of a ban on the granting of O.D.P.s in the region. Central London will again be the hardest hit. At the end of 1974 controls were still strictly applied with apparently severe restrictions on speculative building but a number of very large schemes given permission during the year has given rise to some doubt about the policy.

17 See for example National Council for Social Service, *Dispersal: An Enquiry into the Advantages and Feasibility of the Permanent Settlement Out of London and the Other Great Cities of Offices and Clerical and Administrative Staff* (Oxford: Oxford University Press, 1944). For a more detailed discussion of the period 1948–63 see E. Hammond, *op. cit.*, pp. 266–70.

18 *Dispersal of Government Work from London, op. cit.*, p. 22.

19 *Ibid.*, p. 12.

20 The index of concentration expresses each region's share of civil servants as a percentage of its share of population. E. Hammond, *op. cit.*, pp. 260–2.

21 J. J. Chapman, 'A criticism of the Hardman Report on the dispersal of Government work from London, with special reference to South Yorkshire', Paper read at Regional Studies Association Conference, *op. cit.*

22 J. B. Goddard, 'Office employment, urban development and regional policy', Paper presented at Regional Studies Association Conference on Office Location Policy, London, 3 February 1973. Concentration of Government office dispersal in a limited number of centres in the Netherlands (4) and Sweden (15) is indicative of the importance of this approach. See J. Toby, 'Regional development and Government office location in the Netherlands', and B. Thorngren, 'Communication studies for Government office dispersal in Sweden', in M. J. Bannon (ed.), *Office Location and Regional Development* (Dublin: An Foras Forbartha, 1973), pp. 37–46 and pp. 47–58.

23 'Average trade-off' represents the benefit per unit of damage to be derived from dispersing the whole Department or part of it to the proposed location.

24 It has since been discovered that Bletchley cannot receive all the posts allocated to it under the preferred solution. This leaves some 6000 posts to be distributed elsewhere and it has been decided that they will be moved to Glasgow. This makes the 'regional' solution more satisfactory.

25 The Hardman Report is a consultative document and as such has received a good deal of criticism. It would not be appropriate to discuss these in detail here, but the main difficulty has been the unequal distribution of jobs to the regions and to individual cities. A number of the assumptions about the multiplier effects of office development in reception areas have also been criticized.

26 J. Rhodes and A. Kan, *op. cit.*, pp. 69–81. E. Hammond, *op. cit.*, pp. 270–3. P. Cowan *et al.*, *The Office: A Facet of Urban Growth* (London: Heinemann, 1969), pp. 130–88. P. W. Daniels, *op. cit.*, pp. 176–7. C. R. Wareham, 'The pattern of office development', *Chartered Surveyor*, vol. 105 (1973), pp. 352–4. J. B. Goddard, 'Civil Service for the regions', *Town and Country Planning*, vol. 41 (1973), pp. 451–4. D. Burtenshaw, M. Bateman and A. Duffet, 'Office decentralization—ten

years' experience', *The Surveyor*, vol. 143 (1974), pp. 23–5.

27 G. Manners, 'On the mezzanine floor: Some reflections on contemporary office location policy', *Town and Country Planning*, vol. 40 (1972), p. 212.

28 *Ibid.*, p. 213.

29 Location of Offices Bureau, *op. cit.* (1973), Table 8, p. 37 and Table 11, p. 39.

30 This was cited by the financial offices which have moved to Bristol, see n. 10.

31 J. Rhodes and A. Kan, *op. cit.*, p. 17.

32 *Ibid.*, Table 2.3, p. 18.

33 D. Morris, 'The impact of relocation on office communications patterns', Paper read at Symposium on Office Location Policy, Institute of British Geographers Annual Conference, Norwich, 3 January 1974. J. B. Goddard and D. Morris, *The Communications Factor in Office Decentralization* (London: Department of Geography, London School of Economics and Political Science, 1974), pp. 47–153.

34 Unpublished statistics made available by the Location of Offices Bureau (personal communication). See also Interscan Ltd., *Report on a Survey of Non-Movers* (London: Location of Offices Bureau, 1967).

35 J. Rhodes and A. Kan, *op. cit.*, pp. 6–7.

36 Economic Consultants Limited, *Office Classification Systems* (London: Report prepared for Location of Offices Bureau, 1974), Appendix A, pp. 141–4. A useful list of legal and administrative business unit terminology is also included in this Report, see pp. 8–15.

37 J. R. O'Meara, *Corporate Moves to the Suburbs: Problems and Opportunities* (New York: The Conference Board, 1972), p. 1. One of the first detailed studies was undertaken by D. L. Foley, *The Suburbanization of Offices in the San Francisco Bay Area* (Berkeley: University of California, Bureau of Business and Economic Research, 1957). See also 'Should management move to the country', *Fortune*, vol. 66 (1952), p. 142 *et seq.* G. Manners, 'Decentralization in metropolitan Boston', *Geography*, vol. 45 (1960), pp. 276–85. G. Manners, 'Urban expansion in the United States',

Urban Studies, vol. 2 (1965), pp. 51–66. Some Australian data is given in A. D. Sorenson, 'Office activities as an economic base for urban decentralization in Australia', *Royal Australian Planning Institute Journal*, vol. 12 (1974), pp. 51–7.

38 J. R. O'Meara, *op. cit.*, pp. 10–11.

39 This has also happened in Britain, particularly in Government offices.

40 J. R. O'Meara, *op. cit.*, pp. 14–15.

41 R. Vernon, *Metropolis 1985* (Cambridge, Mass.: Harvard University Press, 1960), pp. 19–20.

42 D. E. Jones, 'Offices: An element of urban geography—the case of Minneapolis' (University of Minnesota, unpublished M.A. Thesis, 1970), Table 8.

43 B. Gooding, 'Roadblocks ahead for the great corporate move out', *Fortune*, vol. 86 (1972), pp. 78–83, *et seq.* B. K. Goodman, 'More users than tenants: Suburban owners struggle to fill empty spaces', *National Real Estate Investor* (1972), pp. 74–7. B. Cohen, 'A Look at suburban office space', *Skyscraper Management*, vol. 56 (1971), pp. 6–10. 'The swing back from the suburbs', *Vision*, vol. 31 (1972), p. 106.

44 New York City Planning Commission, *Headquarters Relocation in New York City and the Region* (New York: City Planning Commission, 1972), p. 1. New York City Planning Commission, *The Demand for Office Space in Manhattan* (New York: City Planning Commission, 1971), pp. 11–12. P. Herrera, 'That Manhattan exodus', *Fortune*, vol. 81 (1967), pp. 106 *et seq.* 'Moving to the suburbs', *Fortune*, vol. 86 (1972), p. 278.

45 A. E. Callahan, *The Migration of Corporations from New York to Suburban Areas and to Other Regions of the Country* (Washington: U.S. Department of State, 1971).

46 C. G. Burke, 'Houston is where they're moving', *Fortune*, vol. 85 (1971), pp. 91–7.

47 See also D. E. Jones and R. K. Hall, 'Office suburbanization in the United States', *Town and Country Planning*, vol. 40 (1972), pp. 470–3.

48 G. Manners, *The Office in Metropolis: An Opportunity for Shaping Metropolitan America* (Harvard: Joint Centre for Urban Studies, Working Paper, no. 22, 1973), pp. 4–7.

CHAPTER 11

The Impact of Changing Office Location Patterns

Changes in the location of office floorspace and employment do not take place in a vacuum. They give rise to questions about alternative strategies for suburban office growth; the multiplier effects created by the development of office activities in receiving centres; the impact on employment levels in the C.B.D. or in the areas to which offices are moving; and the impact on the mobility, housing or journey to work charac-teristics of office workers affected by re-location decisions. A number of studies which examine some of these issues have appeared during the last few years. They provide an opportunity to assess whether voluntary or 'planned' office re-location is beneficial to urban development, to regional policies, and to individual companies and their office employees.

IMPACT ON THE C.B.D.

The most important effect of office migration from the C.B.D. should be a reduction, or at least a slowing down, in the growth of office employment. Assuming that other employment in the C.B.D. is already declining, a reduction in office employment should further help to ease the congestion and other problems distinctive of the central area. It is difficult, however, to be precise about the changes in employment brought about by office movement. The earliest attempts to estimate decentralization have relied heavily on the derivation of lists from L.O.B. records or have been based on field and postal surveys of office buildings.[1] The subsequent statistics are inadequate both in areal coverage and, in the case of L.O.B. records, probably only cover 50 per cent of the offices which have actually moved.

Hall has attempted to overcome these difficulties by estimating office decentralization on the basis of a sample survey of firms which, according to *Kelly's Directories*, appeared to have decentralized during the period 1963-9.[2] Of the 1729 firms in central London which had changed address, 121 had moved to addresses outside the area. The original sample of firms was 6 per cent, hence the true total of decentralized firms should lie between 1560 and 2525 which is substantially higher than the 430 offices recorded as complete moves by L.O.B. during the same period. Hall then conducted a postal survey of the complete movers to establish their employment and the results were used to estimate the total number of jobs moved out of central London. Between 44,000 and 72,000 jobs appear to have been moved and allowing for survey errors and firms missed from the original sample it is likely that this is an underestimate. Similar data were obtained for partial moves with the true total ranging between 543 and 693 firms and 40,990 to 51,560 decentralized jobs.[3]

The jobs moved by central government do not require estimates because precise information is available. Hence, between mid-1963 and late 1969 some 124,500-167,500 commercial and Government office jobs had been moved out of central London (Table 53). This represents between 16 and 22 per cent of the 755,500 office workers in central London in 1966 and is clearly large scale decentralization of jobs. It cannot be assumed, however, that this means that the total number of office jobs in central London has been reduced. The jobs moved out are replaced by endogenous growth of employment in firms remaining there, by the birth of new firms requiring

194

office space and workers, and by in-migration of office users from other locations in Britain, from Europe, or from overseas.[4] Although total employment in central London is falling, this is mainly caused by reductions in industrial employment; office jobs represent a growing proportion of the total jobs which remain and are probably increasing in absolute terms despite decentralization. This in no way represents failure of the office decentralization policy because continued expansion of office employment, but at a much higher rate, would undoubtedly have occurred in the absence of controls.

of the region's total office employment will decrease from 52·4 to 41·3 per cent as growth accelerates in the intermediate and outer rings and decentralization of some office activities takes place.

The 50 major corporate headquarters which have left Manhattan, or have announced their intention of doing so, represent a loss of just 4000 jobs annually.[7] This represents less than 25 per cent of the annual projected growth of office employment up to 1980 and it affects a very small fraction of Manhattan's 200 m. ft² of floorspace. Headquarters re-location only makes a partial contribution to the impact on office jobs. Middle

TABLE 53
ESTIMATED DECENTRALIZATION OF
FIRMS AND OFFICE JOBS FROM
CENTRAL LONDON—mid-1963 to late-1969

Type of move	No. of firms		No. of jobs	
	Upper	Lower	Upper	Lower
Complete	2525	1560	71519	44229
Partial, leaving large office	346	272	51650	40990
Partial, leaving small office	427	336	24339	19152
Central government	—	—	15059	15059
Nationalized industries	—	—	5000	5000
Totals	3298	2168	167567	124430

Note: The figure of 5000 jobs for Nationalized industries is an estimate. Upper and lower limits are expressed at the 99 per cent confidence level.
Source: R. K. Hall, 'The movement of offices from central London', *Regional Studies*, vol. 6 (1972), Table 2, p. 389.

The impact of office employment decentralization on Manhattan is less clear. In terms of floorspace changes there is no evidence for a strong element of decentralization; in 1963, 50·9 per cent of the New York Region's office space was in Manhattan and 50·8 per cent of the new office floorspace started in 1963/70 was also located there.[5] Manhattan has retained its attraction for office floorspace although, allowing for increased employee/floorspace ratios, it cannot be concluded that employment has remained equally stable. In common with central London, it is anticipated that office employment will continue to increase in Manhattan, from 950,000 in 1967 to 1,440,000 in 2000, while production and other employment decreases.[6] But Manhattan's share

and local market jobs are more likely to follow population decentralization because of their dependence on regional and lower order activities. Hence, headquarters office jobs in Manhattan are expected to double between 1965 and 2000 but middle market jobs will only increase by approximately 50 per cent and local market jobs will decrease by approximately 13 per cent, largely due to differential growth and decentralization.[8] While the precise impact of decentralization is unclear because of the absence of suitable records, there is mounting concern in New York about the loss of tax revenues, the reduction in employment opportunities for less skilled office workers who cannot afford to live in the distant suburbs, and the absence of a co-ordinated public policy to deal with these problems.

Office migration from the C.B.D. also releases floorspace for occupation by new, expanding or in-moving offices. This is regarded as one of the major weaknesses of decentralization policies affecting central London. Reduction of office employment in central London, or elsewhere, can only be really effective if the reoccupation of vacated office premises is controlled.[9] But few surveys have been undertaken of what actually happens to premises vacated by office firms which have left central or Greater London. The information which has been collected suggests that an embargo on the occupation of vacated C.B.D. office premises would not solve any problems.[10] This conclusion is largely derived from the results of two surveys completed by L.O.B. in 1966–7, and in August/October 1969, in which premises made vacant by decentralized offices were visited to establish whether they had been reoccupied by movement from another location, by birth of a new firm or by expansion of a firm or firms already in the premises.

Both surveys showed that vacant office space occupied by new firms was 3–6 per cent of the total available at the time. Replacement of decentralized offices by in-migrants appears to be negligible and not likely to have serious consequences for the attraction of sufficient office work to replace all the jobs which have been decentralized. Some replacement staff will be required but many will be recruited from amongst office workers previously employed in the C.B.D. by decentralizing firms. Much of the demand for vacated office floorspace is therefore derived from inside the C.B.D., from the firms which have only partially decentralized, and from complete moves within the C.B.D. by some companies.[11] In both cases, the firms are usually taking the opportunity to improve their space standards and the fact that vacated space is reoccupied cannot be directly equated with an equivalent increase in office employment. Hence, a ban on the use of vacated office premises would deprive offices remaining in the C.B.D. of the chance to improve their working conditions; to reorganize themselves more efficiently; and to achieve a better functional distribution of central area activities. Office buildings also represent substantial investment and the removal of many good quality buildings from the office market would represent an inefficient utilization of existing resources and also place an onerous demand for compensation, at public expense, by the G.L.C.[12]

STRATEGIES FOR SUBURBAN OFFICE GROWTH

It has been demonstrated that the suburbs are the major recipients of the growing outflow of office, retail, wholesale, and manufacturing activities from the central areas of cities. It has therefore become important, in the interests of the decentralizing activities and the suburbs, to ensure a rational, efficient, and well planned pattern of distribution and growth. The way in which suburbs respond to the process of decentralization will, to a large degree, determine the success or failure of movement from the centre. Activities leave the C.B.D. because they foresee particular advantages arising from a suburban location so that the problem facing the suburbs is how offices, or other activities, should be distributed within the suburban fabric.

There appear to be two courses of action; dispersal of activities or concentration into a limited number of major growth centres. The particular location requirements of office activities makes the nucleated solution more satisfactory and this seems to be the consensus amongst metropolitan areas faced with accommodating rapid suburban growth and change. The preparation of broad planning strategies which provide a framework for detailed local planning of individual centres is a relatively recent approach to suburban growth problems. Consequently, early suburban office development has often taken place without the benefit of a strategic framework. Between 1958 and 1965 the decentralization trend began to 'scatter the outskirts of London with a host of banal and unrelated office blocks' which were located largely at points with access to good transport facilities and pockets of office workers.[13] Apart from self-generating clusters such as Wembley, Ealing or Croydon, most of the early suburban decentralized office buildings were part of a dispersed pattern of development which, in the case of some speculative buildings, did not always attract clients. Some buildings may have remained empty because the rents were too high, but bad location relative to supporting services such as restaurants, shopping facilities, office services, banks, and hotels discouraged many firms from leasing space in such buildings. As suggested in Chapter 9, the various plans produced since 1951 for the County, and later, Greater London have invariably recommended concentration of growth into named suburban centres but the lists are rarely comparable, although some centres such as Croydon consistently appear.[14] The importance of relating suburban office centres to good communications and adequate local transport facilities has always been emphasized, however, and this has promoted more rapid development of some suburban nodes than others.

An inherited pattern of dispersed and concentrated office development has therefore shaped contemporary planning strategies for suburban London. The *Greater London Development Plan* recommends that decentralized activities should be concentrated, as far as possible, within selected suburban centres, particularly the 28 centres defined as being of 'strategic' importance.[15] Most are existing shopping centres suitably spaced around central London and in relation to each other, as well as possessing the accessibility attributes so important for their viability. By concentrating office development in these centres, it is hoped to avoid problems of multi-directional journey to work movements, excessive competition for labour between centres, and inefficient use of scarce resources, particularly land. Preferred locations for office development are also suggested; six 'major strategic' centres selected from the 28 'strategic' units; Croydon, Ealing, Ilford, Kingston, Lewisham, and Wood Green. Provided that sufficient infrastructure investment is forthcoming, these suburban centres should complement central London in terms of the range of services and facilities conducive to a flourishing office complex. It will be necessary to ensure, however, that these centres do not generate office commuter movements, for example, which create congestion comparable with that which exists in central London. Some suburban centres, particularly Croydon, are already facing serious transport problems which are largely a product of the volume of office development and employment growth permitted during the last ten years.

The expected growth of office floorspace and employment in the strategic centres is not specified precisely. The strategic centres are almost exclusively distributed as distinct units within individual boroughs and although borough boundaries have no real meaning in employment terms it was decided that floorspace targets for complete administrative areas were more realistic.[16] During the preparation of the G.L.D.P. each borough submitted estimates of its office floorspace requirements but these often exceeded the space allocated to them in the proposed strategy. Consequently, the suburban boroughs have been left to decide how to allocate the office floorspace permitted by this strategy to the preferred locations in their area. The realization of the objectives, based on demand estimates, will only be achieved if sufficient proposals are forthcoming from office developers. If a firm policy can be agreed by the suburban boroughs it is more likely to lead to development proposals which fit their requirements.

In 1970, about 50 m. ft^2 of office floorspace in the New York Region was concentrated into 15 suburban centres; this was equal to less than 25 per cent of Manhattan's total (Fig. 47).[17] This amounted to some 13 per cent of the Region's office floorspace but only 8 per cent of new construction between 1963–70 was located in the 15 centres. The *Second Regional Plan* places great emphasis on expansion of these centres both to contain further urban sprawl and to prevent overconcentration in Manhattan. The four major centres in the Core area of the Region (outside the C.B.D.), Newark, Downtown Brooklyn, Jersey City, and Jamaica–Rego Park, contained almost 33 per cent of the total office floorspace in the zone. They received 54·5 per cent of the new floorspace constructed between 1963 and 1970 and by 2000 will have over half the office jobs and office floorspace. The picture in the Inner Ring suburbs is rather different and, in common with suburban London, the trend has been for greater dispersal than concentration of office growth. The major centres, Central Nassau,

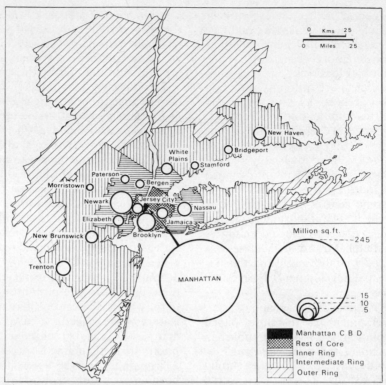

Fig. 47   Location of Office Floorspace in the New York Region—1970
(After R. B. Armstrong, *The Office Industry: Patterns of Growth and Location*, 1972, with the permission of the Regional Plan Association, New York)

Elizabeth, Central Bergen, Paterson-Clifton, and White Plains contained 19·6 per cent of the total floorspace in the Inner Ring in 1970 with most of the space in Central Nassau. These centres only received 9·3 per cent of the 1963–70 floorspace increment and the remainder was distributed amongst widely scattered suburban locations. If policies are pursued to concentrate suburban office growth in centres, as recommended by the *Second Regional Plan*, the major centres in the Inner Ring will contain 36 per cent of the total office floorspace in 2000. The distribution will be even more dispersed in the Intermediate Ring where the major centres, New Brunswick, New Haven, Bridgeport, Trenton, Stamford, and Morristown will have 27 per cent of the floorspace in 2000, if policy recommendations are implemented. There is no detailed information for the Outer Ring but Poughkeepsie could become an office centre with 3 m. ft^2 by 2000.

A policy of concentrated suburban office growth is one of a number of alternatives, each of which have different implications for the areas affected (Table 54). The first alternative has already been outlined. It is based on the assumption that 40–50 per cent of the growth in headquarters office jobs, 60 per cent of the middle market jobs, and 20 per cent of the local market jobs will locate in the 15 suburban centres between 1970 and 2000. Hence, Newark would increase its floorspace from 14·2 m. ft^2 in 1970 to 23·6 m. ft^2 at the end of the century, or New Haven and Trenton would grow from 4 to 12 m. ft^2. If existing trends are continued, however, the second alternative would occur; only 10 per cent of the floorspace increment would accrue to the 15 major centres and 54 per cent would be dispersed, particularly on open plan sites in the Inner, Intermediate, and Outer rings. This 'trend' alternative reduces by approximately 80 m. ft^2 the amount of office floorspace allocated to the major centres by the 'policy' alternative. A third alterna-

TABLE 54
ALTERNATIVE ALLOCATION OF NEW OFFICE FLOORSPACE
IN THE NEW YORK REGION—1970–2000

	Alternatives							
Area	1 (policy) Floorspace[1]	%	2 (trend) Floorspace	%	3 Floorspace	%	4 Floorspace	%
Manhattan C.B.D.	153	33	153	33	200	43	55	12
Major centres (15)	118	25	49	10	98	21	118	25
Other centres	22	5	13	3	19	4	22	5
Dispersed	177	37	255	54	153	32	275	58
Total for region	470	100	470	100	470	100	470	100

Note: 1. Floorspace — m. ft^2 gross. No allowance is made for alterations or replacement of existing
stock and new buildings completed during 1970–3 are included.
Source: R. B. Armstrong, *The Office Industry: Patterns of Growth and Location* (Cambridge, Mass.:
M.I.T. Press, 1972), Table 5.23, p. 153.

tive rests on the assumption that Manhattan continues to expand its office floorspace at the 1963–70 rate and it also attracts an extra 50 m. ft^2 and 200,000 additional office workers over and above that allocated to it by the first and second alternatives. This recognizes that a continuation of existing locational behaviour is possible but with more emphasis on suburban office centres than the unadulterated 'trend' figures which include a large proportion of dispersed development. The most extreme alternative is the fourth. This assumes that new commuter flows from the suburbs to Manhattan will remain constant and, consequently, its share of the region's 1970–2000 floorspace increment is reduced to 12 per cent which could be met by new construction completed by 1975. Over 58 per cent of the suburban growth would be at dispersed locations and the major centres would receive 25 per cent. This totally ignores the major social and economic problems already facing the core area of New York and which would be enhanced if suburban office expansion took place almost entirely at the expense of continuing long-term growth in Manhattan.

Most of the comparative costs of the four alternatives are derived from the land requirements of dispersed as opposed to concentrated office development and the different transport implications. Concentration in suburban nodes, advocated in three of the alternatives, will save approximately 5,000–7,000 acres and

400–500 lane-miles of expressway, but will place heavier commuting and housing costs on office workers.[18] The predominantly dispersed pattern of the fourth alternative will require at least 250–300 miles of 4-lane expressway or one-sixth of the New York Region's existing expressway network. Office centre location therefore has major implications for investment in suburban development.

Unfortunately, only limited work, mainly from the standpoint of office employees, has been undertaken on the benefits attached to alternative strategies. New York seems to have intuitively adopted a concentration policy and this is best illustrated by the behaviour of office developers who continue to invest in Manhattan, while it has also been adopted as official New York City policy.[19] If, as expected, much of the decentralization and new office growth continues to take place outside New York City, it is important that the suburban areas affected adopt an equally positive policy, using the *New York Regional Plan* as a guideline. Cities elsewhere in the United States have also become conscious of the need to estimate future demand for suburban office development and to fit it into efficient patterns of growth. Major metropolitan areas such as Houston, St Louis, and Atlanta have examined the problem, as well as some of the smaller metropolitan municipalities affected by suburban expansion of office activities such as Southfield on the fringes of Detroit.[20] The latter has analysed existing office development in the area and considered future prospects for growth with reference to projected demand and competition from adjacent centres such as Troy and Dearborn.

OFFICE PARKS

Low density, dispersed suburban office development of the type prevalent in New York and other major metropolitan regions reflects, to a considerable degree, the aspirations of firms leaving the central area. Firms are attracted by the possibility of enjoying the suburban 'countryside' with lawns, trees, and landscaping forming an integral part of the working environment. Such conditions are more difficult to satisfy in the higher density, embryonic suburban office centres which are located within existing urban development and are a part of urban renewal schemes. It is not surprising, therefore, that the business, or office, park has proved very attractive to decentralized and other offices.[21] Industrial parks were the first to group together compatible uses in an attractive environment and once the headquarters of large industrial corporations began to move to the suburbs in the early 1950s, office parks became viable. The outmigration by large headquarters offices encouraged smaller offices activities such as those involved in research, publishing and various professional services to follow, thus making office parks successful operating units.[22] Although office parks largely comprise clusters of office buildings on the same suburban site, it has been increasingly recognized that easy access to shopping and other facilities is also important. Hence, office, retail, and recreational facilities can usefully occupy the same site and prevent wasteful investment in such facilities at separate locations.

With large tracts of land in the outer suburbs priced by the acre rather than the square foot, the location of office parks has been crucial to their success. Sites accessible to local freeways and major highways are most sought after by developers and tenants because of the easy access from adjacent suburbs and areas outside the city, as well as to the C.B.D. (Fig. 48). Areas adjacent to circumferential and radial freeway intersections therefore experience the heaviest demand for office park sites. A second location factor is

access to airport facilities which is an asset for marketing office space in office parks although the benefits to individual firms may be perceived rather than real. McKeever notes that only seven of the 41 parks in an Urban Land Institute survey considered airports to be an important factor in local office space demand. Finally, quality of the surroundings is an important factor

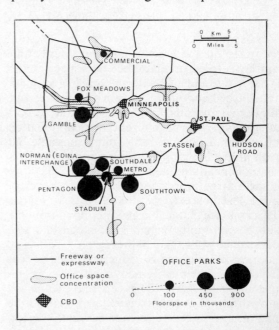

Fig. 48   Location of Office Parks in Minneapolis— 1973 (Data: Twin Cities Metropolitan Council, *Office Space: An Inventory and Forecast for the Twin Cities Metropolitan Area*, 1973)

in site selection, this helps to give the office parks an element of prestige, particularly if they are in or near high quality residential areas. Some developers also refer to the journey to work of office workers and the need to provide access to other facilities as being equally important to satisfactory office park development.

Probably the major disadvantage of office

parks is that they consume large areas of land; in 1970 the average size was 70 acres.[23] Only between 10 and 15 per cent of the area is usually occupied by buildings, the remainder is devoted to open spaces and car parks. The latter may absorb more than 50 per cent of the site acreage and this underlines the heavy dependence of office parks upon private transport. Only 25 per cent of the parks studied by the Urban Land Institute were served by public transport and this proportion may well decrease in the future. Within the over-all framework of suburban expansion the need to cater for predominantly car-based movements demands heavy investment in highway networks over a wide area.

It might be more fruitful to channel such investment into carefully selected suburban centres, accessible by private and public transport, and allowing office workers from inner and outer metropolitan areas equal access to employment opportunities. Examples of office park development are given by McKeever, Long, and Hartshorne; they are an accepted form of suburban office development in New York, Chicago, San Francisco, Minneapolis, Atlanta, Boston and many other smaller cities.[24] In Minneapolis, almost 30 per cent of the 9·5 m. ft^2 of office floorspace in 14 major suburban concentrations is located in 12 office parks (see Fig. 48).

CROYDON: AN OUTER SUBURBAN OFFICE CENTRE

Individual office parks may contain up to 1 m. ft^2 of floorspace but much post-war suburban expansion has taken place in pre-existing centres and on a larger scale than in office parks. A good example of an outer suburban office centre based on an established nucleus is Croydon which is approximately 15 min. from central London by fast train.[25] The London Borough of Croydon has a population of over 300,000 and central Croydon had a long established business, administrative, and retail function before 1956 when office development began to become important. Central Croydon has better train and bus connections along radial and cross-radial routes than many other suburban centres and this has made it more accessible from a variety of residential areas and for various types of office staff both within and outside its administrative boundaries. It also benefits from a good range of shopping and cultural facilities within easy reach of the main office area. The initiative and drive of Croydon Corporation has also been instrumental in promoting and encouraging the continued expansion of the office complex which forms a compact but linear distribution (Fig. 49).

The advent of Croydon as an office centre was initiated by the *Croydon Corporation Act, 1956*, which allowed the Corporation to acquire land in the central area which was in multiple ownership (two acres). This land adjoined two acres already in Corporation ownership and which was

then leased to private developers for office and shop development. Some of the land was also used for road widening in George Street (see Fig. 49), the construction of an underpass, and various other public works. The development which resulted was almost exclusively office space, 192,000 ft^2, compared with only 1500 ft^2 of shops. The space was provided in three buildings, Essex House, Suffolk House, and Norfolk House, at the core of the present office complex (see Fig. 49). This embryonic demand for office space in central Croydon coincided with the adoption of decentralization policies by the L.C.C. and Croydon was able to allocate 45 acres in the centre for office development to accommodate firms leaving central London. Most of this area, in the north-eastern quadrant of the town centre, has now been redeveloped for offices and the demand has been such that several buildings have been allowed outside the specified area and beyond the central area boundary. By mid-1971, 5·5 m. ft^2 had been completed with a further 1 m. ft^2 approved but not started. It is estimated that the completed space provides employment for 25,000 office workers with a potential capacity of more than 30,000. They are employed in 50 office buildings which make a distinctive physical, as well as socio-economic, contribution to the suburban landscape of South London. The momentum of growth has, however, slowed down in recent years because of the O.D.P. restrictions.

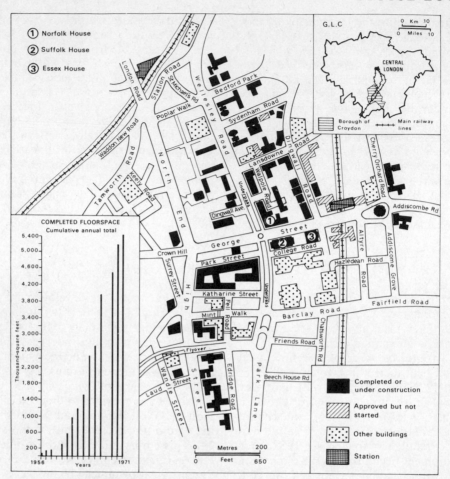

Fig. 49   Plan of Croydon Office Centre (After London Borough of Croydon, with the permission of the Director, Department of Development)

The development of office parks can be programmed to absorb the transport movements which they generate but this is more difficult with suburban office centres which have grown by aggregation. Many of the early office buildings in Croydon included very limited provision for car parking so that there has been an increasing trend towards on-street parking and over 7000 cars are parked in and around the fringes of the central area during the average working day. In an attempt to control this problem five out of ten planned multi-storey car parks have been completed with their location closely integrated with the office area and the main traffic routes, particularly the ring road around the central area. Because of its excellent accessibility to central London, Croydon's transport problems are also accentuated by conflicting demands; local office workers require daily car parking space and public transport, while central London office workers also use public transport to reach East Croydon station, as well as private cars to make longer journeys from outlying areas before transferring to fast trains into central London. The latter generate demand for parking space which does not directly arise from Croydon's office centre function. A third source of demand arises from Croydon's importance as a shopping centre which also generates public and, more particularly, private transport trips requiring parking facilities. All new office development is now required to include one car space for every 1000 ft^2 of lettable floorspace in order to cater for the needs of 'essential' users. Assuming that each employee occupies 250 ft^2 and 50 per cent of the office workers drive to work, this requirement can only partly satisfy the demand for parking facilities.

Large suburban office centres also distort the suburban/C.B.D. wage rate differential because of the competition for staff, many of whom demand higher wages to compensate for long suburban journeys to work, or as compensation for moving with their firms from the C.B.D. Suburban wage rates will depend also on the quality of staff and Child suggests that most employers can attract staff to suburban offices at a wage rate differential not less than the cost of transport to the C.B.D.[26] Uncontrolled expansion may also lead to local housing problems as commercial development often displaces residential development as well as putting great pressure on local housing markets.

LA DÉFENSE: INNER SUBURBAN RENEWAL AND OFFICE GROWTH

Major suburban office centres may also be located within a short distance of the C.B.D. Urban renewal through comprehensive redevelopment of an outdated inner city fabric can be made economic by incorporating a large proportion of office development. This is well illustrated by the La Défense scheme in Paris. The area involved is some 2 miles from the centre of the city and covers 750 acres of former warehouses, low quality housing, and industry (Fig. 50).[27] It incorporates parts of the municipalities of Nanterre, Puteaux Courbevoie and its development is controlled by L'Etablissement Public pour l'Aménagement de la Région de la Défense (E.P.A.D.). E.P.A.D. prepares development plans, is responsible for re-housing inhabitants and industrial undertakings, and provides various infrastructure investments. The scheme is controlled by the State but with extensive local community involvement and is financed by granting concessions to private developers for offices, retail, residential, and recreational development. It is hoped that when completed La Défense will be a counter-magnet to central Paris for shopping and leisure activities as well as for offices. Hence, space is provided for a variety of retail activities, including large departmental stores, and hotels. Residential development will provide housing for 20,000 people, many of whom will work in the office and service activities.

La Défense was started in 1958 but the first offices were not brought into use until 1964. The projected office floorspace is 16 m. ft^2 in 30 office buildings able to accommodate a projected 100,000 office jobs. Existing development in La Défense already represents 50 per cent of the completed office floorspace in Croydon, or 2·8 m. ft^2 in eight buildings. Approximately 17,000 office employees worked in La Défense at the end of 1972 and a further 4·3 m. ft^2 of office space was under construction. Despite the importance of office space in the overall scheme, it occupies less than 10 per cent of the total developed area because of the emphasis on skyscraper buildings. The majority of firms occupying the existing offices have moved from central Paris and most have moved their headquarters. There is no marked rent differential to attract offices, as in Croydon, and at 500 francs/m^2 the rents are only exceeded in small parts of central Paris such as Champs-Elysées, Opera, and Vendome.

It seems that firms are attracted to La Défense by the prospect of better facilities and less congestion. In contrast to Croydon, there are also good transport reasons for choosing La Défense which is probably the best served suburban nucleus in the metropolitan area. It is accesible by express underground from central Paris, has its own railway station, and is served by 11 bus routes. The major office and residential areas are surrounded by a peripheral access road system opened in 1971. More than 6000 parking bays are operational and 32,000 will be available when the project is completed. The road system is linked to the Paris motorway network and La

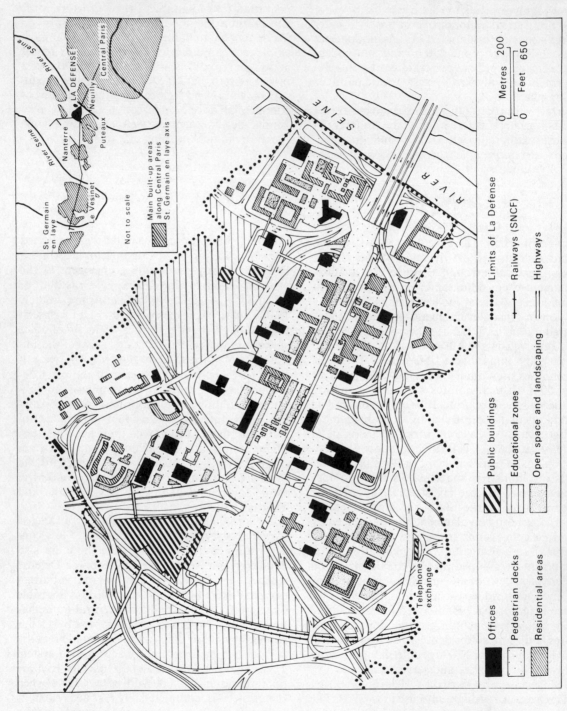

Fig. 50 La Défense (After *Information Review No. 10*, 1972, with the permission of Établissement Public Pour L'Aménagement De La Région De La Défense)

Défense is therefore very accessible for most types of journey to work, particularly from the western side of Paris. Pedestrian/transport segregation is also an important feature of the development with office and other buildings surrounded by a pedestrian deck with controlled access to public and private transport facilities beneath.

La Défense therefore represents an integrated approach to inner suburban office development. Conditions attractive to office activities are produced in a similar way, but on a much larger scale, to office parks with the additional advantage that comprehensive urban renewal is also achieved. Similar, although less comprehensive, inner suburban office centres have been proposed for Downtown Brooklyn, Downtown Newark and Jamaica (Queens).[28] All three are well served by existing public and private transport systems with large potential office worker catchment areas. This should make them attractive to headquarters offices of the type which have moved into La Défense, a process which it is hoped will slow down the out-migration of middle and upper income households and jobs.

The demand for suburban offices can therefore be satisfied by a number of alternative strategies. Most of the major metropolitan areas which are actively considering the problem seem to favour concentrated development, limiting dispersed growth to the needs of local market offices.[29] Such a pattern offers benefits to both employers and employees. The former achieve lower rentals, superior staff accessibility, and office linkages at lower cost; the latter benefit from increased job opportunities and choice, the highest possible level of transport accessibility, and minimum social disruption. It is clearly impossible to focus all new office development in suburban nodes because some office space is associated with industrial plants which have a different suburban location pattern, but the aim should be to achieve as high a level of concentration as possible. One of the outstanding problems, however, is how to establish the optimum size of office centre, in terms of employment and floorspace, which optimizes social and economic goals.

THE LOCAL IMPACT OF OFFICE DEVELOPMENT

New office development, whether concentrated or dispersed in suburban areas or located in towns and cities beyond a metropolitan area, will have consequences for local employment, housing, and traffic. Interest in the local impact of office development has been stimulated by the volume of office decentralization during the last decade. Much of the research has been undertaken in Britain and has been approached in one of two ways; case studies of individual offices which have moved to new locations[30] and case studies of groups of offices in individual towns or cities.[31] These two groups may be further sub-divided into those which consider as many aspects as possible of the local effects of new offices, and those which analyse specific components such as the journey to work or housing. The main objective of most of these studies has been to provide an empirical/descriptive analysis of the changes introduced by new offices. More detailed statistical analysis of the local income effects of migrant offices has only recently been

attempted.[32] Yannopoulos has attempted to analyse these effects in relation to the private and public economies of three reception towns for decentralized offices; Bootle, Hemel Hempstead and Reading. Although the sample is small and many simplifying assumptions are made, it appears that office moves do generate net economic and fiscal benefits for reception towns.

Local employment

The local employment effects of new offices will depend on the demand for labour which they generate and the supply of labour in the area.[33] Labour demand will depend upon the distance moved from area of origin, the type of office in terms of industrial classification, whether a partial or complete move is undertaken, the number of jobs in the office, and the percentage of staff transferred from the old to the new location. The latter is linked with the distance moved from area of origin in that the proportion of staff prepared to be geographically mobile decreases as distance moved increases.[34] If central London is taken as the origin of most new offices in other areas, centres within 40 miles receive a wider range of office activities than places further away. Because the offices are moving short distances they also bring a larger proportion of their previous staff, thus reducing the pressure of demand on local supply. The large number of offices which move short distances does, however, tend to diversify the range of demand for all office worker grades. Large offices often move furthest from origin and because they take with them a small proportion of their total staff requirements they create substantial demand in the reception area. The type of office workers required from local sources will depend on the occupation characteristics of employees moving with an office. Most firms are anxious to bring with them the key personnel such as managers, accountants, systems analysts, executives, and some senior clerical workers. Such staff are more likely to consider moving than junior male or female clerical workers but the distance moved often effects the success of this policy.[35] Junior clerical personnel, especially females, such as typists, secretaries, clerks and cashiers are therefore the major recruits at the new locations.[36]

An office can recruit staff from three main sources: from office workers employed by other firms in the local area; by diverting office workers employed in surrounding towns and cities; and as a result of an increase in the number of office workers resident in the reception area. The major source of supply is recruitment from other local employers, some of whom may have previously moved into the area themselves. Inducements such as higher wage rates are often necessary to attract suitable staff from other employers, particularly at locations near to the origin of in-migrant offices or in areas with a low proportion of office workers in the total labour force. Similar recruitment problems apply to staff attracted from other towns or adjacent suburbs but this is normally a second order source of supply. The accessibility of the new office location from surrounding areas is an additional factor governing the supply of suitable staff from surrounding areas. An increase in the number of resident office workers is a more long-term source of supply. Population growth through natural increase is never likely to be rapid enough to keep up with the possible short-term demand for office workers but growth by migration can be relevant in new or expanding towns. This has been demonstrated in Basingstoke.[37] An increase in female activity rates can also increase the supply of office workers without an increase in the number of resident population. Female activity rates will vary between towns according to the number of female jobs available locally.[38] In areas with below average activity rates, an increase in female office employment opportunities will lead to more females entering the job market and a greater demand for female workers as local employers' attitudes change. School leavers and previously unemployed office workers are also an important source of labour with the former particularly important for offices which move into Development Areas.[39]

Given knowledge of the sources and factors influencing the supply of office workers, the potential supply in the reception area can be calculated by using census data which relate to population, occupation, and journey to work characteristics. Such data can be used to assess the availability of office staff from each of the three main sources already mentioned. It will show whether supply will meet demand for individual office moves or for planned office development programmes for reception areas. Data relating to demand for office workers is more difficult to obtain and must usually be provided by individual firms and by projection of previous trends.

Housing

The relationship between new offices and local housing demand will largely depend on the number of office workers changing address in order to retain access to their places of work. Employees transferring with the firm are likely to be most mobile but the tendency to change address will be directly related to the distance moved by the office. The demand for housing in more distant centres is therefore limited although a move by a large office to a small town may cause local difficulties.[40] There is also an element of time lag to be considered; Hammond notes that many civil servants moving from London to Durham initially transferred from rented private accommodation in London to rented local authority houses in Durham. Eventually, however, they purchased new houses when they became available, or after becoming more familiar with the area. Both Carey and Bateman *et al.* have also noted a trend towards owner-occupation and a higher housing standard amongst migrant office workers. Before the move of an office from London to Ipswich, 80 per cent of the migrants (72 out of 90) owned their own houses or flats; in Ipswich the proportion rose to 97 per cent. In London, 11 migrants rented a flat or a house but only three did so in Ipswich.[41] Some 36 per cent (42) of the respondents in a survey of an Ashford decentralized office rented local authority houses or flats at the time of the original study, some five months after the main part of the move had been completed. A later survey of the same office revealed a movement away from this type of accommodation into owner-occupied properties.[42]

Demand for housing therefore becomes polarized as a result of decentralization with strong emphasis on owner-occupation of detached and semi-detached houses. Availability of rented accommodation is likely to be more restricted anyway outside major urban areas but polarized demand also reflects the dominance of senior and managerial personnel amongst office migrants. They are able to afford the kind of housing they seek and are prepared to consider travelling long distances to work in order to satisfy their objectives. This is partly a product of the perception of the reception area and its constituent parts as a place in which to live. Each migrant office worker attempts to live in an area which is considered most acceptable to his standards. Bateman and Burtenshaw note, however, that there is a considerable gap between perceived areas of residential preference and the actual residential distribution of migrants.[43] One-third of the migrants at a Portsmouth office lived in areas which had negative scores as potential areas where migrants might choose to live and only 6 per cent had succeeded in obtaining a house in areas with the highest rankings. The ability to achieve residential aspirations amongst migrant

office workers is partly controlled by the aid provided by firms. Disturbance allowances, bridging loans, help with mortgage arrangements and removal costs are frequently provided by firms to encourage staff to move, but the value of aid often varies according to status. Many decentralized office workers are attracted by the prospect of lower cost housing in the areas of reception but in practice the savings in housing costs are often negligible. Many of the junior staff take out a mortgage for the first time, but take out a larger mortgage than they might otherwise have done to cover the cost of better, more spacious, residential facilities. In the South East, the differential between metropolitan and non-metropolitan house prices has narrowed as population has become more widely dispersed and this has further reduced potential savings in house costs.[44] Over 40 per cent of the migrant households in the Ashford survey had incurred costs of moving which exceeded by more than £100 the contribution made by the company.[45]

Re-location allowances which cover all stages of the process are also used by American companies, most of whom are anxious to retain as many city employees as possible when they decentralize.[46] Existing owner-occupiers or employees buying for the first time may be allowed six-month equity loans at no interest or five-year loans at 5 per cent interest. Help in obtaining lower interest rates from banks or building societies, repayment of conveyancing, and other fees, or mortgage interest differential allowances, is also provided. Removal costs are also paid, although limits related to salary and status are often used. Some firms also make special payments in order to retain as many staff as possible; salary increases, various bonus schemes, and money for the purchase of a second car are typical examples. O'Meara refers to one company in which an employee having to pay more for his new home than he received for his old one was allowed the difference in the form of a loan. If, at the end of a three-year period after the office had moved, the employee was still with the company, one-third of the loan was written off. It does seem, however, that most migrant office workers only achieve marginal benefits in the form of lower housing costs as a result of offices moving to new locations.

Journey to work

Liepmann has suggested that the journey to work 'is a test of urban layout, excessive costs and hardships of daily travelling can be taken as a symptom that something is wrong with the form of towns or the conurbations and the location of industry plays an important part in this respect'.[47] In the context of this statement, offices have become just as important and, indeed, one of the main reasons for promoting decentralization has been the easing of transport congestion in the C.B.D. Until recently, however, comparatively little has been known about the traffic generated by offices either at new or existing locations. This is also true of the journey to work changes experienced by office employees. It is now recognized that 'planning the "best" location for changes or growth of employment and population must ideally require a knowledge of the journey to work patterns which are likely to result'.[48] The journey to work patterns generated by suburban office nuclei, for example, may begin 'dominating and obsolescing prevailing concepts about the relationship between employment location and the journey to work' while it is also possible that they will produce local congestion problems which rival those of the C.B.D.[49]

Without recourse to case or special studies, statistical evidence about transport and journey to work changes associated with new patterns of office location is difficult to produce. The 1961, 1966, and 1971 Censuses provide a general source of comparative information on the journey to work to employment centres outside central London but the aggregate form of the data and the problem of identifying nuclei within administrative areas makes it difficult to be precise about the changes which are taking place.[50] Transportation studies could be another data source but, in many cases, it is difficult to isolate travel patterns in relation to specific types of land use or to individual office buildings. It is therefore left to case studies to provide the detailed data which are not available at the macro-level.

Space does not permit a detailed discussion of the growing number of studies of the relationship between office location and the journey to work during the last five years. It is apparent, however, that studies of this type have their origins in the United States, particularly with reference to industrial establishments and to a study of the peripheral journey to work in Chicago by Taafe et al.[51] Most of the studies in relation to offices, particularly decentralized offices, have been undertaken in Britain, either as an integral part of wide ranging analyses which include reference to housing or occupation changes as well as the journey to work,[52] or in the form of studies devoted exclusively to analyses of the journey to work.[53] The accumulated evidence suggests that the emphasis on use of public transport by office workers travelling to the C.B.D. changes to heavy dependence on private transport at suburban and extra-metropolitan locations. One of the most frequently quoted advantages of office decentralization is that it promotes shorter and less arduous journeys to work and, in general, there are indeed some marked improvements in the trip times and distances travelled by office employees in such offices. But the benefits which accrue are not consistently distributed and account must be taken, for example, of where the office employees worked before, whether they change place of residence in response to the change of job location, the location of the office in relation to transport routes, or the distance moved by offices from their zones of origin. Expressed in aggregate at individual office locations, the journey to work changes have important implications for local transport demand. It is also clear that there are spatial variations in journey to work changes which must be considered when evaluating the impact of office development on areas of reception.

Some of these points can be clarified in the context of 63 decentralized offices which moved from central London to locations throughout Britain between 1963 and 1969. The sample includes Government and commercial offices and 32 per cent moved to locations within Greater London. Journey to work and related data was obtained from 5809 office employees with reference to both their previous and present workplace locations and analysed, initially, within the framework of six distance zones around central London.[54]

It is commonly assumed that improvements in trip time for the journey to work will increase as offices decentralize further from London (Fig.

51). A negative relationship certainly exists between mean trip time for the present journey to work and distance moved when all 63 offices are included and r (-0.46) is significant at the 0.05 level. But this conceals some major variations between the zones, so that while there is a clear trend towards shorter trip times as distance from the centre increases ($r = 0.52$ in zone 1 which coincides approximately with Greater London), it is by no means continuous and trip times increase in the outer zones. The difference between previous and present mean trip times at each office emphasizes further the dichotomy between the inner (South East) zones and the outer (provincial) zones. It clearly emerges that offices which move to the outer parts of the South East are the ones which are most likely to produce trip time benefits for their employees. At offices within Greater London, the mean trip time differences are lower than elsewhere in the South East, but the value of r (0.46) is the highest for any of the zones and suggests that distance from the C.B.D. is one of the more important controls on trip time improvement within metropolitan areas. An analysis of the distance travelled by office employee produced broadly similar conclusions.[55]

The inter-zonal variations in trip time changes illustrated in Fig. 51 are partly due to differences in the distribution of office employees by occupation and previous place of work. It has already been noted that office employees previously

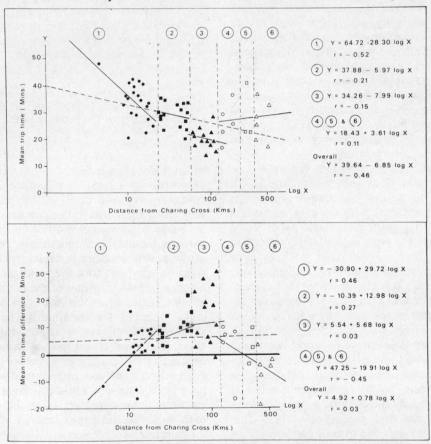

Fig. 51 Relationship Between Distance Moved by Decentralized Offices and Changes in Employee Trip Times for the Journey to Work (After P. W. Daniels, 'Some changes in the journey to work of decentralized office workers', *Town Planning Review*, 1973, with the permission of the Editor)

employed in central London will only accompany their offices if they move short distances. Hence, the larger the proportion of this group in the sample the higher the probability of large trip time savings at the new location. On average, central London employees had previous journeys to work which took twice the time of those undertaken by staff recruited locally or from elsewhere (Fig. 52). At the decentralized location, the central London employees achieve trip times which are similar to the local distribution but which represent a major improvement on their previous journeys. Not surprisingly, local employees have only achieved marginal trip time benefits. Indeed, in the provincial zones they are spending, on average, more time travelling to work. New offices moving into an area often provide better working conditions and higher salaries than other competitors for office labour and local employees seem prepared to spend more time and to travel further, in many cases, to utilize these opportunities. Central London employees now working in suburban London save approximately 30 min each day on their journey to work; a total of $2\frac{1}{2}$ hr for the working week. This increases to an average of 4 and 6 hr in zones 2 and 3 respectively.[56]

The relevance of the occupation variable for the journey to work is widely recognized with higher income groups showing less concern for transport costs or with distance minimization. Managerial, professional, and supervisory, technical, assistant professional office workers in the sample have all achieved positive time changes of at least 10 min for the average one way trip (Fig. 52). It is also apparent that average trip times decrease with distance from central London, except in the case of clerical workers. Clerical employees spent an average of 33 min for their previous journeys to work, compared with 45 min for managerial and professional staff. But when present times are compared the situation is reversed; in the outer zones clerical employees actually have higher mean trip times than managerial and professional staff. This occurs, even though the overall distribution of present trip times for clerical workers is little different to the previous distribution; approximately 30 min for the former and 25 min for the latter. Therefore, clerical employees are prepared

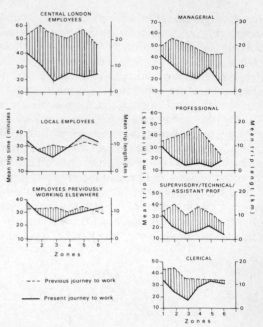

Fig. 52 Relationship Between Occupation Group and Previous Place of Work and Trip Time, Trip Length Changes of Decentralized Office Employees (After P. W. Daniels, see Fig. 51)

to, or have to, spend more time travelling to decentralized offices, particularly in the provincial zones. Residential location patterns probably affect these results because managerial and professional personnel, most of whom previously worked in central London, usually choose to live in the towns or cities to which their organizations have moved with the result that trip times are much shorter. Many of the clerical workers at offices in the provincial zones are also entering employment for the first time and because of the shortage of employment opportunities in some areas, they must travel further and spend more time than the average for all clerical workers. The occupation structures of decentralized offices in provincial locations are dominated by clerical workers; there were over 1000, the majority female, amongst the respondents in zones 5 and 6, for example. Approximately, 19 and 14 per cent respectively spent an additional 25 min on their journey to work to a decentralized office. Such increases will almost certainly add to the cost of the journey to work for the employees affected, whether measured in fiscal terms or as the time deducted from available leisure time outside working hours.

Travel mode changes for the journey to work represent the most tangible impact of decentralized offices on reception areas. The most important characteristic is the transfer from public to private transport modes, irrespective of previous workplace or occupation (Fig. 53). Private transport trips in all the zones are almost exclusively made by employees driving to the

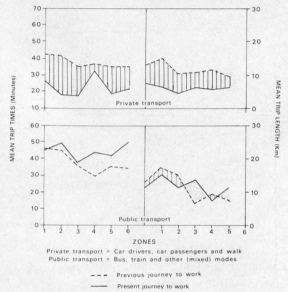

Fig. 53 Travel Mode Changes by Decentralized Office Employees (After P. W. Daniels, see Fig. 51)

office or travelling as car passengers. The largest proportional contribution to the increase in these trips is attributable to central London employees. Their previous journeys to work were dominated by public transport; 86 per cent of the respondents in Greater London, for example, previously travelled to central London by public transport, mainly by train and the underground. The figure at decentralized locations is less than 50 per cent with almost 40 per cent able to drive to their suburban offices. This proportion is lower than in zones 2 and 3 where public transport alternatives are far less satisfactory than in Greater London, so that 87 per cent of the trips by central London employees in zone 3 are made by private transport. While over 80 per cent of the

office workers previously travelling to work by car have continued to do so for the present journey to work, only between 10 and 15 per cent of those travelling by train have continued using this mode. The largest proportion, 20·4 per cent, travel to offices in suburban London where the location of individual offices influences the modal split. An office at Mitcham, 3·3 km from the nearest suburban station and poorly served by bus routes, generated private transport trips by more than 60 per cent of its employees, compared with 16 per cent at a Harrow office with direct access to the underground and a good range of bus services.[57] Townsley suggests, however, that the degree of parking control in the locality of an office block has a greater influence on modal choice than public transport availability.[58]

Office development at suburban locations provides an opportunity for retaining the role of public transport for the journey to work. There is no reason why this could not take place despite the established trend, much more strongly developed in the United States, towards private transport trips.[59] The net of commuter railways into central London, which are fed at several nodal points by suburban bus routes or crossed by radial and cross-radial roads, should provide the framework for locating offices at public transport nodes. If suburban office workers continue to transfer to private transport, the congestion on suburban roads will increase and will only be reduced by investment in appropriate road space or encouragement of public transport trips. By choosing public transport orientated locations it should be possible to counter-balance the disutilities of slower trip times and general inconvenience of public transport with the possibility of direct trips to the destination offices. It would reduce the need for expensive car parking provision and help to generate a more clearly defined pattern of journey to work movement in suburban London (Fig. 54). The desire lines for the present journey to work of employees at seven decentralized locations clearly demonstrate the complexity of movement in the suburbs with large offices having wider catchment areas than smaller units. Such a pattern is superimposed on the radial movements of office workers and others into central London. The

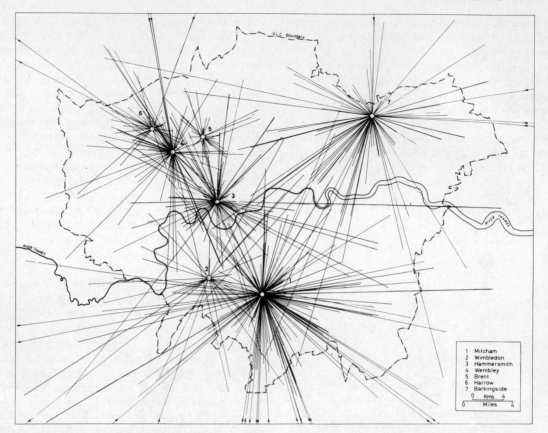

Fig. 54   Journeys to Work to Decentralized Offices in Suburban London (Data: Survey of decentralized office employees by the Author, 1969)

conflict between the two could be reduced, particularly where radial and cross-suburban traffic flow meet, by channelling as many suburban office workers as possible along similar routes and using similar modes as central London office workers, i.e. public transport, especially the railways. Many of the office staff in suburban decentralized offices do not change address when they move jobs but already live in areas with good access to rail facilities because of a previous need to travel to work in central London. It is inevitable that a certain proportion of suburban office employees will wish, or have, to travel to work by car but the remainder might be persuaded to use public transport if offices were suitably located.

But the general *malaise* of public transport is deep-seated and not confined to offices which

have decentralized to suburban London (Table 55). Although the overall role of public transport is greater in the provincial zones, in accordance with the larger proportion of young clerical employees who are captive users, its relative status has declined. Even local employees have abandoned public transport in favour of the car, particularly if the offices have moved to the suburban areas of the larger provincial cities such as Glasgow or Manchester. The lower settlement densities, the influence of existing travel patterns in the provincial conurbations, the size of the centres to which some large offices have moved, and the distances which previously unemployed staff are prepared to travel to obtain work, makes it difficult to provide services which are a viable alternative to the private car. Hence, it is estimated that the sample decentralized offices

TABLE 55
ESTIMATED CHANGES IN THE NUMBER OF
(A) CAR DRIVER AND (B) BUS TRIPS
TO DECENTRALIZED OFFICES
IN SIX ZONES—GREAT BRITAIN, 1969

Zone[1]	Additional trips to local networks	E.F.[2]	Estimated additions	Previous total trips external to networks	% change
(A) CAR DRIVERS					
1	548 (30·6)[3]	1·66	909	505	+80·0
2	420 (33·4)	1·85	777	344	+125·9
3	272 (27·8)	1·62	441	204	+116·2
4	113 (24·4)	1·72	194	53	+266·0
5	68 (21·4)	2·74	186	99	+87·9
6	161 (15·3)	1·85	298	148	+101·3
Total	1582	—	2805	1353	+107·3
(B) BUS					
1	138 (7·7)	1·66	229	256	−10·5
2	115 (9·1)	1·85	213	196	+8·7
3	19 (1·9)	1·62	31	134	−76·9
4	60 (12·9)	1·72	103	93	+10·8
5	14 (4·4)	2·74	38	107	−64·4
6	109 (17·6)	1·85	202	302	−33·1
Total	455	—	816	1088	−25·0

Notes: 1. See n. 54.
2. Expansion factor.
3. Values in brackets are additional trips to local networks
   expressed as a percentage of all present trips in each zone.
Source: P. W. Daniels, 'Office decentralization from London: The
   journey to work consequences' (University of London, unpublished Ph.D. Thesis, 1972).

have generated 2805 additional trips by car drivers.[60] This is an increase of 107·3 per cent compared with the number of car driver trips prior to decentralization. The level of change is considerably higher in zones 2 and 4. Buses are the most important post-decentralization mode of public transport and using these trips as an index, there has been a decrease in public transport trips of at least 25 per cent compared with previous public transport trips external to local networks. This means that although new public transport journeys have been added to the local networks around decentralized offices, they are at a lower level than expected from previous travel behaviour of the respondents. These results probably understate the true extent of the

transfer to private transport because car passenger trips, some of which do not involve sharing with other office employees, have been excluded from the estimates.

The Greater London Council, in an attempt to assess more objectively the applications received for office development in the suburbs, have conducted detailed studies of traffic generated by a sample of suburban office blocks.[61] This includes not only the journey to work, but non-work trips, business trips, and servicing trips by goods vehicles. The relationship between gross floorspace/employment and traffic generation by travel mode, two hour peaks, trip distance or trip time, for example, is examined using linear regression techniques.

Although the sample is small, most of the results are statistically significant and permit a more objective analysis of the likely effects of new office development on transport demand at locations in the outer suburbs. It is much more difficult to conduct a similar exercise on housing and employment demand.[62]

at all levels are minimized but the variables involved are so numerous that no attempt has yet been made to evaluate the consequences of office decentralization in this way. The costs and benefits are more easily calculated for some variables than others, in particular transport.

The actual costs of providing for the transport

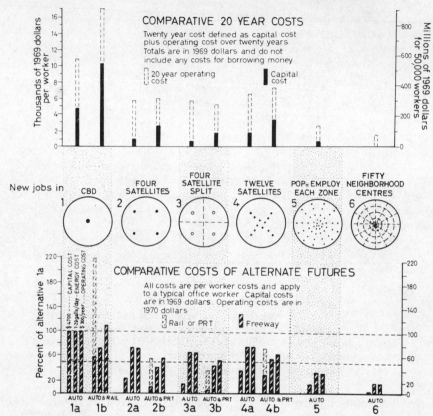

Fig. 55   Comparative Costs of Providing Transport Facilities for Different Types of Office Location Patterns (After R. C. Harkness, *Telecommunications Substitutes for Travel: A Preliminary Assessment of their Potential for Reducing Transportation Costs by Altering Office Location Pattern*, 1973, with the permission of the Author)

The growing pool of information about the effects of changing office location patterns on office workers and the impact on areas of new development is an invaluable aid to an evaluation of the costs and benefits. The Hardman Report on Civil Service office dispersal viewed the net costs to be incurred by the Exchequer but there are also costs, as existing research shows, to be met by the local community and individual office workers. It is vital that the costs incurred

demands generated by new distributions of office employment have been estimated by Harkness (Fig. 55).[63] Capital investment for transport facilities, annual operating costs, and energy consumption is examined with reference to six alternative patterns of office distribution, including the case of all office employment being in the C.B.D. The other alternatives range from a pattern of four satellites to totally dispersed neighbourhood centres; the latter representing the most efficient distribution for the journey to work assuming that population equals employment in every zone. Using the hypothesized patterns, it is then possible to calculate the freeway and public transport requirements of each alternative and the associated costs.[64] Operating and energy cost calculations are based on the person/miles travelled by each mode and published statistics on energy consumption per vehicle mile.

The generally lower costs of the suburban alternatives are clearly evident in Fig. 55. Harkness estimates that over 20 years it would cost about $17,000 in capital and operating costs to provide a rail/freeway service for a C.B.D. office worker; this is reduced to $6000 for an office in a suburban satellite. Suburban centres therefore produce a saving of almost two-thirds in the provision of transport facilities. The cost per office worker decreases even further to $2700 in the event of widespread dispersion leading to the number of jobs equalling the number of workers in every zone. In the case of 50 neighbourhood centres the ability to use existing local streets and the short work trips which are possible means that capital expenditures on transport are unnecessary. The costs of travelling by car are the only ones incurred and amount to $1300 per office worker. Some trips could probably be made on foot, while the fragmentation which such a low cost pattern of office location implies assumes efficient communications and more flexible organizational structure than exist at present.

The ratio of public transport (rapid transit) to freeways required by each alternative distribution also has a major influence on capital costs. The former are estimated by Harkness to cost three and a half times as much per route mile as freeways. The limited dependence of the suburban centres on public transport may not be totally unsatisfactory therefore because it helps to keep costs down. Construction costs per mile of a suburban freeway are also lower than equivalent costs for inner city or C.B.D.-orientated freeways while it is also assumed that the social benefits of each circumferential freeway mile are twice those of radial freeways of similar size. This reflects the heavy congestion of existing radial freeways and rail facilities into the C.B.D. during peak periods and the excess capacity in the reverse direction. Any trips which utilize such excess capacity can therefore fill existing road or rail space and no new facilities are required; consequently no social benefit is achieved.

These conclusions are based on hypothetical distributions of new office employment and activity in a city or a region. There are several assumptions built in to the calculations which make them rough approximations in some cases. Despite any errors which must inevitably introduce 'noise' into models of this type, Harkness has provided a good guide to the general relationship between alternative office distributions. In terms of transport investment the advantages of encouraging future office employment in suburban locations or beyond are clear enough.

A SUBURBAN OFFICE ALLOCATION MODEL

Any preferred patterns of suburban or regional office growth ultimately depend for their success on effective allocation of dispersed and other office floorspace. Model-based techniques can usefully be used to allocate future office growth and a simple model for allocating space to the suburban areas of a major city is outlined below. It is assumed that future office location patterns will be influenced by journey to work demands and other variables are not considered.[65]

Existing transportation survey zones can be utilized as a frame for locating existing office floorspace distributions and work trip patterns by destination land use. It has been demonstrated earlier that the future potential growth of office space is closely related to the distribution of existing office space and the same principal is used here for the calculation of the number of trips attracted to each office centre. It can be postulated that the larger, existing, office concentrations in the suburbs will attract office workers from further away than smaller centres and that this will influence the distribution of work trips from any zone i. Competition between centres for trips from any origin zone i can then be expressed as follows:

$$C_i = \sum_{\text{all } j} \left(\frac{D_j}{t_{ij}{}^x} \right),$$

where C_i is the competition for trips from zone i; D_j is the total office space at zone j; and t_{ij} is the travel time between zone i and zone j, where x is a travel time exponent. C_i is used to allocate total work trips to any zone j, using a gravity model formula as follows:

$$AT_j = \sum_{\text{all } j} \left\{ \left[\left(\frac{D_j}{t_{ij}{}^x} \right) C_i \right] T_i \right\},$$

where AT_j is the total trips attracted to zone i; and T_i is the total origins in zone i. The zonal values of AT_j can be used to define a trip distribution surface for the study area. The predictive accuracy of the model is then checked through calibration and the actual and predicted distribution of work trips to office space compared. The travel time exponent, which may be calculated according to the relative importance of car and public transport travel times, is varied and its effect on closeness of fit evaluated. This stage of model development also allows the possible inclusion of other variables, such as income, socio-economic characteristics, or a land availability constraint, to be considered.

Given the present distribution of office centres and journey to work distributions a number of future office centre sizes are then identified. The additional floorspace involved is added to existing space on the assumption that no regional growth of population and employment has occurred and that the demand for new office space remains constant. This simplifying assumption is necessary if the model is to remain fairly basic but it could be relaxed in more advanced versions of the model. After the projected office space information is added to the existing office space in each zone, the new work trip distributions generated by the incremented zones are calculated. With an assumption that no regional growth has taken place, this stage indicates whether the additions to existing floorspace will be justified and, if the answer is positive, where such development should take place. In this respect, it would certainly be useful to include a land availability constraint in the model. The present and predicted work trips to any zone j are then compared and the difference between the two allocation values represents the trip potential (tp) of zone j. The tp values for each j are then aggregated and averaged into tp values for different areas of the city. The best zone for additional office development (Z) is that zone with the highest tp value within that area of the city with highest average trip potential.

This method ensures that the best zone, in relation to the journey to work, is selected. The office centre size projections can be varied to assess their effect on the location of the best office zone and this allows the locational attributes of centres of differing sizes to be compared. It may well be that the best location indicated by the model will be inadequate in terms of the travel times of the additional trips generated or the levels of congestion which might arise. It is therefore necessary to specify a maximum trip generation rate (mt) for the different sized office centres in the projections. If the trip potential (tp) of the best office zone (Z) selected by the model exceeds mt, that zone is rejected for additional office development and another zone selected until a suitable one has been located.

Further zones for office development are located iteratively until either, no further zones qualify, or all projected growth has been accommodated. As each centre is identified and new floorspace added to the existing office space the trip potential surface is changed because new centres create competition for the existing office concentrations. The competition variable therefore changes before each iteration and this ensures that floorspace allocation does not exceed the total number of work journeys available for distribution between centres. The distribution of office space predicted by the model can then be compared with the actual distribution, along with any further planned development for the future. If the results are considered acceptable, it is possible to move on to the forecast stage of the model.

For the forecast phase a certain time period is assumed to have elapsed and the pattern of demand for office space to have changed. There will be a larger number of work trips available for distribution and because the demand for office space is measured in terms of work trip generation rates, these must be recalculated for the forecast period. Changes in travel time between zones as well as in the range of travel mode choice should also be allowed for. New floorspace is then allocated in the same way and when all the available journey to work trips have

been distributed, the model is complete. The possibility of forecasting the location of new office space over a series of limited time periods may make the model more useful than if it is used to forecast the position at the end of a long time period, say 20 or 25 years.

REFERENCES

1   Economist Intelligence Unit, *A Survey of Factors Governing the Location of Offices in the London Area* (London: Economist Intelligence Unit, 1964). J. V. Aucott, 'Dispersal of offices from London', *Town Planning Review*, vol. 31 (1960), pp. 39–44. P. W. Daniels, 'Office decentralization from London: Policy and practice', *Regional Studies*, vol. 3 (1969), pp. 172–6.

2   R. K. Hall, 'The movement of offices from London', *Regional Studies*, vol. 6 (1972), pp. 387–91.

3   The techniques for estimating partial moves are explained in detail in R. K. Hall, *op. cit.*, pp. 388–9.

4   R. K. Hall, 'The vacated offices controversy', *Journal of the Town Planning Institute*, vol. 56 (1970), pp. 298–300.

5   R. B. Armstrong, *The Office Industry: Patterns of Growth and Location* (Cambridge, Mass.: The M.I.T. Press, 1972), p. 122.

6   *Ibid.*, Table 5.17, p. 133.

7   New York City Planning Commission, *Head-quarters Relocation in New York and the Region* (New York: City Planning Commission, 1972), pp. 2–4.

8   R. B. Armstrong, *op. cit.*, Table 5.14, p. 130.

9   M. W. Wright, 'Provincial office development', *Urban Studies*, vol. 4 (1967), pp. 250–1.

10 E. J. C. Griffith, 'Moving industry from London', *Town Planning Review*, vol. 26 (1956), pp. 54–9. E. Hammond, 'Dispersal of Government offices: A survey', *Urban Studies*, vol. 4 (1967), pp. 271–2. Standing Conference on London Regional Planning, *Office Employment in the Conference Area* (London: Standing Conference, LRP 279, 1964), n. 10. R. K. Hall, *op. cit.* (1970), pp. 298–300.

11 R. K. Hall, *op. cit.* (1970), Table 4, p. 300.

12 Greater London Council, *Greater London Development Plan: Statement* (London: Greater London Council, 1969), p. 20.

13 O. Mariott, *The Property Boom* (London: Hamish Hamilton, 1967), pp. 178–9.

14 London County Council, *A Plan to Combat Congestion in Central London* (London: London County Council, 1957), p. 15. Ministry of Housing and Local Government, *The South East Study* (London: Her Majesty's Stationery Office, 1964), p. 41. South East Economic Planning Council, *A Strategy for the South East* (London: Her Majesty's Stationery Office, 1967), pp. 52–5.

15 Greater London Council, *Greater London Development Plan: Report of Studies* (London: Greater London Council, 1969), p. 103.

16 Greater London Development Plan Inquiry, *Industrial and Office Floorspace Targets, 1972–76* (London: Greater London Council, Background Paper, no. B.452, 1971), pp. 48–53.

17 R. B. Armstrong, *op. cit.*, Table 5.22, pp. 147–66.

18 *Ibid.*, pp. 154–66. Armstrong assumes that a 1 m. ft^2 office building requires 1·35 track miles of railway in Manhattan, 2·2 lane miles of expressway in a major suburban centre, and 7·9 lane miles elsewhere on suburban land. This is equivalent to an investment of $12 m. in Manhattan, $3·1 m. in a major centre, and $4·7 m. on suburban land for each 1 m. ft^2 increment.

19 New York City Planning Commission, *Plan for New York City: Part 1, Critical Issues* (Cambridge, Mass.: The M.I.T. Press, 1969).

20 E. W. Kersten and D. R. Ross, 'Clayton: A metropolitan focus in the St Louis area', *Annls Assn. Amer. Geographers*, vol. 58 (1968), pp. 637–49. F. A. Tarpley, L. S. Davidson and D. D. Clark, 'Flight to the fringes: A study of shifting office locations in Atlanta', *Review of Regional Studies*, vol. 1 (1970), pp. 117–40. Houston City Planning Department, *Major Office Areas, 1960–1990* (Houston: City Planning Department, 1971). Southfield City Planning Commission, *Southfield Office Study* (Southfield: Vulcan-Leman and Associates Inc., 1972).

21 'The office park: A new concept in office space', *Industrial Development*, vol. 15 (1965), pp. 9–14. F. B. Moore, 'Downtown office building versus the office park complex', *Skyscraper Management*, vol. 54 (1969), pp. 15–17. J. R. McKeever, *Business Parks* (Washington D.C.: Urban Land Institute,

Technical Bulletin 65, 1970), pp. 7–44. G. R. Long, 'Office park development', *Urban Land*, vol. 32 (1973), pp. 10–17.

22 F. P. Clark, 'Office buildings in the suburbs', *Urban Land*, vol. 13 (1954), pp. 3–10.

23 J. R. McKeever, *op. cit.*, p. 15.

24 *Ibid.*, pp. 45–82, G. R. Long, *op. cit.*, pp. 14–15. Twin Cities Metropolitan Council, *Office Space: An Inventory and Forecast for the Twin Cities Metropolitan Area* (St Paul: Twin Cities Metropolitan Council, 1973), pp. 9–16. D. B. Knight and T. Ito, 'Office parks: The Oak Brook example', *Land Economics*, vol. 58 (1972), pp. 65–9. T. A. Hartshorne, 'Industrial/office parks: A new look for the city', *Journal of Geography*, vol. 72 (1973), pp. 33–45. P. W. Daniels, 'New offices in the suburbs', in J. H. Johnson (ed.) *Suburban Growth: Geographical Processes at the Edge of the Western City* (London: Wiley, 1974), pp. 184–6.

25 London Borough of Croydon, *Office Development* (Croydon: Borough Engineer, Surveyor and Planning Officer's Department, 1968). O. Marriott, *op. cit.*, pp. 185–90. P. W. Daniels, *op. cit.* (1974), pp. 189–91.

26 P. Child, *Office Development in Croydon: A Descriptive and Statistical Analysis* (London: Location of Offices Bureau, Research Paper, no. 5, 1971).

27 Etablissement Public pour l'Aménagement de la Défense, *Travaux* (Paris: E.P.A.D., 1972), p. 3. 'Aménagement de la Région de la Défense', *Techniques and Architecture*, vol. 34 (1971), pp. 61–82.

28 New York Regional Plan Association, *The Second Regional Plan* (New York: Regional Plan Association, 1968).

29 See also R. M. Pierce, 'Towards an optimum policy for office location' (University of Wales, unpublished M.Sc. Thesis, 1972).

30 S. J. Carey, *Relocation of Office Staff: A Study of the Reactions of Office Staff Decentralized to Ashford* (London: Location of Offices Bureau, Research Paper, no. 4, 1969). E. Hammond, *London to Durham: A Study of the Transfer of the Post Office Savings Certificate Division* (Durham: Rowntree Research Unit, 1968). M. Bateman, D. Burtenshaw and R. Hall, *Office Staff on the Move* (London: Location of Offices Bureau, Research Paper, no. 6, 1971). Location of Offices Bureau, *Case Studies of Decentralized Offices: A Summary* (London: Location of Offices Bureau, 1972).

31 Economic Consultants Limited, *Demand and Supply for Office Workers and the Local Impact of Office Development* (London: Report prepared for Location of Offices Bureau, 1971). See also H. Murray *et al.*, *The Location of Government Review: Human Aspects of Dispersal* (London: Tavistock Institute of Human Relations, 1972), E. Sidwell, *The Problems for Employees in Office Dispersal: A Methodology* (London: London School of Economics, Discussion Paper No. 48, Department of Geography, 1974).

32 G. Yannopoulos, *The Local Impact of Decentralized Offices* (London: Location of Offices Bureau, Research Paper, no. 7, 1973). G. Yannopoulos, 'Local income effects of office relocation', *Regional Studies*, vol. 7 (1973), pp. 33–46.

33 Economic Consultants Limited, *op. cit.*, pp. 4–11.

34 M. Bateman *et al.*, *op. cit.*, pp. 77–8. P. W. Daniels, 'Office decentralization from London: The journey to work consequences' (University of London, unpublished Ph.D. Thesis, 1972a).

35 National Opinion Polls Limited, *White Collar Commuters: A Second Survey* (London: Location of Offices Bureau, Research Paper, no. 1, 1967), pp. 38–74.

36 P. W. Daniels, *op. cit.* (1972a), Ch. 3.

37 Economic Consultants Limited, *op. cit.*, pp. 22–7.

38 J. Bowers, *The Anatomy of Regional Activity Rates* (London: National Institute for Economic and Social Research, 1970).

39 P. W. Daniels, *op. cit.* (1972a), Ch. 3. E. Hammond, *op. cit.* (1968), pp. 95–127.

40 E. Hammond, *op. cit.* (1968), pp. 39–59.

41 M. Bateman *et al.*, *op. cit.*, pp. 37–8.

42 S. J. Carey, *Relocation of Office Staff: A Follow-up Survey* (London: Location of Offices Bureau, Research Paper, no. 4a, 1970).

43 M. Bateman and D. Burtenshaw, 'Sponsored white collar migrants', *Town and Country Planning*, vol. 39 (1971), pp. 554–7.

44 M. Bateman and D. Burtenshaw, 'Sponsored migration and residential change', Paper read at Institute of British Geographers Urban Study Group Conference, Sheffield, 25 September 1973. E. Sidwell, *op. cit.*, pp. 3–6.

45 S. J. Carey, *op. cit.* (1969), Table 4, p. 8.

46 J. R. O'Meara, *op. cit.*, pp. 24–7.

47 K. Liepmann, *The Journey to Work* (London: Routledge, 1945), p. 85.

48 J. S. Wabe, 'An econometric analysis of the factors affecting the journey to work in the London Metropolitan Region and their significance' (University of Oxford, unpublished D.Phil. Thesis, 1966), p. 3.

49 A. Ganz, 'Emerging patterns of urban growth and travel', *Highway Research Record*, vol. 203 (1968), p. 22. See also R. B. Mitchell and C. Rapkin, *Urban Traffic: A Function of Land Use* (New York: Columbia University Press, 1954), pp. 120–3.

50 General Register Office, *Census of Population 1961: Usual Residence and Workplace Tables* (London: Her Majesty's Stationery Office, 1964). *Sample Census 1966, Great Britain: Transport Tables* (London: Her Majesty's Stationery Office, 1969). Special tabulations for the journey to work characteristics of workers in employment concentrations (comprised of the appropriate aggregated E.D.s) are available from the 1971 Census.

51 J. W. Martin and J. L. Johnson, 'Labour market boundaries: Inter-county commuting to employment', *Current Economic Comment*, vol. 17 (1955), pp. 29–37. J. H. Thompson, 'Commuting patterns of manufacturing employees', *Industrial Labor Relations Review*, vol. 10 (1956), pp. 70–80. R. E. Lonsdale, 'Two North Carolina commuting patterns', *Economic Geography*, vol. 42 (1966), pp. 114–138. E. J. Taafe, B. J. Garner, and M. H. Yeats, *The Peripheral Journey to Work: A Geographic Consideration* (Evanston: North Western University Press, 1963). E. J. Burtt, *Plant Relocation and the Core City Worker* (Washington D.C.: U.S. Department of Housing and Urban Development, 1967).

52 Kent County Council, *A Pilot Survey and Analysis of Some Office Firms in Kent* (Maidstone: County Planning Department, 1967), pp. 40–70. E. Hammond, *op. cit.* (1968), pp. 116–20. S. J. Carey, *op. cit.* (1969), pp. 9–12. M. Bateman *et al.*, *op. cit.*, pp. 39–41 and pp. 55–9.

53 J. S. Wabe, 'Dispersal of employment and the journey to work', *Journal of Transport Economics and Policy*, vol. 1 (1967), pp. 345–61. P. W. Daniels, 'Employment decentralization and the journey to work', *Area*, vol. 1 (1970), pp. 47–51. P. W. Daniels, 'Transport changes generated by decentralized offices', *Regional Studies*, vol. 6 (1972b), pp. 273–289. P. W. Daniels, 'Some changes in the journey to work of decentralized office workers', *Town Planning Review*, vol. 44 (1973), pp. 167–88.

54 The six zones are defined as follows: 1. Less than 16 miles; 2. 17–47 miles; 3. 48–94 miles; 4. 95–156 miles; 5. 157–235 miles; 6. More than 235 miles.

55 P. W. Daniels, *op. cit.* (1973), pp. 170–2.

56 These values compare favourably with the average time saving of four hours per week for all employees, irrespective of previous workplace, at an Epsom decentralized office. See J. S. Wabe, *op. cit.* (1967), p. 357.

57 P. W. Daniels, *op. cit.* (1972a), Ch. 6.

58 C. H. Townsley, *Traffic Generation of Suburban London Offices* (London: Greater London Council, Department of Planning and Transportation Research Memorandum 398, 1973), pp. 24–30.

59 Department of the Environment, *Greater London Development Plan—Report of Panel of Inquiry*, vol. 1 (London: Her Majesty's Stationery Office, 1973), pp. 100–5.

60 The total trips made by bus and by car drivers for the previous and present journey to work are calculated and then expanded to produce an estimate of the actual increase or decrease in the number of trips made by each mode (the employee response rate averaged 60 per cent at each office). A distinction is drawn between trips already made in the local networks of the reception area and the new trips introduced following office migration. Therefore, all the trips by local employees have been deducted from the total number of present trips made by car drivers or by bus. The number of previous trips made outside the local network has also been calculated in order to calculate absolute and percentage change. The expansion factor equals the total office employees at time of survey divided by the number of respondents at each office. P. W. Daniels, *op. cit.* (1972b), pp. 278–9.

61 C. H. Townsley, *op. cit.*, pp. 3–35. See also M. J. Croft, *Offices in a Regional Centre: Follow-up Studies on Infra-Structure and Linkage* (London: Location of Offices Bureau, Research Paper, no. 3, 1969), pp. 24–31. C. H. Townsley, *Traffic Generation of Central London Offices* (London: Greater London Council, Department of Planning and Transportation Research Memorandum 399, 1974).

62 Economic Consultants Limited, *op. cit.*, pp. 37–40.

63 R. C. Harkness, 'Telecommunications substitutes for travel: A preliminary assessment of their potential for reducing urban transportation costs by altering office location pattern' (University of Washington, unpublished Ph.D. Thesis, 1973).

64 The costs attributable to office workers are based on a complex 'costing philosophy' which, broadly, assumes that 'new office workers' should pay a prorated share of the cost of new facilities equal to the percentage of total users of those facilities which they constitute, *ibid.*, p. 514.

65 P. W. Daniels, *Offices in the Suburbs* (London: University College London, Department of Geography Occasional Papers, no. 7, 1970), pp. 11–15.

CHAPTER 12

Conclusions

Office activities and employment will continue to grow, probably at a reduced rate, for some time into the future. The transformation of society which has created a new, and ever widening, range of 'élite' and 'routine' office work is not yet complete. The transactional environments within which offices operate are becoming more efficient yet more complex as information and communications systems are improved. Changes in office technology have been particularly beneficial for the growth of 'élite' office occupations which now seem to be expanding at the expense of 'routine' functions. This has taken place at a time when some important location changes have also become evident. The 'élite' functions are becoming characteristic of the centre of cities while the 'routine' functions are becoming more widely dispersed.

Offices have therefore emerged as a major factor in the evolution of urban form. They have become an integral, and increasingly crucial, part of urban and to some extent regional systems and planning. They respond to, and help to generate, changes in the system through the birth, death, division, expansion, locational adjustment, and migration of establishments. These events are a response to national and to regional economic trends; to the steadily increasing share of office work in total employment; and to locational trends within individual cities or at the regional level. It remains difficult, however, to separate offices from the dominance of the urban context in which most of them exist, even though it has been shown that they have an important contribution to make to the resolution of regional economic and social disequilibrium.

Office geography is still mainly concerned with collection, description, and analysis of published and other empirical observations. This has been one of the points to consistently emerge during the preparation of this book. This is certainly a vital preliminary step in the evolution of a subject which is now able to pass from an embryonic to a more formative stage of its development. Much of the descriptive work has helped to make the role of office activities in urban and regional studies more comprehensible to geographers, planners, and others.

The next step in the office study continuum must be to test more rigorously the hypotheses about growth and location which have been derived from empirical observations. Cowan, Goddard and a few others have already made efforts in this direction but much remains to be done. It must be recognized, however, that offices are inter-linked with other parts of the urban and regional system and modelling which concentrates only on office activities is likely to be less useful than a more integrated approach. At a time when urban areas are involved in, or will in future embark upon, major structural and land use changes, it is vital to be able to assess the contribution of office activities as accurately as possible and to incorporate them in a more comprehensive fashion in plans and models. This task is not made any easier by the fact that, initially, material has had to be synthesized from many disparate sources. From their respective viewpoints, geographers, sociologists, economists, economic historians, organization theorists, and planners have all, at various times, dabbled in office studies. Collectively, these fragmented contributions may be useful but they have also retarded the evolution of office studies *per se*, particularly the understanding of office location and the development of theory. Perhaps geographers, because of their particular interest in spatial patterns, and a growing awareness of the policy implications of their work, are amongst the best qualified to advance our understanding of the role of office activities in urban and regional development. Remarkably few have grasped the nettle.

AN INADEQUATE DATA FRAME

It is worth reiterating that one of the major obstacles to the study and analysis of office activities in Britain and elsewhere is the totally inadequate supply of relevant, comprehensive, and easily accessible statistics. The problems and deficiencies associated with the use of existing data have already been documented in the relevant chapters. Probably the most serious deficiency is found in the classification of most employment data by industry rather than occupation. The identification of separate office establishments as well as offices attached to manufacturing and other buildings is also universally difficult, while floorspace statistics leave a great deal to be desired. The net effect is to make the study of most aspects of office activity a precarious affair in which imperfect, or incompatible, data sets are the rule rather than the exception. Such basic difficulties influence the level of confidence which can be placed in the most elementary forecasting models for office employment or floorspace, for example. It is not surprising that it remains virtually impossible to devise more general models of office location using published empirical information.

It is therefore frequently necessary to generate special data sets for particular studies. The best example of this is the Regional Plan Association's Study for the New York Region which uses detailed and comprehensively researched data from many diverse sources. Much of the very basic and time-consuming work which this involved could easily have been avoided if suitable national census data had been available or had been collected by official agencies for publication or construction of special tabulations upon demand. Less ambitious studies by Goddard and others in Britain certainly demonstrate clearly that specially collected empirical data can usefully be utilized in models of specific parts of the urban and office system. Such data has helped to generate hypotheses about office location and is of immediate value to planners and policymakers interested in short-term changes. Over the longer-term, however, data from fragmented sources or for special purposes is not very helpful in the task of office location analysis or in the evolution of theoretical constructs. Therefore, standardization and a more comprehensive range of office sector statistics is a major priority. More consistency, over a reasonable period of time, is also required in definition and measurement of elements such as occupation or floorspace. Effective measurement of systematic themes such as the journey to work or office employment changes is impossible without statistics collected regularly over 10–20 years in censuses.

OFFICE LOCATION FACTORS

In common with other economic activities, offices select locations within the framework of a number of constraints. These can be classified as internal, and therefore to some extent easier to predict and control, and external. Internal controls on location are a product of the structure of office activities and the context within which individual organizations operate. Organizational context refers to the legal structure, type of industry, number of employees, number of divisions, or the products and technology used by each company. Context will to some extent affect organizational structure and both will affect the performance of office activities. If performance is good and an activity is able to expand or to become more efficient, this may create opportunities or a demand for locational adjustments. Conversely, if performance is deteriorating, perhaps because of the existing distribution of office premises used by an activity, locational changes may also be required. Few companies are aware, however, of the effects of organizational changes or performance on their office space requirements and changes in location are rarely pre-planned but occur when and where the pressures at existing locations become acute.

Office activities cannot move to locations of their choice at will but exist in competition with other office and non-office establishments. It is in this situation that the external constraints on office location become far more important than internal considerations. The office component of every economic activity generates demand for office floorspace (or premises), for labour, and for communications, both physical and non-physical. These three elements of demand are balanced by supply of the same three variables at any given location. Each office attempts to obtain that location which optimizes its supply/demand equation in relation to the limited number of sites or premises available in a city at any one time. Economic rent theory, based on the accessibility concepts described by Haig, provides the basis for understanding the outcome of this competition for limited space. It is largely reflected in the office market by rents which, in general terms, decrease with distance from the major office areas in the C.B.D. The three basic supply/demand variables also operate along similar lines irrespective of the markets served by different types of office activity. Different market requirements effectively circumscribes the locational choice of individual offices to particular parts of a city or region so that a hierarchical pattern of location also emerges.

There are also other external influences which, through their effects on supply and demand variables, can affect office location. These are the controls usually applied in the 'public interest' and designed to prevent excessive concentration of offices within specific parts of an urban area or to guide office development to certain locations or areas in the interests of regional planning. Such controls are exemplified by Britain's O.D.P. system but also include more general land use and other planning controls used by planning agencies to guide the spacing, detailed location, height, appearance and other aspects of office development. In addition to their indirect effects on the location patterns of offices, planning controls also affect the ability of office developers to respond to market requirements for space. Market demand only rarely parallels the pattern of development permitted in strategic or local plans. The role of the developer should not be underestimated; he will only provide space where it is viable to do so on economic grounds *vis-à-vis* a fair return on investment and the ability of a project to attract finance from the in-

stitutions. The actual location requirements of office organizations might almost be considered secondary and their actual behaviour will be governed by the developer's assessment of demand. This is especially true in the United States where market forces operate more freely. Although land use controls, in addition to regional office location policies, are much stronger in Britain than in most other countries, they should still take into account the effects on office market and the way in which developers are likely to respond.

It would be useful to be able to measure the relative effects of the internal and external constraints upon office location. There have been no comprehensive attempts to deal with this problem in a way which might lead to a model of office location. Office location research has followed particular channels, in particular the influence of communications on location. Detailed analysis of the role of labour supply and demand, or the distribution of different types of office floorspace, for example, have been almost completely ignored so that the location behaviour of offices can only remain partially understood. The volume of literature on communications studies suggests that this might be the most important single control on office location. It could be, however, that this is one of the easier variables to measure. The significance of communications varies between different office activities and those with weaker communications ties with the C.B.D. are not necessarily more footloose. The other, less understood and researched location variables, might well discourage any apparent freedom of movement.

It remains difficult to make general statements about the location behaviour of offices in the urban system. The empirical evidence which has been gathered in increasing quantities during the last 15 years seems to suggest that a recognizable pattern is emerging. The most obvious and important feature is the influence of centrality on office location and expansion in a way which affects only a very small part of a city. Although the highly centralized clusters of office buildings and activities blur at the edges into other land uses, particularly in the case of lower order offices with weaker locational constraints, or may shift location through time, they are self-perpetuating because of their strong attraction for other office activities. These may replace activities which have vacated office space in a cluster or they will occupy new space within or adjacent to a cluster. This has led Cowan to conclude that, for short time periods at least, it is possible to predict with some confidence when and where new office space will come on to the market. Planning approvals for new office development are not random, initial permissions received by developers generate clusters of other events and these tend to multiply steadily through time. Recent decentralization trends have not caused centrality to become less important for offices, they have simply distributed the demand for centrality more widely than before. There is no reason to believe that it will become less relevant for the future location of offices.

REGIONAL PATTERNS AND FUTURE LOCATION STRATEGIES

Disequilibrium in the regional distribution of office employment is a universal phenomenon. The reasons for this important characteristic stem mainly from the location requirements of office activities and the constant search for centrality. Regional polarization tends to increase as the proportion of total national employment in office work grows. This is the process which has presented some major challenges to urban and regional planners.

Urban planners in metropolitan areas are disturbed about the growing disparity between the location of homes and workplaces. Office workers are at the forefront of the population exodus from central cities but this is not matched by a similar movement of office jobs in sufficient numbers to divert office workers who still need to travel to the central area to obtain work. Central area congestion and related problems have therefore been perpetuated and office activities are largely responsible. Intra-metropolitan redistribution of office employment and floorspace has therefore become at least as important as movement to more distant centres in the regions.

Regional planners comprehend a diminishing range of employment opportunities in regions where long established manufacturing industries are prone to decline and are reducing their labour requirements. National trends are rarely reflected in regional office employment growth and this, in turn, has encouraged out-migration of existing or potential white-collar workers to the 'centre' regions and the major cities. Thus, the peripheral regions become even less attractive for expansion by indigenous office activities, as well as for in-migration of offices decentralizing from the congested regions. This is a negative form of Myrdal's theory of cumulative causation. Yet, both groups of planners have been comparatively slow to recognize the symptoms and the consequences of the office location patterns which have been emerging since the war.

Attempts to achieve regional redistribution of commercial office activities in Britain have met with very limited success. Offices are reluctant to decentralize further than is absolutely necessary and many firms prefer to endure the congestion and costs of a central London location. It seems that the disadvantages are more than outweighed by the advantages. Legislation introduced to stimulate redistribution has usually been one step behind market processes and has sometimes caused the opposite effect to that intended. Decentralization has already begun on a voluntary basis some years before controls were introduced in 1964 in an attempt to increase the volume of out-movement. Hindsight suggests that market forces combined with strict control on the issue of planning permissions would operate more successfully than O.D.P.s. The growth of office employment in central London has certainly been curbed but the redistribution which this reflects has only partially fulfilled regional requirements. Office job availability in suburban London and the remainder of the South East has been substantially improved. This is a desirable outcome but the regions outside the South East still deserve a much larger share of the decentralized jobs available simply to keep pace with growth at the centre.

It may be that London's suburbs have received more decentralized jobs than they really need immediately. The short-term needs of the regions are far more pressing but they have received a fluctuating slice of the decentralization cake in recent years; a slice which has also tended to get smaller, not larger. The image of the regions in the minds of potential movers, difficulties of recruitment, the costs of training office staff, postal and telecommunications problems, inadequate housing, and the reluctance of key staff to move far from London have all been advanced at one time or another as an explanation for the poor performance of the regions. Recent research suggests, however, that many of these problems are imagined rather than real disincentives to decentralization and they do not stand up to detailed scrutiny. Firms are anxious, for example, to retain, and to maintain, business contacts as efficiently as possible on a face-to-face basis, or to be near to the major markets for their services in London and the South East. This would appear to be an overwhelming reason for allowing offices to remain and to expand in London. But modern communications technology already allows some of these constraints to be 'stretched' in a way which would benefit regional development without necessarily damaging the viability of individual office organizations.

The apparent disadvantages of the regions mainly affects the location behaviour of commercial offices. Government offices in Britain, the Netherlands and Sweden have a good record of long distance decentralization. This may be an attempt to pave the way for commercial sector offices. Alternatively, Government departments may be constrained rather less by economic considerations and the effects of competition with rivals than their commercial counterparts. Government offices can act as a magnet for attracting certain types of non-Government office activities but, unfortunately, this does not seem to be happening to any marked degree outside major metropolitan areas like London. The Hardman Report reiterates the important role of Government offices in regional office policies. However, many of the arguments and alternative proposals included in that Report do not adequately reflect the current, let alone the future, requirements for office employment in the regions. Each Economic Planning Region considers that it has a special case and that it deserves the largest possible share of the already

limited number of jobs considered to qualify for decentralization to the peripheral regions.

British experience also suggests that office decentralization to metropolitan suburbs or regions with employment problems should form part of a clearly defined strategy for national, urban, and regional development. It is comparatively easy to provide financial inducements or to apply negative planning controls. It is much more difficult, but very necessary, to identify a comparatively small number of regional urban centres or suburban nuclei which best meet the particular locational requirements of decentralizing activities. Office 'centres' should be a clearly defined component of decentralization strategies. There has been much *ad hoc* decentralization which has created a patchwork of dispersed and concentrated reception centres; the latter arising by accident rather than design in most cases. This is true of both London's suburbs and areas further away and causes unnecessary costs to be incurred by individual office establishments, by the developers providing office space, and by the community at large. Basic facilities and services have been duplicated at several locations instead of at a limited number of centres where new transport, telecommunications, and other services could be provided as efficiently as possible.

Recent research into the effects of offices on the journey to work, the residential behaviour of office employees, or into communications patterns also points to the role of strategic centres where offices can enjoy economies of scale and other benefits similar to those in central London. Such centres would also act as an attraction for additional office activities as well as providing a viable base for a wide range of supporting services. Expansion should not be allowed to proceed beyond a threshold level, however, for it is clearly important to avoid creating conditions which begin to resemble those from which firms are trying to escape. But strategic centres cannot depend entirely upon decentralized offices for their expansion; they will almost certainly need to encourage growth of indigenous office activities which will also help to keep office workers in the regions. Office centres could be incorporated in growth pole policies for regional economic development. This conclusion has been slowly emerging from the late 1960s onwards and seems to be favoured by France, Sweden, the Netherlands, Ireland and in the proposals for the future development of the New York Region.

It must be emphasized that strategic office centres will not usurp existing major office concentrations such as central London or Manhattan. They will simply help to stabilize and distribute more equitably the benefits of office employment growth which are at present enjoyed by too few concentrations in metropolitan areas. Hence, the Regional Plan Association, while advocating planned expansion of regional office centres, also envisages continued expansion of Manhattan as a focus for office activities. The major problem is how to estimate the optimum size of a strategic office centre for given levels of transport, employment potential, housing, or telecommunications facili-

ties in a way which minimizes social and environmental costs. There has been no research for example, on the optimum size and location of an office centre, in terms of floorspace or employment, which will generate the highest possible level of public transport trips for the journey to work. This is the kind of specific problem which requires urgent examination before a strategy for office location and development in relation to general patterns of urbanization can be devised.

Interest in office studies has steadily increased during the last decade as urban and regional development issues have come to occupy an important place in public policy. It can only be hoped that the momentum of this work will be retained for some time ahead and that it will provide solutions to some of the location questions and policy problems outlined in this book.

Bibliography

P. Abercrombie, *Greater London Plan 1944* (London: His Majesty's Stationery Office, 1945).

R. B. Armstrong, *The Office Industry: Patterns of Growth and Location* (Cambridge, Mass.: The M.I.T. Press, 1972).

J. V. Aucott, 'Dispersal of offices from London', *Town Planning Review*, vol. 31 (1960), pp. 37–51.

B. H. Bagdikian, *The Information Machines: their Impact on Men and Media* (London: Harper & Row, 1971).

G. R. Bailey, 'Functional design of office buildings', *Appraisal Journal*, vol. 24 (1956), pp. 173–86.

A. W. Baker and R. L. Davis, *Ratios of Staff to Line Employees and Stages of Differentiation of Staff Functions* (Columbus: Ohio State University, Bureau of Business Research, 1954).

E. F. Baker, *Technology and Women's Work* (New York: Columbia University Press, 1964).

L. L. H. Baker and J. B. Goddard, 'Inter-sectoral contact flows and office location in central London', in A. G. Wilson (ed.) *London Studies in Regional Science*, vol. 3 (London: Pion, 1972).

M. J. Bannon, 'The changing centre of gravity of office establishments within central Dublin, 1940 and 1970', *Irish Geogr.*, vol. 6 (1972), pp. 480–4.

M. J. Bannon, *Office Location in Ireland: The Role of Central Dublin* (Dublin: An Foras Forbartha, 1973).

M. J. Bannon, 'Office location and regional development in Ireland', in M. J. Bannon (ed.), *Office Location and Regional Development* (Dublin: An Foras Forbartha, 1973).

M. Bateman, D. Burtenshaw and R. K. Hall, *Office Staff on the Move* (London: Location of Offices Bureau, Research Paper, no. 6, 1971).

M. Bateman and D. Burtenshaw, 'Sponsored white-collar migrants', *Town and Country Planning*, vol. 39 (1971), pp. 554–7.

S. Bliven, *The Wonderful Writing Machine* (New York: Random House, 1954).

British Institute of Management, *Office Relocation: A Report on a Series of Cost Studies of Firms which have Decentralised from London* (London: British Institute of Management, 1971).

British Market Research Bureau, *Communications and the Relocation of Offices: Report of a Depth Investi-*

gation among Manufacturing Companies (London: Location of Offices Bureau, 1968).

E. J. W. Buckler, *Bank Finance for Property Development* (London: Institute of Bankers, 1966).

Buildings: Their Uses and Spaces About Them (New York: Regional Survey of New York and Its Environs, 1931).

C. G. Burke, 'Houston is where they're moving', *Fortune*, vol. 85 (1971), pp. 91–7.

T. Burns, 'Management in action', *Operations Res. Quarterly*, vol. 8 (1957), pp. 45–60.

E. M. Burrows, 'Office employment and the regional problem', *Regional Studies*, vol. 7 (1973), pp. 17–31.

E. M. Burrows and S. Town, *Office Services in the East Midlands* (Nottingham: East Midlands Economic Planning Council, 1971).

D. Burtenshaw, M. Bateman, and A. Duffet, 'Office decentralization—ten years' experience', *The Surveyor*, vol. 143 (1974), pp. 22–5 and 21–3.

E. J. Burtt, *Plant Relocation and the Core City Worker* (Washington D.C., U.S. Department of Housing and Urban Development, 1967).

A. E. Callahan, *The Migration of Corporations from New York to Suburban Areas and to other Regions of the Country* (Washington: U.S. Department of State, 1971).

S. J. Carey, *Relocation of Office Staff: A Study of the Reactions of Staff Decentralized to Ashford* (London: Location of Offices Bureau, Research Paper, no. 4, 1969).

S. J. Carey, *Relocation of Office Staff: A Follow-up Survey* (London: Location of Offices Bureau, Research Paper, no. 4a, 1970).

E. B. Carne, 'Telecommunications: Its impact on business', *Harvard Business Review*, vol. 50 (1972), pp. 125–32.

E. Carruth, 'Manhattan's office building binge', *Fortune*, vol. 83 (1969), pp. 114–17 *et seq.*

E. Carruth, 'New York hangs out the For-Rent sign', *Fortune*, vol. 85 (1971), pp. 86–90 *et seq.*

D. Carter, 'Reactions to open plan offices', *Built Environment*, vol. 1 (1973), pp. 465–7.

R. Cassidy, 'Oak Brook: Planning for polo not people', *Planning*, vol. 40 (1974), pp. 34–7.

Central Statistical Office, *Standard Industrial Classifi-*

cation (London: Her Majesty's Stationery Office, 1968).

C. Cherry; 'Electronic communication: A force for dispersal', *Official Archit. and Planning*, vol. 33 (1970), pp. 773–6.

P. Child, *Office Development in Croydon: A Descriptive and Statistical Analysis* (London: Location of Offices Bureau, Research Paper, no. 5, 1971).

M. Chisholm and G. Manners (eds), *Spatial Policy Problems of the British Economy* (London: Cambridge University Press, 1971).

City of Manchester, *Central Manchester Office Survey, 1971* (Manchester: City Planning Department, 1972).

C. Clark, *The Conditions of Economic Progress* (London: Macmillan, 1940).

F. P. Clark, 'Office buildings in the suburbs', *Urban Land*, vol. 13 (1954), pp. 3–10.

W. M. Clarke, *The City in the World Economy* (London: Institute of Economic Affairs, 1965).

B. Cohen, 'A look at suburban office space', *Skyscraper Management*, vol. 56 (1971), pp. 6–10.

Communications Study Group, *The Scope for Person-to-Person Telecommunications in Government and Business* (London: Communications Study Group, Joint Unit for Planning Research (University College London), 1973).

S. Connell, *The 1973 Office Communications Survey* (London: Communications Study Group, Joint Unit for Planning Research (University College London), 1974).

Control of Office and Industrial Development Act 1965 (London: Her Majesty's Stationery Office, 1965).

P. Cowan, 'The growth of offices in London', *Transactions, Bartlett Soc.*, vol. 6 (1967), pp. 27–39.

P. Cowan, J. Ireland, and D. Fine, 'Approaches to urban model-building', *Regional Studies*, vol. 1 (1967), pp. 163–72.

P. Cowan, D. Fine, J. Ireland, C. Jordan, D. Mercer, and A. Sears, *The Office: A Facet of Urban Growth* (London: Heinemann, 1969).

G. L. Coyle, *Present Trends in Clerical Occupations* (New York: The Woman's Press, 1928).

M. J. Croft, *Offices in a Regional Centre: Follow-up Studies on Infra-structure and Linkage* (London: Location of Offices Bureau, Research Paper, no. 3, 1969).

F. Croner, 'Salaried employees in modern industry', *International Labour Review*, vol. 44 (1954), pp. 97–110.

J. B. Croxton and H. B. Goulding, 'The effectiveness of communication at meetings: A case study', *Operational Res. Quaterly*, vol. 17 (1967), pp. 45–7.

M. Crozier, *The World of the Office Worker* (Chicago: University of Chicago Press, 1965).

A. Custerson, 'Telecommunications: The key to the non-city?', *Built Environment*, vol. 2 (1973), pp. 403–406.

A. Custerson, 'Telecommunications: The office node', *Built Environment*, vol. 2 (1973), pp. 647–9.

J. R. Dale, *The Clerk in Industry* (Liverpool: Liverpool University Press, 1962).

Dallas Chamber of Commerce, *A Guide to Dallas Office Buildings* (Dallas Chamber of Commerce, 1973).

P. W. Daniels, 'Office decentralization from London: Policy and practice', *Regional Studies*, vol. 3 (1969), pp. 171–8.

P. W. Daniels, *Offices in the Suburbs* (London: University College London, Department of Geography Occasional Papers, no. 7, 1970).

P. W. Daniels, 'Employment decentralization and the journey to work', *Area*, vol. 1 (1970), pp. 47–51.

P. W. Daniels, 'Office decentralization from London: The journey to work consequences' (University of London, unpublished Ph.D. Thesis, 1972).

P. W. Daniels, 'Transport changes generated by decentralized offices', *Regional Studies*, vol. 6 (1972), pp. 273–89.

P. W. Daniels, 'Some changes in the journey to work of decentralized office workers', *Town Planning Review*, vol. 44 (1973), pp. 167–88.

P. W. Daniels, 'New offices in the suburbs', in J. H. Johnson (ed.), *Suburban Growth: Geographical Processes at the Edge of the Western City* (London: Wiley, 1974), pp. 177–200.

J. A. Davey, *The Office Industry in Wellington: A Study of Contact Patterns, Location and Employment* (Wellington: Ministry of Works, 1972).

J. A. Davey, 'Wellington's office industry', *Pacific Viewpoint*, vol. 14 (1973), pp. 45–60.

J. A. Davey, 'Office location and mobility in Wellington', *New Zealand Geographer*, vol. 29 (1973), pp. 120–133.

D. R. Denman, 'Frustrated development', *Westminster Bank Quarterly Review*, November (1970), pp. 43–54.

Department of Employment, *Computers in Offices, 1972* (London: Her Majesty's Stationery Office, Manpower Studies, no. 12, 1972).

Department of Employment, *Classification of Occupations and Directory of Occupational Titles (CODOT)* (London: Her Majesty's Stationery Office, 1972).

Department of the Environment, *Statistics for Town and Country Planning, Series II, No. 2, Floorspace* (London: Her Majesty's Stationery Office, 1972).

Department of the Environment, *Greater London Development Plan: Report of Panel of Enquiry, Vol. 1* (London: Her Majesty's Stationery Office, 1973).

T. K. Derry and T. I. Williams, *A Short History of Technology* (Oxford: Clarendon Press, 1960).

C. L. Detoy and S. L. Rabin, 'Office space: Calculating the demand', *Urban Land*, vol. 31 (1972), pp. 4–13.

E. Devons, *British Economic Statistics* (London: Cambridge University Press, 1961).

D. Diamond, 'The location of offices', *Town and Country Planning*, vol. 39 (1971), pp. 106–9.

A. Dickens, *Structural and Service Systems in Office Buildings: A Background Review* (Cambridge: Centre for Land Use and Built Form Studies, Working Paper, no. 35, 1970).

P. F. Drucker, *Technology, Management and Society* (London: Heinemann, 1970).

F. Duffy and D. Wankum, *Office Landscaping: A New Approach to Office Planning* (London: Anbar Publications, 1966).

J. H. Dunning and E. V. Morgan (eds), *An Economic Study of the City of London* (London: Allen & Unwin, 1971).

Economic Consultants Limited, *Demand and Supply for Office Workers and the Local Impact of Office Development* (London: Report prepared for Location of Offices Bureau, 1971).

Economic Consultants Limited, *Office Classification Systems* (London: Report prepared for Location of Offices Bureau, 1974).

Economist Intelligence Unit, *A Survey of Factors Governing the Location of Offices in the London Area* (London: Economist Intelligence Unit, 1964).

M. Elton and R. Pye, *Travel or Telecommunicate? The Comparative Costs* (London: Communications Study Group, Joint Unit for Planning Research (University College London), 1974).

A. W. Evans, 'Myths about employment in central London', *J. Transp. Econ. and Policy*, vol. 1 (1967), pp. 214–25.

A. W. Evans, 'The location of headquarters of industrial companies', *Urban Studies*, vol. 10 (1973), pp. 387–95.

M. V. Facey and G. B. Smith, *Offices in a Regional Centre: A Study of Office Location in Leeds* (London: Location of Offices Bureau, Research Paper, no. 2, 1968).

R. M. Fisher, *The Boom in Office Buildings: An Economic Study of the Past Two Decades* (Washington: The Urban Land Institute, Technical Bulletin, no. 58, 1968).

D. L. Foley, 'Factors in the location of administrative offices', *Papers and Proceeding, Regional Science Assoc.*, vol. 2 (1956), pp. 318–26.

D. L. Foley, *The Suburbanization of Offices in the San Francisco Bay Area* (Berkeley: University of California, Bureau of Business and Economic Research, 1957).

L. R. Ford, 'The skyscraper: urban symbolism and city structure' (University of Oregon, unpublished Ph.D. Thesis, 1970).

L. R. Ford, 'Individual decisions in the creation of the American Downtown', *Geography*, vol. 58 (1973), pp. 324–7.

Fortune: The Fortune Directory (*Annual Supplement*) (New York: Time Inc.).

V. R. Fuchs, *The Service Economy* (New York: Bureau of Economic Research, 1968).

W. Galenson, 'Economic development and the sectoral expansion of employment', *International Labour Review*, vol. 87 (1963), pp. 505–19.

R. E. Galtman and T. J. Weiss, 'The service industries in the nineteenth century', in V. R. Fuchs (ed.), *Production and Productivity in the Service Industries* (New York: Studies in Income and Wealth, 1969).

A. Ganz, 'Emerging patterns of urban growth and travel', *Highway Res. Record*, vol. 203 (1968), pp. 21–37.

J. B. Goddard, 'Changing office location patterns within central London', *Urban Studies*, vol. 4 (1967), pp. 276–84.

J. B. Goddard, 'Multivariate analysis of office location patterns in the city centre: A London example', *Regional Studies*, vol. 2 (1968), pp. 64–85.

J. B. Goddard, 'Functional regions within the city centre: A study by factor analysis of taxi flows in central London', *Trans. Inst. Brit. Geogr.*, vol. 49 (1970), pp. 161–82.

J. B. Goddard, 'Office communications and office location: A review of current research', *Regional Studies*, vol. 5 (1971), pp. 263–80.

J. B. Goddard, *Office Linkages and Location* (Oxford: Pergamon, 1973).

J. B. Goddard, 'Civil Service for the regions', *Town and Country Planning*, vol. 41 (1973), pp. 451–4.

J. B. Goddard and D. Morris, *The Communications Factor in Office Decentralization* (London: London School of Economics and Political Science, Department of Geography, 1974).

B. Gooding, 'Roadblocks ahead for the great corporate move out', *Fortune*, vol. 86 (1972), pp. 78–83, *et seq.*

W. Goodwin, 'The management center in the United States', *Geographical Review*, vol. 55 (1965), pp. 1–16.

J. Gottman, *Megapolis: The Urbanised Northeastern Seaboard of the United States* (Cambridge, Mass: The M.I.T. Press, 1961).

J. Gottman, 'Why the skyscraper?' *Geographical Review*, vol. 51 (1966), pp. 190–212.

J. Gottman, 'Urban centrality and the interweaving of quarternary activities', *Ekistics*, vol. 29 (1970), pp. 322–31.

J. Gottman, 'The new geography of transactions and its consequences for planning' in M. J. Bannon (ed.), *The Application of Geographical Techniques to Physical Planning* (Dublin: An Foras Forbartha, 1971), pp. 3–16.

J. Gottman, 'The dynamics of large cities', *Geographical Journal*, vol. 140 (1974), pp. 254–61.

J. Gottman, *The Evolution of Urban Centrality: Orientations for Research* (Oxford: Department of Geography Research Papers, no. 8, 1974).

Greater London Council, *Greater London Development Plan: Statement* (London: Greater London Council, 1969).

Greater London Council, *Greater London Development Plan: Report of Studies* (London: Greater London Council, 1970).

Greater London Council, *Offices in London* (London: Greater London Council, Department of Planning and Transportation, Research Bibliography, no. 48, 1973).

Greater London Development Plan Inquiry, *Industrial and Office Floorspace Targets, 1972–76* (London: Greater London Council, Background Paper, no. B452, 1971).

H. I. Greenfield, *Manpower and the Growth of Producer Services* (New York: Columbia University Press, 1966).

E. J. C. Griffith, 'Moving industry from London', *Town Planning Review*, vol. 26 (1956), pp. 51–63.

Guides to Official Sources No. 2, Census Reports of Great Britain 1801–1931 (London: His Majesty's Stationery Office, 1951).

R. M. Haig, *Major Economic Factors in Metropolitan Growth and Arrangement* (New York: Committee on Regional Plan for New York and Its Environs, Regional Survey, vol. 1, 1927).

M. Haire, 'Biological models and empirical histories of the growth of organizations', in M. Haire (ed.), *Modern Organization Theory* (New York: Wiley, 1959).

J. M. Hall, 'Office growth in London', *New Society*, vol. 27 (1974), pp. 124–26.

R. K. Hall, 'The vacated offices controversy', *Journal of the Town Planning Institute*, vol. 56 (1970), pp. 298–300.

R. K. Hall, 'The movement of offices from central London', *Regional Studies*, vol. 6 (1972), pp. 385–92.

F. E. I. Hamilton, 'Industrial location models', in R. J. Chorley and P. Haggett (eds), *Models in Geography* (London: Methuen, 1967).

E. Hammond, 'Dispersal of Government offices: A survey', *Urban Studies*, vol. 3 (1967), pp. 258–75.

E. Hammond, *London To Durham: A Study of The Transfer of the Post Office Savings Certificate Division* (Durham: Rowntree Research Unit. 1968).

R. C. Harkness, 'Communications substitutes for intra-urban travel', *Transportation Engineering Journal*, vol. 98 (1972), pp. 585–98.

R. C. Harkness, *Communication Innovations, Urban Form and Travel Demand: Some Hypotheses and a Bibliography* (Seattle: University of Washington, Department of Urban Planning and Civil Engineering, Research Report, no. 71–2, 1972).

R. C. Harkness, 'Telecommunications substitutes for travel: A preliminary assessment of their potential for reducing urban transportation costs by altering office location pattern' (University of Washington, unpublished Ph.D. Thesis, 1973).

T. A. Hartshorne, 'Industrial/office parks: A new look for the city', *Journal of Geography*, vol. 72 (1973), pp. 33–45.

D. Hawkes, *Offices: A Digest of Data* (Cambridge: Centre for Land Use and Build Form Studies, Working Paper, no. 10, 1968).

D. Hawkes, *Building Bulk Legislation: A Description and Analysis* (Cambridge: Centre for Land Use and Built Form Studies, Working Paper, no. 4, 1969).

P. Herrera, 'That Manhattan exodus', *Fortune*, vol. 81 (1967), pp. 106 *et seq.*

I. R. Hoos, 'When the computer takes over the office', *Harvard Business Review*, vol. 38 (1960), pp. 102–112.

E. M. Hoover and A. Vernon, *Anatomy of a Metropolis* (Cambridge, Mass: Harvard University Press, 1959).

E. M. Horwood and R. R. Boyce, *Studies of the Central Business District and Urban Freeway Development* (Seattle: University of Washington Press, 1959).

Houston City Planning Department, *Major Office Areas, 1960–1990* (Houston: City Planning Department, 1971).

R. S. Howard, *The Movement of Manufacturing Industry in the United Kingdom 1945–65* (London: Her Majesty's Stationery Office, 1968).

International Labour Office, *International Standard Classification of Occupations* (Geneva; International Labour Office, 1958).

Interscan Ltd., *Report on a Survey of Non-Movers* (London: Location of Offices Bureau, 1967).

Interscan Ltd., *Survey of Offices in the Central Area* (London: Location of Offices Bureau, 1970).

C. R. Jennings, 'Predicting demand for office space', *Appraisal Journal*, vol. 33 (1965), pp. 377–82.

J. H. Johnson, 'The geography of the skyscraper', *Journal of Geography*, vol. 55 (1956), pp. 349–63.

D. E. Jones, 'Offices: An element of urban geography — The case of Minneapolis' (University of Minnesota, unpublished M.A. Thesis, 1970).

D. E. Jones and R. K. Hall, 'Office suburbanization

in the United States', *Town and Country Planning*, vol. 40 (1972), pp. 470–3.

D. W. Jones, *Must We Travel? The Potential of Communication as a Substitute for Travel* (Stanford: Stanford University, 1973).

D. E. Keeble, 'Industrial decentralization and the metropolis: The North West London case', *Trans. Inst. Brit. Geogr.*, vol. 44 (1968), pp. 1–54.

Kent County Council, *A Pilot Survey and Analysis of Some Office Firms in Kent* (Maidstone: County Planning Department, 1967).

E. W. Kersten and D. R. Ross, 'Clayton: A metropolitan focus in the St Louis area', *Annls Ass. Amer. Geographers*, vol. 58 (1968), pp. 637–49.

D. B. Knight and T. Ito, 'Office parks: The Oak Brook example', *Land Economics*, vol. 58 (1972), pp. 65–69.

M. Lengelle, *The Growing Importance of the Service Sector in Member Countries* (Geneva: Organization for Economic Co-operation and Development, 1966).

H. S. Levin, *Office Work and Automation* (New York: Wiley, 1956).

R. Lewis, *The New Service Society* (London: Longman, 1973).

R. M. Lichtenberg, *One-tenth of a Nation* (Cambridge, Mass.: Harvard University Press, 1960).

H. G. Lind, 'Location by guesswork', *J. Transport Econ. and Policy*, vol. 1 (1967), pp. 154–63.

A. Ling, 'Office buildings in big cities', *Town and Country Planning*, vol. 24 (1956), pp. 521–6.

A. Ling, 'Skyscrapers and their siting in cities', *Town Planning Review*, vol. 34 (1963), pp. 7–18.

'List of key occupations for statistical purposes (KOSP)', *Department of Employment Gazette*, vol. 80 (1972), pp. 799–803.

Location of Offices Bureau, *Annual Reports, 1964–74* (London: Location of Offices Bureau, 1974).

D. Lockwood, *The Blackcoated Worker* (London: Allen & Unwin, 1958).

London Borough of Croydon, *The Redevelopment of Central Croydon* (Croydon: Borough Engineer, Surveyor and Planning Officer's Department, 1971).

London County Council, *A Plan to Combat Congestion in Central London* (London: London County Council, 1957).

London. Employment: Housing: Land (London: Her Majesty's Stationery Office, Cmd 1952, 1963).

G. R. Long, 'Office park development', *Urban Land*, vol. 32 (1973), pp. 10–17.

R. E. Lonsdale, 'Two North Carolina commuting patterns', *Econ. Geography*, vol. 42 (1966) pp. 114–28.

G. D. McDonald, *Office Building Construction in Manhattan, 1947–67* (New York: Real Estate Board, 1964).

J. C. McDonald, *Impact and Implications of Office Automation* (Ottawa: Department of Labour, Occasional Paper, no. 1, 1964).

J. R. McKeever, *Business Parks* (Washington D.C.: Urban Land Institute, Technical Bulletin 65, 1970).

C. W. McMahon and G. D. N. Worswick, 'The growth of services in the economy', in D. H. Aldercroft and P. Fearon (eds), *Economic Growth in Twentieth Century Britain* (London: Macmillan, 1969).

W. McQuade, 'A daring new generation of skyscrapers', *Fortune*, vol. 87 (1973), pp. 78–89, 150–2.

G. Manners, 'Decentralization in metropolitan Boston', *Geography*, vol. 45 (1960), pp. 276–85.

G. Manners, 'Service industries and regional economic growth', *Town Planning Review*, vol. 33 (1963), pp. 293–303.

G. Manners, 'Urban expansion in the United States', *Urban Studies*, vol. 2 (1965), pp. 51–66.

G. Manners, 'On the mezzanine floor: Some reflections on contemporary office location policy', *Town and Country Planning*, vol. 40 (1972), pp. 210–15.

G. Manners, *The Office in Metropolis: An Opportunity for Shaping Metropolitan America* (Harvard: Joint Centre for Urban Studies, Working Paper 22, 1973).

G. Manners, D. Keeble, B. Rodgers, and K. Warren, *Regional Development in Britain* (London: Wiley, 1972).

P. Manning (ed.), *Office Design: A Study in Environment* (Liverpool: Pilkington Research Unit, 1965).

W. F. Manthorpe, 'The limitation of employment in central London', *Journal of the Royal Institute of Chartered Surveyors*, vol. 34 (1954), pp. 389–9.

O. Marriot, *The Property Boom* (London: Hamish Hamilton, 1967).

J. W. Martin and J. L. Johnson, 'Labour market boundaries: Inter-county commuting to employment', *Current Economic Comment*, vol. 17 (1955), pp. 29–37.

R. L. Meier, *A Communications Theory of Urban Growth* (Cambridge, Mass: The M.I.T. Press, 1962)

A. Meonard and A. Vigarie, 'Les interrelations dans la tertiaire superieur Nantais', *Cahier Nantais*, no. 7 (1973), pp. 5–120.

R. H. Merriman, 'Office movement in central Christchurch 1955–65', *New Zealand Geographer*, vol. 23 (1967), pp. 117–31.

C. W. Mills, *White Collar* (New York: Oxford University Press, 1953).

Ministry of Housing and Local Government, *The South East Study* (London: Her Majesty's Stationery Office, 1964).

Ministry of Housing and Local Government, *Statistics for Town and Country Planning, Series II, No. 1, Floorspace* (London: Her Majesty's Stationery Office, 1969).

Ministry of Labour, *Computers in Offices* (London: Her Majesty's Stationery Office, Manpower Studies, no. 4, 1965).

Ministry of Labour, *Occupational Changes 1951–61* (London: Her Majesty's Stationery Office, Manpower Studies No. 6, 1967).

Ministry of Labour, *Growth of Office Employment* (London: Her Majesty's Stationery Office, Manpower Studies No. 7, 1968).

Ministry of Town and Country Planning, *The Redevelopment of Central Areas* (London: His Majesty's Stationery Office, 1947).

F. B. Moore, 'Downtown office building versus the office park complex', *Skyscraper Management*, vol. 54 (1969), pp. 15–17.

W. T. W. Morgan, 'The growth and function of the general office district in the West End of London' (Northwestern University, Illinois, unpublished Ph.D. Thesis, 1960).

W. T. W. Morgan, 'Office regions in the West End of London', *Town and Country Planning*, vol. 29 (1961), pp. 257–9.

W. T. W. Morgan, 'A functional approach to the study of office distributions', *Tijdschrift voor Economische en Sociale Geografie*, vol. 52 (1961), pp. 207–10.

W. T. W. Morgan, 'The geographical concentration of big business in Great Britain', *Town and Country Planning*, vol. 30 (1962), pp. 122–4.

A. E. J. Morris, 'Skyscrapers', *Official Archit. and Planning*, vol. 32 (1970), pp. 55–7.

L. Mumford, *The Culture of Cities* (London: Secker & Warburg, 1939).

E. Mumford and O. Banks, *The Computer and the Clerk* (London: Routledge & Kegan Paul, 1967).

H. Murray *et al.*, *The Location of Government Review: Human Aspects of Dispersal* (London: Tavistock Institute of Human Relations, 1972).

National Council for Social Service, *Dispersal: An Inquiry into the Advantages and Feasibility of the Permanent Settlement Out of London and the other Great Cities of Offices and Clerical and Administrative Staff* (Oxford: Oxford University Press, 1944).

National Opinion Polls Limited, *White-Collar Commuters: A Second Survey* (London: Location of Offices Bureau, Research Paper, no. 1, 1967).

New York City Planning Commission, *The Demand for Office Space in Manhattan* (New York: City Planning Commission, 1971).

New York City Planning Commission, *Headquarters Relocation in New York City and the Region* (New York: City Planning Commission, 1972).

North West Industrial Development Association, *London Pay Weighting and Regional Policy* (Manchester: North West Industrial Development Association, 1974).

J. R. O'Meara, *Corporate Moves to the Suburbs: Problems and Opportunities* (New York: The Conference Board, 1972).

Offices: A Statement by Her Majesty's Government (London: Her Majesty's Stationery Office, 1964).

Office Decentralization to the New Towns (London: Location of Offices Bureau, mimeo, 1974).

'Office review', *Town and Country Planning*, vol. 42 (1974), pp. 465–7.

B. G. Orchard, *The Clerks of Liverpool* (London: Collinson, 1871).

G. F. Parsons, 'The giant manufacturing corporations and balanced regional growth in Britain, *Area*, vol. 4 (1972), pp. 99–103.

J. K. Pierce, *Symbols, Signals and Noise: The Nature and Process of Communication* (New York: Harper & Row, 1961).

R. M. Pierce, 'Towards an optimum policy for office location' (University of Wales, unpublished M.Sc. Thesis, 1972).

C. A. Prendergast, 'Decentralization: The pattern changes', *Investors Chronicle* (1972), pp. 44–53.

W. B. Proudfoot, *The Origin of Stencil Duplicating* (London: Hutchinson, 1972).

R. Pye, *The Communications Factor in Dispersal: An Overview* (London: Communications Study Group, Joint Unit for Planning Research (University College London), 1972).

R. Pye, *A Cost Minimization Model for Choosing Office Locations* (London: Communications Study Group, Joint Unit for Planning Research (University College London), 1973).

R. Pye, *The End of the Journey to Work: Fact or Fiction? A Preliminary Assessment of Existing Knowledge and Necessary Research* (London: Communications Study Group, Joint Unit for Planning Research (University College London), 1974).

J. Rannells, *The Core of the City* (New York: Columbia University Press, 1956).

C. Rapkin, *Urban Traffic: A Function of Land Use* (New York: Columbia University Press, 1954).

E. R. Rausch, *Principles of Office Administration* (Columbus: Merrill, 1964).

W. J. Reader, *Professional Men: The Rise of the Professional Classes in Nineteenth Century England* (London: Wiedenfeld & Nicolson, 1966).

G. Rees and R. Wiseman, 'London's commodity markets', *Lloyds Bank Review*, January (1969), pp. 22–45.

A. Reid, *Face-to-Face Contacts in Government*

Departments (London: Communications Study Group, Joint Unit for Planning Research (University College London), 1971).

Report of Heights of Buildings Commission (New York, 1913).

Report of the Royal Commission on the Distribution of the Industrial Population (London: His Majesty's Stationery Office, Cnd 6153, 1940).

H. A. Rhee, *Office Automation in Social Perspective* (Oxford: Blackwell, 1968).

J. Rhodes and A. Kan, *Office Dispersal and Regional Policy* (London: Cambridge University Press, Department of Applied Economics Occasional Papers, no. 30, 1971).

K. T. L. Rhodes, 'Moving out of London', *Town and Country Planning*, vol. 37, pp. 68–71.

S. M. Robbins and N. E. Terleikyj, *Money Metropolis* (Cambridge, Mass: Harvard University Press, 1960).

H. B. Schechter, 'An analysis of commercial construction', *Land Economics*, vol. 26 (1950), pp. 115–35.

E. Schultz and W. Simmons, *Offices in the Sky* (New York: Bobbs-Merrill, 1959).

M. Scott, *American City Planning Since 1890* (Berkeley: University of California Press, 1969).

R. K. Semple, 'Recent trends in the spatial concentration of corporate headquarters, *Econ. Geography*, vol. 49 (1973), pp. 309–18.

E. Sidwell, *The Problems for Employees in Office Dispersal: A Methodology* (London: London School of Economics, Department of Geography, Discussion Paper, no. 48, 1974).

H. A. Simon, *The Shape of Automation for Men and Management* (New York: Harper & Row, 1960).

C. Sladen, 'Banks move head offices out of London', *Administrative Management*, vol. 27 (1973), pp. 23–25.

P. R. Smethurst and R. U. Redpath, *Central London Workers: Changes in Distribution of Residence* (London: Greater London Council, Research Paper S.R.1, 1966).

D. M. Smith, *Industrial Location: An Economic Geographical Analysis* (London: Wiley, 1971).

G. M. Smith, *Office Automation and White-Collar Employment* (Rutgers University: Institute of Management and Labour Relations, Bulletin, no. 6, 1959).

A. D. Sorenson, 'Office activities as an economic base for urban decentralization in Australia', *Royal Australian Planning Institute Journal*, vol. 12 (1974), pp. 51–7.

South East Economic Planning Council, *A Strategy for the South East* (London: Her Majesty's Stationery Office, 1967).

South East Joint Planning Team, *Strategic Plan for the South East* (London: Her Majesty's Stationery Office, 1971).

Southfield City Planning Commission, *Southfield Office Study* (Southfield: Vulcan-Leman and Associates Inc., 1972).

D. J. Spooner, 'Industrial movement and the rural periphery: The case of Devon and Cornwall', *Regional Studies*, vol. 6 (1972), pp. 197–215.

Standing Conference on London Regional Planning, *Office Employment in the Conference Area* (London: Standing Conference, LRP 279, 1964).

D. F. Stevens, 'The central area', in J. T. Coppock and H. C. Prince (eds), *Greater London* (London: Faber, 1964).

R. Stewart, *How Computers Affect Management* (London: Macmillan, 1971).

G. J. Stigler, *Trends in Employment in the Service Industries* (Baltimore: John Hopkins Press, 1956).

E. J. Taafe, B. J. Garner, and M. H. Yeates, *The Peripheral Journey to Work: A Geographic Consideration* (Evanston: North Western University Press, 1963).

F. A. Tarpley, L. S. Davidson, and D. D. Clark 'Flight to the fringes: A study of shifting office locations in Atlanta', *Review of Regional Studies*, vol. 1 (1970), pp. 117–40.

S. Taylor, 'A study of post-war office developments', *Journal of the Town Planning Institute*, vol. 52 (1963), pp. 54–6.

The Dispersal of Government Work from London (The Hardman Report) (London: Her Majesty's Stationery Office, Cmd 5322, 1973).

The Times 1000 Leading Companies in Britain and Overseas 1971–72 (London: Times Newspapers Ltd, 1972).

J. H. Thompson, 'Commuting patterns of manufacturing employers', *Industrial Labor Relations Review*, vol. 10 (1956), pp. 70–80.

C. Thomsen, 'How high to rise', *Appraisal Journal*, vol. 32 (1966), pp. 585–91.

B. Thorngren, 'Regional economic interaction and flows of information', in *Proceedings of the Second Poland-Norden Science Seminar* (Warsaw, 1967).

B. Thorngren, 'How do contact systems affect regional development?', *Environment and Planning*, vol. 2 (1970), pp. 409–27.

B. Thorngren, 'Communication studies for Government office dispersal in Sweden', in M. J. Bannon (ed.), *Office Location and Regional Development* (Dublin: An Foras Forbartha, 1973).

J. Toby, 'Regional development and Government office relocation in the Netherlands', in M. J. Bannon (ed.), *Office Location and Regional Development* (Dublin: An Foras Forbartha, 1973).

G. E. Törnqvist, 'Flows of information and the location of economic activities', *Geografiska Annaler*, vol. 50 (1968), pp. 99–107.

G. E. Törnqvist, 'Contact requirements and travel facilities: Contact models of Sweden and regional development alternatives in the future', in A. R. Pred and G. E. Törnqvist, *Systems of Cities and Information Flows* (Lund: Gleerup, Lund Studies in Geography, Series B, 1973), pp. 81–121.

Town and Country Planning Association, *The Paper Metropolis* (London: Town and Country Planning Association, 1962).

C. H. Townsley, *Traffic Generation of Suburban London Offices* (London: Greater London Council, Department of Planning and Transportation, Research Memorandum 398, 1973).

C. H. Townsley, *Traffic Generation of Central London Offices* (London: Greater London Council, Department of Planning and Transportation, Research Memorandum 399, 1974).

R. Turvey, *The Economics of Real Property* (London: Allen & Unwin, 1957).

Twin Cities Metropolitan Council, *Office Space: An Inventory and Forecast for the Twin Cities Metropolitan Area* (St Paul: Twin Cities Metropolitan Council, 1973).

R. Vernon, *The Changing Economic Function of the Central City* (New York: Committee for Economic Development, Supplementary Paper, no. 1, 1959).

R. Vernon, *Metropolis 1985* (Cambridge, Mass.: Harvard University Press, 1960).

J. S. Wabe, 'Office decentralization: An empirical study', *Urban Studies*, vol. 3 (1966), pp. 35–55.

J. S. Wabe, 'Dispersal of employment and the journey to work', *J. Transport Econ. and Policy*, vol. 1 (1967), pp. 345–61.

C. R. Wareham, 'The pattern of office development', *Chartered Surveyor*, vol. 105 (1973), pp. 350–6.

H. D. Watts, 'Giant manufacturing corporations: Further observations on regional growth and large corporations', *Area*, vol. 4 (1972), pp. 269–75.

M. Waugh, 'The changing distribution of professional and managerial manpower in England and Wales between 1961 and 1966', *Regional Studies*, vol. 3 (1969), pp. 157–69.

J. Westaway, *Contact Potential and the Occupational Structure of the British Urban System 1961–66: An Empirical Study* (London: London School of Economics and Political Science, Geography Department Discussion Paper, no. 45, 1973).

B. P. Whitehouse, *Partners in Property* (London: Birn, Shaw, 1964).

K. B. Williams, 'The factual basis of office policy in South East England' (University of London, unpublished M.A. Thesis, 1965).

L. Woodbury, *The Future of Cities and Urban Redevelopment* (Chicago: University of Chicago Press, 1953).

M. W. Wright, *Office Development outside the South East* (London: Department of Economic Affairs, 1965).

M. W. Wright, 'Provincial office development', *Urban Studies*, vol. 4 (1967), pp. 213–57.

Yorkshire and Humberside Economic Planning Board, *The Service Industries: Prospects in Yorkshire and Humberside* (Leeds: Department of the Environment, 1972).

G. Yannopoulos, *The Local Impact of Decentralized Offices* (London: Location of Offices Bureau, Research Paper, no. 7, 1973).

G. Yannopoulos, 'Local income effects of office relocation', *Regional Studies*, vol. 7 (1973), pp. 33–46.

Index

iothèqu
D'

brar
151